MARKETING PLACES AND SPACES

ADVANCES IN CULTURE, TOURISM AND HOSPITALITY RESEARCH

Series Editor: Arch G. Woodside

Recent Volumes:

Volumes 1–2:   Advances in Culture, Tourism and Hospitality Research –
Edited by Arch G. Woodside

Volume 3:   Perspectives on Cross-Cultural, Ethnographic, Brand
Image, Storytelling, Unconscious Needs, and Hospitality
Guest Research – Edited by Arch G. Woodside,
Carol M. Megehee and Alfred Ogle

Volume 4:   Tourism-Marketing Performance Metrics and Usefulness
Auditing of Destination Websites – Edited by
Arch G. Woodside

Volume 5:   Tourism Sensemaking: Strategies to Give Meaning to
Experience – Edited by Arch G. Woodside

Volume 6:   Field Guide to Case Study Research in Tourism,
Hospitality and Leisure – Edited by Kenneth F. Hyde,
Chris Ryan and Arch G. Woodside

Volume 7:   Luxury Fashion and Culture – Edited by Eunju Ko and
Arch G. Woodside

Volume 8:   Tourists' Perceptions and Assessments – Edited by
Arch G. Woodside and Metin Kozak

Volume 9:   Tourists' Behaviors and Evaluations – Edited by
Arch G. Woodside and Metin Kozak

ADVANCES IN CULTURE, TOURISM AND HOSPITALITY
RESEARCH   VOLUME 10

MARKETING PLACES AND SPACES

EDITED BY

ANTÓNIA CORREIA
CEFAGE, University of Algarve, Faro, Portugal

JUERGEN GNOTH
Otago University, Dunedin, New Zealand

METIN KOZAK
Dokuz Eylül University, Izmir, Turkey

ALAN FYALL
University of Central Florida, Orlando, USA

Emerald

United Kingdom – North America – Japan
India – Malaysia – China

Emerald Group Publishing Limited
Howard House, Wagon Lane, Bingley BD16 1WA, UK

First edition 2015

Copyright © 2015 Emerald Group Publishing Limited

Reprints and permissions service
Contact: permissions@emeraldinsight.com

British Library Cataloguing in Publication Data
A catalogue record for this book is available from the British Library

ISBN: 978-1-78441-940-0
ISSN: 1871-3173 (Series)

Printed and bound by CPI Group (UK) Ltd, Croydon, CR0 4YY

ISOQAR certified
Management System,
awarded to Emerald
for adherence to
Environmental
standard
ISO 14001:2004.

Certificate Number 1985
ISO 14001

INVESTOR IN PEOPLE

CONTENTS

LIST OF CONTRIBUTORS   *ix*

LIST OF REVIEWERS   *xi*

PREFACE   *xiii*

EDITORIAL BOARD   *xv*

INTRODUCTION   *xix*

**PART I: PLACES, PERCEPTIONS AND CO-CREATIVE
DEVELOPMENT**

LOCAL STUDENTS' PERCEPTIONS OF SPACES FOR
TOURISTS AND LOCALS IN A SHOPPING DISTRICT:
PHOTO-BASED RESEARCH
  Taketo Naoi, Shoji Iijima, Akira Soshiroda and   3
  Tetsuo Shimizu

RESIDENTS' PERCEPTIONS OF MOUNTAIN
DESTINATIONS
  Carla Silva, Elisabeth Kastenholz and José Luís Abrantes   19

ATTITUDES OF SUCCESSORS IN DAIRY FARMS
TOWARD EDUCATIONAL TOURISM IN JAPAN
  Yasuo Ohe   33

RESIDENTS' PERCEPTIONS OF THE IMPACT OF SHIP
TOURISM AND THEIR PREFERENCES FOR
DIFFERENT TYPES OF TOURISM
  Giacomo Del Chiappa and Giuseppe Melis   45

WEDDING-BASED TOURISM DEVELOPMENT:
INSIGHTS FROM AN ITALIAN CONTEXT
Giacomo Del Chiappa and Fulvio Fortezza   61

CONCEPTUALIZING THE VALUE CO-CREATION
CHALLENGE FOR TOURIST DESTINATIONS: A
SUPPLY-SIDE PERSPECTIVE
Giuseppe Melis, Scott McCabe and Giacomo Del Chiappa   75

PART II: IMAGE AND COMPETITIVE STRATEGIES

THE EMOTIONAL ATTACHMENT BUILT THROUGH
THE ATTITUDES AND MANAGERIAL APPROACH TO
PLACE MARKETING AND BRANDING – "THE
GOLDEN CITY OF KREMNICA, SLOVAKIA"
Marica Mazurek   93

HOSPITALITY SERVICESCAPES SEEN BY VISUALLY
IMPAIRED TRAVELERS
Alma Raissova   107

DETERMINANTS OF TOURISM DESTINATION
COMPETITIVENESS: A SEM APPROACH
Cristina Estevão, João Ferreira and Sara Nunes   121

EVENTS AS A DIFFERENTIATION STRATEGY
FOR TOURIST DESTINATIONS: THE CASE OF
ALLGARVE
Inês Miranda, Nuno Gustavo and Eugénia Castela   141

FROM TOURISM SPACE TO A UNIQUE TOURISM
PLACE THROUGH A CONCEPTUAL APPROACH
TO BUILDING A COMPETITIVE ADVANTAGE
Kamila Borseková, Anna Vaňová and   155
Katarína Petríková

PART III: MARKETING PLACES – TOWARDS A COOPERATIVE STRATEGY

ACHIEVING CONSISTENCY IN DESTINATION
PERSONALITIES: A TRIPARTITE PERSONALITY
CONGRUITY THEORY FOCUSED ON INDUSTRY
PROFESSIONALS
Veronica I. K. Lam and Leonardo (Don) A. N. Dioko   175

MARKETING TO CHILDREN IN TOURISM
INDUSTRY: DESCRIPTIVE ANALYSIS OF KID-
FRIENDLY HOTELS' PRACTICES IN TURKEY
Çağıl Hale Özel   193

THE INFLUENCE OF SLOW CITY IN THE CONTEXT
OF SUSTAINABLE DESTINATION MARKETING
Yeşim Coşar, Alp Timur and Metin Kozak   209

CUSTOMER COMMUNICATION FACILITIES WITH
TOURISM: A COMPARISON BETWEEN GERMAN
AND JAPANESE AUTOMOBILE COMPANIES
Yosuke Endo and Yohei Kurata   221

TOURIST SPACES AND TOURISM POLICY IN SPAIN
AND PORTUGAL
Fernando Almeida, Rafael Cortés and Antonia Balbuena   235

PART IV: METHODS IN MARKETING PLACES AND SPACES

ANALYZING SEASONAL DIFFERENCES IN A
DESTINATION'S TOURIST MARKET: THE CASE OF
MINHO
Elisabeth Kastenholz and António Lopes de Almeida   253

MODELLING FERRY PASSENGER NUMBERS:
IMPLICATIONS FOR DESTINATION MANAGEMENT
Carl H. Marcussen   269

YIELDING TOURISTS' PREFERENCES
Jaime Serra, Antónia Correia and Paulo M. M. Rodrigues   281

LAKE-DESTINATION IMAGE ATTRIBUTES:
CONTENT ANALYSIS OF TEXT AND PICTURES
Ana Isabel Rodrigues, Antónia Correia, Metin Kozak and   293
Anja Tuohino

HOW DO TOURISTS TURN SPACE INTO PLACE? – A
CONCEPTUALISATION FOR SUSTAINABLE PLACE
MARKETING
Juergen Gnoth   *315*

LIST OF CONTRIBUTORS

José Luís Abrantes	Polytechnic Institute of Viseu, Portugal
António Lopes de Almeida	University of Aveiro, Portugal
Fernando Almeida	University of Málaga, Spain
Antonia Balbuena	University of Málaga, Spain
Kamila Borseková	Matej Bel University, Slovakia
Eugénia Castela	University of Algarve, Portugal
Antónia Correia	University of Algarve, Portugal
Rafael Cortés	University of Málaga, Spain
Yeşim Coşar	Dokuz Eylül University, Turkey
Giacomo Del Chiappa	University of Sassari, Italy
Leonardo (Don) A. N. Dioko	Institute for Tourism Studies, Macau, SAR China
Yosuke Endo	Tokyo Metropolitan University, Japan
Cristina Estevão	Polytechnic Institute of Castelo Branco – NECE, Portugal
João Ferreira	University of Beira Interior – NECE, Portugal
Fulvio Fortezza	University of Ferrara, Italy
Juergen Gnoth	Otago University, New Zealand
Nuno Gustavo	Estoril Higher Institute for Tourism and Hotel Studies, Portugal
Shoji Iijima	University of the Ryukyus, Japan
Elisabeth Kastenholz	University of Aveiro, Portugal

Metin Kozak	Dokuz Eylül University, Turkey
Yohei Kurata	Tokyo Metropolitan University, Japan
Veronica I. K. Lam	Institute for Tourism Studies, Macau
Carl H. Marcussen	Centre for Regional and Tourism Research, Denmark
Marica Mazurek	Matej Bel University, Slovakia
Scott McCabe	Nottingham University, UK
Giuseppe Melis	University of Cagliari, Italy
Inês Miranda	Estoril Higher Institute for Tourism and Hotel Studies, Portugal
Taketo Naoi	Tokyo Metropolitan University, Japan
Sara Nunes	Polytechnic Institute of Castelo Branco & NECE, Portugal
Yasuo Ohe	Chiba University, Japan
Çağıl Hale Özel	Anadolu University, Turkey
Katarína Petríková	Matej Bel University, Slovakia
Alma Raissova	Lund University, Sweden
Ana Isabel Rodrigues	Polytechnic Institute of Beja, Portugal
Paulo M. M. Rodrigues	Nova School of Business and Economics, Portugal
Jaime Serra	University of Évora, Portugal
Tetsuo Shimizu	Tokyo Metropolitan University, Japan
Carla Silva	Polytechnic Institute of Viseu, Portugal
Akira Soshiroda	Tokyo Institute of Technology, Japan
Alp Timur	Dokuz Eylül University, Turkey
Anja Tuohino	University of Eastern Finland, Finland
Anna Vaňová	Matej Bel University, Slovakia

LIST OF REVIEWERS

Paulo Águas
University of Algarve, Portugal

David Airey
University of Surrey, UK

António Almeida
Madeira University, Portugal

Maria Alvarez
Bogazici University, Turkey

Vitor Ambrósio
ESHTE, Portugal

Luisa Andreu
Valencia University, Spain

Andrés Artal
Cartagena University, Spain

Seyhmus Baloglu
UNVL, USA

Carlos Barros
Technical University of Lisbon, Portugal

Adarsh Batra
Assumption University, Thailand

Michael Bosnjak
Free University of Bozen, Italy

Pedro Brito
University of Porto, Portugal

Antónia Correia
University of Algarve, Portugal

John Crotts
College of Charleston, USA

Alain Decrop
Louvain School of Management, Belgium

João Duque
Technical University of Lisbon, Portugal

Adão Flores
University of Algarve, Portugal

Alan Fyall
University of Central Florida, USA

Jurgen Gnoth
University of Otago, New Zealand

Basak Denizci Guillet
Hong Kong Polytechnic University, SAR, China

Szilvia Gyimóthy
Aalborg University, Denmark

Heather Hartwell
Bournemouth University, UK

Tzung-Cheng Huan
National Chiayi University, Taiwan

Simon Hudson
University of South Carolina, USA

Ken Hyde
AUT University, New Zealand

Gilberto Jordan
CEO, André Jordan Group

Elisabeth Kastenholz
University of Aveiro, Portugal

Metin Kozak
Dokuz Eylül University, Turkey

Sonja Sibila Lebe
University of Maribor, Slovenia

Drew Martin
University of Hawaii at Hilo, USA

Júlio Mendes
University of Algarve, Portugal

Miguel Moital
Bournemouth University, UK

Peter Nijkamp
Free University, Netherlands

Andreas Papatheodorou
Aegean University, Greece

Cody Paris
Middlesex University, Dubai

Harald Pechlaner
European Academy of Bolzano, Italy

Richard Perdue
Virginia Tech University, USA

Joaquim Ramalho
University of Évora, Portugal

Tamara Ratz
Kodolanyi Janos University College, Hungary

Efigénio Rebelo
University of Algarve, Portugal

Arie Reichel
Ben Gurion University of the Negev, Israel

Paulo Rodrigues
Nova University, Portugal

Francisco Silva
Azores University, Portugal

Ercan Sirakaya-Turk
University of South Carolina, USA

Boris Snoj
University of Maribor, Slovenia

Patricia Valle
University of Algarve, Portugal

Andreas Zins
MODUL University, Vienna, Austria

PREFACE

This book continues the testimony of the scientific contributions of the *Advances in Tourism Marketing Conference* (ATMC) series. It compiles papers selected before and after their presentation at the 5th ATMC held in Algarve, Portugal, October 2–4, 2013. Under the conference theme of "Marketing Space and Place: Shifting Tourist Flows," this conference builds on the success of the previous Advances in Tourism Marketing conferences with a series of critical reference books now in existence and beginning to demonstrate impact through citations.

The first conference took place in 2005, in Mugla University in Akyaka (Turkey), which resulted in Kozak and Andreu (2006) *Progress in Tourism Marketing*, a book published by Elsevier. It contains 17 chapters that add to the discussion of pertinent theories and practices critical to marketing research. The second conference was hosted in 2007 by the Universitat de València (Spain) and resulted in the edition of Kozak, Gnoth, and Andreu (2009) *Advances in Destination Marketing*. This second book published by Routledge explores new and emerging topics in destination marketing reinforcing scientific and innovative thinking in tourism marketing. The third conference hosted by Bournemouth University (UK) resulted in a further book by Fyall, Kozak, Andreu, Gnoth, and Lebe (2011) *Marketing Innovations for Sustainable Destinations*. Published by Goodfellow, this volume offers insight into a variety of innovative marketing operations able to enhance tourism development in destinations. The fourth conference was then held in Maribor (Slovenia) leading to a further book Kozak, Andreu, Gnoth, Lebe, and Fyall (2013) *Tourism Marketing: On Both Sides of the Counter*, published by Cambridge Scholars Publishing. This book brings to the discussion tourism marketing strategies and operations through the lenses of industry and tourists. Ahead of its time, the conference and book promote collaboration and co-creation in the particular context of tourism marketing.

Nine years after the launch of the ATMC series, an increasing number of researchers have been attracted to discuss emergent topics across the domain of tourism marketing. During this time, over 500 sets of research, findings, and presentations have been made accessible to the public. In addition to the conferences and books, its steering committee edited three special journal issues and many more individual articles that have found their way into top-ranking tourism journals after first, presentations, followed by collegial critique and discussion at respective ATMC events, as well as further editorial help thereafter. The fifth conference follows the proud tradition of ATMC, enlarging and consolidating an expert worldwide network which, in turn, continues to enrich the body of knowledge in Tourism Marketing.

The editors of this book, with the assistance of many colleagues who gave their time to serve as reviewers for papers submitted to the ATMC 2013, selected the papers for the chapters in this book. The editors would like to acknowledge the contribution of the authors and reviewers to make this achievement possible.

The result is a timely and relevant compendium of chapters that offer to readers topical issues in place marketing and competitive strategies where tourism is discussed as a subjective, performative action contextualized by the geographical and sociocultural characteristics of destinations. The book covers qualitative and quantitative methods as well as case studies, finishing with conceptual papers that offer new avenues of research in image and tourism place marketing. The contributions reflect the vibrancy of ATMC and the high caliber of researchers the conference attracts. Chapters are mostly written by mature researchers, some of them in collaboration with young researchers following the collegial tradition of ATMC of launching new scholars and opening new horizons for future generations of academia and industry.

The book offers itself as a must read for researchers, students of tourism and industry, as well as all the individuals who wish to be updated on topical research issues in Tourism Places Marketing. This book helps trigger new topics in tourism marketing research and deserves your attention. Keep reading is our major advice!

Antónia Correia
Juergen Gnoth
Metin Kozak
Alan Fyall
Co-Editors

EDITORIAL BOARD

INTRODUCTION

This book bridges the gaps between tourism space and place. Space expresses fluidity or contingency, whereas place implies interaction between individuals and the physical location. As space is transformed into place, tourism is all about the reality of experiences that generate flows and impacts.

This book comprises four parts and 21 chapters. These chapters contribute by deconstructing how space takes form in different physical, cognitive, social, and emotional dimensions resulting from interactions between tourists and host environments. These contributions led to further our understanding of tourism flows. The book includes tourists' and marketers' perspectives and is structured into four parts: *Places, Perceptions and Co-Creative Development*; *Image and Competitive Strategies*; *Marketing Places — Towards a Cooperative Strategy*; and *Methods in Marketing Places and Spaces*.

This volume boldly questions the scope and truth of Urry's (1990) gaze or Boorstin's (1961) critique who see tourists' postmodern condition as a "trivial, superficial, frivolous pursuit of vicarious, contrived experiences, [and as] a 'pseudo-event'," to argue that the spatial behavior is intertwined with tourists' own emotional connection to a given place. Questions that give rise to this book are: Is place attachment truly just a contrived and commercially generated notion of feelings of attachment or embeddedness in a place? How does this spatial activity coalesce with their search for authenticity in new places? (Cresswell, 1997; Löfgren, 1999; MacCannell, 1973). Bearing these questions in mind, the book is a collection of groundbreaking and stimulating chapters that explore place marketing through the adoption of a cooperative approach.

PART I: PLACES, PERCEPTIONS AND CO-CREATIVE DEVELOPMENT

The multidimensional nature of tourism phenomena leads the discussion toward the understanding of places perceived by tourists as forms of "valued environments" (Burgess & Gold, 1985). Yet Pearce (1982) defines a "tourist place" as "any place that fosters a feeling of being a tourist." The latter has been understood as a juxtaposition of "outsideness" and "insideness," with one of the tourist's objective of penetrating the insideness or "back region" of the attraction to savor its authenticity (MacCannell, 1973), highlighting its emotional and cognitive content. As Schroeder (2007) proposes, human−nature relationships differ based on how people see themselves, either as part or apart from nature. As such, place attachment may be measured by the extent to which people feel attached or embedded in the places they experience. This assessment is offered in the first six chapters in different contexts; from the urban/shopping districts to the clues of sacred mountains passing through the sea (ship tourism). The resident perspective has been explored to conclude that it is in the encounter in between the locals and the tourists that a touristic place is bordered.

The chapter "Local Students' Perceptions of Spaces for Tourists and Locals in a Shopping District: Photo-Based Research" by Taketo Naoi, Shoji Iijima, Akira Soshiroda, and Tetsuo Shimizu aims to depict the elements that separate tourism spaces from the residential ones. This chapter represents very innovative research as it describes the characteristics of the varied spaces to be connoted as touristic. The characteristics of places are described, enlightening the interactions between people and spaces considering affective and emotional dimensions, by means of photo elicitation. This chapter combines an innovative method with timely research which reinforces that the locals enhance the attractiveness of a tourism space, in particular when locals encounter tourists and contribute to the tourists' sense and charming authenticity of places.

The chapter "Residents' Perceptions of Mountain Destinations" by Carla Silva, Elisabeth Kastenholz, and José Luís Abrantes offers a very similar view in quite a different scenery, namely, mountains. This chapter emphasizes that the image of mountains from the perspective of residents relies on their historic and cultural heritage. It highlights the mysticism that surrounds the mountains' attributes of these places and as holding a sacred and mystic value that represents the attracting clues of its image. This chapter combines qualitative and quantitative methods and is particularly valuable as it uses a cross-country approach to generalize the findings.

Keeping with nature places, the chapter "Attitudes of Successors in Dairy Farms toward Educational Tourism in Japan" by Yasuo Ohe focuses on dairy farms. This chapter shows that farmers' identity moderates tourists' sense of place. Their attitude to their own place forms the launching step and also establishes this emerging social demand for farm tourism in Japan. This chapter thereby emphasizes a new but increasing form of farm tourism led by farmers in which the farmer's identity and own experiences are critical to define the touristic place.

Moving from nature on land to the beauty of the oceans, the chapter "Residents' Perceptions of the Impact of Ship Tourism and Their Preferences for Different Types of Tourism" by Giacomo Del Chiappa and Giuseppe Melis assesses cruise tourism, and researches the identity of the sea as a touristic place. The involvement of local communities and personalized promotions are pivotal to cruise tourism development.

Following the conference aims of assessing touristic places from different perspectives, the chapter "Wedding-Based Tourism Development: Insights from an Italian Context" by Giacomo Del Chiappa and Fulvio Fortezza assesses places in the context of new product development, in this case, weddings, as they enhance the romantic gaze of places. This chapter uses qualitative analysis, critically argues for sustainable development based on emotional and experiential strategies rather than a product/ service-oriented strategy.

Part I of the book closes with the chapter "Conceptualizing the Value Co-Creation Challenge for Tourist Destinations: A Supply-Side Perspective" by Giuseppe Melis, Scott McCabe and Giacomo Del Chiappa, which stresses co-creative strategies as a bridge to sustainable development. This chapter outlines value creation in tourist experiences. The model proposed by the authors puts forward fundamental ideas on how to acknowledge and handle tourists' experiences as a value-based construct to establish a touristic place identity.

PART II: IMAGE AND COMPETITIVE STRATEGIES

Part II of the book discusses place images as the way to develop competitive strategies. This discussion arose under the umbrella of place identity and tourism experience. It assumes that touristic places generate emotive outcomes that may lead to unveil branding (Volo, 2010). As in Schmitt (2002) and Ye, Tussyadiah, and Fesenmaier (2009), sensory, affective, cognitive, physical, and relational dimensions are all assumed to structure tourists' interactions with places. The chapter "The Emotional Attachment Built through the Attitudes and Managerial Approach to Place Marketing

and Branding – "The Golden City of Kremnica, Slovakia"" by Marica
Mazurek fosters that culture and heritage, co-partnerships and strategic
management together set forth the paths of place branding.

Enlightening the relevance of the other senses to define place image, the
chapter "Hospitality Servicescapes Seen by Visually Impaired Travelers"
by Alma Raissova promotes an empirical research within visually impaired
travelers. This chapter demonstrates how visually impaired guests (VIPs)
perceive places and hosts in hospitality spaces. This chapter, grounded on
qualitative methods, suggests that hospitality servicescapes should be developed by understanding VIPs' mobility tactics. Furthermore, it argues that
place image is more than simply design and furniture, and includes smell,
sound, taste, and touch.

Under the five dimensions of touristic places image, Part II of the book
introduces a group of chapters to discuss differentiation strategies and
competitiveness throughout a competitive strategic perspective within different contexts. The chapter "Determinants of Tourism Destination
Competitiveness: A SEM Approach" by Cristina Estevão, João Ferreira,
and Sara Nunes introduces the most relevant determinants of tourism destinations, by means of a SEM approach. This chapter argues that place
images and competitiveness stem from its natural resources counterba-
lanced with their supply and strategic management. This chapter, which
was empirically tested in Portugal, is of utmost importance in the advancement of a cooperative strategy.

Furthermore, the chapter "Events as a Differentiation Strategy for
Tourist Destinations: The Case of *Allgarve*" by Inês Miranda, Nuno
Gustavo, and Eugénia Castela scopes Portugal once again, in this particular case the south (Algarve) of the country assessing how events may contribute to differentiate a destination that is recognized worldwide. The
results of this chapter show that event experiences may contribute to the
consolidation of the brand Algarve, although recognizing that promotional
efforts are still required. Furthermore, connecting a mature sun and sand
image with events is effortless if a huge increase in events and promotion
are not materialized.

As in Part I, Part II of the book closes with a chapter that consolidates
tourism places throughout a competitive approach. The chapter "From
Tourism Space to a Unique Tourism Place through a Conceptual
Approach to Building a Competitive Advantage" by Kamila Borseková,
Anna Vaňová, and Katarína Petríková argues that unique places are
derived from resources creation, exploration, and innovation, moving the
target of the place to tourism.

PART III: MARKETING PLACES – TOWARDS A COOPERATIVE STRATEGY

Part III of the book offers an integrated approach of how hosts, guests, and places may interact to co-create unique tourism places. Literature stresses that marketing tourism places is more effective when a destination personality is set forth. The chapter "Achieving Consistency in Destination Personalities: A Tripartite Personality Congruity Theory Focused on Industry Professionals" by Veronica I. K. Lam and Leonardo (Don) A. N. Dioko stresses that destination personality proves that industry professionals' self-personality are mirrored in destinations' personality although this self-representation suggests that more efforts are needed to enhance the marketing of places. The chapter "Marketing to Children in Tourism Industry: Descriptive Analysis of Kid-Friendly Hotels' Practices in Turkey" by Çağıl Hale Özel proposes a very interesting marketing strategy for children in Turkish hotels through the leveraging of the parents' attitudes toward these touristic places. This chapter probes that the tourism products/places may fit tourists needs, more than generalizing and mass-orienting places. Yet the "must have" strategy is to cluster the tourism places accordingly with its demand expectations. The chapter "The Influence of Slow City in the Context of Sustainable Destination Marketing" by Yeşim Coşar, Alp Timur, and Metin Kozak follows by introducing a timely and relevant dimension, that of slow tourism. The authors posit that the marketing of slow cities struggles against a backdrop of environmental constraints and high levels of saturation. That said, a proper and integrated tourism policy ought to be in place to counter such barriers at the destination level. The essential need for cooperativism in marketing activities is again stressed in the chapter "Customer Communication Facilities with Tourism: A Comparison between German and Japanese Automobile Companies" by Yosuke Endo and Yohei Kurata. This chapter focuses on the incorporation of tourism in the corporate branding strategies of consumer goods companies, in particular in the car manufacturing industry. The innovativeness of this chapter relies on establishing a communication platform that may positively leverage the tourism brand through the inclusion of tourists in road shows or events that simultaneously promote the cars and tourism industry for example.

Aside from the efforts industry commits to the promotion of destinations, a tourism policy is still required which embraces tourism development more fully. This is the subject of the chapter "Tourist Spaces and

Tourism Policy in Spain and Portugal," which closes Part III of the book. This chapter by Fernando Almeida, Rafael Cortés, and Antonia Balbuena shows the existence of two stages of tourism development in Latin America, that of Fordism and post-Fordism, with significant consequences in territory organization, that today are difficult to reverse most notably with efforts to counter the imbalances of mass tourism.

PART IV: METHODS IN MARKETING PLACES AND SPACES

As anticipation is pivotal to promote a balanced and sustainable strategy where all the players may intervene toward tourism development, Part IV, the final part of the book, introduces chapters that provide a valuable foundation for emerging methodologies to marketing places and spaces.

The chapter "Analyzing Seasonal Differences in A Destination's Tourist Market: The Case of Minho" by Elisabeth Kastenholz and António Lopes de Almeida proposes a methodology to measure tourism demand seasonality which was empirically tested in the Minho touristic region in the north of Portugal. This chapter stresses the attention of managers to profile tourists by seasons in order to organize strategies in light of their motivations and attitudes. This, in turn, will contribute to the alleviation of the problems of seasonality. In light of tourism demand modeling and forecasting, the chapter "Modelling Ferry Passenger Numbers: Implications for Destination Management" by Carl H. Marcussen introduces passengers' daily-based forecasts to optimize supply and revenues in the context of destination marketing. In the same fashion, the chapter "Yielding Tourists' Preferences" by Jaime Serra, Antónia Correia, and Paulo M. M. Rodrigues introduces new measures of yield grounded on the stated preferences of tourists.

Furthermore, the chapter "Lake-Destination Image Attributes: Content Analysis of Text and Pictures" by Ana Isabel Rodrigues, Antónia Correia, Metin Kozak, and Anja Tuohino offers an innovative conceptual model to measure lake destination images comprising photo elicitation and content analysis of promotional texts. The authors proposed that lake destination images rely on five dimensions: resource, supply, logistical, organizational, and meaning.

The final chapter "How Do Tourists Turn Space into Place? – A Conceptualisation for Sustainable Place Marketing" by Juergen Gnoth answers the questions that embodied the structure of this compendium. This chapter establishes the close nexus on place marketing. The answer is simple in that tourists need to move or at least imagine to be somewhere else, to co-create meanings. Meanings are the essence of place that are derived from the tourists' interaction with the space. It involves interactions and experiences engrained in emotions and moods. Although meanings entail awareness and consciousness, this is the only way to unveil the uniqueness the place holds. Most of the time the places made by marketers do not converge with tourists' authentic identity of places. As such, leveraging the place as tourists wish to perceive it is critical to ensure tourism places authenticity in the future.

In conclusion, this innovative and critical book contributes to the advancement of knowledge in tourism marketing through approaching spaces and places via multidisciplinary perspective ranging from geography, to economics, marketing, and sociology and promoting a close nexus of the paths to ensure the future development of tourism.

REFERENCES

Boorstin, D. (1961). *The image: A guide to pseudo-events in America*. New York, NY: Harper and Row.

Burgess, J., & Gold, J. R. (1985). Place, the media and popular culture. In J. Burgess & J. R. Gold (Eds.), *Geography, the media and popular culture* (pp. 235–251). Melbourne: Longman Cheshire.

Cresswell, T. (1997). Imagining the nomad: Mobility and the postmodern primitive. In G. Benko & U. Strohmayer (Eds.), *Space and social theory: Interpreting modernity and postmodernity* (pp. 360–379). Oxford: Blackwell Publishers.

Löfgren, O. (1999). *On holiday: A history of vacationing*. Berkeley, CA: University of California Press.

MacCannell, D. (1973). Staged authenticity: Arrangements of social space in tourist settings. *American Journal of Sociology, 79*(3), 589–603.

Pearce, P. (1982). *The social psychology of tourist behavior*. Oxford: Pergamon Press.

Schmitt, B. (2002). *Marketing experimental*. São Paulo: Nobel.

Schroeder, M. A. (2007). *Slaves of the passions*. Oxford: Oxford University Press.

Urry, J. (1990). *The tourist gaze*. London: Sage.

Volo, S. (2010). Bloggers' reported tourist experiences: Their utility as a tourism data source and their effect on prospective tourists. *Journal of Vacation Marketing, 16*(4), 297–311.

Ye, Y., Tussyadiah, I., & Fesenmaier, D. R. (2009). Capturing the phenomenon of tourism experience as a foundation for designing experiential brands. In *Proceedings of the 14th Annual Graduate Student Research Conference in Hospitality & Tourism*. Las Vegas, USA.

PART I
PLACES, PERCEPTIONS AND CO-CREATIVE DEVELOPMENT

LOCAL STUDENTS' PERCEPTIONS OF SPACES FOR TOURISTS AND LOCALS IN A SHOPPING DISTRICT: PHOTO-BASED RESEARCH

Taketo Naoi, Shoji Iijima, Akira Soshiroda and Tetsuo Shimizu

ABSTRACT

This study aims to identify the elements that characterise spaces for tourists and those that characterise spaces for locals in a shopping district based on the perspectives of local students. Forty-five local undergraduates took photographs of settings that impressed them in the shopping district in Naha-shi, Okinawa Prefecture, Japan, and the reasons given by each respondent for photographing a particular setting were recorded. Frequently used nouns and adjectives were extracted for each category. The results suggest the importance of the types of commercial facilities and people on the perspectives of locals. Affordable and mundane products are associated with local spaces, while souvenirs may be regarded as symbols of touristic spaces. The absence of locals and the presence of tourists may be characteristics of touristic spaces whereas

Marketing Places and Spaces
Advances in Culture, Tourism and Hospitality Research, Volume 10, 3–18
Copyright © 2015 by Emerald Group Publishing Limited
ISSN: 1871-3173/doi:10.1108/S1871-317320150000010001

the potential attractiveness of encounters with locals for tourists is also implied.

Keywords: Shopping districts; photo-based research; spaces for locals and tourists

INTRODUCTION

In consideration of Schmidt's (1979) distinction between places that are primarily intended for tourists and those that are not, there seem to be very few tourism destinations of the former category. For example, cities have emerged primarily to accommodate human residential or commercial needs while also serving tourists; consequently, certain spaces that serve tourists may overlap with or be in close proximity to ones serving residents. Snepenger, Murphy, Snepenger, and Anderson (2004) described the differences between places dependent on tourists and those dependent on locals. The authors recognised some places within a large tourism economy that accommodate mainly tourists, ones that focus on a mix of tourists and locals, and others that cater to locals and only incidentally tourists.

The aim of this study is to identify the elements that characterise spaces for tourists and those that characterise spaces for locals in a shopping district based on the perspectives of local students. To the knowledge of the authors, this study represents the first attempt to elucidate empirically the characteristics of the varied spaces in a shopping district based on individual perceptions. Thus, the characteristics of various settings are viewed in light of interactions between people and spaces based on analyses of individuals' views regarding settings that they encounter. As Snepenger et al. (2004) argued, an investigation of the mix of tourists and locals may shed light on the nature of a place. Further, a study of this kind may offer indicators for tourism destination managers who promote tourism in consideration of its influences on shopping districts.

LITERATURE REVIEW

Shopping has been viewed as an important part of the tourism experience (Choi, Chan, & Wu, 1999; Cohen, 1995; Hsieh & Chang, 2006; Kent, Schock, & Snow, 1983; Mak, Tsang, & Cheung, 1999; Snepenger, Murphy,

O'Connell, & Gregg, 2003; Swanson & Horridge, 2004; Timothy, 2005) and as a destination attraction (Ryan, 1991; Timothy & Butler, 1995). Shopping also provides tourists with a taste of local culture (Stobart, 1998, as cited in Hsieh & Chang, 2006, p. 3). Indeed, experiencing a destination and its local culture has been pointed out as one of the key motives for shopping at the tourism destination; other motives include purchasing necessities and meeting social obligations (Moscardo, 2004; Murphy, Benckendorff, Moscardo, & Pearce, 2011).

Venues for shopping that are potential tourist attractions may vary in form. For example, shopping malls are organised intentionally to accommodate tourists; some venues such as supermarkets, however, have not been regarded traditionally as tourist destinations, although many now cater to tourists (Timothy, 2005). Such non-traditional shopping places for tourists can include what Bloch, Ridgway, and Dawson (1994) call tourist shopping habitats, which often vary according to the diversity of small shops reflected in their colours, scents and sounds, and these small businesses enhance the tourism experience by highlighting local customs and culture (Hsieh & Chang, 2006).

This study focuses on a shopping district (shopping habitat) that is not oriented towards tourists. It not only functions as a centre for locals but also attracts tourists (Murphy et al., 2011; Snepenger et al., 2003). Thus, it is a suitable setting for observing relationships between tourists and communities (Snepenger, Reiman, Johnson, & Snepenger, 1988).

A shopping district usually covers a certain geographical expanse, and its sub-areas may have characteristics that are both touristic and local. The lifecycle model for retail spaces proposed by Snepenger et al. (1988) offers some indices reflecting the transition of a shopping district towards a touristic venue. In this model, a shopping district moves through five stages, depending on the numbers of tourists and locals and their purchasing power.

At the first stage of exploration, a shopping district caters to the needs of residents, and there are only a few incidental tourists whose purchases are ordinary. At the involvement stage, shops begin to target tourists while still serving locals. As tourism expands, the district enters the development stage. Then, upscale stores that sell nonessentials for tourists displace local stores. The fourth stage is consolidation, in which the district has ceased to accommodate the everyday needs of local residents. Stores at this stage sell products and mementos that are irrelevant to locals' daily lives or not affordable for residents. When a district enters the final stage of stagnation, locals rarely shop in the district. Development of services such as catering and entertainment businesses usually leads to the displacement of traditional and resident-oriented businesses. This model suggests the shift of core clienteles from locals to tourists, the shift of merchandise from mundane products to nonessentials and mementos, and the shift of prices from affordable to unaffordable for most locals, as the signs of a shopping district changing into a touristic venue.

The concepts of staged authenticity and the collective romantic gaze further suggest that there may be spaces that cannot be typified as spaces solely for tourists or locals. MacCannell (1976) cited main streets and shopping centres as places of staged authenticity; in other words, they appear to be authentic, but they are contrived settings. In contrast, some areas that cater to locals may draw attention from tourists in light of the concept of tourists' collective romantic gaze (Ooi, 2002). This concept suggests that tourists may gaze on local food courts, for example, for their authentic charm, which is strengthened by locals' participation.

In this study, the views of locals regarding features that characterise a shopping district's spaces as suitable for tourists or locals have been elicited. Apart from a few studies, including ones by Snepenger et al. (1988), many past studies have researched tourists' views, rather than locals', regarding shopping areas as tourist attractions. Studies of locals' views are crucial in light of the possible impact that tourists could have on the locals. On the one hand, higher-priced products and the replacement of traditional shopping with tourist-oriented services have been pointed out as possible disrupters for local residents (Getz, 1993). On the other hand, for tourism destination authorities, the creation of shopping areas that persuade customers to visit and even extend their stays may be an important objective (Jones, 1999; Lin, 2004; Yuksel, 2004). Although the locals' approval and disapproval of the influx of tourists into the shopping district is beyond the scope of this study, identification of the characteristics of touristic and local spaces from the viewpoints of locals should provide clues to locals' perceptions of tourism in shopping districts.

This study also focuses on specific features of shopping streets. Studies of shopping places as tourist attractions based on environmental perceptions are still scarce. Some studies include environment-related information, but holistic attributes such as shops' appearance (Yuksel, 2004) and in-store environment (Choi, Liu, Pang, & Chow, 2008) are used as the features for respondents to rate. Some other studies have focused on the detailed characteristics of shops (Heung & Cheng, 2000; Lee, Chang, Hou, & Lin, 2008). However, they have not addressed differences among spaces within a shopping area.

METHODOLOGY

In this study, photographs that respondents took to capture their perceptions of designated places were utilised. Use of still images is a method to present settings of a tourism destination as stimuli to respondents. Indeed, photographs may portray environmental situations more accurately than verbal descriptions (Brown, Richards, Daniel, & King, 1989, as cited in Son & Pearce, 2005, p. 24; Munson, 1993 as cited in Son & Pearce, 2005, p. 24).

Some past studies have utilised photographs prepared by researchers as stimuli. For example, Son and Pearce (2005) required respondents to rate the extent to which photographed features represented the images they had of Australia. Likewise, Prebensen (2007) employed photographs of Norway's attributes. Fairweather and Swaffield (2001, 2002) used the Q method, requiring visitors to state their views about destinations after classifying various photographs. Naoi, Airey, Iijima, and Niininen (2006, 2007) also used photographs of a historical district to conduct personal interviews using the repertory grid and laddering analysis. Regarding more quantitative approaches, some authors (MacKay & Fesenmaier, 1997, 2000; Naoi, Airey, & Iijima, 2009; Naoi & Iijima, 2004) conducted experiments with slides to investigate respondents' evaluations of destinations.

However, the use of photographs taken by researchers may fail to capture fully respondents' evaluations of elements that are relevant to their experiences (Garrod, 2007). Some researchers analysed the contents of photographs taken by respondents for their studies of natural environments (Cherem & Driver, 1983; Oku & Fukamachi, 2006; Taylor, Czarnowski, Sexton, & Flick, 1995), urban environments (Haywood, 1990), historic sites (MacKay & Couldwell, 2004), and a famous seaside resort (Garrod, 2007). The anticipated benefits of this technique are deepened reflections by respondents regarding their views and experiences (Garrod, 2007, 2008; Markwell, 2000) and elicitations of their experiences (Garrod, 2007).

While the studies cited above focused largely on analysing the contents of photographs, evaluations of photographed settings by respondents may be helpful as well. Garrod (2007) has emphasised the importance of the interpretation of photographers' viewpoints reflected in the actual photographs. Dakin (2003) has suggested that the meanings and associations people ascribe to photographed landscapes must be captured. Botterill and his colleagues (Botterill, 1989; Botterill & Crompton, 1987, 1996) asked respondents to describe their travel experiences based on the photographs they took during their trips. Their open-ended views were analysed. Their analyses, though, were based on extremely small sample sizes of one or two respondents.

The shopping district in Naha-shi, Okinawa Prefecture, Japan, was selected as the research site. The archipelagic prefecture is in the western-most part of Japan and is the only Japanese prefecture that lies wholly within the subtropical oceanic climatic zone (Kakazu, 2011). The area in and around the prefecture used to be the independent Ryukyu Kingdom until the middle of the 19th century. The prefecture has an abundance of unique flora and fauna (Kakazu, 2011). Okinawa Prefecture ranked 2nd among Japan's 47 prefectures as a summer tourism destination according to a survey by the Japan Travel Bureau, the largest tour operator in Japan (2009), possibly due to its natural and cultural uniqueness as well as its subtropical climate.

The shopping district in Naha-shi (the prefectural capital) has its roots in the post-war black market. The opening of the municipal market in 1948 marks the beginning of the district, which was followed by the establish-ment of the nearby shopping streets (Domae, 1997). During the 1950s and 1960s, *Kokusai-dori*, the main street, was developed (Domae, 1997). Many shops in and adjacent to these shopping streets were rented out to large-scale stores in the 1980s. While they have been used primarily as souvenir shops since then (Kim, 2009), Kinjo's study (2004) reports a mix of shops targeting tourists and market-type stores selling clothes and food in the dis-trict. The study respondents, therefore, were expected to have opportunities to encounter touristic spaces as well as those with local characteristics.

Forty-five local undergraduates who had graduated from high schools in the prefecture walked around the district for about an hour and took ten or more photographs of settings that impressed them according to four categories:

• Category 1: Spaces for tourists
• Category 2: Spaces that visitors may regard as part of the local lives, but are not
• Category 3: Spaces that are potentially attractive for tourists
• Category 4: Spaces for locals.

Respondents answered open-ended questions to explain their reasons for photographing these settings according to elements they noticed, character-istics of elements they noticed, and their perceptions of 'noticed characteris-tics'. These points were proposed by Koga et al. (1999) as a framework for respondents to state their reasons for photographing certain settings.

The first and second questions were designed to extract the characteristics of a noticed element; the last question was designed to elicit respondents' thoughts about the characteristics of the noticed elements.

With use of KH Coder (Higuchi, n.d.), a text mining software package for Japanese analyses, nouns and adjectives with frequencies of 5% or more relative to the total responses were extracted for each category. It should be noted that some words suggest the presence of certain elements as characteristics of spaces while others may imply the absence of certain elements as characteristics. For instance, 'tourist' may mean that tourists are perceived as characteristic of a setting or that the setting is distinct because tourists are absent. Thus, the context in which the frequent words were used was checked to see whether the presence or absence of each word related to the characteristics of the settings.

FINDINGS

The results of this study are presented in Tables 1–4. Each table number corresponds to each of the four categories explained above. Each table shows the frequently used words extracted (by category) from the reasons given for photographing certain settings. The highlighted words are words for which their absence was mentioned as a characteristic of each category in 50% or more of the cases. For instance, Table 1 shows that the absence of 'local residents' was mentioned as a reason for photographing certain settings for Category 1 in 54.5% of the cases. The following explanations focus on notable results from our analyses.

Regarding Category 1, Table 1 shows that the presence of 'tourists', the absence of 'local' (adjective), the absence (54.5% of the cases) and presence (45.5% of the cases) of 'local residents', and the presence of commercial elements such as shops and souvenirs were mentioned as reasons for photographing certain settings. Regarding Category 2, Table 2 indicates that the presence of 'tourists', the absence of 'local residents', 'local' (adjective) and 'customers', and the presence of commercial elements such as shops, souvenirs, markets and shopping streets were mentioned as the reasons for photographing selected settings. Regarding Categories 1 and 2, 'tourists' and commercial elements were prominent in both. The presence of the main street (*Kokusai-dori*) and the main arcade (*Heiwa-dori*) in responses for both categories may point to the perception of these types of settings as 'front stage' (MacCannell, 1976). As for the difference between Categories

Table 1. Frequent Words (Category 1).

Nouns	Frequencies	%	Negative[a]	Negative%[b]
Tourists	104	68.0	1	1.0
Okinawa	70	45.8	3	4.3
Shops	35	22.9	0	0.0
Souvenirs	34	22.2	2	5.9
People	28	18.3	11	39.3
Shi-sa[d]	27	17.6	2	7.4
Kokusai-dori[e]	23	15.0	0	0.0
Atmosphere	12	7.8	0	0.0
Local residents[c]	11[c]	7.2[c]	6[c]	54.5[c]
Places	11	7.2	0	0.0
Heiwa-dori[f]	10	6.5	1	10.0
Feelings	9	5.9	1	11.1
Shops' signs	8	5.2	0	0.0
Adjectives	Frequencies	%	Negative[a]	Negative%[b]
Intended for	24	15.7	0	0.0
Many	23	15.0	1	4.3
Local[c]	12[c]	7.8[c]	9[c]	75.0[c]
Alike	8	5.2	0	0.0
Famous	8	5.2	0	0.0

[a]Number of times when the absence of a word was mentioned as characteristic of the category.
[b]Percentage of times when the absence of a word was mentioned as a characteristic of the category.
[c]The highlighted words are words for which their absence was mentioned as a characteristic of each category in 50% or more of the cases. For instance, the absence of 'local residents' was mentioned as a reason for photographing certain settings for Category 1 in 54.5% of the cases.
[d]Okinawan lion statues.
[e]The main street.
[f]The main arcade.

1 and 2, Category 2 may also be perceived to have the aspects of 'backstage' in that local elements including 'residences' and 'houses' were recorded.

Regarding Category 3, Table 3 shows that the presence of 'tourists', 'local residents', 'local' (adjective) and commercial elements including shops, cafes, shopping signs and souvenirs were mentioned as reasons for photographing settings. 'Residence' can also be observed in the table. Category 4, which is associated with spaces for locals, is the focus of Table 4. The absence of 'tourists' and the presence of 'local residents' and 'local' (adjective) are mentioned as reasons for photographing settings.

Table 2. Frequent Words (Category 2).

Nouns	Frequencies	%	Negative[a]	Negative%[b]
People	57	58.2	26	45.6
Tourists	50	51.0	6	12.0
Okinawa	37	37.8	10	27.0
Shops	32	32.7	3	9.4
Lives[c]	20[c]	20.4[c]	13[c]	65.0[c]
Places	15	15.3	3	20.0
Souvenirs	12	12.2	1	8.3
Municipal markets	11	11.2	2	18.2
Local residents[c]	10[c]	10.2[c]	8[c]	80.0[c]
Utilisation[c]	10[c]	10.2[c]	7[c]	70.0[c]
Feelings	9	9.2	0	0.0
Markets	9	9.2	0	0.0
Locals	8	8.2	3	37.5
Kokusai-dori[d]	7	7.1	0	0.0
Shopping streets	6	6.1	0	0.0
Food stuff	6	6.1	0	0.0
Heiwa-dori[e]	6	6.1	0	0.0
Customers[c]	6[c]	6.1[c]	5[c]	83.3[c]
Residences	5	5.1	0	0.0
Merchandise	5	5.1	2	40.0
Restaurants	5	5.1	0	0.0
Atmosphere	5	5.1	0	0.0
Naha	5	5.1	1	20.0
Inner parts	5	5.1	0	0.0
Houses	5	5.1	0	0.0
Spots[c]	5[c]	5.1[c]	3[c]	60.0[c]
Roads	5	5.1	0	0.0
Adjectives	**Frequencies**	**%**	**Negative[a]**	**Negative%[b]**
Local[c]	42[c]	42.9[c]	31[c]	73.8[c]
Many	20	20.4	0	0.0
Intended for	12	12.2	1	8.3
No	10	10.2	1	10.0
Few/Little	6	6.1	1	16.7

[a]Number of times when the absence of the word was mentioned as a characteristic of the category.
[b]Percentage of times when the absence of the word was mentioned as a characteristic of the category.
[c]The highlighted words are words for which their absence was mentioned as a characteristic of each category in 50% or more of the cases. For instance, the absence of 'local residents' was mentioned as a reason for photographing certain settings for Category 2 in 80.0% of the cases.
[d]The main street.
[e]The main arcade.

Table 3.   Frequent Words (Category 3).

Nouns	Frequencies	%	Negative[a]	Negative%[b]
Okinawa	48	50.5	2	4.2
Tourists	46	48.4	16	34.8
People	30	31.6	7	23.3
Shops	29	30.5	1	3.4
Places	21	22.1	0	0.0
Attractiveness	17	17.9	2	11.8
Kokusai-dori[c,d]	16[c]	16.8[c]	10[c]	62.5[c]
Atmosphere	10	10.5	1	10.0
Local Residents	7	7.4	0	0.0
Tourism destinations[c]	7[c]	7.4[c]	4[c]	57.1[c]
Lives	9	9.5	0	0.0
Feelings	8	8.4	0	0.0
Residences	8	8.4	0	0.0
Roads	8	8.4	2	25.0
Cafes	6	6.3	0	0.0
Utilisation	6	6.3	1	16.7
Inner parts	6	6.3	0	0.0
Spots	6	6.3	0	0.0
Shops' signs	5	5.3	0	0.0
Parks	5	5.3	0	0.0
Souvenirs	5	5.3	0	0.0
Screening of movies	5	5.3	0	0.0

Adjectives	Frequencies	%	Negative[a]	Negative%[b]
Nice	11	11.6	0	0.0
Local	11	11.6	2	18.2
Many	7	7.4	0	0.0
Alike	7	7.4	1	14.3
New	6	6.3	0	0.0
No	6	6.3	0	0.0
Few/Little	5	5.3	0	0.0
Good	5	5.3	1	20.0

[a]Number of times when the absence of the word was mentioned as a characteristic of the category.
[b]Percentage of times when the absence of the word was mentioned as a characteristic of the category.
[c]The highlighted words are words for which their absence was mentioned as a characteristic of each category in 50% or more of the cases. For instance, the absence of 'tourism destinations' was mentioned as a reason for photographing certain settings for Category 3 in 57.1% of the cases.
[d]The main street.

Table 4. Frequent Words (Category 4).

Nouns	Frequencies	%	Negative[a]	Negative%[b]
Tourists[e]	38[c]	36.5[c]	31[c]	81.6[c]
People	37	35.6	6	16.2
Local residents	35	33.7	0	0.0
Lives	35	33.7	0	0.0
Okinawa	30	28.8	6	20.0
Spots	24	23.1	0	0.0
Shops	24	23.1	1	4.2
Places	17	16.3	0	0.0
Kokusai-dori[c,d]	11[c]	10.6[c]	8[c]	72.7[c]
Utilisation	11	10.6	0	0.0
Feelings	9	8.7	0	0.0
Residences	9	8.7	0	0.0
Houses	9	8.7	0	0.0
Markets	7	6.7	1	14.3
Restaurants	7	6.7	0	0.0
Residents	6	5.8	0	0.0
Atmosphere	6	5.8	0	0.0
Clothes	6	5.8	0	0.0
Shopping	6	5.8	1	16.7
Hanagasa-Shokudo[e]	6	5.8	1	16.7

Adjectives	Frequencies	%	Negative[a]	Negative%[b]
Local	35	33.7	0	0.0
Many	24	23.1	0	0.0
Intended for[e]	10[c]	9.6[c]	6[c]	60.0[c]
No	9	8.7	0	0.0
Reasonable	7	6.7	0	0.0
Good	7	6.7	0	0.0

[a]Number of times when the absence of the word was mentioned as a characteristic of the category.
[b]Percentage of times when the absence of the word was mentioned as a characteristic of the category.
[c]The highlighted words are words for which their absence was mentioned as a characteristic of each category in 50% or more of the cases. For instance, the absence of 'tourists' was mentioned as a reason for photographing certain settings for Category 4 in 81.6% of the cases.
[d]The main street.
[e]A local restaurant that offers Okinawan home cooking.

The table illustrates that the types of commercial elements mentioned in this category are different from commercial elements in the other three categories in that 'souvenirs' are absent, and that 'clothes' and 'Reasonable' are present. When the findings for categories 3 and 4 are compared, the absence of the main street (*Kokusai-dori*) is noticeable in both. Thus, both types of settings associated with these categories might have been regarded as 'backstage' (MacCannell, 1976) and away from the touristic 'front'. Regarding differences, in addition to the absence of tourists, Category 4 indicates local, mundane and reasonable elements as characteristic, which appears to be consistent with the model by Snepenger et al. (1988), which points to affordable prices as characteristic of spaces for locals.

CONCLUSIONS AND IMPLICATIONS

This study sheds light on locals' views of the elements that characterise spaces in a shopping district with touristic and local features. The types of commercial facilities and the types of people (i.e. tourists and locals) appear to be important. Affordable and mundane products are associated with local spaces, while souvenirs may be regarded as symbols of touristic spaces. The results also imply that the absence of locals and the presence of tourists may be characteristics of touristic spaces. Thus, as argued by Snepenger et al. (1988), a shift of core clientele from locals to tourists, the shift of merchandise from commonplace products to nonessentials and mementos, and a shift in prices from affordable to not affordable for most locals are suggested to be indices that a shopping district has become a mecca for tourists.

That being said, the presence of locals was also seen as aspects of touristic spaces by a certain number of respondents. This view implies that locals may enhance the attractiveness of a space for tourists. The importance of human interaction in shopping places has been advocated in tourism studies (Christiansen & Snepenger, 2002; Murphy et al., 2011). The results of this study indicate that the potential attractiveness of encounters with locals for tourists is recognised by locals themselves. Thus, locals appear to have expectations that their existence contributes to tourists' collective romantic gaze, which is directed towards local objects with authentic charm (Ooi, 2002).

The outcomes of this study are expected to provide a foundational framework for future investigations regarding maintaining a proper balance between the expansion of visited areas and the protection of local residents. Particularly, the findings related to potentially attractive spaces for tourists and the potential attractiveness of encounters with locals may be insightful for managers of shopping districts. Such findings suggest that aspects of local culture that are not contrived for tourists may be attractive to tourists. However, many issues could be explored further, such as ensuring that the negative impact of tourism on local residents is kept to a minimum.

Turning to the limitations, the small sample size is attributed to the difficulties associated with gathering subjects at the same place for a long time, and it is a major limitation of this study. Moreover, this study involves local undergraduates, who may not be representative of locals who visit the shopping district. A broader range of residents should be targeted for future studies. Particularly, it would be worthwhile to examine the views of older generations, for whom the state of the shopping district before the 1980s or at the time of its emergence may be remembered. A comparison of their views with the views of respondents in this study would be useful for capturing the changes in touristic and local spaces as perceived by the locals.

Finally, the spatial organisation of spaces has not been a focus of this study. For example, information on whether spaces that are perceived to be touristic are concentrated and/or surrounded by non-touristic spaces or are scattered and/or mingled with non-touristic spaces may help managers of shopping districts expand the areas that tourists visit or minimise the influences of tourists in well-travelled areas. Analyses that associate respondents' perceptions of spaces with the locations that they choose to photograph may contribute to spatial strategies.

ACKNOWLEDGEMENT

This study is funded by the Japan Society for the Promotion of Science.

REFERENCES

Bloch, H. P., Ridgway, M. N., & Dawson, A. S. (1994). The shopping mall as a consumer habitat. *Journal of Retailing, 70*(1), 23–42.

Botterill, T. D. (1989). Humanistic tourism? Personal constructions of a tourist; Sam visits Japan. *Leisure Studies, 8*(3), 281–293.

Botterill, T. D., & Crompton, J. L. (1987). Personal constructions of holiday snapshots. *Annals of Tourism Research, 14*(1), 152–156.

Botterill, T. D., & Crompton, J. L. (1996). Two case studies exploring the nature of the tourist's experience. *Journal of Leisure Research, 28*(1), 57–82.

Brown, T. C., Richards, M. T., Daniel, T. C., & King, D. A. (1989). Recreation participation and the validity of photo-based preference judgments. *Journal of Leisure Research, 21*(1), 40–60.

Cherem, G., & Driver, L. (1983). Visitor employed photography: A technique to measure common perceptions of natural environments. *Journal of Leisure Research, 15*(1), 65–83.

Choi, T. M., Liu, S. C., Pang, K. M., & Chow, P. S. (2008). Shopping behaviors of individual tourists from the Chinese Mainland to Hong Kong. *Tourism Management, 29*(4), 811–820.

Choi, W. M., Chan, A., & Wu, J. (1999). A qualitative and quantitative assessment of Hong Kong's image as a tourist destination. *Tourism Management, 20*(3), 361–365.

Christiansen, T., & Snepenger, D. J. (2002). Is it the mood or the mall that encourages tourists to shop? *Journal of Shopping Center Research, 9*(1), 7–26.

Cohen, E. (1995). Touristic craft ribbon development in Thailand. *Tourism Management, 16*(3), 225–235.

Dakin, S. (2003). There's more to landscape than meets the eye: Towards inclusive landscape assessment in resource and environmental management. *The Canadian Geographer, 47*(2), 185–200.

Domae, K. (1997). Okinawa no Toshi Kukan *[urban spaces in Okinawa]*. Tokyo: Kokin Shoin.

Fairweather, J. R., & Swaffield, S. R. (2001). Visitor experiences of Kaikoura, New Zealand: An interpretative study using photographs of landscapes and Q method. *Tourism Management, 22*(3), 219–228.

Fairweather, J. R., & Swaffield, S. R. (2002). Visitors' and locals' experiences of Rotorua, New Zealand: An interpretative study using photographs of landscapes and Q methods. *International Journal of Tourism Research, 4*(4), 283–297.

Garrod, B. (2007). A snapshot into the past: The utility of volunteer-employed photography in planning and managing heritage tourism. *Journal of Heritage Tourism, 2*(1), 14–35.

Garrod, B. (2008). Exploring place perception: A photo-based analysis. *Annals of Tourism Research, 35*(2), 381–401.

Getz, D. (1993). Tourist shopping village: Development and planning strategies. *Tourism Management, 14*(1), 15–26.

Haywood, K. M. (1990). Visitor-employed photography: An urban assessment. *Journal of Travel Research, 29*(1), 25–29.

Heung, V., & Cheng, E. (2000). Assessing tourists' satisfaction with shopping in the Hong Kong special administrative region of China. *Journal of Travel Research, 38*(4), 396–404.

Higuchi, K. (n.d.). *KH Coder index page*. Retrieved from http://khc.sourceforge.net/. Accessed on July 5, 2010.

Hsieh, A., & Chang, J. (2006). Shopping and tourist night markets in Taiwan. *Tourism Management, 27*(1), 138–145.

Japan Travel Bureau. (2009). *News release: Kono Natu ni Ikitai Nihon no Ryokosaki ha? [Where do you wish to visit in Japan this summer?]*. Retrieved from http://www.jtb.co.jp/myjtb/tabiq/. Accessed on November 12, 2013.

Jones, M. (1999). Entertaining shopping experiences: An exploratory investigation. *Journal of Retailing and Consumer Services, 6*(3), 129–139.

Kakazu, H. (2011). Sustainable island tourism: The case of Okinawa. In J. Carlsen & R. Butler (Eds.), *Island tourism: Sustainable perspectives (ecotourism)* (pp. 171–185). Wallingford: CAB Intl.

Kent, W., Schock, P., & Snow, R. (1983). Shopping: Tourism's unsung hero(ine). *Journal of Travel Research, 21*(4), 2–4.

Kim, J. (2009). Retail system of Okinawa: The existence mechanism of commercial accumulation in Naha, Okinawa. *Regional Studies, 5*, 61–71.

Kinjo, H. (2004). Development of Gabugawa-Chuo shopping district after the river improvement. *The Journal of General Industrial Research, 12*, 25–46.

Koga, T., Taka, A., Munakata, J., Kojima, T., Hirate, K., & Yasuoka, M. (1999). Caption Hyouka Hou ni yoru shimin sanka-gata keiken chousa [Participatory research of townscape, using 'Caption Evaluation Method']. *Journal of Architecture and Planning, 517*, 79–84.

Lee, S., Chang, S., Hou, J., & Lin, C. (2008). Night market experience and image of temporary residents and foreign visitors. *International Journal of Culture, Tourism and Hospitality Research, 2*(3), 217–233.

Lin, Y. I. (2004). Evaluating a servicescape: The effect of cognition and emotion. *International Journal of Hospitality Management, 23*(2), 163–178.

MacCannell, D. (1976). *The tourist: A new theory of the leisure class*. Los Angeles, CA: University of California Press.

MacKay, K. J., & Couldwell, C. M. (2004). Using visitor-employed photography to investigate destination image. *Journal of Travel Research, 42*(4), 390–396.

MacKay, K. J., & Fesenmaier, D. R. (1997). Pictorial element of destination in image formation. *Annals Tourism Research, 24*(3), 537–565.

MacKay, K. J., & Fesenmaier, D. R. (2000). An exploration of cross-cultural destination image assessment. *Journal of Travel Research, 38*(4), 417–423.

Mak, B. F., Tsang, N. K., & Cheung, I. C. (1999). Taiwanese tourists' shopping preferences. *Journal of Vacation Marketing, 5*(2), 190–198.

Markwell, K. W. (2000). Photo-documentation and analyses as research strategies in human geography. *Australian Geographical Studies, 38*(1), 91–98.

Moscardo, G. (2004). Shopping as a destination attraction: An empirical examination of the role of shopping in tourists' destination choice and experience. *Journal of Vacation Marketing, 10*(4), 294–307.

Munson, W. (1993). Perceived freedom in leisure and career salience in adolescence. *Journal of Leisure Research, 25*(3), 305–314.

Murphy, L., Benckendorff, P., Moscardo, G., & Pearce, P. L. (2011). *Tourist shopping villages: Forms and functions*. New York, NY: Routledge.

Naoi, T., Airey, D., & Iijima, S. (2009). Evaluating historical districts: Exploring the use of photographs and slide experiments. *Tourism Analysis, 14*(5), 587–603.

Naoi, T., Airey, D., Iijima, S., & Niininen, O. (2006). Visitors' evaluation of an historical district: Repertory grid analysis and laddering analysis. *Tourism Management, 27*(3), 420–436.

Naoi, T., Airey, D., Iijima, S., & Niininen, O. (2007). Advancing and testing a theory of how visitors assess historical districts: With use of repertory grid analysis and laddering analysis. In A. G. Woodside (Ed.), *Advances in culture, tourism and hospitality research: Volume 1* (pp. 289–319). Amsterdam: Elsevier JAI.

Naoi, T., & Iijima, S. (2004). Effects of the presence of other people on visitors' evaluation[s] of a historical district. *Proceedings of the 14th International Research Conference of the Council for Australian University Tourism and Hospitality Education*, Brisbane, Australia.

Oku, H., & Fukamachi, K. (2006). The differences in scenic perception of forest visitors through their attributes and recreational activity. *Landscape and Urban Planning*, 75(1–2), 34–42.

Ooi, C. S. (2002). *Cultural tourism and tourism cultures: The business of mediating experiences in Copenhagen and Singapore*. Copenhagen: Copenhagen Business School Press.

Prebensen, N. K. (2007). Exploring tourists' images of a distant destination. *Tourism Management*, 28(3), 747–756.

Ryan, C. (1991). *Recreation tourism: A social science perspective*. New York, NY: Routledge.

Schmidt, G. J. (1979). The guided tour: Insulated adventure. *Urban Life*, 7(4), 441–467.

Snepenger, D., Murphy, L., O'Connell, R., & Gregg, E. (2003). Tourists and residents use of a shopping space. *Annals of Tourism Research*, 30(3), 567–580.

Snepenger, D., Murphy, L., Snepenger, M., & Anderson, W. (2004). Normative meanings of experiences for a spectrum of tourism places. *Journal of Travel Research*, 43(2), 108–117.

Snepenger, D., Reiman, S., Johnson, J., & Snepenger, M. (1988). Is downtown mainly for tourists? *Journal of Travel Research*, 36(4), 5–12.

Son, A., & Pearce, P. (2005). Multi-faceted image assessment: International students' views of Australia as a tourist destination. *Journal of Travel & Tourism Marketing*, 18(4), 21–35.

Stobart, J. (1998). Shopping streets as social space: Leisure, consumerism and improvement in an eighteenth-century county town. *Urban History*, 25(1), 3–21.

Swanson, K. K., & Horridge, P. E. (2004). A structural model for souvenir consumption, travel activities, and tourist demographics. *Journal of Travel Research*, 42(4), 372–380.

Taylor, J. G., Czarnowski, K. J., Sexton, N. R., & Flick, S. (1995). The importance of water to Rocky Mountain National Park visitors: An adaptation of visitor-employed photography to natural resources management. *Journal of Applied Recreation Research*, 20(1), 61–85.

Timothy, D. (2005). *Shopping tourism, retailing and leisure*. Tonawanda, NY: Multilingual Matters.

Timothy, D. J., & Butler, R. W. (1995). Cross-border shopping: A North American perspective. *Annals of Tourism Research*, 22(1), 16–34.

Yuksel, A. (2004). Shopping experience evaluation: A case of domestic and international visitors. *Tourism Management*, 25(6), 751–759.

RESIDENTS' PERCEPTIONS OF MOUNTAIN DESTINATIONS

Carla Silva, Elisabeth Kastenholz and
José Luís Abrantes

ABSTRACT

This chapter analyses residents' perceptions of mountain destinations. The aim is to develop a scale for assessing residents' mountain images. An extensive literature review and insights from an empirical study of 315 residents of the Serra da Estrela in Portugal, the Alps in France, Austria and Switzerland, and the Peaks of Europe in Spain show that mountain images held by local people refer to the dimensions: mystic/ sacred, historic-cultural life; health and affective image. Results were obtained by both content analysis of open-ended questions and by a quantitative approach based on scale items identified as belonging to specific dimensions in the literature review, whose relevance was confirmed through a confirmatory factor analysis using LISREL. Discussion is focused on theoretical and practical implications of findings and limitations are also presented.

Keywords: Mountains; destination image; measurement scale

Marketing Places and Spaces
Advances in Culture, Tourism and Hospitality Research, Volume 10, 19–31
ISSN: 1871-3173/doi:10.1108/S1871-317320150000010002

INTRODUCTION

Mountains are cultural, natural, social, and physical spaces (Robertson & Hull, 2001). But they are also socially, cognitively, and emotionally constructed sites (Cronon, 1995; Evernden, 1992; Greider & Garkovich, 1994; MacFarlane, 2003; Soper, 1995), made up of ideas and perceptions that exist in the minds of individuals and which are partly shared with others (Robertson & Hull, 2001). These ideas and associations are thus mirrored in place images, which are held by both visitors/tourists of these areas (destination images) and by local communities referring to these places as their home, however distinct these images may be.

Until very recently, tourism studies concerned with mountain places mainly focused on physical, ecological, and environmental perspectives (Smethurst, 2000). But the notion that places are socially produced suggests that their meaning is anchored in history and culture and not simply in some objective or visible properties. This means that the development of a new perspective of mountains within the corresponding image context is therefore a most interesting endeavor and also that the local community could be the key for a more realistic and differentiated image of certain mountain destinations. Furthermore, residents are an important part of the tourism system, which are many times ignored. Residents have a distinct image of their own place, which could and should be measured and taken into account when promoting mountain tourism (Andriotis, 2005). This is desirable for both guaranteeing sustainable development acknowledging local stakeholders' interests, sensitivities, and identities and for also projecting more powerful, as more shared, credible, and significant images of the destination.

Based on the knowledge that destination image is a total impression of cognitive and affective evaluations (Baloglu, 1996; Baloglu & Mangaloglu, 2001; Baloglu & McCleary, 1999; Hosany, Ekinci, & Uysal, 2007; Mackay & Fesenmaier, 2000; Stern & Krakover, 1993; Uysal, Chen, & Williams, 2000), the study aims to analyze, in a holistic and multidisciplinary approach, residents' images of mountain destinations. The aim is to develop the RMDI (Residents' Mountain Destination Image) Scale in order to assess a wide set of cognitive and affective mountain destination image parameters.

Based on an extensive literature review on destination image (125 studies) and on social and cultural meanings of mountains overtime, the conceptual model integrated seven destination image dimensions regarding mountain places: (1) mystique/sacred, (2) natural/ecological, (3) historic-cultural, (4) social and prestige, (5) sport and leisure, (6) facilities and infra-structures, and (7) affective image.

THEORETICAL CONSIDERATIONS

Mountains occupy about 24 percent of the global land surface (Kapos, Rhind, Edwards, Price, & Ravilious, 2000) and are home to 12 percent of the global population (Huddleston, Ataman, & Fè d'Ostiani, 2003). A further 14 percent live adjacent to mountain areas (Meybeck, Creen, & Vorosmarty, 2001). Mountains, however, are important not only for people living in and adjacent to mountains, but for a very large proportion of the world's population of over 6.5 billion people by providing fresh water, clean air, food, energy, timber, flood and storm protection, and erosion prevention (United Nations Sustainable Development, 1992).

Mountain environments, and the societies that live in and depend on them, are clearly complex and highly diverse, that is also mountain communities are far from homogeneous entities all over the globe. Additionally, they have high internal diversity (Vaccaro & Beltran, 2007). Therefore, mountains are centers of biological and cultural diversity, which linked with their attractive landscapes, are among the key reasons why mountains are also major centres of tourism, the world's largest and fastest growing industry (Godde, Price, & Zimmermann, 2000). Mountains are particularly attractive destinations (Beedie & Hudson, 2003) and many tourist destinations are located in mountain regions. About 20 percent of the tourist industry, per year, is accounted for by mountain tourism. Therefore, the value of mountains to tourism is very significant.

The attractiveness of mountains is linked with their own symbolic nature revealed thorough their symbolic images shared by the residents. Mountain image, as any place/destination image, is a complex and multidimensional variable. "Image is the sum of beliefs, ideas, and impressions that people have of a place or destination" (Baloglu & Brinberg, 1997, p. 11), having thus a cognitive and an affective component. The cognitive component refers to the beliefs or knowledge a person has of the characteristics or attributes of a tourist destination (Baloglu, 1999; Pike & Ryan, 2004), while the affective dimension is represented by the individual's feelings toward the tourist destination (Chen & Uysal, 2002; Kim & Richardson, 2003).

Image assessment involves measuring factual knowledge, personal beliefs, meanings, memories, evaluations, feelings attached to a place and attitudes toward the place (Baloglu, 1996; Chon, 1990; Hu & Ritchie, 1993, Pike & Ryan, 2004). Many studies have suggested a wide variety of scales to measure destination image. A review of 45 studies empirically assessing destination image from the 1970s to the end of the past millennium showed that there is no agreement on the range of attributes to include in a destination image scale, with studies varying considerably both in the number of attributes used and in their content, and some suggesting destination image measurement should be adapted to the type of destination (Kastenholz, 2002).

In any case, to reveal holistic, cognitive, and affective impressions as well as corresponding place expectations and meanings, integrated in such a place image, so as to obtain a global and complete destination image, it is important to consider not only scale ratings, but also a qualitative approach is desirable in the image measurement process, so as to assess more unique and specific place qualities, as well as to understand particular subjective associations (Echtner & Ritchie, 1991). Correspondingly, mountain image should best be measured using both, mountain-specific scales and open-ended questions.

METHOD

The study combines quantitative and qualitative survey techniques. The variables used to assess the cognitive destination image in the survey instrument developed were selected from most used items applied in other destination image studies, which would be adequate to include in a mountain destination image study. This scale was a result of the mentioned literature review related to the constructs of destination image and the social/cultural meanings attributed to mountains. In total, 103 studies regarding cognitive destination image and 22 on affective destination image have been reviewed and pre-established scale items are integrated into the here developed measurement instrument. The initial scales were adjusted to the reality of local residents being inquired as well as to the specificity of the mountain destinations being studied (Serra da Estrela/Portugal, Alps/France, Austria and Switzerland, and the Peaks of Europe/Spain).

Residents were asked to rate the mountain place as a tourism destination on each of a list of 49 attributes on a five-point Likert-type scale ranging from one (offers very little) to five (offers very much). The affective dimension of tourism destination image was measured through nine semantic differential scales, based on a literature review of 22 studies. Additionally, respondents were asked to answer open-ended questions and to suggest three adjectives related to their subjective mountain perceptions in order to identify other holistic or unique characteristics associated with the mountain destination.

The main survey was conducted from March through July 2009 using a kind of cluster sampling approach, defined in space and time (Kastenholz, 2002), specifically trying to interview all residents encountered on certain days in locations were those were most likely to be encountered (constituting a series of clusters in time and space). Residents were approached through personal administration on-site and a total of 315 valid questionnaires were completed.

FINDINGS

Confirmatory Factor Analysis

A confirmatory factor analysis (CFA) was applied using full-information maximum likelihood (FIML) estimation procedures in LISREL. The Chi squared for this model is significant ($\chi^2 = 244.35$, 62 df, $p < .00$). Since the Chi squared statistic is sensitive to sample size, we further analyzed additional fit indices: the Normed Fit Index (NFI), the Comparative Fit Index (CFI), the Incremental Fit Index (IFI), and the Non-Normed Fit Index (NNFI).

The NFI and the NNFI for this model were 0.96. The CFI and the IFI showed a value of 0.97. All constructs present levels of composed reliability (Bagozzi, 1980). Given that the fit indices may be strengthened permitting the existence of more terms to be freely estimated, also the Root Mean Square Error of Approximation (RMSEA) was considered, which incorporates a penalization for lack of parsimony. A value of RMSEA above 0.10 indicates an inacceptable value (Steiger & Lind, 1980). The RMSEA of this measurement model is of 0.097.

Convergent validity is revealed by the significant and high standardized weights of each item in respect to the measured construct (the mean weight is of 0.81). Discriminant validity between the constructs is analyzed by

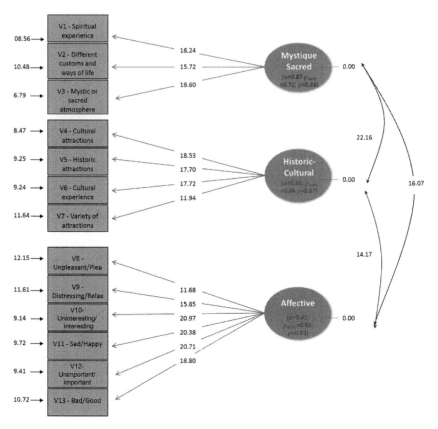

Fig. 1.   Residents' Perceptions of Mountain Destinations.

using the Fornell and Larcker (1981) test, in which all possible construct pairs pass the test (see Fig. 1).

Nomological Validity

In order to assess nomological validity, measures are tested with respect to some other construct to which destination image constructs are theoretically related, such as residents' perceptions of tourism impacts. Destination images and perceptions of tourism impacts are highly related because the perceptions of the effects of tourism development on a destination influence

Table 1. Correlations between Residents' Destination Image Dimensions and Tourism Impact Perceptions.

	Mystique/Sacred	Historic-Cultural	Affective
Positive social and cultural impacts	0.613**	0.569**	0.548**
Positive economic impacts	0.444**	0.517**	0.456**
Negative economic impacts	0.309**	0.347**	0.178**
Negative social impacts	−0.201**	−0.234**	−0.230**

**All correlations are significant at the 0.01 level (2-tailed).

the perception that people globally hold of it (Diedrich & García-Buades, 2009; Zamani-Farahani & Musa, 2008).

For this purpose, data processing and analysis were performed using the programs SPSS and LISREL, in their latest versions.

Table 1 shows the correlations between destination image dimensions and positive socio-cultural impacts, positive economic impacts, negative economic impacts and negative social impacts, which means that the more the residents' mountain destination image is enhanced, the more pronounced will be the perceptions of positive social, cultural, and economic impacts of tourism on the destination. All the correlation coefficients are significant (at $p < 0.01$). Therefore, mountain destination image contributes to forming the perceptions of impacts of tourism in mountain areas and hence there is evidence supporting the nomological validity of the three proposed measures (cf. Cadogan, Diamantopoulos, & de Mortanges, 1999; Cross & Chaffin, 1982).

Content Analysis

In order to assess contents of mountain images held by respondents, the adjective words suggested by the respondents were first categorized and then analyzed within broader categories, which were treated as dimensions of the mountain destination image construct, with frequencies of occurrence revealing the importance of each dimension. From this analysis seven image categories result: (1) affective, (2) mystique/sacred, (3) natural/ecological, (4) historic-cultural, (5) social and prestige, (6) leisure and sport, and (7) life and health. Overall, the categories "mystique/sacred," "life and health," "historic-cultural," and "affective" stood out as the most significant mountain image dimensions held by residents, being followed by "natural/ecological" (see Table 2).

Table 2.   Content Analysis – Frequencies of Mountain Image Dimensions Held by Residents.[a]

Affective image (197)		Beauty (56); relaxing (30); peaceful (17); pleasant (10); freedom (10); cosy (7); fascinating (7); good (5); comfortable (5); familiar (5); happiness (5); dangerous (5); fun (4); magnificent (4); missing of (4); joy (3); grandiose (3); interesting (3); attractive (2); blinding (2); powerful (2); romantic (2); passionate (1); unknown (1); different (1); unusual (1); pleasure (1); respectful (1).
Cognitive image	Mystique/sacred (195)	Sacred (51); uniqueness (19); mythical (18); silence (16); divine (11); spirituality (11); serenity (10); primitive (9); god (8); paradise (8); legendary (7); magical (6); heaven (5); retirement (5); fortress (3); mystery (3); refugee (3); eternal (2).
	Life and health (180)	Well-being (38); healthy (37); harmony (32); health (23); life (17); purity (15); balance (10); quality of life (4); peace of mind (2); quality (2).
	Historic-cultural (171)	Home (28); lore-traditional (21); heritage (17); culture (16); genuine (14); memory (14); history (11); typical (8); rural (8); ancestral (7); simplicity (6); childhood (5); milk (5); cheese (5); symbolic (4); bucolic (2).
	Natural/ ecological (124)	Pure air (11); tranquillity (11); water (10); isolation(10); rest (8); snow (8); scenery (7); wildlife (6); inaccessible (6); lakes (6); authentic (5); natural (5); nature (5); green (5); remote (4); restriction (4); forest (3); glacier (3); sun (2); wild (1); environment (1); ecology (1); ecosystem (1); untouchable (1).
	Leisure and sport (64)	Sport (11); sky (10); tourism (8); adventure (7); climbing (5); hiking (4); tourists (4); entertainment (3); vacation (2); free time (2); snowboard (2); discovery (1); escape (1); leisure (1); mountaineering (1); walks (1); radical (1).
	Social/prestige (14)	Family (8); hospitality (4); friends (1); luxury (1).

[a]Between parentheses are absolute frequencies of each word cited by tourists.

CONCLUSION AND IMPLICATIONS

Mountains are important tourist destinations as well as the home of numerous communities, living in and making use of mountain ecosystems, while simultaneously contributing to their increased accessibility for human leisure and tourism purposes. However, little is known about the image mountain that residents hold of their living space as a tourism destination, however important their involvement in tourism development. This study tries to fill this gap by attempting to present a mountain image scale for measuring residents' image of the place and by additionally assessing more specific meanings of the place, eventually not considered in the literature before through a qualitative approach.

Results from a survey of 315 residents of three European Mountains Destinations – Serra da Estrela (Portugal), Alps (France, Austria, and Switzerland) and Peaks of Europe (Spain) – indicate that tourism mountain perceptions held by residents correspond mainly to the dimensions: (1) mystique/sacred, (2) historic-cultural, (3) life and health, and (4) affective.

The first dimension reflects the fact that, since the most remote times, mountains are the source of legends and myths (McCool, 2002). This seems to be particularly embraced by local mountain communities. Mountains are perceived as sacred places and source of spiritual renewal (Jokinen & Veijola, 2003), an image reflected in their designation as "cathedrals of the world" (Mathieu, 2006).

The second dimension mirrors the meaning of mountains as genuine guardians of a historic and cultural heritage that are a part of local people's identities and thereby presenting a strong touristic value (Goeldner, Ritchie, & McIntosh, 2003). They are perceived as singular, alternative, and prestigious places to visit (Vengesayi & Mavondo, 2004), an image which residents identify with.

Literature confirms that mountains are regarded as places with clean air, pure water, medical plants which makes them a privileged area for enhancing the residents' and visitors' physical and psychological well-being (Liniger, Weingartner, & Grosejean, 1998; Messerli & Ives, 1997), as also visible in the responses of residents interviewed for this study. This dimension named here as "life and health" may also be related to the dimension "natural/ecology," found in the qualitative approach.

Last, but not least, mountains are perceived as affective places inducing strong feelings and emotions to those who live there, which should be naturally related to their attachment to their place of living, providing them with an emotion-loaded place of living, where family and friendship bonds may be as relevant as connection to a particular, typically dramatic and aesthetically appealing, nature and landscape environment and corresponding outdoors experiences may be associated with precious, even sacred meanings.

These findings may help mountain destinations implement innovative positioning strategies, targeted to distinct markets and simultaneously supported by the mountain's communities, as corresponding to their place identity. Specifically, new product development options may arise by, for example, theming the mountain destination experience as a "sacred/mystic" or "cultural" experience, a theme that might require co-creation integrating residents as "cultural brokers" (Cohen, 1988), and thereby addressing tourists who are increasingly looking for meaningful and memorable experiences during their holidays (Chambers, 2009; Richards & Wilson, 2006) and may not be aware of particular cultural meanings of the place they visit. Thereby not only the mountain experience may be enhanced for tourists, improving marketing effectiveness. Simultaneously a better integration of the views of the mountain populations may yield a more sustainable destination development (Nepal & Chipeniuk, 2005). Also Fesenmaier and MacKay (1996) point at the need to consider the residents' perspective, so as to avoid negative consequences of promotional image-creation local communities do not identify with.

However, interesting the possible managerial implications, we have to recognize some limitations of the study. First, and from a theoretical standpoint, despite the extensive literature review, the study might omit and therefore not consider other specific relevant mountain image dimensions that a more thorough in-depth qualitative study might suggest. On the other hand, the conceptual model proposed here is validated only with a limited sample, while the resulting RMDI scale could not be proposed as an image measurement instrument to all mountain destinations, since one of the more relevant dimensions ("life and health"), found in the qualitative approach, could not be confirmed in our model. The replication of this study and corresponding extension of the model to other mountain destinations, particularly out of Europe, would be needed for a more general validation. Finally, tourism destination image is a dynamic concept because images are not static but change overtime (Gallarza, Saura, & Garcia, 2002; Gartner & Hunt, 1987). Therefore, it would seem desirable to carry out longitudinal studies that deal with the process of the formation and changes in image over longer time periods.

Additionally, the mountain destination images held by tourists should be compared with the residents' point of view so as to identify gaps, which may suggest additional need for (internal and external) marketing action, while also different destination images held by distinct tourist groups, which may be more or less culturally distant from the visited mountain communities (Kastenholz, 2010), should be identified and eventually lead to differentiated market approaches. Last, but not least, also the role of relevant constructs like place attachment (Silva, Kastenholz, & Abrantes, 2013) for the residents' mountain destination image formation and its link to the diverse dimensions identified before would be worth of study, as would be the analysis of particular moderating variables, such as age, education level, type of professional activity, on the content of the here studied image.

REFERENCES

Andriotis, K. (2005). Community group's perceptions of and preferences for tourism development: Evidence from Crete. *Journal of Hospitality and Tourism Research, 29*(1), 67–90.

Bagozzi, R. (1980). *Causal models in marketing.* New York, NY: Wiley.

Baloglu, S. (1996). *An empirical investigation of determinants of tourist destination image.* Unpublished dissertation, Virginia Polytechnic University, Blacksburg, VA.

Baloglu, S. (1999). A path-analytical model of visitation intention involving information sources, socio-psychological motivations and destination images. In A., Woodside, G., Crouch, J., Mazanec, M., Oppermann, & L., Sakai (Eds.), *Consumer psychology of tourism, hospitality and leisure* (pp. 63–90). Wallingford: CAB International.

Baloglu, S., & Brinberg, D. (1997). Affective images of tourism destinations. *Journal of Travel Research, 35*(4), 11–15.

Baloglu, S., & Mangaloglu, M. (2001). Tourism destination images of Turkey, Egypt, Greece, and Italy as perceived by US-based tour operators and travel agents. *Tourism Management, 22*(1), 1–9.

Baloglu, S., & McCleary, K. (1999). A model of destination image formation. *Annals of Tourism Research, 26*(4), 868–897.

Beedie, P., & Hudson, S. (2003). Emergence of mountain-based adventure tourism. *Annals of Tourism Research, 30*(3), 625–643.

Cadogan, J., Diamantopoulos, A., & Mortanges, C. (1999). A measures of export market orientation: Scale development and cross-cultural validation. *Journal of International Business Studies, 30*(4), 689–707.

Chambers, E. (2009). From authenticity to significance: Tourism on the frontier of culture and place. *Futures, 41*, 353–359.

Chen, J., & Uysal, M. (2002). Market positioning analysis: A hybrid approach. *Annals of Tourism Research, 29*, 987–1003.

Chon, K.-S. (1990). The role of destination image in tourism: A review and discussion. *Revue du Tourisme, 2*, 2–9.

Cohen, E. (1988). Authenticity and commoditization in tourism. *Annals of Tourism Research, 15*(3), 371–386.

Cronon, W. (1995). *Uncommon ground: Rethinking the human place in Nature.* New York, NY: W. W. Norton.

Cross, E., & Chaffin, W. (1982). Use the binomial theorem in interpreting results of multiple tests of significance. *Educational and Psychological Measurement, 42*, 25–34.

Diedrich, A., & García-Buades, E. (2009). Local perceptions of tourism as indicators of destination decline. *Tourism Management, 30*, 512–521.

Echtner, C., & Ritchie, R. (1991). The meaning and measurement of destination image. *The Journal of Tourism Studies, 2*(2), 2–12.

Evernden, N. (1992). *The social creation of nature.* Baltimore, MD: The Johns Hopkins University Press.

Fesenmaier, D., & MacKay, K. (1996). Deconstructing destination image construction. *Revue de Tourisme, 51*(2), 37–43.

Fornell, C., & Larcker, D. (1981). Evaluating structural equation models with unobservable variables and measurement error. *Journal of Marketing Research, 18*(1), 39–50.

Gallarza, M., Saura, I., & Garcia, H. (2002). Destination image: Towards a conceptual framework. *Annals of Tourism Research, 29*(1), 56–72.

Gartner, W., & Hunt, J. (1987). An analysis of state image change over a twelve-year period (1971–1983). *Journal of Travel Research, 26*(2), 15–19.

Godde, P., Price, M., & Zimmermann, F. (2000). Tourism development in mountain regions: Moving forward into the new millennium. In P., Godde, M., Price, & F., Zimmermann (Eds.), *Tourism and development in mountain regions* (pp. 1–25). Wallingford: CABI Publishing.

Goeldner, C., Ritchie, J., & McIntosh, R. (2003). *Tourism: Principles, practices and philosophies* (9th ed.). New York, NY: Wiley.

Greider, T., & Garkovich, L. (1994). Landscapes: The social construction of nature and the environment. *Rural Sociology, 59*(1), 1–24.

Hosany, S., Ekinci, Y., & Uysal, M. (2007). Destination image and destination personality. *International Journal of Culture, Tourism and Hospitality Research, 1*(1), 62–81.

Hu, Y., & Ritchie, B. (1993). Measuring destination attractiveness: A contextual approach. *Journal of Travel Research, 32*(2), 25–34.

Huddleston, B., Ataman, E., & Fè d'Ostiani, L. (2003). *Towards a GIS-based analysis of mountain environments and populations*. Rome: FAO.

Jokinen, E., & Veijola, S. (2003). Mountains and landscapes: Towards embodied visualities. In D. Crouch & N. Lubbren (Eds.), *Visual, culture and tourism*. New York, NY: Berg.

Kapos, V., Rhind, J., Edwards, M., Price, M., & Ravilious, C. (2000). Developing a map of the world's mountain forests. In M., Price & N., Butt (Eds.), *Forest in sustainable mountain development: A state-of-knowledge report for 2000* (pp. 4–9). Wallingford: CAB International.

Kastenholz, E. (2002). *The role and marketing implications of destination images on tourist behavior: The case of Northern Portugal*. Ph.D. thesis, Universidade de Aveiro, UMI dissertation service.

Kastenholz, E. (2010). "Cultural proximity" as a determinant of destination image. *Journal of Vacation Marketing, 16*(4), 313–322.

Kim, H., & Richardson, S. (2003). Motion picture impacts on destination images. *Annals of Tourism Research, 30*(1), 216–237.

Liniger, H., Weingartner, R., & Grosejean, M. (1998). *Mountains of the world: Water towers for the 21st century*. Part I. Bern: Institute of Geography, University of Bern.

MacFarlane, R. (2003). *Mountains of the mind: How desolate and forbidding heights were transformed into experiences of indomitable spirit*. New York, NY: Pantheon Books.

Mackay, K. J., & Fesenmaier, D. R. (2000). An exploration of cross-cultural destination image assessment. *Journal of Travel Research, 38*(4), 417–423.

Mathieu, J. (2006). The sacralization of mountains in Europe during the modern age. *Mountain Research and Development, 26*(4), 343–349.

McCool, S. (2002). Mountains and tourism: Meeting the challenges of sustainability in a messy world. *Celebrating Mountains: Proceedings of an international year of mountain conference*, Jindabyne, Australia (pp. 311–318).

Messerli, B., & Ives, J. (1997). *Mountains of the world: A global priority.* New York, NY: Parthenon Publishing Group.

Meybeck, M., Creen, P., & Vorosmarty, C. (2001). A new typology for mountains and other relief classes: An application to global continental water resource and population distribution. *Mountain Research and Development, 21*(1), 34−45.

Nepal, S., & Chipeniuk, R. (2005). Mountain tourism: Toward a conceptual framework. *Tourism Geographies, 7*(3), 313−333.

Pike, S., & Ryan, C. (2004). Destination positioning analysis through a comparison of cognitive, affective and conative perceptions. *Journal of Travel Research, 42*(4), 333−342.

Richards, G., & Wilson, J. (2006). Developing creativity in tourist experiences: A solution to the serial reproduction of culture? *Tourism Management, 27*, 1209−1223.

Robertson, D., & Hull, R. (2001). Which nature? A case study of Whitetop mountain. *Landscape Journal, 20*(2), 176−185.

Silva, C., Kastenholz, E., & Abrantes, J. L. (2013). Place attachment, destination image and impacts of tourism in mountain destinations. *Anatolia: An International Journal of Tourism and Hospitality Research, 24*(1), 17−29.

Smethurst, D. (2000). Mountain geography. *The Geographical Review, 90*(1), 35−56.

Soper, K. (1995). What is Nature? Cambridge: Blackwell.

Steiger, J. H., & Lind, J. M. (1980). Statistically based tests for the number of factors. Paper presented at the Annual Meeting of the Psychometric Society, Iowa City, IA.

Stern, E., & Krakover, S. (1993). The formation of composite urban image. *Geographical Analysis, 25*(2), 130−146.

United Nations Sustainable Development. (1992). Managing fragile ecosystems: Sustainable mountain development. Agenda 21 (Chapter 13), *United Nations Conference on Environment & Development,* Brazil.

Uysal, M., Chen, J., & Williams, D. (2000). Increasing state market share through a regional positioning. *Tourism Management, 21*(1), 89−96.

Vaccaro, I., & Beltran, O. (2007). Consuming space, nature and culture: Patrimonial discussions in the hyper-modern era. *Tourism Geographies, 9*(3), 254−274.

Vengesayi, S., & Mavondo, F. (2004). Aspects of reputation and human factors as determinants of tourist destination attractiveness. *ANZMAC conference proceedings,* Wellington (pp. 1−5).

Zamani-Farahani, H., & Musa, G. (2008). Residents' attitudes and perceptions toward tourism development: A case study of Masooleh, Iran. *Tourism Management, 29*(6), 1233−1236.

ATTITUDES OF SUCCESSORS IN DAIRY FARMS TOWARD EDUCATIONAL TOURISM IN JAPAN

Yasuo Ohe

ABSTRACT

Educational tourism in agriculture is attracting growing attention. It is expected that educational activities can create a new social role for agriculture. However, farmers need to refine their identity to embark on this emerging activity. On the basis of a questionnaire survey, the present study has statistically clarified how a farmer's identity determines their attitude toward educational tourism by focusing on mainly family-run Educational Dairy Farms in Japan. The results show that those farmers who have a wider perspective on the activity domain conduct educational tourism more positively than those who do not. The findings also indicate how the next-generation farm successors view the educational activity; that is, whether they consider themselves to be simply conventional milk producers or rather farm resource managers with a wider scope of new social demand that is connected to farmers' identity. The latter

Marketing Places and Spaces
Advances in Culture, Tourism and Hospitality Research, Volume 10, 33–44
Copyright © 2015 by Emerald Group Publishing Limited
All rights of reproduction in any form reserved
ISSN: 1871-3173/doi:10.1108/S1871-317320150000010003

redefinition will be increasingly necessary when farm successors conduct tourism-related activity.

Keywords: Rural tourism; educational tourism; identity; farm diversification; farm tourism

INTRODUCTION

Educational tourism in agriculture is attracting growing attention as a potential new market segment of rural tourism along with mounting demands for experience-oriented tourism. This activity is an emerging opportunity for farm operators to expand their activities from traditional ordinary farm production to farm activity that involves direct communication with consumers by providing intangible educational services as a measure of farm diversification amid stagnant consumption of farm products. This educational activity also can be expected to create a new social role for the farm sector by informing consumers about the close connection between life and food, and about rural heritage − factors that are often forgotten in the modern urban daily routine.

This educational activity, however, is not always economically viable because some farmers provide the educational services free of charge on a voluntary basis, while others levy a service charge. As a result, it is necessary to clarify operator's attitudes of the activity toward these differences in charging behavior because this point is crucial to the sustainable development of educational tourism in agriculture. Thus, this chapter examines the attitudes of farm operators toward the educational activity by focusing on the next-generation successors who are already involved in the operations of an Educational Dairy Farm (EDF, hereafter). The EDFs comprise a network of dairy farmers in Japan that aims to provide educational services, and is one of the most advanced and organized programs of farmers that provide educational services to farm visitors.

The hypothesis here is that a farmer's identity determines their attitude toward educational tourism. Unless a farmer's identity changes from that of a conventional farm producer to that of a farm resource manager with a wider perspective on conducting tourism, a new activity such as educational tourism is not well implemented.

Traditionally, issues of capability building have mostly focused on improving the skills of operators who are already involved in tourism activity. In the arena of an emerging new category of tourism such as educational tourism, however, it is difficult to simply apply a traditional capability-building approach to trying to motivate farmers toward embarking on the realization of a viable educational activity. Instead, the concept of identity may be effective in addressing this issue. To my knowledge, the concept of identity has not been fully applied in empirical research on tourism, especially on educational tourism in agriculture or rural tourism, which is the reason that I conducted this study.

LITERATURE REVIEW

Examples of such activities that already have been implemented are the Farming And Countryside Education (FACE) program in the United Kingdom (Graham, 2004; for more recent developments, Gatward, 2007), Ferme Pédagogique in France, Fattorie Didattiche in Emilia-Romagna in Italy (Canavari, Huffaker, Mari, Regazzi, & Spadoni, 2009), children's gardening in the United States (Moore, 1995) and educational dairy farms (EDFs) in Japan (Ohe, 2007). Although these preceding studies made meaningful contributions to let people know the significance of the educational value of agriculture, these studies were case studies. Thus, we can say that we need more theoretical exploration and empirical evidence based on the statistical verification.

In this context, the author considers that the concept of identity is a key to address this new field. Especially, identity was not explored fully in economics, which is the author's discipline. Economic approaches to identity issues were initially explored fully by Akerlof and Kranton (2000, 2002, 2010), who first defined identity as a person's sense of self and proposed the utility function that identity is associated with different social categories and with how people in these categories should behave (Akerlof & Kranton, 2000). They went on to investigate the connections between school and work (Akerlof & Kranton, 2002), and also considered gender and race issues in connection with work and minority poverty (Akerlof & Kranton, 2010). Furthermore, Akerlof (2007) dealt with the relationship between norms and macroeconomics. Nevertheless, empirically agriculture and tourism have not been explicitly studied in relation to identity issues. Educational tourism in agriculture has not been extensively explored except for studies by Ohe (2011, 2012), which mainly dealt with internalization of the educational externality generated by dairy farming, not directly with the identity aspect of farmers.

To summarize, the relationship between identity and educational activity especially in agriculture has not been examined, yet. Thus, conceptual and empirical evaluations on this issue are necessary.

METHODOLOGY

Definition of Identity and Hypothesis on Operator's Identity

I define the identity of operators conducting the educational tourism; the identity sets a norm of operators about what domain of activity is undertaken as an economic activity. If the operators conduct an activity within their norm, they are willing to do it and they gain high satisfaction, and therefore the activity will be conducted efficiently. If the activity is not within their norm, the operators are less willing to do it and thus the performance of that activity will not be performed so efficiently.

Keeping this in mind, I consider the relationship between a farmer's identity and the degree of diversification of the activity, that is, milk production and the educational activity, based on observation of the EDF operators' behaviors. To simplify the discussion, suppose that a farmer might have two types of identity: traditional identity and enlarged identity. For those with traditional identity, the norm is that their main activity is farm production, so that the educational service is just a voluntary activity offered free of charge in their spare time. Thus, their managerial aim is to maximize milk production to the best possible extent because milk production is their main original activity.

On the other hand, for those with enlarged identity, the norm is that they should engage in multiple economically viable activities including the educational service. Therefore, they will levy a service charge for the educational service in order to make it viable. Their aim is, thus, to attain overall managerial efficiency in farm resource allocation among all activities; this means that operators with enlarged identity have a wider perspective toward farm-resource management and farm diversification than those with traditional identity.

In reality, however, we cannot observe identity itself, but solely behaviors that reflect our own identities. In practice, if operators levy a charge for an educational service, we can say that they are oriented toward the viability of that service. For this reason, it is considered that operators who charge have enlarged identity. In contrast, if operators do not levy a charge, we can say that they have traditional identity. In this respect, whether a farmer levies a service charge is an easily observable criterion that indicates the identity of that farmer.

Although identity can change with time, once it has been established, in general, it is hard to change and it can be passed down through generations. Even if a policy framework promotes farm diversification eagerly, efficient farm management will not be achieved unless a farmer enlarges their identity. Although this does not mean that those who conduct diversified activities as a volunteer do not engage in efficient farm resource management, those with enlarged identity regard farm resource management more as economic behavior than those with traditional identity. Within each identity, the clearer the identity that a farmer possesses, whether it is traditional or enlarged identity, the better able that farmer can perform farm resource management. To put it differently, a farmer cannot realize efficient farm resource management if the activity is conducted beyond the scope of that farmer's own identity.

Data and Method

Although the majority of EDFs are family farms, this organization does include public ranches run by municipalities and agricultural high school and university, and ranches run by cooperatives and dairy industry. The author sent a questionnaire survey to EDFs that were mainly run by families to narrow data variations for the purpose of this chapter. This survey was done in conjunction with the Japan Dairy Council, which gave the designation of EDFs to selected farms and financed this survey. The survey was sent by surface mail to 248 of the 309 EDFs and returned from September to December 2012. The response rate was 141 farms (56.8%). I conducted statistical tests, Chi-squared and *t*-tests, to examine the relationship between successors' attitudes, educational behavior and dairy farm activity.

FINDINGS

Outline of the Program of the Educational Dairy Farms

The EDF program was established in 2000 by the Japan Dairy Council, which is a national organization for promotion of the dairy industry.

The purpose of this program is to provide accurate information on what dairy farms do to enable the public to understand the roles dairy farming play in society. The aim of EDFs is not only to promote an open-door policy of the farmyard to the general public but also to enhance the educational value of dairy farming through teaching where milk comes from and showing the life of milk cows on the farm. People learn what food is and the close connection between food and life from these experiences, which is an advantage of milking cows as opposed to other types of farming such as field crop and rice production. In this respect, a farmer's role is crucial to actualize the high educational value that milking cows and dairy farms have, and thus a farmer is called a facilitator in this program.

To be a facilitator for the EDFs, a farmer or a farm employee must attend a course on principles, safety, hygiene, and communication skills, as well as a presentation of a case study provided by the Council. The Council administers certification for recognition as an EDF, and presents various capacity-building courses for those with certified EDF farms as well as for dairy farmers in general in Japan. There were 309 EDFs as of 2011.

Time series statistics show that the number of visitors to EDFs has increased yearly and reached nearly 880,000 in 2009, which is a 3.89-fold increase from the number in 2003 (Table 1). School children and family visitors are the two main pillars of demand. This increase was far more rapid than the increase in the number of EDFs, which grew only 1.5-fold during the same period. As a result, the average number of visitors per farm increased from 1,353 to 3,421, a 2.53-fold increase that is mainly attributed to an increase in the first half of the period from April to

Table 1. Trend in Number of EDFs and Visitors.

Year	No. of EDFs	No. of Visitors		Total	No. of Visitors per Farm
		First half (April–September)	Second half (October–March)		
2003	167	162,484	63,392	225,876	1,353
2004	174	254,542	89,600	344,142	1,978
2006	200	421,855	133,285	555,140	2,776
2007	217	465,593	225,114	690,707	3,183
2008	249	473,220	232,348	705,568	2,834
2009	257	662,629	216,600	879,229	3,421
2009/2003 ratio	1.54	4.08	3.42	3.89	2.53

Source: Japan Dairy Council.

September. These facts suggest that the demand for farm experience has steadily grown to reach a certain market level or at least has the potential to do so. I assume that this mounting demand indicates a new social role that dairy farmers can play in society and subsequently gain a new income source amid stagnant prices of dairy products and intensifying global competition in farm trade.

Statistical Test Results

Statistical tests on the respondents' attributes and attitudes toward educational activities and farm diversification were compared between those successors who did and those who did not levy service charges for the educational activities among EDFs. There were no statistically significant differences in terms of age and sex, academic background of successors, and farm size according to the number of milk cows, size of land holdings, and the amount of milk production. These results indicate that tourism activity is not stipulated by farm size. A previous study (Ohe, 2011) also pointed out this neutrality of farm size, which has the important implication that educational activities can be carried out on any size of dairy farms, either small or large despite the common trend of enlargement in farm size in any type of farming.

Regarding the EDF activity between farms that did and did not levy charges, which represents operator's identity, I found that the number of visitors and types of educational services offered were significantly greater in the dairy farms that levied charges, indicating that those farms were more active in performing the educational activities (Table 2). There was a statistically significant difference in how the educational service is provided between those who charge and those who do not. This is because the majority of those who do not charge provide only an individual task or "menu," such as feeding or milking separately, whereas those who charge provide a combined menu of individual tasks that comprise, for example, experience of dairy operation, butter making, and butter tasting successively. There is no doubt that the combined menu has higher educational benefit as compared with the individual menu although it takes more time to implement the menu, skills, and ideas. In this regard, it is well conceived that those operators who charge have better skills as facilitators than those who do not.

Interestingly, the proactive attitude taken by those who charge enables them to have better feedback from visitors and results in the operators

Table 2.   Comparison of EDF Activity between Operators Levying
Charges and Those Not Charging.

Items	Levying Charges			Test Result	Method of Test
	Yes	Magnitude relation	No		
No. visitors (% of respondents)					
−50	14.5	<	50.9	***	Chi-square
500−1000	17.1	>	1.8	***	Chi-square
Types of educational services offered (% of respondents)					
Solely individual menu	26.3	<	52.6	***	Chi-square
Combined individual menu	46.1	>	7.0	***	Chi-square
Changes in consciousness after starting the EDF activity (average score evaluated from 1 to 5)					
Enhancement of self-confidence	4.4	>	3.8	N***	*t*-test
Valuation of farm and farm resources	4.1	>	3.5	N**	*t*-test
Extension of human network	4.0	>	3.3	N***	*t*-test
Discovery of new farm resources	3.9	>	3.3	E**	*t*-test
Enjoyment of teaching children	3.8	>	3.4	N*	*t*-test
New sales channel for products	2.9	>	1.9	E***	*t*-test
New farm sector	2.9	>	2.1	E***	*t*-test
Income source	2.8	>	1.9	E***	*t*-test

Source: A questionnaire survey to the Educational Dairy Farms conducted by the author from
September to December 2012. Sample size was 141.
Notes: E = equal variance, N = unequal variance.
***, **, * indicate 1%, 5%, 10% significance, respectively.

experiencing more positive changes in themselves since starting the EDF
activity. Among the changes that were evaluated most highly were enhancement of self-confidence, valuation of farm and farm resources, expansion
of human networks, and enjoyment of teaching children (Table 2). These
results were obtained via a Likert scale, ranging from one, indicating the
least value, to five, indicating the highest value. These facts clearly demonstrate that those who charge obtain higher satisfaction, wider perspectives
on their own farm and farm resources, and more extensive networks
beyond their own local community as compared with those who do not
charge. However, none of these highly valued changes were related to the
economics of the activity. Economic aspects, such as a new sales channel
for products and a new income source, were not evaluated highly.

In short, those who charge were proactive toward the educational activity and gained higher satisfaction and enjoyment, even though these are

non-economic aspects. Presumably, the resulting positive mental changes work as factors that promote farm diversification. To examine this, I also looked at how the successors are diversifying farm activity.

As expected, because of their positive attitude toward the educational activity, those respondents levying charges were active in other diversified activities such as self-processing and selling of dairy products, making and selling soft ice cream or ice cream, making sweets, and opening farm cafés and restaurants (Table 3). Provision of accommodation is not common among the EDFs because farm visitors are mostly locals who come on a day trip to the farm yard. Subsequently, Table 3 also indicates that those levying charges do not consider that the activity should be done voluntarily; only 6.6% thought that the activity should be performed voluntarily (or free of charge) while a half of those who do not charge replied to be done voluntarily. Instead, those respondents levying charges were more likely to think of the educational activity as a profitable farm sector than those not levying charges. Most common attitude among those operators who charge, however, were that the EDF activity only needs cost covering rather than profits. Thus, the behavior regarding levying charges represents essential differences in how operators treat the educational activity.

Table 3. Comparison of Successors' Attitudes Toward Educational Tourism and Farm Diversification.

Items	Levying Charges			Test Result	Method of Test
	Yes	Magnitude relation	No		
Conducting diversified activities (% of respondents)					
Soft ice cream or ice cream	38.2	>	12.3	***	Chi-square
Processing and selling dairy products	35.5	>	19.3	**	Chi-square
Sweets	21.1	>	5.3	**	Chi-square
Café	18.4	>	3.5	***	Chi-square
Restaurant	15.8	>	3.5	**	Chi-square
Souvenirs	13.2	>	3.5	*	Chi-square
Present attitudes toward the educational activity (% of respondents)					
Volunteer	6.6	<	50.9	***	Chi-square
Cost covering	43.4	>	22.8	**	Chi-square
Viable sector of farm	17.1	>	0.0	***	Chi-square

Source: A questionnaire survey to the Educational Dairy Farms conducted by the author from September to December 2012. Sample size was 141.
***, **, * indicate 1%, 5%, 10% significance, respectively.

As easily expected from the above results, those respondents who charge
are eager to conduct public relations with various means from traditional
to the latest social network media (Table 4). Public relations through farm's
own website is most popular among respondents who charge while nearly 8
out of 10 respondents who do not charge do not do anything for public
relations. Finally, issues regarding the development of the educational
activity were not scored highly, and thus were not considered so important,
although there were a few significant differences between the two groups
(Table 4). Specifically, how to increase the number of visitors, a shortage of
manpower for the educational activity, and a shortage of toilets for visitors
were issues of significantly greater concern to those who did levy charges
than those who did not.

To summarize, those who levied charges expressed positive attitudes
toward not only the educational activity, but also farm diversification by
expanding networks outside the farmyard. This finding indicates how farm
successors treat the educational activity, that is, whether they consider

Table 4. Method of Public Relations and Issues of EDF Activity.

Items	Levying Charges			Test Result	Method of Test
	Yes	Magnitude relation	No		
Method of public relations (% of respondents)					
Through on web site	46.1	>	12.3	***	Chi-square
Twitter/blog	23.7	>	10.5	*	Chi-square
Facebook	19.7	=	12.3	ns	Chi-square
Making leaflet	22.4	>	7.0	**	Chi-square
Publicity	22.4	>	5.3	***	Chi-square
Nothing in particular	31.6	<	77.2	***	Chi-square
Others	15.8	>	3.5	**	Chi-square
Issues concerned with the educational activity (average score evaluated from 1 to 5)					
Shortage of manpower for educational services	3.5	>	3.1	E*	*t*-test
Need more toilets	3.2	>	2.6	E**	*t*-test
Low capability for increase in no. visitors	3.0	>	2.4	E***	*t*-test
Unstable no. visitors	3.0	>	2.4	E**	*t*-test
Fee collection for educational services	2.0	<	2.7	N***	*t*-test

Source: A questionnaire survey to the Educational Dairy Farms conducted by the author from
September to December 2012. Sample size was 141.
Notes: E = equal variance, N = unequal variance.
***, **, *, ns indicate 1%, 5%, 10% significance and not significance, respectively.

themselves to be simple conventional milk producers or farm resource managers with a wider scope of new social demand that is connected with farmers' identity. Consequently, we can say that these findings back up empirically the idea that levying charges can be a practical criterion that draws a line between the two identities.

CONCLUSION AND IMPLICATION

The farm visit program is attracting growing interest among the younger generation and families who do not know much about rural life. The farm sector has now started to realize that farm activity has an educational value, and can provide both a new social role and a potential income source. From this perspective, based on survey data obtained via a questionnaire sent to next-generation successors who are already involved in an EDF, this chapter has shed light on how a successor's identity is connected with the educational activity and farm diversification. We have defined two contrasting types of identity that stipulate different levels of educational activity and farm diversification, namely, a traditional identity and an enlarged identity.

The statistical results in this chapter indicate that new educational activities provide an opportunity for farmers to redefine their identity from that of a volunteer to that of a provider of a new educational service, because those who have enlarged identity are proactive toward the educational activity and farm diversification. The statistical results also demonstrate that this redefinition will be increasingly necessary for operators to be able to cope with the new social needs of dairy farming. When policy-makers try to induce farmers to take this new social direction, if this redefinition is not well done, it will be difficult to attain these policy goals.

Consequently, policy-makers should take this identity issue into account when promoting educational tourism as a means of farm diversification. This consideration will increasingly become important in effective policy design toward the promotion of farm tourism faced with emerging social demands. Redefinition of farmer's identity should be included in the category of capability building to expand the social role of the farm sector especially in the case of tourism-related activity. Further investigation is necessary on the relationship between operator's identity and the overall outcomes of farm resource management when conducting the educational activity.

ACKNOWLEDGMENTS

The author is grateful to review comments on the early draft of this study. This chapter was presented at 5th ATMC and improved with the support of the ATMC scientific committee. The questionnaire survey for this research was financed by the Japan Dairy Council and the subsequent analysis was funded by Grants-in Aid for Scientific Research No. 24658191, Japan Society for the Promotion of Science (JSPS).

REFERENCES

Akerlof, G. A. (2007). The missing motivation in macroeconomics. *The American Economic Review, 97*(1), 3−36.

Akerlof, G. A., & Kranton, R. E. (2000). Economics and identity. *The Quarterly Journal of Economics, 115*(3), 715−753.

Akerlof, G. A., & Kranton, R. E. (2002). Identity and schooling: Some lessons for the economics of education. *Journal of Economic Literature, 40*(49), 1167−1201.

Akerlof, G. A., & Kranton, R. E. (2010). *Identity economics: How our identities shape our work, wages, and well-being.* Princeton, NJ: Princeton University Press.

Canavari, M., Huffaker, C., Mari, R., Regazzi, D., & Spadoni, R. (2009). Educational farms in the Emilia-Romagna region: Their role in food habit education. *Symposium on 'food, agri-culture and tourism'*, University of Göttingen, December 15, pp. 1−24.

Gatward, G. (2007). The society's charitable activities. *Journal of the Royal Agricultural Society of England, 168*, 1−8.

Graham, B. (2004). The work of farming and countryside education (FACE). *Journal of the Royal Agricultural Society of England, 165*, 1−8.

Moore, R. C. (1995). Children gardening: First steps towards a sustainable future. *Children's Environments, 12*(2), 222−232.

Ohe, Y. (2007). Emerging environmental and educational service of dairy farming in Japan: Dilemma or opportunity? In E. Tiezzi, J. C. Marques, C. A. Brebbia, & S. E. Jørgensen (Eds.), *Ecosystems and sustainable development VI* (pp. 425−436). Southampton: WIT Press.

Ohe, Y. (2011). Evaluating internalization of multifunctionality by farm diversification: Evidence from educational dairy farms in Japan. *Journal of Environmental Management, 92*, 886−891.

Ohe, Y. (2012). Evaluating operators' attitudes to educational tourism in dairy farms: The case of Japan. *Tourism Economics, 18*(3), 577−595.

RESIDENTS' PERCEPTIONS OF THE IMPACT OF SHIP TOURISM AND THEIR PREFERENCES FOR DIFFERENT TYPES OF TOURISM

Giacomo Del Chiappa and Giuseppe Melis

ABSTRACT

This study aims to investigate how residents in Cagliari (a port of call in the island of Sardinia, Italy) perceive the economic, environmental and socio-cultural impacts (both positive and negative) of cruise tourism and to what extent they would like to support the idea of further cruise tourism development within the destination, also making a comparison with other types of tourism. Findings show that residents have overall a positive attitude towards cruise tourism development, and also very little concern when negative impacts are considered. However, cruise tourism is not the most preferred when compared with other types of tourism. Further, they highlight that significant differences based on socio-economic and demographic characteristics exist in residents' perceptions and attitudes towards cruise tourism development and in their

Marketing Places and Spaces
Advances in Culture, Tourism and Hospitality Research, Volume 10, 45–60
ISSN: 1871-3173/doi:10.1108/S1871-317320150000010004

preferences for different types of tourism development. Implications for policymakers are discussed and suggestions for further research are given.

Keywords: Cruise tourism; residents' preferences; socio-economic and demographic characteristics; tourism island destinations; port of call; Mediterranean area

INTRODUCTION

The cruise industry has been experiencing remarkable growth worldwide in the last few decades (Chin, 2008). In 2011, the total contribution of the global cruise industry to the European economy rose to a record €36.7 billion, from €35.2 billion in 2010 (European Cruise Council, 2012). In the Mediterranean area cruise tourism represents 12% of the overall cruise industry (CLIA, 2008) with Italy ranking second after Spain (Risposte Turismo, 2011). Cruise tourism in Italy is concentrated in five main regions (i.e. Latium, Liguria, Veneto, Campania and Sicily) with a total number of cruise passengers of 9.356 million in 2010 (Risposte Turismo, 2011).

Cruise tourism still represents a dilemma and a serious problem for a small island with small landfill potential (Wilkinson, 1999). Further, concerns have been expressed (Wilkinson, 1999) that the pressure of cruise lines can keep the taxes so low that they are not able to cover the direct costs which governments need to shoulder in order to attract those tourist flows (e.g. dredging, pier construction and maintenance, security services, etc.), thus also generating crowding-out effect in other relevant projects (Brida, Del Chiappa, Meleddu, & Pulina, 2012a, 2012b).

Prior to 2000 academic research on cruise tourism was limited to few publications (Wild & Dearing, 2000). However, over the last few years the number of academic papers dealing with this topic has been significantly increasing, especially in social sciences (mainly business and management, sociology, psychology and economics). Cruise tourism currently represents a novel and evolving research domain (Papathanassis & Beckmann, 2011).

Papathanassis and Beckmann (2011) highlighted that four main relevant cruise-related research domains can be considered, namely: cruise passengers, cruise staff, destinations, cruise operators and cruise vessels. In line with this analysis, a significant number of published papers aim to analyse the several impacts (both positive and negative) that cruise activity can produce on the host destination from an economic, environmental, political and socio-cultural point of view (e.g. Brida & Zapata, 2010; Dwyer, Douglas, & Livaic, 2004; Dwyer & Forsyth, 1998; Klein, 2009). Further research analysed the so-called 'show casing effect' (Gabe, Lynch, & McConnon, 2006), which refers to the likelihood of cruise passengers returning to visit the destination as independent land tourists and/or to recommend the destination to others.

Broadly, it could be argued that when studying the tourism phenomenon, it is pivotal to analyse the interactions between tourists and host places and to evaluate the impacts that these tourist flows have on the destination, objectively and as perceived by residents. Policymakers and destination marketers need to incorporate a host community's perceptions and attitudes towards cruise tourism development to ensure that residents support tourism projects and tourism planning is sustainable in the long term (Jackson, 2008; Mowforth & Munt, 2003).

This explains why recently academic research has also been devoted to the perceptions and attitudes of residents towards cruise tourism development (e.g. Brida et al., 2012a, 2012b; Brida, Riaño, & Zapata-Aguirre, 2011; Del Chiappa & Abbate, 2013; Diedrich, 2010; Gatewood & Cameron, 2009; Hritz & Cecil, 2008), thus contributing to the development of a cruise-related research domain which was unexplored until recently (Papathanassis & Beckmann, 2011). However, most of them focus on arctic/polar tourism destinations and/or they do not compare the residents' attitudes towards cruise tourism and other segments of tourism development.

Therefore, the present study was carried out to fill the research gap, presenting and discussing the findings of an empirical analysis on a convenience sample of 1,039 residents living in Cagliari, a port of call in the South of Sardinia (Italy).

LITERATURE REVIEW

There is huge consensus in the literature that collaborative policymaking is needed to achieve tourism sustainability, which suggests that local authorities, government agencies, businesses and host communities should collaborate and integrate to plan and regulate tourism development (Vernon, Essex, Pinder, & Curry, 2005). As a consequence, residents' perceptions and attitudes towards the impact of cruise tourism development should be taken into account when planning the future of any cruise tourism destination (Mowforth & Munt, 2003).

Further, when studying the sustainability of cruise activity other relevant issues emerge, namely, how far the views of stakeholders who most influence local tourism development converge with each other and whether they are able to keep up with those of local residents (Del Chiappa, 2012; Del Chiappa, Gallarza, & Zaragoza Viguer, 2013; Presenza, Del Chiappa, & Sheean, 2013).

The literature has categorised factors affecting residents' attitudes towards tourism into extrinsic and intrinsic factors (Faulkner & Tideswell, 1997). The former refers to the characteristics of the location with respect to its role as a tourist destination such as: the degree or stage of tourism development (Doxey, 1976; Gursoy & Rutherford, 2004), the level of economic activity in the host area (Johnson, Snepenger, & Akis, 1994), the degree of tourism seasonality (Fredline & Faulkner, 2000), the tourist-guest ratio (Doxey, 1976) and the type of tourist visiting the destination (Nyaupane, Morais, & Dowler, 2006).

The intrinsic factors refer to the characteristics of the host community members such as: geographical proximity to activity concentrations (Fredline & Faulkner, 2000), length of residency (Gu & Ryan, 2008), proximity to tourist zone, degree of tourism concentration (Pizam, 1978), level of contact with tourists, economic reliance and tourism dependence (Ap, 1992; Smith & Krannich, 1998), socio-demographic characteristics (Belisle & Hoy, 1980) and the perceived balance between positive and negative impacts (Dyer, Gursoy, Sharma, & Carter, 2007).

When cruise tourism development is considered, residents' perceptions and attitudes towards cruise tourism development are reported as being differentiated based on several socio-demographic characteristics of residents (e.g. age, gender, income and level of education), reliance on cruise tourism, residence-port distance, residence-tourism area distance and contact with cruise tourists (Brida et al., 2012a, 2012b; Del Chiappa & Abbate, 2012; Del Chiappa & Abbate, 2013; Del Chiappa, Meleddu, & Pulina, 2012; Pulina, Meleddu, & Del Chiappa, 2013).

For example, Del Chiappa and Abbate (2013) showed that in Messina (Sicily) further developments of the cruise tourism market appeared to be most wanted by residents whose income depended on the cruise sector, middle-aged people, the highly educated, living close to the tourism area, residing in the city for less than five years and interacting intensively with tourists. Del Chiappa, Meleddu, and Pulina (2013) made similar findings in the context of Olbia, a port of call in north-east Sardinia (Italy). In another comparative study, Brida et al. (2012b) showed that residents' perception and attitudes towards cruise activity in Messina and Olbia are not significantly different despite these two ports of call being at different stages of the life cycle of their cruise tourism development.

In their study on Key West, Hritz and Cecil (2008) found residents fearing that cruise tourism may threaten the laid-back atmosphere of their location and asking for greater involvement in tourism planning. Diedrich (2010) reported residents preferring to attract stay-over tourists over cruisers. Other research found that the majority of the local community preferred the development of historic/cultural tourism, while few people wished to experience a growth in cruise tourism in their destination (Gatewood & Cameron, 2009). Similarly, Del Chiappa and Abbate (2013), in their study in Messina, showed that the local community would rather see the development of historic/cultural tourism, followed by sea, sun and sand tourism, cruise tourism and sport tourism.

Brida, Riaño, and Zapata-Aguirre (2011) carried out a cluster analysis of residents' attitudes towards the cruise tourism development in Cartagena de Indias. They considered just economic and socio-cultural impacts. Overall, the study revealed a positive recognition of the economic impacts. The same was also true for social-cultural impacts, even if to a lower degree.

They found four different clusters, namely: 'opponents', 'neutrals', 'developers' and 'tourism workers'. The opponents were mainly women, older age residents, with a bachelor or master degree, living not far from the area visited by cruise passengers and not having a job related to the tourism industry. Neutrals were mostly males, less than 45 years of age and not having a job related to the cruise sector. The majority of supporters did not work in a cruise-related sector and were in the lowest income bracket. Finally, 'tourism workers' were mostly working in a related sector and interact frequently with cruise passengers.

METHODOLOGY

Cagliari was chosen as the researched site of this study for several reasons. Firstly, Sardinia is the second largest island in the Mediterranean Sea. Secondly, as Cagliari is 11 miles from the Gibraltar-Suez line, it represents one of the key points for the transshipment activities in the western Mediterranean. The number of cruise passengers increased from 16,607 in 2001 to 232,300 in 2011, thus making Cagliari the eleventh most popular cruise tourism destination in Italy (Risposte Turismo, 2012).

In this study, we adopted the questionnaire used in prior research (Brida et al., 2012a, 2012b; Del Chiappa & Abbate, 2012, 2013). Specifically, the questionnaire included 49 questions and was divided into three sections.

The first focused on socio-demographic information (17 items, 9 of which were used in this study). The second section listed 26 items concerning residents' perceptions towards the impacts generated by cruise tourism development. Finally, the third part asked respondents to express to what extent they agree or disagree with a list of five statements specifically chosen to investigate their attitudes towards further cruise tourism development. A 5-point Likert scale was used (1 = completely agree; 5 = completely disagree) to indicate their answers. The third part also asked respondents to what extent they would support different types of tourism (cruise tourism, sport tourism, cultural tourism and sea, sun and sand tourism) by using a 5-point Likert (1 = not at all, 5 = very much).

Data were coded and analysed using SPSS (version 17.0), then a series of non-parametric tests (Mann−Whitney: U, and Kruskal−Wallis: H) were applied, where appropriate, to identify whether there were any significant differences in residents' perceptions, attitudes and preferences based on gender, age, reliance on cruise-related employment, level of education, geographical proximity to tourist areas and port, length of residency and frequency of interaction with tourists.

FINDINGS

The majority of respondents were male (51.4%), while females accounted for 48.6% of respondents. Most respondents reported not being economically dependent on cruise tourism (95.7%), having a secondary school qualification (51.3%) and being administrative workers (27.1%). The majority of residents belonged to the 18−25 age group and reported a length of residency above 31 years (48%) and living 3−5 km from the main tourist area (33.2%) and the port (39.8%).

Table 1 shows that respondents think that, on the whole, cruise tourism is bringing more benefits than costs ($M = 3.54$, SD = 1.135). Respondents reported a positive attitude towards the idea of further cruise tourism development and particularly favoured local institutions incentivising this kind of tourism through subsidies, tax cuts ($M = 4.34$, SD = 1.146) and revitalisation of the city centre ($M = 3.94$, SD = 1.146).

Table 1. Mean Scores for the Questionnaire Items and Results of Non-Parametric Tests.

Statements: Cruise Tourism	Mean	S.D.	Gender U	Age H	Employment Reliance U	Level of Education H	Residence-port Distance H	Residence-Tourism Area H	Length of Residency H	Contact with Tourists H
Positive economic impacts										
Increases public investments and infrastructures	3.27	1.187	128952.52	0.066	14.110**	0.129	3.418	3.040	7.045	4.933
Increases private investments and infrastructures	3.26	1.118	132719.5	1.709	19645.5	0.010	2.184	2.427	2.501	1.691
Increases job opportunities	3.63	1.191	128583.5	0.675	16.571*	0.055	7.341	2.972	2.026	10.128*
Increases the income of local people	2.92	1.195	132.930	3.020	15383.5**	0.001	2.187	2.532	6.200	5.840
Positive socio-cultural impacts										
Enhances the quality of life	2.98	1.113	131295.5	0.183	−3.060**	2.016	3.052	1.021	1.604	1.817
Allows for the meeting of new people and experience new culture	3.70	1.060	131485.5	1.628	18.013	0.472	4.660	2.904	5.596	6.966
Enhances the local offer of cultural entertainment activities and attractions	3.51	1.056	13.3973	0.533	15.687**	1.268	1.559	8.722	8.075	15.158**
Makes the best of this location's identity and authenticity	3.77	1.030	131.260	3.795	15770.5**	0.077	2.520	0.260	2.502	5.578
Enhances the quality of restaurants, hotels and retail facilities	3.68	1.024	134076.5	3.068	16893.5*	0.314	1.821	1.975	1.428	5.260
Improves the safety and security of the city	3.16	1.038	130.475	0.436	18208.5	0.845	0.908	6.306	2.866	1.376

Table 1. (Continued)

Statements: Cruise Tourism	Mean	S.D.	Gender U	Age H	Employment Reliance U	Level of Education H	Residence-port Distance H	Residence-Tourism Area H	Length of Residency H	Contact with Tourists H
Enhances social and cultural life for local people	3.30	1.068	129.758	4.577	17.081*	0.000	2.706	5.391	4.792	4.705
Positive environmental impacts										
Incentivises the preservation of the environment	2.91	1.119	130333.5	9.076*	16.813*	0.017	2.724	3.164	11.636*	1.764
Incentivises better infrastructures (roads, water supply, etc.)	2.94	1.717	130830.5	0.874	−16.668*	0.298	1.529	2.202	7.116	1.994
Enhances the quality of public services	3.00	1.151	130491.5	1.163	16405.5*	0.456	1.678	3.831	4.358	5.387
Allows for the preservation and exploitation of local cultural heritage	3.50	1.088	133297.5	4.076	17087.5*	0.129	1.519	2.930	2.586	4.640
Enhances the physical and socio-cultural settings	3.19	1.113	131964.5	6.173*	17.855	0.042	4.309	5.622	4.699	2.063
Negative economic impacts										
Increases the cost of living	2.65	1.173	126260.5	1.682	17283.5	0.210	7.824	14.405**	4.985	3.288
Produces benefits that go to external business investors for the most part	3.14	1.217	129134.5	3.216	19.204	1.028	4.338	2.950	3.230	3.783
Subtracts financial resources from other potential and relevant projects	2.39	1.091	131.176	1.210	19881.5	2.747	2.929	9.232	9.237	4.254

Negative socio-cultural impacts										
Increases car traffic	1.91	0.964	130.677	1.692	20.447	0.476	4.220	13.847**	5.334	3.483
Increase the number of minor crimes	1.91	0.937	132953.5	5.309	19088.5	0.177	2.955	15.281**	4.326	2.641
Forces me to change the way I manage my daily life	1.66	0.902	133.375	4.726	19613	0.766	4.833	10.235*	15.626**	6.991
Negative environmental impacts										
Alters the ecosystem (sand erosion, flora and fauna are damaged, etc.)	2.16	1.125	133.659	0.985	19.750	0.317	11.713*	5.028	8.896	3.876
Increases air and marine pollution	2.40	1.180	128.193	4.214	20275.5	0.071	9.273	4.465	18.210**	2.243
Makes local entertainment facilities and public areas overcrowded	2.25	1.110	128170.5	1.549	19655.5	0.252	6.585	1.940	4.003	1.971
Produces significant levels of waste/rubbish	2.41	1.204	133115.5	2.606	20382.5	0.201	6.283	5.824	7.899	0.766
Overall opinion about tourism										
Overall, it brought more benefits than costs	3.54	1.135	124963.5*	2.403	13909.5**	0.310	11.251*	11.620*	3.084	6.281
Support for cruise tourism development										
The number of cruise ships that arrive in our city should be limited/stopped	2.48	1.266	130.612	3.136	17.586	0.019	4.021	13.171**	7.670	9.069
Local institutions should attract (through subsidies, tax cuts, etc.) cruise ships	4.34	0.875	132254.5	20.742**	16249.5*	0.037	1.594	3.867	10.357*	5.246

Table 1. (*Continued*)

Statements: Cruise Tourism	Mean	S.D.	Gender U	Age H	Employment Reliance U	Level of Education H	Residence-port Distance H	Residence-Tourism Area H	Length of Residency H	Contact with Tourists H
The revitalisation of retail facilities in the city centre would be useful to attract more cruise tourism	3.94	1.146	132681.5	19.722**	19946.5	0.001	2.275	3.310	5.771	8.016
The revitalisation of retail facilities outside the city centre would be useful to attract more cruise tourism	3.64	1.307	131709.5	13.447**	15.448**	0.160	7.342	3.439	3.807	16.085**
Which type of tourism would you support the most?										
Cruise tourism	3.40	1.155	130960.5	2.748	12.446**	0.023	1.079	2.136	7.501	27.284**
Sport tourism	3.49	1.118	129.964	15.319**	19981	5.401*	2.549	3.086	3.209	6.446
Sea, sun and sand tourism	4.05	0.994	130863.5	4.206	18280	1.818	6.171	6.076	5.606	7.368
Historical/cultural tourism	4.32	0.882	127853.5	8.139*	19522	0.121	4.925	8.284	4.926	4.150

*Significant at 0.05 level, **significant at 0.01 level.

Further, they slightly agree with the idea that external business investors benefit most from cruise tourism (M = 3.27, SD = 1.199), suggesting that they view cruise tourism development as somehow endogenous-driven.

At the same time, respondents displayed positive attitudes towards some of the economic, socio-cultural and environmental impacts of cruise tourism. The benefits of cruise tourism in terms of improvement in private investments and infrastructure (M = 3.26, SD = 1.118), job creation (M = 3.63, SD = 1.191), improved quality of restaurants, hotels and retail facilities (M = 3.68, SD = 1.024), increasing the opportunities of cultural exchange (M = 3.70, SD = 1.060) and exploitation of local identity/authenticity (M = 3.77, SD = 1.030) were highly ranked by the respondents.

Respondents were also asked whether they would support additional cruise tourism development. They had a positive attitude about this possibility. In particular, they believed that local institutions should incentivise this kind of tourism through subsidies, tax cuts (M = 4.34, SD = .875) and revitalising the area inside (M = 3.94, SD = 1.146) and outside the city centre (M = 3.64, SD = 1.307). However, cruise tourism is not the favourite type of tourism development they would support. The local community would prefer historic/cultural tourism (M = 4.32; SD = .882), followed by sea, sun and sand tourism (M = 4.05, SD = .994), sport tourism (M = 3.49, SD = 1.118) and cruise tourism (M = 3.40, SD = 1.155).

When the statement 'Overall, cruise tourism brought more benefits than costs' is considered, significant differences were found based on gender (U = 124963.5, $p < 0.05$), employment reliance (U = 13909.500, $p < 0.01$) and geographical proximity to the tourism area (U = 11.620, $p < 0.05$) and the port (H = 11.251, $p < 0.05$).

Specifically, female (Mean rank = 538.55, Sum of ranks = 271966.5) cruise-related employed residents (Mean rank = 663.52, Sum of ranks = 28531.50) and those living closer to the tourism area (Mean rank = 492.72) and port (Mean rank = 481.82) assess the balance between positive and negative impacts more positively than non-cruise-related employed residents (Mean rank = 497.41, Sum of ranks = 480004,50), and those living far from the tourism area (Mean rank = 492.72) and port (Mean rank = 534.54). Further, the analysis reveals that all the socio-demographic variables considered can be taken to be a discriminator of residents' perceptions and attitudes towards cruise tourism development.

When the different statements used to investigate to what extent residents would support further cruise tourism development are considered, all but two of the socio-demographic variables (level of education and geographical proximity to port) were found to discriminate the residents' perceptions.

Finally, all but four of the socio-demographic variables (gender, geographical proximity to tourism area and port, length of residency) were found to discriminate the extent to which respondents would support the four types of tourism considered in the study. Cruise tourism was preferred by those people with economic reliance on cruise tourism (Mean rank = 688.17) and interacting closely with tourists in their daily life (Mean rank = 666.82). On the other hand, middle-aged residents (36−56 years old) supported more sport tourism (Mean rank =548.58) than those aged 18−35 (Mean rank = 515.43) or older than 57 years (Mean rank = 441.11) ($H = 15.319, p < 0.01$).

CONCLUSION AND IMPLICATIONS

The aim of this study was to investigate residents' perceptions towards the development of cruise tourism in the city of Cagliari, a cruise port of call in the south of Sardinia (Italy). Further, it aimed to compare the residents' attitudes towards cruise tourism and other segments of tourism development (cultural tourism, sport tourism and sun and sea tourism). Given the importance of residents' input in tourism development (Gursoy & Rutherford, 2004), our findings can usefully contribute to the academic debate on community-based tourism and also support policymakers in their efforts to develop a more sustainable model for cruise tourism destinations.

Findings show that residents have overall a positive attitude towards cruise tourism development, and also very little concern when negative impacts are considered. However, cruise tourism is not the most preferred when compared with other types of tourism. Further, they highlight that significant differences based on socio-economic and demographic characteristics (age, gender, reliance on cruise-related employment, level of education, geographical proximity to tourist areas and port, length of residency and frequency of interaction with tourists) exist in residents' perceptions and attitudes towards cruise tourism development and in their preferences for different types of tourism development.

Our findings are relevant for researchers, destination managers, policymakers and cruise operators/companies. From a theoretical perspective, the study adds to the growing literature in the field of residents' perceptions towards cruise tourism development and the emergent research aimed at investigating the residents' preferences for different types of tourism. Despite minor differences, overall our findings seem to confirm research carried out in other ports of call and in different geographical areas. This allows us to consider socio-demographic characteristics as being common moderator factors on residents' perceptions and attitudes towards cruise tourism development.

From a marketing perspective, our results provide useful information for policymakers and destination marketers attempting to run effective and personalised internal marketing operations with the aim of increasing the favourableness of residents' attitudes towards cruise tourism. To achieve this aim, policymakers, destination managers and cruise companies should be conscious of the necessity to deliver personalised messages which focus as much as possible on the positive balance between the potentially positive and negative impacts of cruise tourism (Perdue, Long, & Allen, 1990).

According to Brida et al. (2012b), Del Chiappa and Abbate (2013) and Pulina et al. (2013), these internal marketing operations and messages should rely on objective measure of costs and benefits of each type of tourism (e.g. the number of employees and entrepreneurs who are involved in cruise activity, the amount of financial resources that were and still need to be invested in developing infrastructures, etc.). This is needed because residents cannot be expected to be fully cognisant of the impacts arising from cruise tourism development and/or they could evaluate these impacts more negatively. In accordance with Social Exchange Theory (Ap, 1992), residents would be willing to support further cruise tourism development only if brings more benefits than costs to their community.

It has been argued (Del Chiappa & Abbate, 2013) that persuasive communication should not simply reaffirm prior beliefs (e.g. cruise tourism created new jobs), but strengthen the evaluation aspects of these beliefs (e.g. stating that creating new jobs is important given the high rate of unemployment in the area). In an attempt to increase the credibility of these messages, the local institutions and policymakers should involve impartial sources of information (such as universities, research centres or organisations which do not belong to the local community). By doing this, local institutions and policymakers can avoid being accused of delivering 'politically minded' messages (Del Chiappa & Abbate, 2013; Lindberg & Johnson, 1997).

Overall, the findings underline the importance of involving the local community in tourism planning and monitoring how residents' perceptions of cruise tourism change over time as tourism develops, and comparing them with those towards other types of tourism development.

Although these findings contribute to a somewhat neglected area in tourism research, the study does have some limitations. In particular, although interviewers were instructed to conduct interviews in the different areas/neighbourhoods of the city, a convenience sample was employed. Contrariwise, it could be argued that an 'area sample' should be considered as being more advisable. Further research should also consider the role that other intrinsic variables (e.g. community involvement, community attachment) and extrinsic factors (e.g. the tourism seasonality and the level of economic activity in the area) can exert in discriminating residents' perceptions and attitudes towards cruise tourism development and other types of tourism segment.

Future research should also be aimed at monitoring whether and how residents' preferences and perceptions change over time along with each stage of cruise tourism life cycle, as well as after particular critical events.

REFERENCES

Ap, J. (1992). Residents perceptions on tourism impacts. *Annals of Tourism Research*, *19*(4), 665–690.

Belisle, F. J., & Hoy, D. R. (1980). The perceived impact of tourism by residents: A case study in Santa Maria, Columbia. *Annals of Tourism Research*, *12*(1), 83–101.

Brida, J. G., Del Chiappa, G., Meleddu, M., & Pulina, M. (2012a). The perceptions of an island community towards cruise tourism: A factor analysis. *Tourism: An International Interdisciplinary Journal*, *60*(1), 29–42.

Brida, J. G., Del Chiappa, G., Meleddu, M., & Pulina, M. (2012b). A comparison of residents' perceptions in two cruise ports in the Mediterranean. *International Journal of Tourism Research*, *16*(2), 180–190.

Brida, J. G., Riaño, E., & Zapata-Aguirre, S. (2011). Resident's attitudes and perceptions towards cruise tourism development: A case study of Cartage de Indias (Colombia). *Tourism and Hospitality Research*, *11*(3), 187–202.

Brida, J. G., & Zapata, A. S. (2010). Cruise tourism: Economic, socio-cultural and environmental impacts. *International Journal of Leisure and Tourism Marketing*, *1*(3), 205–226.

Chin, C. B. N. (2008). *Cruising in the global economy: Profits, pleasure and work at sea.* Aldershot: Ashgate.

CLIA (Cruise Lines International Association). (2008). *Cruise market overview.* Statistical cruise industry data through 2007. Retrieved from http://www.cruising.org/press/overview2008/printPDF.cfm. Accessed on October 25, 2009.

Del Chiappa, G. (2012). Community integration: A case study of Costa Smeralda, Italy. In E. Fayos-Sola (Ed.), *Knowledge management in tourism: Policy and governance applications bridging tourism theory and practice* (Vol. 4, pp. 243–263). Bridging Tourism Theory and Practice. Bingley, UK: Emerald Group Publishing Limited.

Del Chiappa, G., & Abbate, T. (2012). Resident's perceptions and attitude toward the cruise tourism development: insights from an Italian tourism destination. In J. C. Andreani & U. Collesei (Eds.), *Proceedings of the XII international conference marketing trends, 2012*, Marketing Trends Association, Paris-Venice.

Del Chiappa, G., & Abbate, T. (2013). Island cruise tourism development: A resident's perspective in the context of Italy. *Current Issues in Tourism.* doi:10.1080/13683500. 2013.854751

Del Chiappa, G., Gallarza, M. G., & Zaragoza Viguer, A. (2013). Cruise tourism development in Valencia (Spain): Stakeholders' views and residents' attitude. In J. C. Andreani & U. Collesei (Eds.), *Proceedings of the XIII international conference marketing trends*, Marketing Trends Association, Paris-Venice.

Del Chiappa, G., Meleddu, M., & Pulina, M. (2013). Cruise tourism development. A community perspective. In M. Kozak & N. Kozack (Eds.), *Interdisciplinary tourism research*. Newcastle: Cambridge Scholars Publishing.

Diedrich, A. (2010). Cruise ship tourism in Belize: the implications of developing cruise ship tourism in an ecotourism destination. *Ocean & Coastal Management, 53*(5–6), 234–244.

Doxey, G. (1976). When enough's enough: The natives are restless in old Niagara. *Heritage Canada, 2*, 26–27.

Dwyer, L., Douglas, N., & Livaic, Z. (2004). Estimating the economic contribution of cruise ship visit. *Tourism in Marine Environments, 1*(1), 5–16.

Dwyer, L., & Forsyth, P. (1998). Economic significance of cruise tourism. *Annals of Tourism Research, 25*(2), 393–415.

Dyer, P., Gursoy, D., Sharma, B., & Carter, J. (2007). Structural modelling of resident perceptions of tourism and associated development on the Sunshine Coast, Australia. *Tourism Management, 28*(2), 409–422.

European Cruise Council (2012). *The cruise industry: Contribution of cruise tourism to the economies of Europe 2012 edition.* Retrieved from http://www.europeancruisecouncil. com/content/economic%20report.pdf. Accessed on August 25, 2012.

Faulkner, B., & Tideswell, C. (1997). A framework for monitoring community impacts of tourism. *Journal of Sustainable Tourism, 5*(1), 3–28.

Fredline, E., & Faulkner, B. (2000). Host community reactions: A cluster analysis. *Annals of Tourism Research, 27*(3), 763–784.

Gabe, T., Lynch, C., & McConnon, J. (2006). Likelihood of cruise ship passenger return to a visited port: The case of Bar Harbor, Maine. *Journal of Travel Research, 44*(3), 281–287.

Gatewood, J. B., & Cameron, C. M. (2009). Belonger perceptions of tourism and its impacts in the Turks and Calcos Islands [Research project report]. Retrieved from: http://www. lehigh.edu/~jbg1/Perceptions-of-Tourism.pdf

Gu, H., & Ryan, C. (2008). Place attachment, identity and community impacts of tourism: The case of Beijing Hutong. *Tourism Management, 29*(4), 637–647.

Gursoy, D., & Rutherford, D. (2004). Host attitudes toward tourism: An improved structural model. *Annals of Tourism Research, 31*(3), 495–516.

Hritz, N., & Cecil, A. (2008). Investigating the sustainability of cruise tourism: A case study of key west. *Journal of Sustainable Tourism, 16*(2), 168–181.

Jackson, L. (2008). Residents' perceptions of the impacts of special event tourism. *Journal of Place Management and Development, 1*(3), 240–255.

Johnson, J. D., Snepenger, D. J., & Akis, S. (1994). Residents' perceptions of tourism development. *Annals of Tourism Research, 21*(3), 629–642.

Klein, R. A. (2009). *Paradise lost at sea: Rethinking cruise vacations.* Halifax: Fernwood Publishing.

Lindberg, K., & Johnson, R. L. (1997). Modeling resident attitudes toward tourism. *Annals of Tourism Research, 24*(2), 402–424.

Mowforth, M., & Munt, I. (2003). *Tourism and sustainability: Development and new tourism in the Third World* (2nd ed.). London: Routledge.

Nyaupane, G. P., Morais, D. B., & Dowler, L. (2006). The role of community involvement and number/type of visitors on tourism impacts: A controlled comparison of Annapurna, Nepal and Northwest Yunnan, China. *Tourism Management, 27*(6), 1373–1385.

Papathanassis, A., & Beckmann, I. (2011). Assessing the poverty of cruise theory hypothesis. *Annals of Tourism Research, 38*(1), 153–174.

Perdue, R. R., Long, P. T., & Allen, L. (1990). Resident support for tourism development. *Annals of Tourism Research, 17*(4), 586–599.

Pizam, A. (1978). Tourism's impacts: The social costs to the destination community as perceived by its residents. *Journal of Travel Research, 16*(4), 8–12.

Presenza, A., Del Chiappa, G., & Sheean, L. (2013). Residents' engagement and local tourism governance in maturing beach destinations: Evidence from an Italian case study. *Journal of Destination Marketing and Management, 2*(1), 22–30.

Pulina, M., Meleddu, M., & Del Chiappa, G. (2013). Residents' choice probability and tourism development. *Tourism Management Perspectives, 5*, 57–67.

Risposte Turismo. (2011). *Il traffico crocieristico in Italia nel 2010.* Retrieved from http://www.rispesteturismo.it/riviste.php?pag=4#. Accessed on June 15, 2011.

Risposte Turismo. (2012). *Il traffico crocieristico in Italia nel 2011.* Retrieved from http://www.rispesteturismo. Accessed on March 25, 2012.

Smith, M., & Krannich, R. (1998). Tourism dependence and resident attitudes. *Annals of Tourism Research, 25*(4), 783–802.

Vernon, J., Essex, S., Pinder, D., & Curry, K. (2005). Collaborative policymaking. Local sustainable projects. *Annals of Tourism Research, 32*(2), 325–345.

Wild, P., & Dearing, J. (2000). Development of and prospects for cruising in Europe. *Maritime Policy and Management, 27*(4), 315–333.

Wilkinson, P. F. (1999). Carribean cruise tourism: Delusion? Illusion? *Tourism Geographies, 1*(3), 261–282.

WEDDING-BASED TOURISM DEVELOPMENT: INSIGHTS FROM AN ITALIAN CONTEXT

Giacomo Del Chiappa and Fulvio Fortezza

ABSTRACT

Over the past two decades, wedding tourism has been booming. Despite this, very little research has investigated this phenomenon. This chapter discusses the findings of 15 in-depth interviews with Italian wedding planners, which were carried out to analyse their views on what a destination wedding is, and how frequently they are able to influence the final choice of a site. Further, it discusses four case studies of the most important Italian wedding destinations in order to analyse their offer and related marketing strategy. Findings revealed that wedding destinations can be considered as a complex cluster of interrelated stakeholders; hence, a high degree of coordination and cooperation is needed for destination competitiveness. Further, results suggest that wedding destinations are currently opting for a product/service-oriented strategy with very little attention to a more appropriate experiential and emotional approach.

Keywords: Wedding; destinations; wedding planner; experiential approach; Italy

Marketing Places and Spaces
Advances in Culture, Tourism and Hospitality Research, Volume 10, 61–74
ISSN: 1871-3173/doi:10.1108/S1871-317320150000010005

INTRODUCTION

Over the past two decades, there has been increasing scholarly interest and scientific research on an event that is a relevant motivator of tourism, and figures prominently in enhancing the appeal of a destination (Getz, 2008). In this scenario, weddings have attracted the attention of both researchers and practitioners.

According to the Fairchild Bridal group (cited in Daniels & Loveless, 2007), 86% of couples would be willing to choose a destination wedding, 16% of whom opted for this type of celebration. Wedding tourism is booming and several destinations are currently positioning themselves in this lucrative market. Among them, we could cite Las Vegas, Hawaii, the Caribbean, Mexico, Fiji, Jamaica, Europe (Daniels & Loveless, 2007), New York and New Zealand (Johnston, 2006). UK citizens took part in 45,000 weddings abroad in 2005, with an average per capita spending of $12,000. Italy could be considered as still at an early stage in the development of this tourism and has great potential that needs to be exploited through a strategy creating specific package and marketing activities.

According to the International Journalism Observatory, 8% of Italy's 44 million tourists visit the country due to a wedding, honeymoon, or anniversary. The main Italian wedding destinations are Verona, Venice, Florence, Rome, the Amalfi Coast and Capri. In 2012, 6,180 weddings of foreign couples were celebrated in places throughout Italy, thus generating 1.221 million of overnight stays and a total revenue of more than 315 million euros (JFC, 2012).

Some researchers have analysed tourism and honeymoons (e.g. Jang, Lee, Lee, & Hong, 2007; Kim & Agrusa, 2005), but very little research exists on wedding-based tourism, despite its growing importance in many destinations.

This chapter aims to contribute to the scientific debate surrounding the topic by adopting a supply-side perspective. Specifically, it presents and discusses the findings of 15 in-depth interviews with Italian wedding planners, which were carried out with the aim of analysing their views on what a destination wedding is and how it should be organised, and how frequently they are able to influence the final choice of a site. Further, it discusses four case studies of the most important Italian wedding destinations (namely, Verona, Venice, Florence and Palermo) in order to consider what they offer and related marketing strategy.

LITERATURE REVIEW

The relatively recent and growing interest of researchers in weddings as a motivator of tourism flows is generating a new strand of research in the context of event management and event tourism (Getz, 2008). Weddings can be considered as belonging to the category of religious and/or civil and private events (Goldbatt, 2002).

A destination wedding is a wedding ceremony celebrated outside the bride and groom's home town (Daniels & Loveless, 2007). According to Johnston (2006, p. 199), 'The destination wedding entwines sexuality with a sensory appreciation of landscape', thus representing a means by which consumers shape and experience the destination identity.

Wedding-based tourism can be defined as tourist flows arising from participation in weddings that are held at a different location from where the bride and groom, or just one of them, live (Daniels & Loveless, 2007; Del Chiappa, forthcoming). Another type of wedding flow is when the event takes place in a bride and groom's home town and guests arrive from other places (Del Chiappa, forthcoming). The market is made up of marriages (first-time, second or even more), same-sex marriages, commitment ceremonies and renewal of vows (Major, McLeay, & Waine, 2010).

Similarly to other types of tourism (e.g. Brida, 2010), and according to the literature on event tourism (e.g. Bowdin, Allen, O'Toole, Harris, & McDonnel, 2006; Daniels & Loveless, 2007), wedding-based tourism has direct, indirect and induced economic effects on the economy of the destination.

The direct effect is on a supplier who sells goods and services directly to the bride and the groom, who need them to organise their wedding, and/or the guests when they are at the destination. Indirect effects result from the purchases of direct suppliers, such as goods from other companies. Induced effects arise from the expenditures of direct and indirect recipients as a result of their increased incomes that wedding-based tourism brings to the destination.

Further, various social, environmental and marketing impacts and benefits may potentially benefit the host destination in terms of exploitation of local heritage, local identity and authenticity, promotion of local food and wine, increase in the number of visitors, enhancement of destination brand awareness and image and achieving broader tourism seasonality

(Bowdin et al., 2006; Daniels & Loveless, 2007; Fortezza & Del Chiappa, 2012). Finally, it produces the so-called 'show casing effect' (Gabe, Lynch, & McConnon, 2006), which refers to the likelihood of guests returning to visit the wedding destination as independent tourist and/or recommending it to friends and relatives both offline and online via comments, pictures and videos uploaded to some social media platform (Del Chiappa, 2011, 2013).

Several key drivers of sector growth and current trends in destination weddings can be considered. Specifically, they can be categorised into: cost-related factors, socio-cultural factors, supply-side and demand-side characteristics (Fig. 1). On the one hand, we can consider the lower costs of travelling, the rising number of wedding ceremonies and receptions worldwide and the fact that in recent times, and in some cultures (e.g. Korea), the wedding is perceived as being more 'couple-oriented' than 'family oriented'. Thus, for couples, it is increasingly acceptable to get

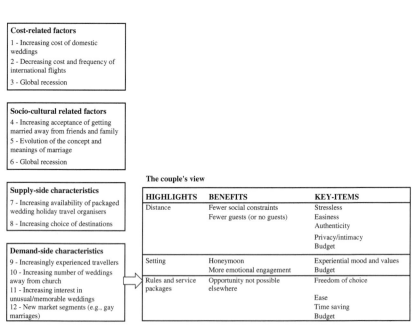

Fig. 1. Key Drivers of Wedding-Based Tourism. *Source*: Our adaptation from Major et al. (2010, p. 253).

married away from friends and relatives (Major et al., 2010), in order to enjoy their wedding wherever they wish (Schumann & Amado, 2010).

On the other hand, destination weddings can be more affordable, exotic, intimate, unique, experiential and memorable (Major, McLeay, & Waine, 2010), which is something intrinsic to the needs of couples getting married (Chadiha, Leber, & Veoff, 1998). They can allow couples to escape any social and family obligations that are a latent part of the wedding as well as the couple's triangulation with wedding officials and state, such as those that do not allow gay marriage (Freeman, 2002; Johnston, 2006; Schumann & Amado, 2010).

Further, destination weddings usually save on cost due to the smaller number of people who are willing to travel to participate in the ceremony and/or the possibility of couples combining their wedding with their honeymoon (Schumann & Amado, 2010). Finally, they may allow the bride and the groom to enjoy their experience with participants, thus avoiding the anxiety or detachment that the couple could experience when leaving for their honeymoon (Ingraham, 1999).

In an attempt to interpret a destination wedding relying on the experiential approach, we could refer to the so-called 'metaphor of theatre' (Pencarelli & Forlani, 2002; Pine & Gilmore, 1999). Thus, it may be argued that a destination wedding requires someone (a wedding planner, a wedding agency, or the couple themselves) who can integrate and coordinate several types of private and public service providers ('who'), so that it is possible to package the different ingredients of the experience ('what'), in a specific location ('where') based on specific rules (how), to make the final result very unique and memorable (Fig. 2).

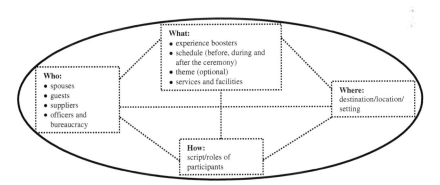

Fig. 2. The Overall Value of the Wedding Experience. *Source*: Our elaboration.

Based on Bieger's (1996) approach, a wedding destination can be defined as a geographical, economic and social unit consisting of all these firms, organisations, activities, areas and installations, which are intended to package an overall wedding experience able to serve and satisfy the specific needs of the couple and their guests.

Given the almost complete lack of research on the topic, further studies are needed to extend investigation into the wedding tourism phenomenon adopting both supply-side and demand-side perspectives (Del Chiappa, forthcoming). The present study aims to fill this gap adopting a supply-side perspective in the context of Italy, in order to increase understanding of how the wedding destination experience can be created, integrated and positioned in the market.

METHODOLOGY

This study discusses the results of 15 in-depth interviews we carried out with Italian wedding planners belonging to the Italian Wedding Planner Association, to understand better the type of services that are needed to organise a destination wedding, to analyse the nature of the cooperation that could exist between wedding planners and local institutions and to assess the extent to which planners influence the destination wedding selection. A semi-structured questionnaire with open-ended questions and closed questions was sent out with the cooperation of the Italian Wedding Planner Association to its current members (at the time of the data collection they were 15).

Further, a case study approach was adopted to investigate four wedding destinations in the context of Italy (Verona, Florence, Palermo and Venice). To this end, we adopted a case study approach given the mainly exploratory nature of the research around the topic (Bregoli & Del Chiappa, 2013; Yin, 2009).

Specifically, for each case study, the analysis was based on both primary (one semi-structured interview with the manager responsible for the wedding-based tourism development of the destination) and secondary data (DMO internal data and documents).

Interviews with the DMO and local authorities took place at their place of work, were recorded and transcribed immediately after the interview. Verona, Florence and Venice were selected because they are three of the most important wedding destinations, and because they share the same characteristics. These are: (a) a strong brand image internationally as romantic destinations; (b) the ability to rely on strong networks of local stakeholders involved in delivering products, services and experiences to couples. Palermo, a city in Sicily, in the South of Italy, was selected because it is in the very early stage of the wedding-based tourism life cycle, thus representing an interesting case for comparison with others.

FINDINGS

The research results were grouped into two sections. On the one hand, the aim was to analyse briefly the wedding planners' views about destination weddings and their influence on the site selection process. On the other hand, the purpose was to discuss four case studies of the most important Italian wedding destinations (namely, Verona, Florence, Palermo and Venice) in order to describe what they offer and their marketing strategies.

The Wedding Planners' Views

In this study, 15 in-depth interviews were carried out to understand better the type of services that are needed to organise a destination wedding, to analyse the nature of the cooperation that could exist between wedding planners and local institutions and to assess the extent to which planners influence the destination wedding selection.

Based on the interviews, the process of planning a destination wedding can be compared to a wheel where the wedding event is at the centre and all the specialist suppliers (venue providers, transport operators, accommodation, photographers, wedding planners, catering providers, make-up artists, etc.) are the spokes delivering the other 'peripheral' services.

The number and/or type of private and public stakeholders are different based on the type of wedding (e.g. religious vs. civil wedding) and of the needs, desires and cultural background of the bride and the groom. Wedding planners claim that strong cooperation with the local institutions is pivotal especially in the case of a civil wedding, and, broadly, when it is necessary to know in advance whether any specific rules can influence the organisation of the wedding, for example, in terms of permission to celebrate the event in a special venue.

The offices with which the interaction is higher are those responsible for banns and/or to book days and places for weddings. It is peculiar that all of the wedding planners we interviewed did not refer at all to some forms of cooperation (co-marketing) with offices responsible for the promotion of the destination. Indeed, it could be argued that wedding planners play a pivotal role in influencing the site selection and support, based on the co-creation paradigm (Prahalad & Ramaswamy, 2004; Sfandla & Bjork, 2013; Shaw, Bailey & Williams, 2011), the development of the destination wedding experience that should be promoted in the international market.

When respondents were asked to assess how often, in their view, they were able to influence the final choice of site (never, almost never, sometimes, almost always and always), the answers were as follow: seven do this almost always, six sometimes and two never. There emerges a kind of marketing myopia of local institutions towards the idea of weddings being a motivator of tourist flows and towards the relevant role of wedding planners in promoting wedding destinations.

DESTINATION WEDDINGS: CASE STUDIES FROM THE CONTEXT OF ITALY

The Verona Case Study

In 2012, a total of 941 weddings were celebrated in Verona, 124 of which involving couples not residing in the city (Italians and foreigners), the most part from Europe.

It is interesting to note that a specific project ('Sposami a Verona') and tourism product club ('Wedding and Emotions in Verona') have existed since 2009 to promote wedding-based tourism. The project 'Sposami a Verona' was started by the municipality which was aware of:

- the position of Verona internationally as a romantic city, thanks to the myth of 'Romeo and Juliet';
- the great appeal of Verona to many Italians and international wedding planners, who had already been advertising Verona to their customers as 'The city of Romeo and Juliet';
- the great appeal of Verona to numerous couples coming from many countries all aiming at experiencing their own individual wedding experience.

The most important strengths of Verona as a wedding tourism destination are the following:

– beautiful and charming surroundings (11) to host the rite of marriage and the wedding party (with a maximum rate of 1000€), including the most famous one, that is, 'The House of Romeo and Juliet', besides 'The Notary's Chapel', 'Tapestry Room', 'Guarenti Hall' and seven charming villas;
– the ability of the municipality to deliver a complex wedding package which includes the management of paperwork and rite of marriage, special floral decorations, live music entertainment, drinks and several other details such as the recital of poetry during the rite to boost the whole wedding experience;
– a strong and effective tourist guide service that allows couples to discover, before the wedding, the great potential of the city as a wedding destination and the magic and emotional myths of the area;
– the ability to customise and enrich the wedding experience through the services offered by the wedding tourism product club, such as accommodation, restaurants, catering, musicians, travel agencies, event and entertainment, etc. Couples, of course, can customise the wedding experience on their own or with the help of their personal wedding planner as well;
– the possibility for the spouses to get married also on New Year's Day, thus increasing the glamour of the experience.

Further, the city of Verona is able to offer other types of experiences which are correlated to the wedding business, such as anniversaries, blessings and promises of love. Moreover, some specific touristic packages, for example, New Year's Eve of Love and Valentine's Day of Love, are made possible by using the product club mentioned above.

The goal is to attract as many different tourist target groups from all over the world, relying mainly on the romantic allure of 'The House of Juliet'.

The Venice Case Study

In Venice, destination weddings are an especially interesting aspect of marriage celebration. In 2010, 55.6% of civil weddings were celebrated by couples not residing in the city; 74.6% of these were Italian or other European couples, 5% American couples and 1% Asian couples.

Venice as a wedding destination adopts a service-oriented strategy, which consists of delivering services to organise effective and efficient events in one of the four locations available to host the rite of marriage (the most expensive is the 'Sala cuoi d'oro - Ca' Vendramin'; at a rate of 5000€). The services include managing the paperwork and the rite, standard floral decorations and music (not live) and, if required, providing an interpreter and broadcasting the ceremony on the website of the municipality for family and friends who follow the marriage from their home.

It could be argued that at the moment Venice is not adopting any experiential and emotional marketing approach when promoting itself as a wedding destination. The role played by the municipality is about facilitating the rite of marriage, while leaving completely to couples all the organisation of their own wedding experience.

From this point of view, the local policy makers are aware of what the Venice surroundings can offer couples wishing to enjoy a romantic time. Recently, local institutions have been researching and developing a project to measure the economic and marketing impacts of wedding tourism on the city.

The Florence Case Study

In terms of wedding-based experience, Florence is in the early stages of tourism development. In 2012, a total of 902 weddings were celebrated there, 205 of which involving foreign couples (mainly American, British, Russian and Japanese), and 159 couples where either the bride or groom was foreign.

Overall similar to Venice, the city of Florence offers locations (six at the moment, at a maximum rate of 5000€ for the 'Salone de' Cinquecento' at 'Palazzo Vecchio') and basic services. The goal is to increase further the number of locations (applying different rates), giving couples the opportunity to get married in surroundings that are even more charming and unforgettable.

The city is currently lacking a clear vision and strategy about the way it could position itself as a wedding destination and what it should target. Nevertheless, policy makers are interested – like Verona – in hosting not just weddings but also other romantic experiences (e.g. blessings and anniversaries) in a way that will achieve additional international recognition and enhance the image of Florence as a wonderful place to visit and stay.

The Palermo Case Study

Palermo is at a very early stage of the wedding-based tourism development. Here, the policy makers really trust in the advantages that hosting the marriages of people from other parts of Italy and abroad can allow, especially in terms of repositioning the city as a tourism destination. From this point of view, the main goals are the following:

– To promote the Mediterranean authenticity of the destination, making possible a profound change in the way people view Sicily and Palermo.
– To boost business opportunities for the local network of touristic operators. In order for this to happen, the municipality is evaluating the creation of a touristic product club. Moreover, a specific website could be created to make the local operators aware of the business opportunities coming from hosting marriages. In this case, a kind of 'wedding list' could be uploaded each time on the website. By doing so, this would also appeal to the so-called '2.0 couples', like Verona does. These are people who aim at customising their wedding experience, with no support from wedding planners or other agencies.

A specific brand ('Palermo I do') has already been created and three amazing surroundings have been selected by recovering unused places. These are:

– a deconsecrated church;
– a farmhouse alongside the famous beach of Mondello;
– an abandoned foundry.

A very particular aspect of the wedding package created by the municipality of Palermo is that every couple getting married there can adopt a tree as a symbolic way to keep in touch with the wedding destination.

CONCLUSION AND IMPLICATIONS

Our findings firstly revealed that wedding destinations can be considered, as any other tourism destination, as a cluster of interrelated stakeholders (both public and private) offering an amalgam of tourism products and services to couples and their guests (Baggio, Scott, & Cooper, 2010; Del Chiappa & Presenza, 2013). As a consequence, a high degree of coordination and cooperation is needed for destination competitiveness (Bregoli & Del Chiappa, 2013; Wang & Xiang, 2007).

In all the analysed case studies, policy makers act as conveners and 'facilitators' to initiate collaboration (Jamal & Getz, 1995) and to strengthen the natural appeal that the destination may have for couples looking for a special marriage experience. In doing so, they seek to increase wedding tourism mainly by acting on civil rites because these are under the direct control of the municipalities.

The main driver of the competitiveness of the analysed destination weddings is certainly the local setting and surroundings. Then, policy makers exploit the value of this asset by making it quick and easy to perform the bureaucratic steps of the wedding and making it possible to choose the best location for the rite of marriage from a wide range of appealing options (perhaps from a list of different rates).

In general, policy makers and DMOs in our study do not seem to play a proactive role in selecting and involving local businesses in the design of the wedding experience to be delivered to couples and their guests. The only exception is Verona where such a role is played. Further, among the different case studies, Verona appears particularly relevant as an example of Italian destination weddings with a clear and effective position as an 'experiential romance city' where weddings and other romantic experiences can be organised and experienced in a memorable and unique way.

This is in part due to the effective pre-wedding experience that couples can enjoy before their wedding thanks to the tourist ride through the city organised by the municipality. Further, couples here can personalise their experience by relying on the touristic product club, which is promoted and offered by the municipality.

Overall, findings seem to suggest that currently there is a certain type of marketing myopia in the way local institutions and DMOs are trying to exploit such a market and monitoring its impact on the host destination. It seems that wedding destinations are currently opting for a product/service-oriented strategy when promoting themselves with very little attention to a more appropriate experiential and emotional approach that would be definitely more appropriate to attract events (weddings) that are experiential and emotional in nature. The only destination wedding that seems to be currently adopting an experiential approach is Verona.

Our findings revealed further myopia in the way policy makers and destination marketers are currently trying to develop wedding-based tourism in their area. In this regard, it is relevant to highlight that they are not proactively seeking the cooperation of wedding planners to co-create and to promote the wedding package and experience to their market. This seems to be unreasonable given the strong influence that wedding planners seem to play in influencing the site selection process of the couples.

This study, which is exploratory in nature, is not free of limitations and it should just be considered as an attempt to deepen understanding of the wedding-based tourism phenomenon by adopting a supply-side perspective. Further researches are definitely needed to analyse in detail other international case studies, the role of wedding planners, the motivations that push couples to opt for specific destination weddings and, finally, the overall impact generated by this type of event.

REFERENCES

Baggio, R., Scott, N., & Cooper, C. (2010). Improving tourism destination governance: A complexity science approach. *Tourism Review, 65*(4), 51−60.

Bieger, T. (1996). *Management von Destinationen und Tourismusorganisationen.* Munich: R. Oldenbourg Verlag.

Bowdin, G., Allen, J., O'Toole, W., Harris, R., & McDonnel, I. (2006). *Events management* (2nd ed.). Oxford: Elsevier.

Bregoli, I., & Del Chiappa, G. (2013). Coordinating relationships among destination stakeholders: Evidence from Edinburgh (UK). *Tourism Analysis, 18*(2), 145−155.

Brida, J. G. (2010). Cruise tourism: Economic, socio-cultural and environmental impacts. *International Journal Leisure and Tourism Marketing, 1*(3), 205−226.

Chadiha, L. A., Leber, D., & Veoff, J. (1998). Newlywed's narrative themes: Meaning in the first year of marriage for African American and white couples. *Journal of Comparative Family Studies, 29*(1), 115−130.

Daniels, M., & Loveless, C. (2007). *Wedding planning & management.* Oxford: Elsevier.

Del Chiappa, G. (2011). Trustworthiness of travel 2.0 applications and their influence on tourist behaviour: An empirical investigation in Italy. In R. Law, M. Fuchs, & F. Ricci, (Eds.), *Information and communication technologies in tourism 2011* (pp. 331−342). Vienna, Austria: Springer.

Del Chiappa, G. (2013). Internet versus travel agencies: The perception of different groups of Italian online buyers. *Journal of Vacation Marketing, 19*, 55−66.

Del Chiappa, G. (forthcoming). Wedding-based tourism. In J. Jafari & H. Xiao (Eds.), *Encyclopedia of tourism.* Springer.

Del Chiappa, G., & Presenza, A. (2013). The use of network analysis to assess relationships among stakeholders within a tourism destination. An empirical investigation on Costa Smeralda-Gallura (Italy). *Tourism Analysis, 18*(1), 1−13.

Fortezza, F., & Del Chiappa, G. (2012, October 18−19). Il wedding-based tourism come leva di valorizzazione territoriale. In *Referred electronic conference proceedings of XXIV Convegno annuale di Sinergie Il territorio come giacimento di vitalità per l'impresa,* Università del Salento, Lecce (pp. 329−342).

74 GIACOMO DEL CHIAPPA AND FULVIO FORTEZZA

Freeman, E. (2002). *The wedding complex: Forms of belonging in modern American culture*. London: Duke University Press.

Gabe, T., Lynch, C., & McConnon, J. (2006). Likelihood of cruise ship passenger return to a visited port: The case of Bar Harbor, Maine. *Journal of Travel Research, 44*(3), 281–287.

Getz, D. (2008). Event tourism: Definition, evolution, and research. *Tourism Management, 29*(3), 403–428.

Goldbatt, J. (2002). *Special events: Twenty-first century global event management*. New York, NY: Wiley.

Ingraham, C. (1999). *White weddings: Romancing heterosexuality in popular culture*. New York, NY: Routledge.

Jamal, T. B., & Getz, D. (1995). Collaboration theory and community tourism planning. *Annals of Tourism Research, 22*(1), 186–204.

Jang, H., Lee, S., Lee, S., & Hong, S. (2007). Expanding the individual choice-sets model to couples' honeymoon destination selection process. *Tourism Management, 28,* 1299–1314.

JFC. (2012). *Wedding tourism*. Retrieved from http://www.jfc.it/blog/wedding-tourism-sposarsi-in-italia/. Accessed on January 25, 2014.

Johnston, L. (2006). "I do down-under": Naturalizing landscapes and love through wedding tourism in New Zealand. *ACME, 5*(2), 191–208.

Kim, S. S., & Agrusa, J. (2005). The positioning of overseas honeymoon destinations. *Annals of Tourism Research, 32*(4), 887–904.

Major, B., McLeay, F., & Waine, D. (2010). Perfect weddings abroad. *Journal of Vacation Marketing, 16*(3), 249–262.

Pencarelli, T., & Forlani, F. (2002). Il marketing dei distretti turistici-sistemi vitali nell'economia delle esperienze. *Sinergie, 58,* 231–277.

Pine, B. J., & Gilmore, J. H. (1999). *The experience economy: Work is theatre and every business a stage*. Boston, MA: Harvard Business School Press.

Prahalad, C. K., & Ramaswamy, V. (2004). *The future of competition: Co-creating unique value with customers*. Boston, MA: Harvard Business School Press.

Schumann, F. R., & Amado, C. (2010). Japanese overseas weddings in Guam: A case study of Guam's first hotel wedding chapel. *South Asian Journal of Tourism and Heritage, 3*(1), 173–181.

Sfandla, C., & Bjork, P. (2013). Tourism experience network: Co-creation of experiences in interactive processes. *International Journal of Tourism Research, 15,* 495–506.

Shaw, G., Bailey, A., & Williams, A. M. (2011). Service dominant logic and its implications for tourism management: The co-production of innovation in the hotel industry. *Tourism Management, 32*(2), 207–214.

Wang, Y., & Xiang, Z. (2007). Toward a theoretical framework of collaborative destination marketing. *Journal of Travel Research, 46*(1), 5–85.

Yin, R. K. (2009). *Case study research: Design and methods*. Thousand Oaks, CA: Sage.

CONCEPTUALIZING THE VALUE CO-CREATION CHALLENGE FOR TOURIST DESTINATIONS: A SUPPLY-SIDE PERSPECTIVE

Giuseppe Melis, Scott McCabe and Giacomo Del Chiappa

ABSTRACT

To date, most studies on value co-creation processes in tourism have thus far focused on the company—customer relationship. Tourism experiences are produced by a number of firms and organizations collaboratively. Hence, there is a need to further develop knowledge about co-creation issues also adopting the perspective of the network of relationships between local stakeholders (both public and private) which are involved in tourism development within a certain tourist destination. This conceptual study applies the theoretical approaches of Prahalad and Ramaswamy (2004a) and Ramaswamy and Gouillart (2010) in an attempt to identify a set of constructs that could influence the way local stakeholders can co-create the tourism offer. Specifically, the contribution of this chapter is placed on the development of a possible empirical application of the DART model to analyse the co-creation paradigm by

Marketing Places and Spaces
Advances in Culture, Tourism and Hospitality Research, Volume 10, 75–89
ISSN: 1871-3173/doi:10.1108/S1871-317320150000010006

adopting a supply-side perspective, which is still a quite non-common approach in tourism literature.

Keywords: Tourist destination; co-creation; supply-side perspective; DART model; network analysis

INTRODUCTION

The global marketing environment faces one of the most profound and important upheavals as technology development and adoption coupled with a dynamic consumer market have shifted the balance of power from producers to consumers. These transitional states have been equated to a paradigm shift by marketing theorists (e.g. Vargo & Lusch, 2004). Firms and academicians have attempted to redefine what amounts to a radical reinterpretation of our understanding of the fundamental basis of value exchange in consumer markets (Prahalad & Ramaswamy, 2004a). This paradigm shift has led to an understanding that in order to establish competitive advantage, firms must collaborate with consumers to produce meaningful services (Frow, Brodie, Little, & Payne, 2010; Pels, Polese, & Brodie, 2012; Verhoef, Reinartz, & Krafft, 2010).

As a multi-faceted and complex service sector, tourism has recently begun to explore the concept that tourist experience value is intrinsically co-created between firms and customers synchronously, contextually and collaboratively (Shaw, Bailey, & Williams, 2011). To date, most studies on value co-creation processes in tourism have thus far focused on the company–customer relationship and on how individual companies can gain competitive advantage by implementing activities to engage customers in more proactive ways (Grissemann & Stokburger-Sauer, 2012; Hoyer, Chandy, Dorotic, Ktafft, & Singh, 2010).

However, tourism experiences are most frequently produced by a number of firms and organizations collaboratively, and there is a need to further develop knowledge about co-creation issues from the perspective of the network of relationships between individual organizations, both public and private, which are all, more or less directly or indirectly, involved in the development of the tourist supply system, in its reference markets.

More specifically, the purpose of this chapter is to lay the foundation for thinking about how the logic of co-creation can be investigated and applied, adopting a supply-side perspective consistent and compatible with other theoretical contributions that are relevant to the dynamic tourism market, such as the experience economy (Pine & Gilmore, 1999), total relationship marketing (Gummesson, 1999) and network analysis (Scott, 2013; Wasserman & Faust, 2009). To achieve this aim, our focus will be on the complex network of relationships that is created, or which would be useful to create between companies and stakeholders (public and private) in various capacities in order to encourage customer collaboration in the development of innovative value propositions, as is precisely the case of tourist destinations (Baggio, Scott, & Cooper, 2010; Del Chiappa & Presenza, 2013).

Relying on these general considerations, the present work is organized around two main research questions: QR1. Is it possible to extend the value co-creation theory by adopting a macro perspective (tourism destination) instead of a micro perspective (single stakeholders)? QR2. If the answer is positive, is it possible to devise a conceptual model to assess the degree of co-creation of value for a destination?

To date, regarding the first question, there have been few attempts that have explored the possibility of extending co-creation theory to more complex systems than single enterprises, such as tourism destinations (Sfandla & Bjork, 2013; Tussyadiah & Zach, 2013).

Tourism destinations are characterized by a multitude of actors, often very different from each other both for nature and size, bound together not by hierarchical, but only through competitive and/or cooperative relationships. The complexity of tourism destinations is interesting because (a) the tourist experience is the result of the action of a plurality of actors working in a specific destination and (b) because the actors are independent entities, often very different, both in nature and size, free to adopt strategies and actions that are not necessarily mutually consistent, even within the same territorial context in which they operate (inter-independence perspective).

These entities, in other words, are not linked by hierarchical relations but only through competitive and/or cooperative relationships; sometimes these relationships are simultaneously characterized by cooperation and competition giving rise to the so-called 'coopetition' (Hamel, Doz, & Prahalad, 1989). Similarly, the ways in which relationships between complex networks of actors are managed warrant further attention because of the possible effects on the emergence of co-creative capacities. For example, Banks and Humphreys (2008, p. 407) argued that 'emerging co-creators cannot be managed and directed as employees, since 'imposing' control over them may risk losing their creative participation'.

In view of the destination, the challenge to improve competitiveness is embodied in the combination of the appropriate mix of decisions and actions so that all the actors operate together to coordinate their activities and having as their objectives customer satisfaction, winning the loyalty of tourists and, possibly, of their benevolence in terms of judgement on the reputation of the destination. This chapter presents a discussion of the conceptual issues relating to co-creation theory and tourism experience value. Through a review of the theoretical issues surrounding value co-creation, it aims to develop a conceptual model that explains how co-creation might be applied to complex organizational systems.

LITERATURE REVIEW

The Value Co-Creation Theory

The basic idea of the value co-creation theory is based on the active involvement of the customer who is no longer considered an external business process of design, production and distribution of the product-service, but is increasingly a referee (Priem, 2007) and active, central player in the creation of value in consumer experience (Prahalad & Ramaswamy, 2004a, 2004b; Ramaswamy & Gouillart, 2010; Vargo & Lusch, 2008a, 2004). In fact, while *'in the conventional value creation process, companies and consumers had distinct roles of production and consumption'* and *'products and services contained value, and markets exchanged this value, from the producer to the consumer ... as we move toward co-creation this distinction disappears'* (Prahalad & Ramaswamy, 2004a, p. 10).

According to Prahalad and Ramaswamy (2004b, p. 5), *'increasingly, consumers engage in the processes of both defining and creating value'*. To sum up, it can be argued that while in the traditional perspective value creation occurred outside markets, in the co-creative approach, the experience of the consumer becomes the very basis of value (Prahalad & Ramaswamy, 2004a). At the same time, Vargo and Lusch (2008b) were arguing that marketing faces such structural challenges, that in the future, competition would be determined by those companies who could reorient their offers towards a new Service Dominant Logic. Specifically, they argued *'the locus of value creation ... moves from the "producer" to a collaborative process of co-creation between parties'* (Vargo & Lusch, 2008b).

In particular, they emphasize the fact that the service is based on the concept of 'value in use', in contrast to the traditional view based on the 'exchange value'. In other words, they suggested that the attention of the business entity that wants to create value, therefore, must not be focused on the product (*operand resources*) and its construction, but the process leading to its design, development and distribution; it should no longer focus on the exchange between producers and buyers, but on the relationships between the actors and the knowledge and skills they invest in consumption experiences (*operant resources*) (Etgar, 2008; Grönroos, 1997, 2008; Payne, Storbacka, & Frow, 2008). Systems, therefore, should then be able to access and integrate these resources together to create value through knowledge (Vargo & Lusch, 2004, 2008b).

In other words, the process of value creation starts to take form only when a customer consumes or uses the product or service rather than when it is built (Grissemann & Stokburger-Sauer, 2012; Payne et al., 2008; Vargo & Lusch, 2004, 2008a).

Yet as a foundational principle, Vargo and Lusch (2008a, p. 3) underline that '*all social and economic actors are resource integrators*'. According to this thinking, each actor can be a beneficiary of the economic relationship and each beneficiary is always a resource integrator but, as they noted, they are '*all of the external service providers, each creating its own service-providing resources through its own resource-integrating activities*' (Vargo & Lusch, 2011, p. 184).

A consequence of this approach is that '*S-D logic points towards a need to think about value creation taking place in and central to the emergence of service ecosystems*' (Vargo & Lusch, 2011, p. 185). A service eco-system '*is a spontaneously sensing and responding spatial and temporal structure of largely loosely coupled, value-proposing social and economic actors interacting through institutions, technology and language to (1) co-produce service offering, (2) engage in mutual service provision, and (3) co-create value*' (Vargo & Lusch, 2011, p. 185).

Tussyadiah and Zach (2013) summarize the main issues succinctly when they argue that firms and organizations need to look beyond the immediate boundaries of the value chain to actively engage in collaborative exchanges and integrate resources in order to maximize competitive advantage.

Applications in Tourism Destinations

In the tourism literature it is widely recognized that destination competitiveness demands an effective collaborative and cooperative behaviour among the different local stakeholders (both public and private) delivering products and services to tourists (Del Chiappa & Presenza, 2013). All these theories focus the attention on the cooperative behaviour of the different actors of the destination.

Cooperation may be defined as '*a process of joint decision making among autonomous, key stakeholders of an inter-organizational, community tourism domain to resolve planning problems of the domain and/or to manage issues related to the planning and development of the domain*' (Jamal & Getz, 1995, p. 188). This process is expressed on several levels: between institutions/administrations, between companies/organizations and within communities. It is so important to recognize that cooperation in a competitive environment germinates only if certain basic conditions are fulfilled.

Alter and Hage (1993, p. 86) argue that cooperation can be identified as '*the quality of the relationships between human actors in a system of mutual understanding, shared goals and values, capacity to work together on a common task*'. Elbe (2002) identifies three levels of cooperation: (a) limited, when it is characterized by a very low contribution of resources – in terms of time and money invested – and a poor mutual adaptation of operational activities among stakeholders; (b) moderate, when it is restricted to one or limited aspects of the business, with some commitment in terms of resource allocation, but a simple, surface-level adaptation of operational activities; (c) large, when the cooperation is of a long-term, strategic nature and is for the stakeholders at the heart of business growth.

The cooperation can be activated from each of the three levels, but the reality is developed primarily through a step by step process that starts from limited forms to reach the most complex. To ensure that the process develops properly, the role of 'coordinator' needs to be recognized and legitimized (Elbe, Hallen, & Axelsson, 2009, p. 287).

Collaboration and cooperation can be based on formal relationships (mainly based on contracts) or informal relationships between members (mainly based on personal and social relationships). In attempting to apply these theoretical considerations to the case of tourist destinations, Beritelli (2011) argues that both configurations can be detected. The presence of one or another depends mainly on the specific nature of the agreements and the particular circumstances in which they were established.

Firstly, a recognition that '*cooperative behaviour among actors and stakeholder groups in tourism destinations is an interpersonal business*' (Beritelli, 2011, p. 623). Secondly, the greater discrimination between different destinations is not represented by formal rules, but rather by the presence of specific key players and their past experiences, which directly influence future behaviour. Thirdly, Beritelli argued that the simple exchange of information does not directly necessarily lead to a reciprocal understanding among stakeholders and to an effective collaboration among them. The reason is that 'cooperation processes require reciprocal sympathy' (Beritelli, 2011, p.624).

As part of the literature on collaborative marketing applied to tourism, another important contribution is provided by D'Angella and Go (2009), which developed a model for assessing the orientation to the tourist market, applying stakeholder theory. These authors analyse the relationships between DMOs (Destination Management Organization) and tourism enterprises. In particular, they address two important questions: what are the intentions and the interrelationships of the DMO in the complex realities of tourism in which they appear? To what extent are tourism companies satisfied by the actions implemented by the DMO?

D'Angella and Go (2009, p. 429) define a tourism destination as 'an open-social system of multiple and interdependent stakeholders', with this interdependence being a response to certain critical elements. Among these, they referred to the shortage of resources (mostly financial) of the destinations, to the risk of disastrous events that could harm the reputation of the entire territory, and to the fragmented nature of the tourist offer. The need to overcome these difficulties leads to the conclusion that coordinating organizations in tourism (i.e. the DMO), should take a more proactive role in driving the relationships within the network and to generate systematic and on-going feedback about their work from stakeholders involved.

In order to innovate, the DMO should facilitate formal institutional network collaboration between individual actors and organizations, and a level of participation that is bounded by the agreed lines in which the stakeholders can act (D'Angella & Go, 2009, p. 430). Based on an extensive literature review, Bregoli and Del Chiappa (2013) identified the following: social norms, communication, interlocking directorates, common staff, planning control systems, incentive and selection systems and information systems.

For the purpose of our study, a very significant contribution in the field of tourism is provided by Sfandla and Bjork (2013). This chapter aims to create a new framework that explores the co-creation of tourist experiences. The authors note a change of orientation of the tourist literature of recent years: from a competitive approach to a systemic approach, identifying the potential benefits in reorienting thinking about the roles of individual businesses as parts of a larger network. In this sense, tourism businesses are understood as involved in a challenge to jointly create tourist experiences between firms, despite the innate resistance brought on by the nature of competition.

The focus of modern tourism marketing must therefore be reoriented towards for whom and how it creates value by adopting a new mind-set that sees '*the actors as facilitators of experiences and consumers-tourists as active contributors*' involved in the management of services (Sfandla & Bjork, 2013, p. 496). When they introduce the concept of 'facilitators of experiences' the authors refer to people or firms who are able to transform the value of tourist services and capture the experiences in a systematic way (Sfandla & Bjork, 2013, p. 498).

Based on these considerations, they note that the traditional models of tourism network are inadequate because they generally exclude consumers from their structures. The new model proposed transfers basic aspects of SD logic to the marketing of tourist services in a framework based on the creation of experiences.

This model, referred to as TEN (Tourism Experience Network) shows some similarities, albeit with some differences, with the so-called ESC (Experience Supply Chain). In fact, the ESC, according to the authors, is concerned only with linear relationships and takes into account tourists as mere members, but remaining under the control of the network. The TEN, however, also promotes non-linear relationships between the actors and, in particular, those that guide both horizontal and vertical movements of the value (Sfandla & Bjork, 2013, p. 496). In essence, tourists are no longer mere consumers of package holidays offered by tourism industry network stakeholders, but they are involved and wish to be even more actively so, in the process of co-creation of experiences.

Sfandla and Bjork (2013) recognize the importance of the contribution of Porter to the notion of value, but in agreement with Vargo and Lusch (2004), they integrate these ideas in two value configurations: the 'value-in-exchange' (relevant for enterprises in the process of co-creation) and 'value-in-use' (vital for tourists to create their own value) after Prahalad and Ramaswamy (2004a). Today's tourists are not content to play the role as of a passive source of exchange value. They also stress the need for the presence of one or more 'facilitators' who are able to understand how to engage tourists in experience co-creation from a logic based on value.

Specifically they argue that '*firms, in their facilitations processes, are inter-linked through adding and exchanging value to support the co-creation of experiences with tourists, whereas tourists, in their processes, are inter-linked in using firms' resources, performances and experiential components for achieving positive experiences. The co-creation of experiences here arises during exchanges, usage and interactions between facilitators and tourists in relational processes supported by value notions and value-in-conceptions'* (Sfandla & Bjork, 2013, p. 502).

Finally, more recent research has tried to assess the organizational capacity for co-creation at the level of the DMO (Tussyadiah & Zach, 2013). Particularly, the first goal of this study was to *'conceptualize and measure destinations' capacity for co-creation'* and due to the development in information and communication technology (Tussyadiah & Zach, 2013, p. 243), including the influence of social media strategies on destinations' capacity for consumer co-creation.

As many scholars have argued (Bronner & De Hoog, 2010; Litvin, Goldsmith, & Pan, 2008), consumers are even more committed in using social media, before, during and after their trip, to search for information and opinions of other consumers for trip planning and to post their own experiences online thus contributing to co-create tourism experiences. Because of this, ICTs, information systems and social media could be considered as important coordination mechanisms and platforms that allow information to flow more easily across the destination and through the stakeholders facilitating processes such as consensus-based tourism planning, knowledge sharing and co-creation (Baggio & Del Chiappa, 2014; Micera, Presenza, Splendiani, & Del Chiappa, 2013).

Despite this, Tussyadiah and Zach (2013) applied the theory of absorptive capacity to assess whether destinations had the knowledge, skills and capacity to transfer information in a co-creative sense, and they found that there was limited scope for knowledge acquisition and transfer amongst DMOs. Overall, these findings underline a need for further research aimed at analysing how the interrelationships among local stakeholders can be managed and enhanced in an attempt to increase the co-creation of value at a tourism destination level.

A FRAMEWORK PROPOSAL: THE CO-CREATION THEATRE AND ITS DETERMINANTS

One could interpret the co-creation theory in tourism destinations by adopting a systemic perspective that integrates elements of 'collectivism' and 'individualism' together (Hofstede, 1983). Any measure of the degree of co-creation implies an effort to understand how in reality these two apparently contradictory 'forces' are implemented. The orientation towards either collectivism or individualism may not be determined solely by national cultural traits. Inversely, we argue that such leanings can be localized and partly determined by key actors within destinations and their influence in shaping the way network actors engage with destination development and marketing.

In other words, we need to understand not simply whether co-creation exists within a destination, or if the destination has the resources and capacity to integrate co-creation value logic into its development and marketing programmes. There is also a need to understand much more about the dynamics between network stakeholders to assess how a destination can move from a value creation perspective towards a value co-creation perspective.

In today's world, a destination that is able to respond positively to the challenges of the market is one that has a high capacity to be 'experience-centric' (Prahalad & Ramaswamy, 2004a). This idea appears to be highly congruent with the DART model proposed by Prahalad and Ramaswamy (2004a). This model suggests that when co-creation is considered the following facilitators should take place: dialogue, access, transparency and risk assessment (from these the acronym DART was coined). As the authors argued, 'dialogue means interactivity, engagement, and a propensity to act − on both sides. Dialogue is more than listening to customers: it implies shared learning and communication between two equal problem solvers. Dialogue creates and maintains a loyal community' (Prahalad & Ramaswamy, 2004a).

Consequently, they define access as the possibility to have both available proper information and tools, while risk assessment refers to the fact that if consumers are well informed and they increasingly participate in many of the firm's processes, they should assume the responsibility of their choices together with companies. So that customers *will insist that businesses inform them fully about risks, providing not just data but appropriate methodologies for assessing the personal and societal risk associated with products and services'* (Prahalad & Ramaswamy, 2004c, p. 7).

Finally, transparency concerns a relationship between companies and customers based on reciprocity. This is because the conventional asymmetry is rapidly disappearing: firms can no longer assume opaqueness of prices, costs and profit margins. And as information about products, technologies and business systems becomes more accessible, creating new levels of transparency becomes increasingly desirable and important.

Based on such a strand of research, Ramaswamy and Gouillart (2010) later focus their attention on the preconditions that allow companies to put in use the value co-creation approach and suggested to consider the following: context of interactions, engagement platform, experience mind-set and network relationships.

Based on these two conceptual models, we propose to consider what we call 'the co-creation theatre' (Fig. 1); a theoretical model to be used as a basis to measure and to assess the co-creation phenomenon within a complex network system, such as a tourist destination.

The variables of the model as well as a context of interactions (CI) between the different actors within the area are, respectively:

– A network of formal and informal relationships (NR) between the local stakeholders;
– An engagement platform (EP) where both the stakeholders and consumers can share knowledge that can be useful to co-create the tourism experiences to be delivered to the market;
– A systemic consciousness and experience mind-set (EM) that is based on social values driving single stakeholders towards more collaborative and cooperative actions;
– A constant and continuous dialogue (D) between the different actors involved in the design, construction and implementation of the value proposition of the destination;
– An easy accessibility (A) for all the relevant actors to the main information (i.e. marketing plans, marketing reports, etc.) needed to evaluate the performance of the DMO and to those that allow them to have a better

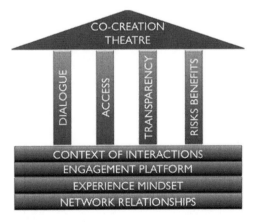

Fig. 1. The Co-Creation Theatre. *Source*: Our elaboration from Prahalad and Ramaswamy (2004a) and Ramaswamy and Gouillart (2010).

knowledge about the different stakeholders working within the destination;

- Transparency (T) of information and documents that can allow each actor to be able to feel 'safe' with respect to the work of others;
- The evaluation of the benefits and costs arising from the support (R) given to run the macro-marketing activities at the destination level.

The co-creation phenomena in a tourism destination (Co-C) can be considered as being a function of the variables considered in Prahalad & Ramaswamy (2004a) and Ramaswamy and Gouillart (2010), thus resulting in the following expression:

$$Co\text{-}C = f(D, A, R, T, EM, EP, NR, CI)$$

Further research is needed to define for each of these variables/ constructs a specific set of items to be used to carry out empirical research aimed at testing the conceptual framework among local stakeholders working within specific tourism destinations.

CONCLUSION AND IMPLICATIONS

This conceptual discussion applies the theoretical approaches of Prahalad and Ramaswamy (2004a) and Ramaswamy and Gouillart (2010) in an attempt to identify a set of constructs that could influence the way local stakeholders can co-create the tourism offer that the destination as a whole is able to offer to its market target. In this way, the contribution of this chapter is placed on the development of a possible empirical application of the DART to analyse the co-creation paradigm by adopting a supply-side perspective, which is still a quite non-common approach in tourism literature.

Once empirically tested, our model could suggest relevant managerial implications. Indeed, based on that policy makers and destination marketers could identify what are the main constructs that the local stakeholders are considering as being more important to enhance the co-creation and co-innovation ability at the destination as a whole.

As a consequence, policy makers and destination marketers could better understand if the resources invested for the tourism development channelled correctly and/or if they should differently prioritize in an attempt to increase the destination competitiveness. Perhaps more investment needs to be placed on developing awareness of and encouraging cooperation, collaboration and dialogue among the various systemic actors, rather than directing attention to the construction of adequate and appropriate 'platforms of contact' between them. Or, perhaps more attention needs to be given to the reorganization of processes to encourage better and more effective and transparent flow of relevant information, or even on adequate information campaigns aimed to change the perception of risk on the part of individuals to induce them to be more cooperative in the construction and implementation of the strategies defined by the DMO.

REFERENCES

Alter, C., & Hage, J. (1993). *Organizations working together*. London: Sage.

Baggio, R., & Del Chiappa, G. (2014). Opinion and consensus dynamics in tourism digital ecosystems. In Z. Xiang & I. Tussyadiah (Eds.), *Information and communication technologies in tourism 2014*. Vienna, Austria: Springer.

Baggio, R., Scott, N., & Cooper, C. (2010). Network science: A review focused on tourism. *Annals of Tourism Research, 37*(3), 802−827.

Banks, J., & Humphreys, S. (2008). The labour of user co-creators: Emergent social network markets? *The International Journal of Research into New Media Technologies, 14*(4), 401−418.

Beritelli, P. (2011). Cooperation among prominent actors in a tourist destination. *Annals of Tourism Research, 38*(2), 607−629.

Bregoli, I., & Del Chiappa, G. (2013). Coordinating relationships among destination stakeholders: Evidence from Edinburgh (UK). *Tourism Analysis, 18*(2), 145−155.

Bronner, A. E., & De Hoog, R. (2010). Consumer-generated versus marketer-generated websites in consumer decision making. *International Journal of Market Research, 52*, 231−248.

D'Angella, F., & Go, F. M. (2009). Tale of two cities' collaborative tourism marketing: Towards a theory of destination stakeholder assessment. *Tourism Management, 30*, 429−440.

Del Chiappa, G., & Presenza, A. (2013). The use of network analysis to assess relationships among stakeholders within a tourism destination: An empirical investigation on Costa Smeralda-Gallura, Italy. *Tourism Analysis, 18*(1), 1−13.

Elbe, J. (2002). *Utveckling av turistdestinationer genom samarbete [Developing tourist destinations through cooperation]*. Doctoral thesis No. 96, Department of Business Studies, Uppsala University, Uppsala, Sweden.

Elbe, J., Hallen, L., & Axelsson, B. (2009). The destination-management organization and the integrative destination-marketing process. *International Journal of Tourism Research, 11*, 283−296.

Etgar, M. (2008). A descriptive model of the consumer co-production process. *Journal of the Academy of Marketing Science, 36*(1), 97−108.

Frow, P., Brodie, R. J., Little, V., & Payne, A. (2010, September). *Collaboration, resource integration and value co-creation within the S-D logic: Exploring research issues*. FMM

2010 – The Forum on Markets and Marketing: Extending Service-dominant Logic. Working paper. University of Cambridge, Cambridge.

Grissemann, U., & Stokburger-Sauer, N. (2012). Customer co-creation of travel services: The role of company support and customer satisfaction with the co-creation performance. *Tourism Management*, *33*, 1483–1492.

Grönroos, C. (1997). From marketing mix to relationship marketing: Towards a paradigm shift in marketing, *Management Decision*, *35*(4), 322–339.

Grönroos, C. (2008). Service logic revisited: Who creates value? And who co-creates? *European Business Review*, *20*(4), 298–314.

Gummesson, E. (1999). *Total relationship marketing: Rethinking marketing management: Form 4Ps to 30Rs*. London: Heinemann.

Hamel, G., Doz, Y. L., & Prahalad, C. K. (1989). Collaborate with your competitors and win. *Harvard Business Review, January–February*, 133–139.

Hofstede, G. (1983). National cultures in four dimensions: A research-based theory of cultural differences among nations. *International Studies of Management & Organisations*, *13*(1–2), 46–74.

Hoyer, W. D., Chandy, R., Dorotic, M., Ktafft, M., & Singh, S. S. (2010). Consumer co-creation in new product development. *Journal of Service Research*, *13*(3), 283–296.

Jamal, T. B., & Getz, D. (1995). Collaboration theory and community tourism planning. *Annals of Tourism Research*, *22*(1), 186–204.

Litvin, S. W., Goldsmith, R. E., & Pan, B. (2008). Electronic word-of-mouth in hospitality and tourism management. *Tourism Management*, *29*, 458–468.

Micera, R., Presenza, A., Splendiani, S., & Del Chiappa, G. (2013). SMART destinations. New strategies to manage tourism industry. In G. Schiuma, J. C. Spender, & A. Pulic (Eds.), *Proceedings of international forum on knowledge asset dynamics* (pp. 1405–1422). Zagreb, Croatia: Distribution IFKAD.

Payne, A. F., Storbacka, K., & Frow, P. (2008). Managing the co-creation of value. *Journal of Academy Marketing Science*, *36*, 83–96.

Pels, J., Polese, F., & Brodie, R. J. (2012). Value co-creation: Using a viable systems approach to draw implications from organizational theories. *Mercati e Competitività*, *1*, 19–38.

Pine, B. J. I., & Gilmore, J. H. (1999). *The experience economy*. Boston, MA: Harvard Business School Press.

Prahalad, C. K., & Ramaswamy, V. (2004a). *The future of competition: Co-creating unique value with consumer*. Boston, MA: Harvard Business School Press.

Prahalad, C. K., & Ramaswamy, V. (2004b). Co-creation experiences: The next practice in value creation. *Journal of Interactive Marketing*, *18*(3), 5–14.

Prahalad, C. K., & Ramaswamy, V. (2004c). Co-creating unique value with customers. *Strategy and Leadership*, *32*(3), 4–9.

Priem, R. L. (2007). A consumer perspective on value creation. *Academy of Management Review*, *32*(1), 219–235.

Ramaswamy, V., & Gouillart, F. (2010). *The power of co-creation: Build it with them to boost growth, productivity, and profits*. New York, NY: Free Press.

Scott, J. (2013). *Social network analysis*. London: Sage.

Sfandla, C., & Bjork, P. (2013). Tourism experience network: Co-creation of experiences in interactive processes. *International Journal of Tourism Research*, *15*, 495–506.

Shaw, G., Bailey, A., & Williams, A. M. (2011). Service dominant logic and its implications for tourism management: The co-production of innovation in the hotel industry. *Tourism Management, 32*(2), 207–214.

Tussyadiah, I., & Zach, F. (2013). Social media strategy and capacity for consumer co-creation among destination marketing organisations. In L. Cantoni and Z. Xiang (Eds.), *Information and communication technologies in tourism 2013 proceedings of the international conference* in Innsbruck (pp. 243–253). Vienna, Austria: Springer.

Vargo, S. L., & Lusch, R. F. (2004). Evolving to a new dominant logic for marketing. *Journal of Marketing, 68*(1), 1–17.

Vargo, S. L., & Lusch, R. F. (2008a). Service-dominant logic: Continuing the evolution, *Journal of the Academy of Marketing Science, 36*(1), 1–10.

Vargo, S. L., & Lusch, R. F. (2008b). From goods to service(s): Divergences and convergences of logics. *Industrial Marketing Management, 37*(3), 254–259.

Vargo, S. L., & Lusch, R. F. (2011). It's all B2B … and beyond: Toward a systems perspective of the market. *Industrial Marketing Management, 40*, 181–187.

Verhoef, P. C., Reinartz, W. J., & Krafft, M. (2010). Customer engagement as a new perspective in customer management. *Journal of Service Research, 13*(3), 247–252.

Wasserman, S., & Faust, K. (2009). *Social network analysis: Methods and applications.* Cambridge: Cambridge University Press.

PART II
IMAGE AND COMPETITIVE STRATEGIES

THE EMOTIONAL ATTACHMENT BUILT THROUGH THE ATTITUDES AND MANAGERIAL APPROACH TO PLACE MARKETING AND BRANDING – "THE GOLDEN CITY OF KREMNICA, SLOVAKIA"

Marica Mazurek

ABSTRACT

A singular place (a destination) is a product with multiple characteristics and multifunctional utility for different customers; however, some places offer the same type of utility and compete for the same customers. For this reason, the competitiveness of a place as a livable space, a space for investments, tourism, etc. has caused the emergence of the innovative managerial approaches to place governance. One such approach, which has been primarily used in production and which could be applied also in destination management, is the concept of branding.

The chapter summarizes the impact of place branding (our main focus) and place marketing (in more broad concept) on destinations, underlines

Marketing Places and Spaces
Advances in Culture, Tourism and Hospitality Research, Volume 10, 93–105
Copyright © 2015 by Emerald Group Publishing Limited
All rights of reproduction in any form reserved
ISSN: 1871-3173/doi:10.1108/S1871-317320150000010007

the importance of culture and history in a place branding concept and highlights the importance of creation of partnerships in destinations by envisioning some useful concepts of co-operation in tourism destinations with a goal to create a positive image.

Keywords: Place marketing; branding; culture; history; co-creation; partnerships

INTRODUCTION

Knowledge, interactions, and relations as well as motivation as has been stated by Porter (1998), are the qualities of the innovative managerial approach to a destination. The authors Pine and Gilmore (1999) mentioned a need to change the attitude to consumer behavior in places, especially a need to be more consumer focused and to create more effective partnerships between the territorial management, consumers of a territory, and the entrepreneurial bodies. Place governance requires strong co-creation principles and mutual understanding and the will to co-operate. In addition, a place has to be able to implement into its marketing strategies such comparative advantage characteristics as their own culture and history. As a result, a strong image and reputation based not only on the economic performance of a place, but especially on the experiences and attitudes to a specific place, might be beneficial for places and help them to improve their competitive position.

THEORETICAL CONSIDERATIONS

The customers' emotional attachment to a brand has become a significant marketing advantage. Places are the biggest brands and the attachment of visitors might be a source of variable benefits and growing loyalty to repeat visits and to spend more money in destinations (as the multiplication factor and beneficial impact of multiple visitations). Some authors, for example Berry (2000), mentioned that brands are connected emotionally and perceived by a customer as an authentic experience. Psychographic factors and their effects on consumption led marketers and academics such as Westwood, Morgan, Pritchard, and Ineson (1999), Veblen (1912), and Lurry (1998) to the recognition of benefits of self-expression in marketing and branding. Branding focuses on the creation and communication of brand vision, forming of partnerships, and measuring of branding results. It could be understood as "the glue that holds the broad range of marketing functions together" (Ries & Ries, 1998). The emotional attachment of customers to the specific places and self-expression concepts focused on finding some similarities between a place and a customer personality (for instance brand personality concept) are becoming more meaningful in tourism, especially due to growing competition among destinations, places, and spaces.

Morgan, Pritchard, and Pride (1999) suggest that a successful brand builds an emotion link between a product and consumer, and the useful tool for it is mood marketing and the emotional relationship among places and customers. Emotional attachment to the tourist destinations can be fulfilled via attitudes and attributes of a place, especially through the sophisticated management of tourism system in a place (place branding and management) and the management of brand attributes, for example natural environment, history, culture, heritage as well as quality of services offered in tourism destinations. Morgan, Pritchard, and Piggot (2003) mentioned that "the battle for customers in tomorrow's destination market place will be fought over hearts and minds," for this reason branding might be an effective tool of success in tourism competition. The destination brand winners appear as those places that are rich in emotional meaning that have great conversational value and hold high anticipation for potential tourists (Prideaux & Cooper, 2002). Great conversational value could be achieved through the implementation of messages promoting the cultural and historical icons as well as distinctive destination natural resources into marketing strategies. The managerial cohesive approach might be achieved by the creation of partnerships and strategic alliances in destinations (private and public sector mutual co-operation in strategic planning and marketing of destinations).

General marketing and branding theoretical sources (e.g., Aaker, 1991; Bertham, Hulbert, & Pitt, 1999, cited in Ekinci & Hosany, 2000) and destination branding concepts (e.g., Crouch and Ritchie, 2003; Hankinson, 2004) define branding of destinations as the set of marketing activities that (1) support the creation of a name, symbol, logo, word mark, or other graphic that readily *identifies* and *differentiates* a destination; that (2) consistently convey the *expectation* of a memorable travel *experience* that is uniquely associated with the destination; that (3) serve to *consolidate* and *reinforce* the *emotional connection* between the visitor and the destination; and that (4) reduce consumer search costs and perceived risk. Collectively, these activities serve to create a *destination image* that positively influences consumer *destination choice* (Blain, Levy, & Ritchie, 2005, p. 331).

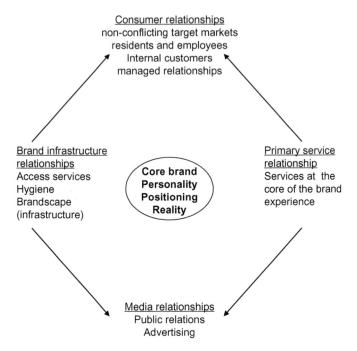

Consumer relationships
non-conflicting target markets
residents and employees
Internal customers
managed relationships

Brand infrastructure
relationships
Access services
Hygiene
Brandscape
(infrastructure)

Core brand
Personality
Positioning
Reality

Primary service
relationship
Services at the
core of the brand
experience

Media relationships
Public relations
Advertising

Fig. 1.   The Relational Network Brand. *Source*: Hankinson (2004).

Based on the Hankinson's relational network brand and place branding (Fig. 1), concepts such as the success of branding and brand equity depend on the coexistence and co-operation of brand creators and brand users and the congruency of their perceptions and attitudes about the attributes offered by tourism destinations. Building a destination brand and creating brand equity requires the fulfillment of expected experience and promise. Brand's function is not only to promote a name, logo, and symbol characterizing a destination, but it requires feeling of a promise of superlative travel experience and the recollection of memories after a visit.

METHODOLOGY

We searched how three associated components of comparative advantage (strategic management – creation of partnerships, historical and cultural perspective) have been used in a historical and cultural tourism destination Kremnica, Slovakia.

The concepts of branding and tourism partnerships were developed in a case study from Europe, an example of Slovakian historical city Kremnica known in the past as a gold mining icon of the Austrian-Hungarian Empire. We tried to use the concepts discussed above dealing with the influence and impact of the unique history, culture, and natural resources on competitiveness; and especially how important is the creation of a specific image in places, which are rich in history and culture (Fig. 2). Additionally, this case study tried to highlight some concepts and especially obstacles of partnerships in Kremnica and the problems with the implementation of the principles of marketing and branding. This is mostly caused by a lack of knowledge of what branding really is and how it should be implemented into the destination marketing strategies.

We applied a combination of qualitative and quantitative methods in primary and secondary data collection. Primary data collection has been conducted during interviews from July 12 to July 31, 2008 in the form of focused groups (city representatives as a mayor and public sector employees, entrepreneurs in tourism, for example, owners of hotels, restaurants, entertainment facilities). In-depth interviews have been performed with the focused group of entrepreneurs, especially semi-structured interviews and individual discussions. Secondary data have been collected during the period of years 2005–2008, especially statistical data (some have been added

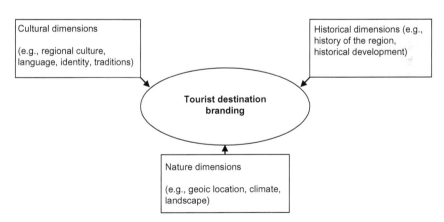

Fig. 2. Tourism Destination Branding Model Incorporating Culture, History, Nature. *Source*: Iliachenko (2005, p. 6).

also during the last stages of research), government documents, published articles, internet materials, and local documents offered by the authorities. Repeated focused group interviews have been conducted recently (2010–2011 and in 2012 as well), especially among the representatives of the town and some entrepreneurs in tourism. The last interview with a major entrepreneur from the city who is the owner of one hotel was just finished last month (2013) and he explained a contemporary state of problem in Kremnica, especially from the point of view of the entrepreneurial position.

A major discussion forum has been conducted during the election of a new mayor of the city among the old and new representatives of the town and tourism supply side representatives. In further research, it might be interesting to add the demand side perspective and the image and expectations of visitors to Kremnica. However, this will be done in further research activities planned for this year while finishing the thesis proposal dealing with place marketing, and one of places chosen in this study is Kremnica. The mapping of the existing state of negotiations and co-operation will be monitored and searched for in dialogues between the representatives of public sector, entrepreneurs, and the community.

FINDINGS

Kremnica is a small town in Slovakia, which definitely has a strong potential to be a competitive town with the ability to succeed, but the chaotic managerial approach and lack of attention from the side of the government and in some aspects also the attitudes of citizens are reasons why this "golden" city suffers from a high unemployment rate and economic stagnation. This town has an enormous potential to become an icon of tourism in Slovakia and benefit from its economic strength given by the ownership of gold resources; however, a city is not able to use it properly especially due to lack of the attention of government and local municipal authorities. Positioning and differentiation strategy is based on the attributes as history and culture, and in the marketing strategy mentioned "the golden history" of the city. Despite of it the win–win scenario is not a result in Kremnica due to a different vision of development and strategy in the town.

Kremnica, in the 16th century, became a symbolic "Centre of Europe" and was called "Golden Kremnica." In the past, the city was famous for its gold mining industry. The town and region, its architecture, mining technology (technical works, water-conduit, and underground electric power station), mint production, and culture have become an inseparable part of European culture. The town was given town privileges in 1328 along with its mining and mint privileges. In 1400, Kremnica became the second most important town in the Kingdom of Hungary and gold and silver production boomed in that period of time. Since the 15th century, Kremnica has experienced a constant decline of mining and gold exploration. The former communist government in Czechoslovakia decided to stop mining in this city and closed the mines. However, the increase in the price of gold and especially the exploration of new mines and new exploration technologies (surface mining) allowed to open a new prosperous era for Kremnica. The question is if this potential could be implemented into the local development strategies.

Another strong comparative advantage of this city is its magnificent scenery and the surrounding mountains, historical monuments, and cultural icons of the town. Despite of this wealth, the city is in a state of decline and recession. For this reason, we tried to explore why this city is not able to succeed and if we could be somehow useful in the process of improvement of situation in the city. We were interested if town representatives and tourism entrepreneurs utilize branding in their marketing strategy and if there existed an effective communication, co-operation, and partnerships among the municipal representatives and entrepreneurs in tourism. Our findings highlighted the following problems:

1. lack of interest from the public sector (financing, conceptual approach) and private sector (financing, co-operation);
2. an image of Kremnica is based on gold mining and mint industry from previous period; however, contemporary trends to revive gold mining brought up many environmental problems which also influenced the reputation of town as a familiar tourism resort;
3. the existing potential of the town has not been fully implemented in marketing strategies despite of an attempt to create a successful tourism product proposal (theatre festival, mining market, summer organ concerts, museum of mining, excursions to mining galleries, mining drainage equipment, etc.); and the representatives of a municipality and entrepreneurs did not implement branding principles in this city because they are not able to understand them;
4. a unique positioning of Kremnica among the other competitive towns in a triangle of three historical mining towns in Slovakia has not been fully

utilized; for this reason Banska Stiavnica (formerly a silver mining icon and historical town, which was recognized as a distinct town by UNESCO) and Banska Bystrica (formerly a copper mining city and regional historical town) are competitors in a region, which also compli-cates financing of tourism attractions;

5. local entrepreneurs and municipal representatives have developed an interesting project called "Return of the Heart − Project for Europe" with the aim to help a city and a region, but due to a lack of interest and a rejection of some partners the project failed;

6. the implementation of strategic management could improve the access to financial resources and improve the infrastructure; however, the approach of municipal representatives and partners complicates the co-operation and decreases the ability of the town to compete with some other historical mining towns in Slovakia;

7. communication of brand identity of Kremnica is underdeveloped despite an enormous potential; the destination lacks clear vision and synergy of partners in tourism, which is a most disturbing fact and a real obstacle in communication and common consensus. Communication strategy of Kremnica did not clearly define the core values of the town.

The existing situation is even more complicated with the fact that Kremnica is a center of attention for entrepreneurial activity, especially gold mining. The company Ortac started its business in Kremnica in 2009 after the plans of a former Canadian company Tournigan had been refused by local municipality representatives, the community, and environmental-ists. In April 2013 Ortac completed a Šturec Project. The results confirm the economic viability of the Šturec Project with a Net Present Value (NPV) at 8% discount rate (pre-tax) of US$195 million (post tax US$145 million) and Internal Rate of Return (IRR) of 30%, at US$1,343/oz Au Eq net price.

The battle for gold and profit also complicates tourism development. Partnerships are not functional and the public, private sector co-operation with the community is totally ineffective. High unemployment in the town and lack of economic opportunities might be an ironic example of a town "sitting on the gold mining throne" (literally speaking).

The development of the unemployment rate in Kremnica was during the period of 1997−2011 and has been depicted in Fig. 3 indicating a growing unemployment rate for the city, especially in the year 2000 (almost 19%); however even in 2011 unemployment was quite high (12.90%). In comparison to other cities of Slovakia such as Bratislava or

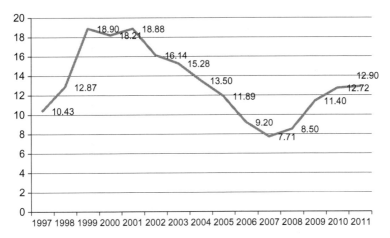

Fig. 3. Development of Unemployment Rate in Kremnica (1997–2011). *Source:* Own chart prepared upon the existing statistical sources (years 1997–2011); http://www.upsvarbs.sk/prispevok/pracovisko-kremnica-nezamestna nost-1991-2011

Trnava (unemployment rate from 6.17 to 9.16%), this unemployment rate is quite high.

Based on the analysis of the existing economic situation in Kremnica, the town could be forced to think more strategically and open more opportunities for gold mining in the future. However, a contemporary phase of dialogue among the public, local authorities and Ortac is still in a phase of negotiations. There has been prepared the so-called Sturecland concept in order to examine the co-creation stage of existing parties in Kremnica region, which is depicted in Fig. 4. Forum Kremnicko, an active citizenship formation has been created in order to support a dialogue between the existing parties. Fig. 4 reveals the existing framework for dialogue based on the principles of co-creation in the city. The existing situation strongly influences the attitudes of citizens and also visitors familiar with the situation about the city.

Despite the existing opposition against the plans to start with mining and further economic activities, the company ORTAC proclaimed that "we are fully committed to the continuing process of openness and transparency and to furthering partnerships with interested parties toward a win-win outcome that would provide long-term benefits to all involved" (www.sturecland.sk). It means that company tries to improve a negative image of

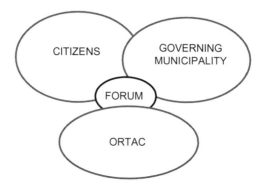

Fig. 4. Co-Creation Concept of Participation of the Existing Parties in Kremnica at the Dialogue Concerning the Economic Development and Gold-Mining Problem. *Source*: www.sturecland.sk

the process of gold exploration in Kremnica (e.g., using of the environmentally unfriendly technologies,) and tries to open more opportunities to build new tourism facilities in the city. It seems to be important for the town representatives to be aware of all necessary contractual relationship (including taking into account the Aarhus Convention dealing with the rights of the public (individuals or associations) with regard to the environment. This convention strongly supports the right of public participation in environmental decision-making, which is the case for Kremnica.

The existing situation complicates the economic development in the city because the city representatives and also a majority of citizens are opposing the exploration of gold; however, some local entrepreneurs are more optimistic and in a favor of the exploration of gold. The image of the city is suffering and despite the willingness of ORTAC to take part in some investments in tourism (skiing complex and swimming pool), a town representatives and the association Kremnica (a non-profit organization) is strongly opposing to this proposal. For this reason, economic development and growth of tourism, attractions, cultural renovations and the improvement of tourism conditions in the town are somehow stacked in the battle for gold. Despite this development, the company plans to invest in Kremnica one million EUR for the improvement of the environmental studies. This case only confirms a need of stronger implementation of social responsibility and the importance of image and reputation into the business environment. Ecimovic, Haw, Esposito, and Mulej (2008) stated that business and society are interwoven rather than distinct entities; therefore, society has certain expectations for appropriate business behavior and outcomes." The importance of image creation and attitudes in the concepts of place marketing and branding are crucial and these aspects cannot be neglected. This case study, which still takes place in small gold mining town Kremnica, is a good example of it.

A repeated sample of results, which has been obtained recently, confirmed that all major concepts of branding, place marketing and partnerships forming or performance are still at the same stage as it was 5 years ago. No major development, no better consensus, has been achieved in this case. It seems that the problem could be somehow resolved in the future, but a question is if the city will be more tourism focused or gold exploration focused (with possible environmental effects), or it might be both, which could be a real beneficial outcome for Kremnica.

CONCLUSION AND IMPLICATIONS

Planning and urban design of places are important factors contributing to a place construction and enhancement. A supply side perspective approach in this case is evident; however, the places are constructed and formed also in the mind of users (demand side approach) by the utilization of places and image forming. Holloway and Hubbard (2001, p. 48) described that the interactions with a place may be "through direct experience or the environment or indirectly through media representations." In order to build a stronger consumer loyalty, confidence, and a long-term attitude, it also requires long-term co-operation of stakeholders in a destination and to understand place marketing and place branding principles. Creation of partnership for ad-hoc reasons cannot create deeper relationships among a destination's stakeholders and visitors. Destinations need to approach a concept of partnerships creation by being more strategic in pooling resources, sharing responsibilities, and developing of a marketing mix that will accept interests of all stakeholders.

New approaches to the DMO's activities and creation of partnerships reveal a necessity of technological changes and implementation of new IT technologies. An important factor is also a changing role of destination marketing organizations toward destination management organizations and implementing of an image creation concept and a public relations approach. In order to be more effective, DMOs have to implement a holistic and pro-active approach in their marketing and management activities.

We searched in Kremnica how these three components of comparative advantage (strategic management – creation of partnerships, historical and cultural conditions) have been used for the improvement of tourism competitiveness. Despite of the existing potential and competitive advantage, tourism representatives seem not to be able to implement branding principles into their marketing strategies and to create functional partnerships in tourism. A marketing strategy for Kremnica lacks the use of branding principles based on the creation of image, a definition of brand identity, positioning, and differentiation, which means a real waste of the enormous cultural and historical potential of this city. One of the reasons is that in the middle of attention in this city is a battle for gold and power. We hope for a stronger tourism growth in this precious historical and cultural town in Slovakia, and our goal is to monitor further studies a development of dialogue among the city representatives, community and developers.

ACKNOWLEDGMENT

The author would like to thank the organizers of the 5th Advances in Tourism Marketing (ATMC) conference in Algarve, Portugal for the possibility to present this article despite of any support of own educational institution and during own vacation. Despite of the obstacles, the article has been presented and published. Thanks to the international academics and colleagues who were able to help me with it and my appreciation to the academic fairness and respect.

REFERENCES

Aaker, D. A. (1991). *Managing brand equity*. New York, NY: The Free Press.
Berry, L. L. (2000). Cultivating service brand equity. *Journal of the Academy of Marketing Science, 28*(1), 128–137.
Berthon, P., Hulbert, J. M., & Pitt, L. F. (1999). Brand management prognostications. *Sloan Management Review, 40*(2), 53–65.
Blain, C., Levy, S. E., & Ritchie, J. R. B. (2005). Destination branding: Insights and practices from destination management organizations. *Journal of Travel Research, 43*, 328–338.
Crouch, G. I., & Ritchie, J. R. B. (2003). *The competitive destination: A sustainable tourism perspective*. Cambridge: CABI Publishing.
Ecimovic, T., Haw, R., Esposito, M., & Mulej, M. (2008). The individual and corporate social responsibility. In *Sustainable future, requisite holism, and social responsibility (against the current abuse of free market society)*. Maribor: IRDO.

Hankinson, G. (2004). The brand images of tourism destinations: A study of the saliency of organic images. *Journal of Product & Brand Management, 1*(13), 6–14. In Henderson, J. (2000). Uniquely Singapore? A case study in destination branding. *Journal of Vacation Marketing, 13*(3), 261–274.

Holloway, L., & Hubbard, P. (2001). *People and place: The extraordinary geographies of everyday life*. Harlow: Pearson Education.

http://www.upsvarbs.sk/prispevok/pracovisko-kremnica-nezamestnanost-1991-2011. Accessed on January 22, 2014.

Iliachenko, E. Y. (2005). Exploring culture, history and nature as tourism destination branding constructs: The case of a peripheral region in Sweden. *The VIII Nordic-Scottish conference on rural and regional development in association with the 14th Nordic Symposium in Tourism and Hospitality Research*.

Lurry, G. (1998). *Brandwatching*. Dublin: Blackhall. In S. Westwood, N. J. Morgan, A. Pritchard & E. Ineson (Eds.). (1999). Branding the package holiday – The role and significance of brands for UK air tour operators. *Journal of Vacation Marketing, 5*, 238–252.

Morgan, N. L., Pritchard, A., & Piggot, R. (2003). Destination branding and the role of the stakeholders: The case of New Zealand. *Journal of Vacation Marketing, 9*, 285.

Morgan, N. L., Pritchard, A., & Pride, R. (1999). *Destination branding: Creating the unique destination position*. Oxford: Butterworth-Heinemann.

Pine, B. J., & Gilmore, J. H. (1999). *The experience economy: Work in theatre and every business a stage: Good and services are no longer enough*. Boston, MA: Harvard Business School Press.

Porter, M. E. (1998). Clusters and new economies of competition. *Harvard Business Review, November–December*, 77–90.

Prideaux, B., & Cooper, C. (2002). Marketing and destinations growth: A symbiotic relationship or simple coincidence? *Journal of Vacation Marketing, 9*(1), 35–48.

Ries, A., & Ries, L. (1998). *Mutable laws of branding*. New York, NY: Harper Business.

Sturecland. *What is Sturecland?* Retrieved from www.sturecland.sk. Accessed on January 10, 2014.

Veblen, T. (1912). The theory of the leisure class. New York, NY: Macmillan. In McCracken, G. (Eds.). (1998). Culture and consumption. Bloomington, IN: Indiana University Press.

Westwood, S., Morgan, N., Pritchard, A., & Ineson, E. (1999). Branding the package holiday: The role and significance of brands for UK air tour operators. *Journal of Vacation Marketing, 5*, 238–252.

HOSPITALITY SERVICESCAPES SEEN BY VISUALLY IMPAIRED TRAVELERS

Alma Raissova

ABSTRACT

Tourism and servicescape are usually figuring in the literature as mobile and seeing as a template for all guests. However, mass-customized servicescapes tend to restrict moves and acts of some groups of customers. The purpose of this research is to understand why manmade servicescapes may create barriers and how restricted customers behave. The research gap is addressed through the specific case of how visually impaired persons (VIPs) act and move in hospitality servicescapes. The study emphasizes the importance of spatial approach in service research.

By utilizing a qualitative approach the research employed go-along observation, individual and focus group interviews to elaborate more on how this thesis relates to mainstream tourism. The empirical data were collected during three years in Sweden and Kazakhstan. Fifty-six visually impaired and blind travelers were interviewed and/or observed. Research results demonstrate that hospitality servicescapes restrict acts and moves

Marketing Places and Spaces
Advances in Culture, Tourism and Hospitality Research, Volume 10, 107–120
ISSN: 1871-3173/doi:10.1108/S1871-317320150000010008

of visually impaired guests. But VIPs resist constraints by developing different tactics to get expected services.

Keywords: Servicescape; constraints; tactics; visually impaired persons (VIPs); time; space

INTRODUCTION

Sometimes there is only the smell of gym, but it is difficult to find the entrance. I might go along the wall for a long time, hearing the sound and smelling the gym or swimming pool, but it takes time to find the entrance. (woman, VIP, focus group interview, Almaty, Kazakhstan, 08.21.2013)

We learned to touch things "without touching" them, for example, touching bread through a napkin. I am not afraid of exploring, but it is important what other people think about what you are doing. (woman, VIP, interview, Limhamn, Sweden, 03.31.2012)

These accounts appear to support the idea that inconveniently designed hospitality servicescapes restrict moves and acts of visually impaired guests. Servicescapes are physical surroundings where services are rendered (Bitner, 1992). Customers evaluate offered services with the help of servicescapes and therefore these evaluations form customers' behavior (Aubert-Gamet, 1996). VIPs are chosen to emphasize the fact that hospitality servicescapes tend to restrict some groups of customers on time and space.

This study illustrates how the combination of themes of servicescape, constraints, and tactics points out importance of time and space dimensions in service research. Servicescape concept explains why this area of human activity is a focus of the study. The concept of constraints identifies why VIPs' physical movement and activities are restricted in service spaces, whereas concept of tactics reasons why customers with disabilities develop different resistive tactics. Servicescape is a phenomenon of the research investigation. Three strands of literature are mutually complemented and considered helpful here: servicescapes of Bitner (1992), a notion of constraints of Hägerstrand's time-geography model (1970), and De Certeau's research on the subversive tactics of ordinary people, as a resistance to the power of space (1984).

By utilizing qualitative approach the research employed go-along observation, individual and focus group interviews to elaborate more on how this thesis relates to mass-customized service places. Empirical data were collected in three stations of hospitality servicescape: lobby, accommodation, and eating place. Fifty-six visually impaired and blind travelers were interviewed and/or observed during three years in Sweden and Kazakhstan. In Sweden the researcher volunteered as an escort person for association of blind and visually impaired persons in Helsingborg, Synskadades riksforbund Fritid (http://www.srf.nu/aktiviteter/srf-fritids-resor/). In Kazakhstan interviewed were members of Republican Library for Blind and VIPs in Almaty (http://www.blindlib.kz/).

LITERATURE REVIEW

Tourism and disability research inform that travelers with disabilities are most oppressed customers (Darcy & Buhalis, 2011; Poria, Reichel, & Brandt, 2011). At the same time people with disabilities are most loyal to destination (Dirita, Parameter, & Stancliffe, 2008). For blind people tourism is more of traveling than sightseeing (Richards, 2011). Hence, tourism is a form of socializing which helps VIPs to explore new interests, take advantages, manage everydayness, increase networking, and accept disability (Yau, McKercher, & Packer, 2004). Traveling for people with disabilities is a chance to participate in decision-making process (Blichfeldt & Nicolaisen, 2011) and to explore sense of independence (Dattilo, 2002). However, built environment is still poorly articulated (Coyle, Shank, & Vilet, 2010; Devine, Cory, & Rauworth, 2010; Higgins, 2004) and customers with disabilities are unable to accomplish their goals in consumption situations (Baker, Gentry, & Rittenburg, 2005). Although vision impairment itself does not barrier traveling (Small & Darcy, 2011), *why manmade servicescapes create barriers and how behave restricted customers?* That knowledge can arise if servicescape theory is complemented with the concept of constraint from Hägerstrand's time-geography model and with De Certeau's notion of tactics.

Servicescapes

Customers form their own opinion on offered services with the help of servicescapes that in turn form customers' behavior (Aubert-Gamet, 1996). Service research recognize servicescapes by three main factors (Baker, 1987; Bitner, 1992). Air quality, temperature, humidity, ventilation, noise, scent, and cleanliness refer to ambient factor. They are noticeable in case of lack or nuisance (Aubert-Gamet, 1996, p. 29). In opposite, design factors can be clearly seen. Architecture, color, scale, materials, texture, shape, style, and accessories are qualified as an esthetic, and layout, comfort, signage, and pattern are functional characteristics of interior design. Audience (other customers), number and appearance (of other customers and staff members), behavior, service personnel belong to social factor (Baker, 1987). All three factors affect in combination and create a service space, and lack of one risks decrease service offerings (Aubert-Gamet, 1996; Bonnin & Goudey, 2012). Whether service providers develop ambient, design, and social cues to drive service process and to create more attractive and memorable service spaces for customers (Kozinets et al., 2002; Ray & Chiagouris, 2009), *why VIPs require extra effort and time to move in service places* (Packer, Small, & Darcy, 2008)?

Examination of time–space approach in modeling consumers' behavior might give a new avenue which can mutually benefit both customers and service providers. Although research on servicescape was overemphasized by behavioral approach, it took less attention on service space as something social (Aubert-Gamet & Cova, 1999). In 1973 Kotler conceptualized an ability of service surroundings to cue "consumer wants" by visual, aural, olfactory, and tactile dimensions (1973, p. 53). Consequently, service providers started to consider customers' spatial understanding of service places and ability to undertake consumer decisions. In 1992 Bitner suggested interesting avenues for analysis of service environment by including ambient conditions, spatial layout and design, signs and symbols in the conceptual framework. She focused on physical surroundings of retail places and took less attention on time dimension. Though she partially considered service space as a personal construct (Aubert-Gamet & Cova, 1999, p. 38).

In the extensive writings on servicescapes, few studies have explicitly examined the relationship among servicescape, time, and space in any detail. Aubert-Gamet (1996) underlined that not only service spaces do act on their users, but users also act to get rendered services. Consequently, clients were regarded as able to change service spaces, because each individual might ascribe different meanings of servicescapes (Aubert-Gamet & Cova, 1999). Although the unity of time and space dimensions was recognized in a varying degree, but mainly in retail area. Aubert-Gamet and Cova (1999) spoke of time and space dimensions for reviving research on value of shopping and suggested consider servicescapes as places of "social ritualization" (1999, p. 40). Tombs and McColl-Kennedy (2010) discussed the ability of customers influencing other customers without any direct interaction, noting a spatial connection between customers and customer's belonging to the servicescapes. Few studies have made cursory mention of time dimension. Yalch and Spangenberg (2000) studied significance of time along with exploration, communication, and satisfaction for customers' approach-avoidance behavior. In a similar vein, Machleit and Eroglu (2000) discussed the ability of personnel to control service spaces by "waiting time" and "retail crowding." In contrast Johnstone (2012) spoke of the inability of personnel to control retail space, because every individual has their own meaning of service place.

All of the above studies discussed various spatio-temporal matters, but none of them had a particular focus on time and space in hospitality servicescapes. In hospitality servicescapes every guest is framed by both: time (temporal stay) and hotel space itself. Taking into account individual' behavioral perception of service space as well as her/his physical ability to move within service encounters, the impact of time and space dimensions on mobility of hotel guests becomes obvious. This line of argument allows considering a time–space approach as important to analyze customer behavior in hospitability servicescapes.

Constraints

Time-geography model (Hägerstrand, 1970) helps to identify emerging constraints while individuals move and act in the allocation of limited time and among activities in space (Miller, 2005). Constraint is something that limits or restricts someone or something (*Oxford Dictionary*), and therefore represents repression of one's own feelings, behavior, or action. Hägerstrand grouped constraints into three classes: capability, coupling, and authority (1970). The grouping of constraints to leisure is quite similar by division on intrapersonal, interpersonal, and structural constraints (Crawford & Godbey, 1987; Daniels, Drogin Rodgers, & Wiggins, 2005). Although individuals may differently react on identical constraints: from non-participation to constraints negotiation (Jackson, Crawford, & Godbey, 1993; White, 2008), constraints to leisure are "far more than the choice to participate or not" (Daniels et al., 2005, p. 920). Drawing from classification of constraints, research explains *why it is not individual's desire, but individual's ability to overcome emerging constraint(s)*.

Capability or Intrapersonal Constraints
Capability constraints include humans' physiological needs and available supplies that individuals can use to get their own goals (Hägerstrand,

1982). Similarly, intrapersonal constraints in leisure research relate individual's psychological state, physical functioning, or cognitive abilities (Daniels et al., 2005, p. 920). Available recourses as a type of capability constraint denote individuals' capability to be in certain location in certain time period (Hägerstrand, 1970; Miller & Bridwell, 2009). Individuals' ability to participate in activities depends from their capability to use physical recourses around. Tourism studies suggest that "length of visit" was a constraining factor for tourists, because their travel opportunities were framed by duration of stay (Shoval, Mckercher, Birenboim, & Ng, 2013). Another research indicated poor weather, air pollution, heavy traffic as limited activities of stop-over visitors (Mckercher, Wong, & Lau, 2006). Tourists are typically unfamiliar with and intimated by the nuances of travel mode (Lew & McKercher, 2006, p. 407) and travel environment. Consequently, availability of recourses in tourism destination manifests tourists' acts and moves.

Coupling or Interpersonal Constraints
Coupling constraints define "where, when, and for how long, the individual has to join other individuals, tools, and materials in order to produce, consume, and transact" (Hägerstrand, 1970, p. 14). Identically, interpersonal constraints to leisure "arise out of social interaction or relationship among people within social context" (Scott, 1991, p. 323). Coupling constraints focus on individuals' interactions with personnel and other guests in hotel facilities. The literature inform that VIPs were uncomfortable to call service personnel (Faria, Silva, & Ferreira, 2012). Blind travelers also shared negative experience when café owner put meal in the mouth of the blind person (Dann & Dann, 2011). Hence, VIPs employed additional time and strength, and it was rather of service space, not disability. Therefore, a dependency from service providers may restrict leisure benefits (Daniels et al., 2005).

Authority or Structural Constraints
Authority constraints refer to "control areas" or "domains." A domain is a time–space entity within which things and events are under the control of a given individual or a given group (Hägerstrand, 1970, p. 16). Authority constraints include rules and norms which limit individuals' access to spatial locations and time period (Yu & Shaw, 2007). Apart from barriers due to regulations a leisure research considers financial challenges, lack of time, ecological and transportation difficulties as structural constraints (Daniels et al., 2005). Majority of people with disability

identify structural constraints as a reason for non-participation in traveling (Small, Darcy, & Packer, 2012). For VIPs inaccessible customs declaration forms and difficulties with currencies (all paper bills were the same size and color) (Yau, Mckercher, & Packer, 2007) regarded authority or structural constraints. Consequently, constructed norms and regulations of service places may restrict some groups of customers by physical inability to follow them.

Constraints in service spaces might be considered as emerging. Customers' trajectories embedded by different barriers are interrelated. These barriers restrict in different degree individuals' ability to move independently (Pred, 1977). Individuals change their own trajectories in hospitality spaces to avoid barriers and get expected services. In fact, emerging constraints limit individual' freedom for the action (Pred, 1977). According to leisure studies clients *negotiate* through constraints to continue leisure participation (Jackson et al., 1993). Though participation in service recovery range from high cooperation to highly resistance (Hibbert, Piacentini, & Hogg, 2012), this research proposes tactics as consumers' acts against restricting service spaces.

Tactics

Despite the diversity of resistance forms (Penaloza & Price, 1993, p. 123) this study selected *tactics*. Although De Certeau probably did not have disability in mind, his characteristics on tactics are taken for the argumentation: (1) Tactics occur in hospitality servicescapes or in *alien territory* (1984). (2) Consumer tactics in essence are *resistance to power* of service providers. People use mass-produced goods, which are "the expressions of strategies" of service providers (Manovich, 2008, p. 322). (3) Tactics are *non-planned* resistance of the weak to the power of space (De Certeau, 1984). Mobility tactics expect to make work with things more "habitable" (Manovich, 2008, p. 322), and therefore time is the focus for the group of weak. While strategies are planned and operated through fixed (own) place, tactics are localized spatially and belong time (Hjorth, 2004).

Customers act by their own will and in the same time risk change their movements due to emerging constraints. Constraints restrict acts and moves of VIPs in servicescapes, but VIPs resist power of service spaces by developing tactics. Hence, temporal nature of VIPs' acts and moves and space-related power of constraints are spatially interrelated.

Method

The study combined participants' observation (*go-along method*) and interview (*individual* and *focus group*). Researcher observed VIPs' spatial practices (Lefebvre, 1991, p. 38) or *how* visually impaired guests walked,
occupied, interacted, networked, and connected places and people in hospitality spaces. Interview data supplied observations with VIPs' comments on
services they had.

The study was a theory-driven (Lofland, Snow, Anderson, & Lofland,
2006, p. 195). Hence, researcher entered the field with pre-understanding of
research problem. Physical environment (ambience and design) of service
spaces as well as interaction with personnel restricted activities of customers with disabilities. That is why servicescapes were considered as generating barriers. Based on codes recommended by literature framework and
selected theories, the researcher suggested her own categories which divided
in two main groups: (1) *exclusion of VIPs from servicescapes because of constraints*; (2) *inclusion of VIPs to servicescape because of their resistive
tactics*.

The field data were collected from November 2010 till August 2013. In
total researcher interviewed or/and observed 56 blind and visually impaired
travelers. In the meantime researcher had conducted three focus group
interviews with eight, six, and three participants, respectively, interviewed
14 VIPs, developed four observation reports on traveling with VIPs as
escort person (Helsingor, Denmark, 1 day with 5 VIPs; Solhaga, Sweden, 3
days with 13 VIPs; Schwerin, Germany, 4 days with 6 VIPs; Almaty,
Kazakhstan, 2 days with 1 VIP). Each focus group interview lasted from
2.5 to 3 hours, whereas individual interview lasted from 45 minutes to 1.5
hours. VIPs' age was ranged from 25 to above.

Findings

Exclusion of VIPs from Servicescapes because of Constraints
With the focus on three types of constraints observations and interviews
highlighted manmade barriers that restrict VIPs' activities. First, the findings revealed that design and ambience of servicescapes can generate intrapersonal constraints. Thus, wide and empty lobbies hinder VIPs by
acoustic. Lack of tactile paths and limited number of contrasting lines
block new arrived to navigate their ways. VIPs could not move along the
walls, because of the drink machines, informational shelves, and big pots of

greenery located on or near the walls (observation, Schwerin, Germany, August 16−19, 2012). Soft covers together with quietness, shadowed corridors, and bifurcated long corridors also make them feel uncomfortable. Noises of air conditioners or refrigerators restrict ability to communicate (focus group Almaty, Kazakhstan, 07.26.2012).

Using a cooled mini-bar in accommodation is rather costly. Price lists are printed on laminated paper. There is no other option than having a blind guest explore the mini-bar by opening the bottles, cans, and packets in order to know what is there. It is also not possible to identify the warm or cool buttons on the air conditioning remote control as well as buttons on TV remote. VIPs have to identify and then memorize relevant buttons by checking air flow temperature and TV channels (observation, Schwerin, Germany, August 16−19, 2012; hotel observation with VIP, Almaty, Kazakhstan, 17.07.2012).

The biggest number of cases on noise was identified in lobby and eating place, and odor mainly restricted VIPs in accommodations. The findings also revealed that intrapersonal constraints seem to be more difficult in accommodation rather than in lobby and eating place. Yet VIPs face difficulties before, during, and subsequent to their travel experience (Poria et al., 2011).

Second, the findings suggest that interaction with non-qualified personnel can generate interpersonal constraints. The researcher heard varying reactions of VIPs to personnel, ranging from total engagement to absolute disgust. The following citation illustrates the latter perspective: *Hotel personnel consider VIPs as extra work. In addition, they are afraid to assist blind guests* (woman, VIP, focus group interview, Almaty, Kazakhstan, 08.21.2013). Personnel "afraid to assist" means that personnel "do not assist." The quotes from individual interviews: *It is always uncomfortable to ask others for help ... we are accustomed to surviving by ourselves; We are like others. There is no need to separate us. We cannot see, but it does not mean that we are inadequate; I lost my vision, but it does not mean that I am dead* (Almaty, Kazakhstan 11.19−21.2010). It is apparent that interactions with non-qualified personnel force VIPs to be "out-of-space" (Kitchin, 1998).

Third, the findings revealed that service place regulations can generate structural constraints. Thus, plastic key and laminated breakfast cards, and a paper card for public transportation were hard to manage for VIPs. All these cards were the same size making it impossible to tell them apart for a person who cannot see. The group was given instructions from the receptionist concerning all these cards at the time of check-in, however, later on one VIP threw away the card for public transportation, because she thought it was trash paper (observation, Schwerin, Germany, August 16–19, 2012).

Inclusion of VIPs to Servicescape because of their Resistive Tactics
What was apparent about moves and acts of observed VIPs is their desire to continue leisure participation (Jackson et al., 1993) by resisting emerging constraints. Visually impaired woman said: *When I come in to unfamiliar hotel I try to listen. Acoustics tell me about size of space. Voices of people talking with personnel, telephone rings, sound of fax machine indicate location of the reception desk. To investigate a new space I move along the wall* (Almaty, Kazakhstan 11.19.2010). This woman wants to be in control and active in her own choices. Control is not only action, but cognition as well (Baker, 2006). Most VIPs ask the hotel "where her/his room is, and is there any code for the door if she/he comes in late?" And VIPs always verify things. They want to be independent "as much as possible" (woman, VIP, interview, Limhamn, Sweden, 03.31.2012, focus group interview, Almaty, Kazakhstan, August 2011). Being visually impaired they, nevertheless, do not apply external assistance, but make their own investigations. VIPs listen, create spatial picture of the place, and then move.

Being asked focus group participants shared navigation experience in hotels: *The noise of the vacuum cleaner is also a reference point, because it helps me to locate where the accommodations are* (man, VIP). *In the hotel I try to find signs for orientation. Sometimes it is difficult to find the room in the long corridor. That is why I just count doors* (woman, VIP). *It is not difficult for me to manage an electronic key. There are only four ways to insert it: two per each side* (man, VIP) (focus group interview, Almaty, Kazakhstan, 08.21.2013). VIPs count the doors to find their own, make mapping by remembering where a "carpet" is or where there is a "turn," use sound and touch for finding their own way to be in control of time and service environment.

CONCLUSION AND IMPLICATIONS

Available resources and *time* are constraints for VIPs' activities in hotel time–space coordinates. Ambience and design of servicescapes can create intrapersonal constraints. When service providers fail to appreciate or are not sensitive to resource limitations of particular groups, consumers face interpersonal and structural constraints.

Previous studies on travelers with disabilities do not conflict with the data presented in the results. Literature suggests that physical surroundings in hotels for VIPs are non-accessible (Poria et al., 2011); furniture disposition in the room often hinder mobility of vision impaired guests (2011, p. 578); hotel lobbies force VIPs to be accompanied (Kaufman-Scarborough, 2001); buffet breakfasts disorient blind guests by inability to find plates and dishes (Bi, Card, & Cole, 2007, p. 207); customers with disabilities felt themselves vulnerable (Yau et al., 2004, p. 957) and socially excluded (Darcy, 2001, 2010). These and many other cases suggest that servicescapes are invented for customers without disabilities. Constraints of hotel servicescapes restrict VIPs' activities, but they resist by developing different tactics. Consequently, tactics is a power for VIPs.

There are few patterns seem to be emerging. Firstly, existing research on servicescape seems to show less attention on space and time awareness in analyzing customer behavior in hospitality servicescapes. Secondly, time–space (spatial) approach suggests another angle for understanding customers' behavior in service encounters. Thirdly, identification of VIPs' mobility tactics from theoretical point of view would lend itself well for use by tourism service providers in order to better understand blind customers. Fourthly, VIPs have a power because of tactics that they are developing. Fifthly, servicescapes are for all, but with different tactics.

REFERENCES

Aubert-Gamet, V. (1996). Twisting servicescapes: Diversion of the physical environment in a re-appropriation process. *International Journal of Service Industry Management, 8*(1), 26–41.

Aubert-Gamet, V., & Cova, B. (1999). Servicescapes: From modern non-places to postmodern common places. *Journal of Business Research, 44*, 37–45.

Baker, J. (1987). The role of the environment in marketing services: The consumer perspective. In J. A. Czepiel, C. Congram, & J. Shanahan (Eds.), *The service challenge: Integrating for competitive advantage* (pp. 79–84). Chicago, IL: American Marketing Association.

Baker, S. M. (2006). Consumer normalcy: Understanding the value of shopping through narratives of consumers with visual impairments. *Journal of Retailing, 82*(1), 37–50.

Baker, S. M., Gentry, J. W., & Rittenburg, T. L. (2005). Building understanding of the domain of consumer vulnerability. *Journal of Macromarketing, 25*(2), 128–139.

Bi, Y., Card, J. A., & Cole, S. T. (2007). Accessibility and attitudinal barriers encountered by Chinese travellers with physical disabilities. *International Journal of Tourism Research, 9*, 2005–2216.

Bitner, M. J. (1992). The impact of physical surroundings on customers and employees. *The Journal of Marketing, 56*(2), 57−71.

Blichfeldt, B. S., & Nicolaisen, J. (2011). Disabled travel: Not easy, but doable. *Current Issues in Tourism, 14*(1), 79−102.

Bonnin, G., & Goudey, A. (2012). The kinetic quality of store design: An Exploration of its influence on shopping experience. *Journal of Retailing and Consumer Services, 19*, 637−643.

Coyle, C. P., Shank, J. W., & Vilet, N. M. (2010). Leisure and rehabilitation. In L. Payne, B. Ainsworth, & G. Godbey (Eds.), *Leisure, health, and wellness: Making the connections* (pp. 264−277). State College, PA: Venture.

Crawford, D. W., & Godbey, G. (1987). Reconceptualizing barriers to family leisure. *Leisure Sciences: An Interdisciplinary Journal, 9*(2), 119−127.

Daniels, M. J., Drogin Rodgers, E. B., & Wiggins, B. P. (2005). "Travel Tales": An interpretive analysis of constraints and negotiations to pleasure travel as experienced by persons with physical disabilities. *Tourism Management, 26*(6), 919−930.

Dann, E., & Dann, G. M. S. (2011). *Sightseeing for the sightless and soundless* (Vol. 16, pp. 1−36). Studies and Reports, Série L. Aix-en-Provence: Centre International de Recherches et D'Etudes Touristiques.

Darcy, S. (2001). People with physical disabilities and leisure. In I. Patterson & T. Taylor (Eds.), *Celebrating inclusion and diversity in leisure* (pp. 59−79). Williamstown, VI: HM Leisure Planning.

Darcy, S. (2010). Inherent complexity: Disability, accessible tourism and accommodation information preferences. *Tourism Management, 31*, 816−826.

Darcy, S., & Buhalis, D. (2011). *Conceptualizing disability, accessible tourism concepts and issues* (p. 316). Bristol, UK: Channels View Publications.

Dattilo, J. (2002). *Inclusive leisure services* (2nd ed.). State College, PA: Venture.

De Certeau, M. (1984). *The practice of everyday life.* Berkeley, CA: University of California Press.

Devine, M. A., Cory, L., & Rauworth, A. (2010). Promoting health and wellness with persons with disabilities: The role of recreation and leisure. In L. Payne, B. Ainsworth, & G. Godbey (Eds.), *Leisure, health, and wellness: Making the connections* (pp. 323−344). State College, PA: Venture.

Dirita, P., Parameter, T., & Stancliffe, R. (2008). Utility economic rationalism and the circumscription of agency. *Journal of Intellectual Disability Research, 52*(7), 618−625.

Faria, M. D. d., Silva, J. F. d., & Ferreira, J. B. (2012). The visually impaired and consumption in restaurants. *International Journal of Contemporary Hospitality Management, 24*(5), 3−33.

Hägerstrand, T. (1970). What about people in regional science? Ninth European congress of the regional science association. *Regional Science Association Papers, 24*(1), 6−21.

Hägerstrand, T. (1982). Diorama, path and project. *Tijdschrift voor Economische en Sociale Geografie, 73*, 323−329.

Hibbert, S. A., Piacentini, M. G., & Hogg, M. K. (2012). Service recovery following dysfunctional consumer participation. *Journal of Consumer Behaviour, 11*, 329−338. doi:10.1002/cb.1391

Higgins, M. A. (2004). *Worldwide, individuals with disabilities want inclusive recreation.* Retrieved from http://www.nrpa.org/story.cfm?story_id=1917&departmentID=79&publicationID=21

Hjorth, D. (2004). Creating space for play/invention — Concepts of space and organizational entrepreneuship. *Entrepreneurship and Regional Development, 16*, 413–432.

Jackson, E. L., Crawford, D. W., & Godbey, G. (1993). Negotiation of leisure constraints. *Leisure Sciences: An Interdisciplinary Journal, 15*(1), 1–11.

Johnstone, M.-L. (2012). The servicescape: The social dimensions of place. *Journal of Marketing Management, 28*(11–12), 1399–1418.

Kaufman-Scarborough, C. (2001). Accessible advertising for visually-disabled persons: The case of color-deficient consumers. *Journal of Consumer Marketing, 18*(4), 303–318.

Kitchin, R. (1998). "Out of Place", "Knowing One's Place": Space, power and the exclusion of disabled people. *Disability and Society, 13*(3), 343–356.

Kotler, P. (1973). Atmospherics as a marketing tool. *Journal of Retailing, 49*, 48–65.

Kozinets, R. V., Sherry, J. F., Deberry-Spence, B., Duhachek, A., Nuttavuthisit, K., & Storm, D. (2002). Themed flagship brand stores in the new millennium: Theory, practice, prospects. *Journal of Retailing, 78*(1), 17–29.

Lefebvre, H. (1991). *The production of space* (D. Nicholson-Smith, Trans.). Oxford: Blackwell Publishers.

Lew, A., & McKercher, B. (2006). Modeling tourist movements a local destination analysis. *Annals of Tourism Research, 33*(2), 403–423.

Lofland, J., Snow, D. A., Anderson, L., & Lofland, L. H. (2006). *Analysing social settings: A guide to qualitative observation and analysis*. Belmont, CA: Wadsworth.

Machleit, K. A., & Eroglu, S. A. (2000). Perceived retail crowding and shopping satisfaction: What modifies this relationship? *Journal of Consumer Psychology, 9*(1), 29–42.

Manovich, L. (2008). The practice of everyday (Media) life: From mass consumption to mass cultural production? *Critical Inquiry, 35*(Winter), 319–331, 2009.

Mckercher, B., Wong, C., & Lau, G. (2006). How tourists consume a destination. *Journal of Business Research, 59*, 647–652.

Miller, H. J. (2005). A measurement theory for time geography. *Geographical Analysis, 37*(1), 17–45.

Miller, H. J., & Bridwell, S. A. (2009). A field-based theory for time geography. *Annals of the Association of American Geographers, 99*(1), 49–75.

Packer, T. L., Small, J., & Darcy, S. (2008). *Tourist experiences of individuals with vision impairment*. Technical Report, CRC for Sustainable Tourism Pty Ltd, Queensland, Australia, pp. 9–35.

Penaloza, L., & Price, L. L. (1993). Consumer resistance: A conceptual overview. In L. McAlister & M. L. Rothschild (Eds.), *Advances in consumer research* (Vol. 20, pp. 123–128). Association for Consumer Research.

Poria, Y., Reichel, A., & Brandt, Y. (2011). Dimensions of hotel experience of people with disabilities: An exploratory study. *International Journal of Contemporary Hospitality Management, 23*(5), 571–591.

Pred, A. (1977). The choreography of existence: Comments on Hagerstrand's time-geography and its usefulness. *Economic Geography, 53*(2), 207–221.

Ray, I., & Chiagouris, L. (2009). Customer retention: Examining the roles of store affect and store loyalty as mediators in the management of retail strategies. *Journal of Strategic Marketing, 17*(1), 1–20.

Richards, V. (2011). (Dis)-embodied tourism experiences of people with vision impairment. Paper presented at the Tourism Futures: Enhancing Creative and Critical Action, Critical Tourism Studies IV, Welsh Centre for Tourism Research.

Scott, D. (1991). The problematic nature of participation in contract bridge: A qualitative study of group-related constraints. *Leisure Sciences: An Interdisciplinary Journal, 13*(4), 321–336.

Shoval, N., McKercher, B., Birenboim, A., & Ng, E. (2013). The application of a sequence alignment method to the creation of typologies of tourist activity in time and space. *Environment and Planning B: Planning and Design, 40*, 1–19.

Small, J., & Darcy, S. (2011). Understanding tourist experience through embodiment: The contribution of critical tourism and disability studies. In D. Buhalis & S. Darcy (Eds.), *Accessible tourism: Concepts and issues* (pp. 73–97). Bristol: Channel View Publications.

Small, J., Darcy, S., & Packer, T. (2012). The embodied tourist experiences of people with vision impairment: Management implications beyond the visual gaze. *Tourism Management, 33*, 941–950.

Tombs, A., & McColl-Kennedy, J. R. (2010). Social and spatial influence of customers on other customers in the social-servicescape. *Australasian Marketing Journal, 18*, 120–131.

White, D. D. (2008). A structural model of leisure constraints. Negotiation in outdoor recreation. *Leisure Sciences, 30*, 342–359.

Yalch, R. F., & Spangenberg, E. R. (2000). Effects of store music on shopping behavior. *Journal of Consumer Marketing, 7*(2), 55–63.

Yau, M. K., McKercher, B., & Packer, T. L. (2004). Traveling with a disability: More than an access issue. *Annals of Tourism Research, 31*(4), 946–960.

Yau, M. K., Mckercher, B., & Packer, T. L. (2007). Understanding the complex interplay between tourism, disability and environmental contexts. *Disability and Rehabilitation, 29*(4), 281–292.

Yu, H., & Shaw, S.-L. (2007). Revisiting Hagerstrand's time-geographic framework for individual activities in the age of instant access. In H. J. Miller (Ed.), *Societies and cities in the age of instant access* (pp. 103–118). Dordrecht: Springer Science.

DETERMINANTS OF TOURISM DESTINATION COMPETITIVENESS: A SEM APPROACH

Cristina Estevão, João Ferreira and Sara Nunes

ABSTRACT

The competitiveness of tourist destinations has been the subject of great research interest in recent decades. Nevertheless, and despite the diversity in the literature, studies focusing on the empirical validation of tourism destination models of competitiveness have still to be completed. Hence, this research project seeks to contribute to filling this shortcoming through the identification and evaluation of the factors underlying tourism destination competitiveness in Portugal. The study methodology adopted requires primary data that were sourced from a questionnaire deployed as a structured research instrument based upon the variables put forward by the Dwyer and Kim model (2003). Through recourse to structural equation models, the results report the existence of significant relationships between resources, supply and tourism destination management as the core and essential factors to the competitiveness of a particular tourist destination.

Keywords: Competitiveness; tourist destinations; structural equation models; Portugal

Marketing Places and Spaces
Advances in Culture, Tourism and Hospitality Research, Volume 10, 121–139
Copyright © 2015 by Emerald Group Publishing Limited
All rights of reproduction in any form reserved
ISSN: 1871-3173/doi:10.1108/S1871-317320150000010009

INTRODUCTION

Competitiveness has been the key focus of many studies across various different sectors and especially since the early 1990s. However, only more recently have researchers turned their attentions to tourism sector competitiveness, both conceptually and empirically, and particularly in terms of tourist destinations (Tsai, Song, & Wong, 2009). How to establish, maintain, protect and strengthen tourist destinations and their respective positions in an increasingly competitive and globalised marketplace represents a major challenge that has proven to be of great relevance to the tourism industry (Crouch, 2007). According to Enright and Newton (2004), relative competitiveness shapes the success of tourist destinations in the global marketplace.

Tourism destination competitiveness proves ever more important to countries seeking to obtain and/or hold a major stake in the growing tourism market and this becomes especially crucial to those strongly dependent on the tourism sector and the travel industry (Echtner & Ritchie, 2003; Navickas & Malakauskaite, 2009). Meanwhile, Malakauskaite and Navickas (2010) maintain that tourism sector competitiveness – as with any other economic sector – is inseparable from the harmonious and sustainable development of tourist destinations. Tourism development requires sustainability not only economically but also in socio-political, technological, natural, ecological and cultural terms (Crouch & Ritchie, 1999; Malakauskaite & Navickas, 2010).

In turn, Crouch and Ritchie (1999) posit how the touristic development potential of any country or region substantially depends on its capacity to maintain its competitive advantage in the supply of goods and services to visitors. Dwyer and Kim (2003) share the same position in stating that the competitiveness of a tourist destination interrelates with its ability to provide better goods and services than its competitors.

The research difficulties and problems inherent to evaluating tourism sector competitiveness have received widespread recognition and are identified and analysed in many scientific studies (Navickas & Malakauskaite, 2009). The tourism industry has seen many studies attempting to measure the levels of competitiveness of different countries and sectors, with some based on primary data (Claver-Cortés, Molina, & Pereira, 2007; Crouch, 2007; Dwyer, Mellor, Livaic, Edwards, & Kim, 2004; Enright & Newton, 2004, 2005; Faulkner, Oppermann, & Fredline, 1999; Gomezelj & Mihalic, 2008; Hudson, Ritchie, & Timur, 2004; Kim & Dwyer, 2003; Kozak &

Rimmington, 1999; March, 2004; Omerzel, 2006) and others on secondary data (ECLAC, 2009; Gooroochurn & Sugiyarto, 2005; WEF, 2007, 2008, 2009, 2010, 2011; Zhang, Gu, Gu, & Zhang, 2011).

However, despite the diversity in these studies, the literature reveals a lack of studies focusing on the empirical validation of tourism destination models of competitiveness. Correspondingly, this research project seeks to contribute to meeting this shortcoming through the identification and evaluation of the factors driving tourism sector competitiveness in the regional areas that have experienced tourism-based development in Portugal.

We have therefore structured this research project as follows: after an initial review of the literature on tourism sector competitiveness, we then proceed to set out not only the methodology applied but also describe the data and the variables applied in the study. Subsequently, we present our analysis and discuss the results obtained before finally putting forward our respective research conclusions.

LITERATURE REVIEW

The concept of competitiveness would at first seem simple to understand; however, its intrinsic complexity becomes clear when seeking to define and analyse it from various perspectives taken in the literature (Cooke & Morgan, 1998; Desrochers & Sautet, 2004; Porter, 1994). Porter (1990) argues that its ambiguity stems from the enormous variety of definitions and different perspectives on competitiveness that combine to render any exhaustive or consensual definition difficult to attain. However, according to his view, the competitiveness of a country derives from the competitiveness of its companies, while a company's competitiveness results from the way in which its business model interrelates with the surrounding environment to produce products and services that aggregate value.

Casadesus-Masanell and Ricart (2010) point out how the majority of the literature on competitiveness concentrates on geographic unity – region, country or even cluster and has served in various ways to foster the creation of virtuous cycles that enable companies to develop the strengths that they subsequently deploy to maintain their level of international competitiveness.

The creation of wealth represents the motor of economic growth and an important leverage of innovation (Dwyer & Kim, 2003). According to

Dwyer et al. (2004), the competitiveness of a nation is not a result in itself but rather the means to attain an end with the final objective of any industry being to generate wealth for the people. Costa, Rita, and Águas (2004), furthermore, advocate how competitiveness represents a transversal concern to contemporary societies. In every activity, and not just the economic based, there is this search for efficiency. Attaining competitiveness is an end and a condition to everything that a society seeks to achieve. Casadesus-Masanell and Ricart (2010) agree that competitiveness is a common concern of many countries and regions before reaching further to affirm that competitiveness proves a means of accelerating development and engaging in international markets.

Competitiveness in the tourism industry proves an equally complex and multidimensional issue (Wong, 2009) and, in the view of Bălan, Balaure, and Veghes (2009), has become one of the most commonly deployed concepts for describing approaches to the sustainable development of tourist destinations in recent years. Part of this complexity derives from the nature of definitions applied to the tourism destination concept conceived as either a place or in the form of a real or perceived borderline, such as the physical boundaries of an island, political borders or even market stipulated limits (Kotler, Bowen, & Markens, 2006). These multidimensional facets incorporate the numerous definitions put forward by many researchers.

Bahar and Kozak (2007), Crouch and Ritchie (1999) and Heath (2003) define tourism sector competitiveness as the capacity for a destination to provide a high standard of living for target residents. Meanwhile, Hassan (2000) refers to the capacities of destinations to create and integrate products adding value that thereby sustain both its resources and its market positioning in relation to its competitors. D'Hauteserre (2000) shares this position while adding that such capacities need improvement over the course of time. In turn, Kim (2000) posits tourism sector competitiveness as the capacity, endowed by the prevailing tourism market conditions, the human resources and the tourism infrastructures of a country, to generate added value and boost national wealth. This author also points out how tourism sector competitiveness incorporates not only the measurement of potential capacity but also an evaluation of the present capacity and performance of the tourism sector.

The interest in studying the competitiveness of tourism destinations reflects in the diverse series of studies. Many of these research projects have set out to identify and diagnose the competitiveness in effect at specific destinations (Crouch, 2007), including the United States (Ahmed & Krohn, 1990), Las Vegas (Chon & Mayer, 1995), European cities (Mazanec, 1995), Southeast Asia (Pearce, 1997), Sun/Lost City in South Africa (Botha,

Crompton, & Kim, 1999), South Australia (Faulkner et al., 1999), a casino in an US resort (D'Hauteserre, 2000), cultural tourism in Toronto (Carmichael, 2002), Mediterranean resorts (Papatheodorou, 2002), South Korea and Australia (Dwyer et al., 2004; Kim & Dwyer, 2003), Spain and Turkey (Kozak, 2003), a ski resort in Canada (Hudson et al., 2004), the Asia-Pacific region (Enright & Newton, 2005), Zimbabwe (Vengesayi, 2005), Slovenia (Gomezelj & Mihalic, 2008), in the Caribbean (ECLAC, 2009) and in Brazil (Ritchie & Crouch, 2010).

Other research projects approached particular facets of destination competitiveness, including the respective destination positioning (Chacko, 1998), management systems (Baker, Hayzelden, & Sussmann, 1996), commercialisation (Buhalis, 2000), pricing (Dwyer, Forsyth, & Rao, 2000a, 2000b, 2000c, 2001, 2002; Stevens, 1992), quality management (Go & Govers, 2000), its environment (Hassan, 2000; Mihalic, 2000), nature-based tourism (Huybers & Bennett, 2003), strategic management (Jamal & Getz, 1996; Soteriou & Roberts, 1998) and organised tour circuits (Taylor, 1995) as well as research based on the development of models and general theories on destination competitiveness (Crouch & Ritchie, 1999; Dwyer & Kim, 2003; Fernando & Long, 2012; Ferreira & Estevão, 2009; Gomezelj & Mihalic, 2008; Heath, 2003; Malakauskaite & Navickas, 2010; Porter, 1990; Vengesayi, 2003).

According to Dwyer and Kim (2003), tourism competitiveness combines various features that may or may not be directly observable and which, on many occasions, are not easily susceptible to measurement. In order to compete in the tourism sector, a destination should not only attain comparative advantages but also competitive advantages and, hence, extending beyond simply deploying a variety, differing to a greater or lesser extent, of tourism products and resources as these additionally need to be efficiently managed over the medium and long term. Thus, Tsai et al. (2009) deem a destination competitive whenever it is able to attract and satisfy potential tourists. Vengesayi (2003) puts forward a concept including the reputation of the tourism destination and how this strengthens competitiveness through its perceived attractiveness.

A destination's attractiveness reflects the feelings and opinions of its visitors as regards its perceived capacity to meet and satisfy their needs. Thus, the greater the capacity of a destination to meet tourist needs, the more attractive it is perceived and the greater the probability of its selection.

The overall competitiveness of the tourism sector stems from many different factors and ranges from the natural environment (geographic location, landscapes, climate etc.), the built environment (tourist transport services, leisure and entertainment infrastructural provision, services, retail outlets, hotel chains etc.) and the level of market globalisation (Navickas & Malakauskaite, 2009). Ritchie and Crouch (2010) also conclude that the resources and attractions are also competitive factors determinant to the success of tourist destinations. Furthermore, Malakauskaite and Navickas (2010) propose that the tourism sector makes a significant contribution to economic development and describe how this results from the synergy of natural and human factors leveraged by tourist destination resources and determined by the effective capacity of tourism sector actors to attract new visitors and raise their expenditure through the provision of quality goods and services as well as highly valued experiences.

Crouch and Ritchie (1999) propose a broad ranging and a sophisticated model for tourism destination management structured around the core theoretical concepts on competitiveness set out by Porter (1990) and introduce the comparative advantage and competitive advantage theories. According to these authors, comparative advantage stems from the factors inherent to tourist destinations, thereby including both those naturally occurring and those purpose built. In turn, competitive advantage incorporates the capacity of tourism destinations to apply their resources efficiently and effectively over the medium and long term. They also add that the destination management component focuses on the activities implemented through the policies for planning and developing the destination and designed to boost the attractiveness of the central resources and points of attraction, strengthening and deepening quality and the efficiency of support factors and resources and best adapting to the constraints and opportunities imposed and shaped by the determining factors of qualification component.

Omerzel (2006) proposes that understanding the competitiveness of tourist destinations inherently requires consideration of both the core factors to comparative advantage as well as the more advanced factors that generate competitive advantage. Comparative advantages therefore constitute the resources available to a destination, whereas the competitive advantages signify the destination's capacity to deploy these resources effectively over the medium and long term.

Dwyer and Kim (2003) put forward an integrated model, which is fundamental in keeping with the aforementioned model while also introducing some important new aspects. Firstly, the resources endowed (both the inherited and the built resources) each individual to have their own identity as do the created and support resources. These factors may in turn be grouped together in a superior structure given that they collectively provide the characteristics that make a tourist destination attractive to visitors and drive the factors that combine to ensure a prosperous tourism industry. These three factors therefore configure the foundations of tourist destination competitiveness. Furthermore, beyond the destination management already incorporated into the aforementioned model, this integrated model considers another relevant dimension to levels of demand and include the three core facets to tourism demand: tourist awareness, perceptions and preferences.

In the opinion of Dwyer and Kim (2003), destination management, the terms of demand and the locally prevailing conditions all wield either a positive or a negative influence on competitiveness. Destination competitiveness is thus shaped by the determinants described above, which, in turn, influence socioeconomic prosperity in the sense that the competitiveness of a destination, in itself, reflects an intermediate objective within the framework of another broader and more important objective, the socioeconomic wellbeing of residents.

Heath (2003) puts forward a tourism competitiveness model based on planning processes and reaching beyond the main indicators proposed by Crouch and Ritchie (1999) and Dwyer and Kim (2003). Ferreira and Estevão (2009) also present a tourism competitiveness model that results from combining the variables from models by Crouch and Ritchie (1999), Dwyer and Kim (2003) and Porter (1990). This incorporates an interactive tourism system that adjusts in accordance with the influences exerted by the three essential components: the tourism product (made up of its resources and attractions), the tourist destination and the tourism cluster. Where the first two components interconnect efficiently then the tourism cluster operates productively.

METHODOLOGY

The methodology adopted for this research project required recourse to primary data, which were gathered through applying a questionnaire research tool and structured in accordance with the Dwyer and Kim model (2003). The instrument applied contained 53 items measured according to the five-point Likert scale and was designed to evaluate issues relating to inherited resources, built resources, support and resource factors, destination management and prevailing levels of demand in addition to a group of socio-demographic factors in order to capture the character of the respondent companies.

The geographic area of study includes the Tourism Development Regions and the Poles on Mainland and Archipelago Portugal (Fig. 1).

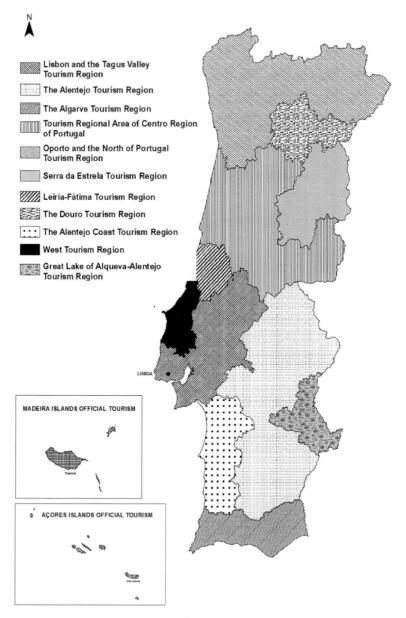

Fig. 1.   Areas and Poles of Tourism Development.

The units of analysis were the companies classified by their CAE identification code for the activities studied and launched prior to 2009 according to the characteristic satellite account as defined by the WTO, OECD, and United Nation and Commission of The European Communities (2001) to a five-digit level of disaggregation. The geographic area underlying the study was the Tourism Development Regions and Poles on Mainland and Archipelago Portugal. These companies were inquired by a questionnaire, the sample size was 4.560 and the response rate was 10.22%. Questionnaire recipients were assured of the privacy and confidentiality of the data submitted and informed of the research project objectives. The collected data were analysed using the software SPSS 21.0.

The study sample featured 446 companies of which 22.4% (100) belonged to the Lisbon and the Tagus Valley Tourism Region, 15.7% (70) to the Oporto and the North of Portugal Region, 11.4% (51) to the Algarve Region and 11% (49) to the Centre Region, with these four tourism regions corresponding to two thirds of the study sample.

We furthermore ascertain that hotels with restaurants represent the CAE class with the highest number of responses with 132 companies (29.6%) in this category, followed by inns/lodgings with restaurants and traditional type restaurants on 6.7% and tourism in rural surroundings on 6%.

In relation to the company's length of service, 37.8% (166) began operations between 2001 and 2010, 27.6% (121) in the final decade of the last century and 15.7% (66) in the 1980s. In terms of their legal registration, almost three quarters (73.6%) of the sample companies operate under quota structures and 18.10% correspond to anonymous firms, with micro-companies (0−9 employees) substantially to the fore − 47.90%, while there are 43.60% small-scale companies and a low level (3.2%) of medium and large companies (100 or more members of staff).

Employment levels ranged from 1 to 527 members of staff with an average of 21 and a median of 10 employees. Over 60% of questionnaire respondents declared that they mostly undertook management functions and were in the main university graduates (55.9%), followed by professional training qualifications and secondary schooling with 20.30% and 19.90%, respectively. Respondent ages broadly ranged from between 30 and 39 (29.20%), 40 and 49 (28.5%) and 50 and 64 (25.70%) with only 58 respondents belonging to the 20−29 age bracket.

FINDINGS

In an initial phase, we carried out factorial analysis of the 53 items under study. Analysis of the indices of internal consistency led to the exclusion of certain items, thereby significantly boosting scale reliability. The remaining 46 items were again subject to the factorial analysis technique and returned a KMO result of 0.901 and a Bartlett TEST score of $p < 0.001$, thereby indicating that the analytical model applied is appropriate to the sample under study. To extract the axes, we made recourse to principal component analysis and applied Cattell's scree plot to determine the number of axes to retain. We correspondingly found that the six retained axes explained 60.0% of total variance. Following Equamax rotation, we obtained the item factor distribution set out in Table 1. In order to facilitate interpretation, we removed all factorial results below 0.3.

Table 1.   Factorial Matrix Obtained Following Equamax Rotation.

Items	Component					
	1	2	3	4	5	6
Company orientation towards growth and innovation policies	0.744		0.327			
Entrepreneurial quality of local businesses	0.721					
Local community support for special tourism events	0.697					
Strong emphasis on product/service research, development and innovation	0.677		0.443			
Proactive attitude of tourism company managers	0.670		0.369			
Communication between tourists and residents	0.626					
Resident hospitality towards visitors	0.597					
Healthcare/medical services for tourists	0.523					
Tourism offices	0.463					0.359
Flora		0.830				
Fauna		0.814				
Footpaths and walkways		0.712				
Activities involving contact with nature		0.707				
National parks, including nature reserves		0.666				
Visitor access to nature areas	0.357	0.629				
Natural wonders/landscapes		0.616		0.333	0.316	
Unspoiled nature		0.607			0.344	
Recreational and leisure quality			0.799			

Table 1. (Continued)

Items	Component					
	1	2	3	4	5	6
Variety in recreation and leisure			0.787			
Fun and theme parks			0.775			
Sporting activities			0.705			
Nightlife (e.g. bars, discos and dance halls)			0.620	0.358		
Special events/festivals			0.585	0.367		
International destination reputation				0.805		
National destination reputation				0.777		
Destination tourism products and services are internationally recognised				0.774		
Recourse to e-mail for marketing and communication	0.301			0.626		
Destination promotion on social networks			0.360	0.617		
Tourism guidance and information	0.433		0.346	0.585		
Attractiveness of climate for tourism				0.494		
Telecommunications systems for tourists	0.416			0.482		
Tourism promotional packages available			0.368	0.431		
Historical/heritage sites					0.727	
Architectonic characteristics					0.699	
Gastronomic variety					0.662	
Customs/traditions		0.354			0.610	
Handicrafts		0.342			0.503	
Good accommodation quality/price relationship						0.649
Appropriate destination access transport facilities					0.380	0.646
Good-quality local tourism transport			0.333			0.643
Efficient local tourism transport			0.363		0.362	0.628
Good-quality accommodation						0.596
Leisure services able to meet tourist demand			0.365			0.543
Restaurant services able to meet fluctuations in local tourist demand						0.510
Sporting facilities/infrastructures available		0.395				0.474
Good 'cleanliness'/sanitation quality levels						0.472

The factorial structure obtained demonstrates how factor 1 gathers items related to orientation towards entrepreneurship and hospitality, factor 2 reports those on natural resources, factor 3 concentrates information on recreational and leisure services, factor 4 centres on promotional marketing, factor 5 deals with inherited resources while factor 6 conveys support and other services.

In order to measure internal consistency, we applied Cronbach's Alpha and gained satisfactory levels: 0.953 for the complete scale; 0.908 for the subscales 'natural resources' and 'promotional marketing'; 0.802 for 'inherited resources'; 0.888 for the subscales 'orientation towards entrepreneurship and hospitality' and 'recreational and leisure services' and 0.787 for 'support and other services'.

To further our analysis of the results obtained, we carried out calculations of the weightings observed for each dimension. In order to ensure the results are comparable, these weightings were calculated according to the number of items that integrate each dimension and to this end assuming a minimum value of one and a maximum value of five. Table 2 reports the core descriptive statistics for each of the dimensions obtained.

We therefore observe how respondents attributed greatest value to the inherited resources item, while the recreational and leisure services factor receives the lowest average weighting level and also gains the lowest level of consensus among respondents. Furthermore, the support and other services factor records the greatest level of heterogeneity.

In a second phase, we applied the structural equations model to the dimensions returned by factorial analysis. We correspondingly made recourse to AMOS 5.0 and, to ensure that the resulting model is fully identifiable, established the averages for all latent variables. Furthermore, we set the weightings for the latent variables resources, supply and destination management relative to the variables F2, F3 and F1, respectively. The criterion deployed was always choosing the model that leads to the highest adjustment quality whenever in accordance with the theoretical fundamentals studied and in keeping with the specifications stipulated by Arbuckle (1997) and Hair, Anderson, Tatham, and Black (1998).

Table 2. Core Descriptive Statistics for the Obtained Dimensions Pondered by the Number of Items.

Factors	No.	Min	Max	Mean	Standard Deviation
Orientation towards entrepreneurship and hospitality	380	1.44	5.00	3.32	0.71
Natural resources	406	1.25	5.00	3.51	0.81
Recreational and leisure services	423	1.00	5.00	3.13	0.88
Promotional marketing	367	1.00	5.00	3.40	0.82
Inherited resources	424	1.40	5.00	3.68	0.69
Support and other services	378	1.56	5.00	3.50	0.66

Estimating the structural equations model, we obtain the model measurements set out in Fig. 2, which details the most accurate estimates for the common factor weightings and their respective covariance levels.

We obtained the following adjustment quality index values: CFI = 0.996, IFI = 0.996, TLI = 0.991, NFI = 0.990 and RMSEA = 0.036 and reported a high level of adjustment quality. All the different variable relationships integrated into the proposed model prove to be statistically significant. We find a strong association between destination management and supply ($r = 0.91$, $P < 0.001$). We also report statistically significant correlations between destination management and resources ($r = 0.77$, $P < 0.001$) and supply and resources ($r = 0.67$, $P < 0.001$).

Analysis of the factorial weightings demonstrates that inherited resources (F5) prove most determinants when considering resources rather than more specifically natural resources (F2), although the latter does also hold major influence over resources. As regards supply, this is strongly

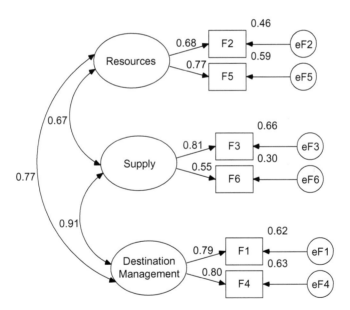

Fig. 2.   Measurement Model for Tourism Destination Competitiveness.
Notes: F1 – orientation towards entrepreneurship and hospitality; F2 – natural resources; F3 – recreational and leisure services; F4 – promotional marketing; F5 – inherited resources; F6 – support and other services. The estimates presented have been subject to standardisation (chi-squared = 9.384; DF = 6).

determined by recreational and leisure services (F3), while destination management very strongly influences promotional marketing (F4) and orientation towards entrepreneurship and hospitality (F1).

Through analysis of the results, we may verify the existence of six factors contributing towards the competitiveness of a tourist destination – 'orientation towards entrepreneurship and hospitality', 'natural resources', 'recreational and leisure services', 'promotional marketing', 'inherited resources' and 'support and other services'. Following analysis of each factor, we may conclude that, on the one hand, natural and inherited resources are awarded extremely high values and therefore recognise how comparative advantages are determinant to tourist destinations.

On the other hand, this highlights the importance of competitive advantages generated by entrepreneurial capacities and the levels of hospitality as well as the promotional marketing of the respective tourist destination that effectively helps in ensuring that destination management entities appropriately leverage their comparative advantages (Crouch, 2007; Crouch & Ritchie, 1999; Dwyer & Kim, 2003; Omerzel, 2006). Furthermore, the 'orientation towards entrepreneurship and hospitality' factor highlights not only the contribution made by innovation and entrepreneurialism to competitiveness but also the attractiveness reflected in the feelings contained in the hospitality and communications between residents and tourist visitors.

CONCLUSIONS AND IMPLICATIONS

We believe that the proposed model of competitiveness may contribute to the creation of value through enabling the calculation of the extent of competitiveness of any particular tourist destination and assist in understanding just which factors underpin its performance. This also demonstrates the complexity and multidimensional nature of tourism sector competitiveness as we correspondingly verify how tourist destination competitiveness depends on a combination of various factors ranging from the resources in place and supply through to the destination management carried out by actors undertaking decision-making processes in a country with various regions displaying their own particular characteristics, as is the case with Portugal. Despite this complexity, the competition prevailing between tourism destinations worldwide has never been so fierce and no destination may avoid engaging with this competitive challenge no matter how difficult this might seem.

We find that the competitiveness of a tourist destination stems from its resources, supply and management with these constructs returning a very high level of association, which thus demonstrates how competitive tourism destinations simultaneously depend on both their comparative and their competitive advantages (Dwyer & Kim, 2003).

We would highlight the strong influence of destination management on the supply in effect at tourist destinations thus serving to demonstrate that, irrespective of being endowed with unrivalled environmental landscapes and unique natural resources, replete with culture and history, the destination still needs entrepreneurs committed and proactively providing recreational and leisure, support and other services while also engaging in the promotion appropriate to these same services and in addition to the human warmth encountered at different tourism destinations and reflected in levels of resident hospitality.

At such a particularly challenging point in time for the Portuguese economy, in which competitiveness, or rather the lack of it, is very much the order of the day, the government needs to intervene more directly and effectively through developing and implementing policies and measures fostering entrepreneurship in order to boost regional development. This requires more direct engagement in management actions enacting strategies enabling Portugal to become a tourism destination of excellence and attain more competitive positions in the tourism sector as the country unquestionably holds all the factors necessary to a competitive tourism industry. Tourism represents an important leverage to the internationalisation of any economy and may here contribute to overcoming the much discussed lack of competitiveness.

We would suggest that future research projects apply the proposed model to tourism regional clusters, ascertaining the specific regional differences before making comparisons between regions, thereby ascertaining whether or not regional factors of competitiveness differ from region to region.

REFERENCES

Ahmed, Z., & Krohn, F. (1990). Reversing the United States' declining competitiveness in the marketing of international tourism: A perspective on future policy. *Journal of Travel Research, 29*(2), 23−29.

Arbuckle, J. (1997). *Amos Users' Guide Version 3.6*. Chicago: SmallWaters Corporation.

Bahar, O., & Kozak, M. (2007). Advancing destination competitiveness research: Comparison between tourists and service providers. *Journal of Travel & Tourism Marketing, 22*(2), 61−71.

136   CRISTINA ESTEVÃO ET AL.

Baker, M., Hayzelden, C., & Sussmann, S. (1996). Can destination management systems pro-
    vide competitive advantage? A discussion of the factors affecting the survival and suc-
    cess of destination management systems. *Progress in Tourism and Hospitality Research*,
    2, 1−13.
Bălan, D., Balaure, V., & Veghes, C. (2009). Travel and tourism competitiveness of the world's
    top tourism destinations: An exploratory assessment. *Annales Universitatis Apulensis
    Series Oeconomica*, *11*(2), 979−987.
Botha, C., Crompton, J., & Kim, S. (1999). Developing a revised competitive position for Sun/
    Lost City, South Africa. *Journal of Travel Research*, *37*(4), 341−352.
Buhalis, D. (2000). Marketing the competitive destination of the future. *Tourism Management*,
    21(1), 97−116.
Carmichael, B. (2002). Global competitiveness and special events in cultural tourism: The
    example of the Barnes exhibit at the art gallery of Ontario, Toronto. *The Canadian
    Geographer*, *46*(4), 310−325.
Casadesus-Masanell, R., & Ricart, J. (2010). Competitiveness: Business model reconfiguration
    for innovation and internationalization. *Management Research: The Journal of the
    Iberoamerican Academy of Management*, *8*(2), 123−149.
Chacko, H. (1998). Positioning a tourism destination to gain a competitive edge, Asia. *Pacific
    Journal of Tourism Research*, *1*(2), 69−75.
Chon, K., & Mayer, K. (1995). Destination competitiveness models in tourism and their appli-
    cation to Las Vegas. *Journal of Tourism Systems and Quality Management*, *1*(2/3/4),
    227−246.
Claver-Cortés, E., Molina, J., & Pereira, J. (2007). Competitiveness in mass tourism. *Annals of
    Tourism Research*, *24*(3), 727−745.
Cooke, P., & Morgan, K. (1998). *The associational economy: Firms, regions and innovation*.
    Oxford: OUP.
Costa, C., Rita, P., & Águas, P. (2004). *Tendências Internacionais em Turismo* (2ª Edição).
    Lisboa: Grupo Lidel.
Crouch, G. (2007). *Modelling destination competitiveness: A survey and analysis of the impact
    of competitiveness attributes*. Australia: National Library of Australia Cataloguing in
    Publication Data. ISBN 9781920965389.
Crouch, G., & Ritchie, J. (1999). Tourism, competitiveness, and societal prosperity. *Journal of
    Business Research*, *44*, 137−152.
Desrochers, P., & Sautet, F. (2004). Cluster-based economic strategy, facilitation policy and
    the market process. *Review of Austrian Economics*, *17*(2−3), 233−245.
D'Hautesserre, A. (2000). Lessons in managed destination competitiveness: The case of
    Foxwoods Casino resort. *Tourism Management*, *21*(1), 23−32.
Dwyer, L., Forsyth, P., & Rao, P. (2000a). Price competitiveness of tourism packages to
    Australia: Beyond the 'Big Mac' index. *Asia Pacific Journal of Tourism Research*, *5*(2),
    50−56.
Dwyer, L., Forsyth, P., & Rao, P. (2000b). Sectoral analysis of destination price competitive-
    ness: An international comparison. *Tourism Analysis*, *5*(1), 1−12.
Dwyer, L., Forsyth, P., & Rao, P. (2000c). The price competitiveness of travel and tourism:
    A comparison of 19 destinations. *Tourism Management*, *21*(1), 9−22.
Dwyer, L., Forsyth, P., & Rao, P. (2001). International price competitiveness of Australia's
    MICE industry. *International Journal of Tourism Research*, *3*(2), 123−139.

Dwyer, L., Forsyth, P., & Rao, P. (2002). Destination price competitiveness: Exchange rate changes versus domestic inflation. *Journal of Travel Research, 40*(Feb), 328–336.

Dwyer, L., & Kim, C. (2003). Destination competitiveness: Determinants and indicators. *Current Issues in Tourism, 6*(5), 369–414.

Dwyer, L., Mellor, R., Livaic, Z., Edwards, D., & Kim, C. (2004). Attributes of destination competitiveness: A factor analysis. *Tourism Analysis, 9*, 91–101.

Echtner, C., & Ritchie, J. (2003). The meaning and measurement of destination image. *The Journal of Tourism Studies, 14*(1), 37–48.

ECLAC. (2009). *An econometric study of the determinants of tourism competitiveness in the Caribbean.* Economic Commission for Latin America and the Caribbean, United Nations.

Enright, M., & Newton, J. (2004). Tourism destination competitiveness: A quantitative approach. *Tourism Management, 25*, 777–778.

Enright, M., & Newton, J. (2005). Determinants of tourism destination competitiveness in Asia Pacific: Comprehensiveness and universality. *Journal of Travel Research, 43*(4), 339–350.

Faulkner, B., Oppermann, M., & Fredline, E. (1999). Destination competitiveness: An exploratory examination of South Australia's core attractions. *Journal of Vacation Marketing, 5*(2), 125–139.

Fernando, I., & Long, W. (2012). New conceptual model on cluster competitiveness: A new paradigm for tourism? *International Journal of Business and Management, 7*(9), 75–84.

Ferreira, J., & Estevão, C. (2009). Regional competitiveness of a tourism cluster: A conceptual model proposal. *Tourism & Management Studies, 5*, 37–51.

Go, F., & Govers, R. (2000). Integrated quality management for tourist destinations: A European perspective on achieving competitiveness. *Tourism Management, 21*(1), 79–88.

Gomezelj, D., & Mihalic, T. (2008). Destination competitiveness – Applying different models the case of Slovenia. *Tourism Management, 29*, 294–307.

Gooroochurn, N., & Sugiyarto, G. (2005). Competitiveness indicators in the travel and tourism industry. *Tourism Economics, 11*(1), 25–43.

Hair, J., Anderson, R., Tatham, R., & Black, W. (1998). *Multivariate data analysis* (5th ed.). Upper Saddle River, NJ: Prentice Hall.

Hassan, S. (2000). Determinants of market competitiveness in an environmentally sustainable tourism industry. *Journal of Travel Research, 38*(3), 239–245.

Heath, E. (2003). Towards a model to enhance destination competitiveness: A Southern African perspective. *Journal of Hospitality and Tourism Management, 10*(2), 124–141.

Hudson, S., Ritchie, J., & Timur, S. (2004). Measuring destination competitiveness: An empirical study of Canadian Ski resorts. *Tourism Hospitality Planning and Development, 1*(1), 79–94.

Huybers, T., & Bennett, J. (2003). Environmental management and the competitiveness of nature-based tourism destinations. *Environmental and Resource Economics, 4*, 213–233.

Jamal, T., & Getz, D. (1996). Does strategic planning pay? Lessons for destinations from corporate planning experience. *Progress in Tourism and Hospitality Research, 2*, 59–78.

Kim, C. (2000). *A model development for measuring global competitiveness of the tourism industry in the Asia-Pacific region.* Seoul: Korea Institute for International Economic Policy.

Kim, C., & Dwyer, L. (2003). Destination competitiveness and bilateral flows between Australia and Korea. *Journal of Tourism Studies, 14*(2), 54–67.

Kotler, P., Bowen, J., & Markens, J. (2006). *Marketing for hospitality and tourism*. Upper Saddle River, NJ: Pearson Prentice Hall.

Kozak, M. (2003). Measuring competitive destination performance: A study of Spain and Turkey. *Journal of Travel and Tourism Marketing, 13*(3), 83–110.

Kozak, M., & Rimmington, M. (1999). Measuring tourist destination competitiveness: Conceptual considerations and empirical findings. *Hospitality Management, 18*, 273–283.

Malakauskaite, A., & Navickas, V. (2010). The role of clusters in the formation process of tourism sector competitiveness: Conceptual novelties. *Economics and Management, 15*, 149–154.

March, R. (2004). *A marketing-oriented tool to assess destination competitiveness*. Australia: National Library of Australia Cataloguing in Publication Data. ISBN 1920704124.

Mazanec, J. (1995). Competition among European tourist cities: A comparative analysis with multidimensional scaling and self-organizing maps. *Tourism Economics, 1*(3), 283–302.

Mihalic, T. (2000). Environmental management of a tourist destination: A factor of tourism competitiveness. *Tourism Management, 21*(1), 65–78.

Navickas, V., & Malakauskaite, A. (2009). The possibilities for the identification and evaluation of tourism sector competitiveness factors. *The Economic Conditions of Enterprise Functioning, 1*(6), 37–44.

Omerzel, D. (2006). Competitiveness of Slovenia as a tourist destination. *Managing Global Transitions, 4*(2), 167–189.

Papatheodorou, A. (2002). Exploring competitiveness in Mediterranean resorts. *Tourism Economics, 8*(2), 133–150.

Pearce, D. (1997). Competitive destination analysis in Southeast Asia. *Journal of Travel Research, 35*(4), 16–25.

Porter, M. (1990). *The competitive advantage of nations*. New York, NY: Free Pass.

Porter, M. (1994). *Construir as Vantagens Competitivas de Portugal* (1ª Edição). Lisboa: Fórum para a Competitividade.

Ritchie, J., & Crouch, G. (2010). A model of destination competitiveness/sustainability: Brazilian perspectives, Brazilian. *Public Administration Review, 55*(5), 1049–1066.

Soteriou, E., & Roberts, C. (1998). The strategic planning process in national tourism organizations. *Journal of Travel Research, 37*(1), 21–29.

Stevens, B. (1992). Price value perceptions of travelers. *Journal of Travel Research, 31*(2), 41–48.

Taylor, P. (1995). Measuring changes in the relative competitiveness of package tour destinations. *Tourism Economics, 1*(2), 169–182.

Tsai, H., Song, H., & Wong, K. (2009). Tourism and hotel competitiveness research. *Journal of Travel & Tourism Marketing, 26*, 522–546.

Vengesayi, S. (2003). A conceptual model of tourism destination competitiveness and atractiveness. *ANZMAC Conference Proceedings Adelaide*, 1–3 December (pp. 637–647).

Vengesayi, S. (2005). *Determinants and outcomes of tourism destination competitiveness and destination attractiveness*. PhD Dissertation, Monash University.

WEF – World Economic Forum. (2007). *Furthering the process of economic*. The Travel & Tourism Competitiveness Report 2007. Geneva, Switzerland.

WEF – World Economic Forum. (2008). *Balancing economic development and environmental sustainability*. The Travel & Tourism Competitiveness Report 2008. Geneva, Switzerland.

WEF – World Economic Forum. (2009). *Managing in a time of turbulence*. The Travel & Tourism Competitiveness Report 2009. Geneva, Switzerland.

WEF – World Economic Forum. (2010). *Managing in a time of turbulence*. The Travel & Tourism Competitiveness Report 2010. Geneva, Switzerland.

WEF – World Economic Forum. (2011). *Beyond the downturn*. The Travel & Tourism Competitiveness Report 2011. Geneva, Switzerland.

Wong, W. (2009). Global competitiveness measurement for the tourism sector. *Current Issues in Tourism, 12*(2), 105–132.

WTO, OECD, & United Nation and Commission of The European Communities. (2001). *Tourism satellite account: Recommended methodological framework*. Luxembourg: OECD Publishing.

Zhang, H., Gu, C., Gu, L., & Zhang, Y. (2011). The evaluation of tourism destination competitiveness by TOPSIS and information entropy – A case in the Yangtze river delta of China. *Tourism Management, 32*, 443–451.

EVENTS AS A DIFFERENTIATION STRATEGY FOR TOURIST DESTINATIONS: THE CASE OF *ALLGARVE*

Inês Miranda, Nuno Gustavo and Eugénia Castela

ABSTRACT

The Algarve is a region located in the South of Portugal and is mostly known for its sun and sea product. In order to strengthen the Algarve's competitiveness, the Allgarve program was launched in 2007. We intend to analyze the importance of events as a differentiation factor of tourist destinations. Questions like loyalty, satisfaction, and perception about the event's program are the main subjects analyzed. This study uses data from a questionnaire applied to 224 individuals who attended "street artist events" and pop music concerts in the 2011 edition of the Allgarve program. Two main techniques were applied: OVERALS and k-means. Despite its flaws, positive conclusions were reached, and after its five editions, the program was finally able to be linked to the region's image, distinguishing it in a wide range of cultural events and entertainment.

Keywords: Strategic management of destinations; events; tourist satisfaction; loyalty; Algarve; Allgarve program

Marketing Places and Spaces
Advances in Culture, Tourism and Hospitality Research, Volume 10, 141–153
ISSN: 1871-3173/doi:10.1108/S1871-317320150000010011

INTRODUCTION

In the last few decades, tourism has become one of the main world economic sectors due to all of its potentially significant economic rewards, and
this has emphasized the importance of improving tourism in destinations
(Crouch & Ritchie, 1999). However, the faster emergence of new destinations and products (especially in the case of seaside destinations) has
brought new competitive conditions and led to the implementation of new
repositioning strategies and to the increased emphasis on factors like quality and innovation.

Tourists are looking for new destinations that provide unforgettable experiences. This new logic highlights the importance of creating competitive advantages and imposed a new concept of tourist destination
management. In this context, the conception of a distinctive destination
brand and the creation of alternative attributes have been receiving significant attention (Echtner & Ritchie, 2003). Radisic and Mihelic (2006) argue,
"the best way to express a destination's identity is through a well-crafted
umbrella brand" (p. 183). This process must be developed with previous
knowledge of the needs and expectations of potential tourists. As emphasized by Djurica and Djurica (2010), "the application of marketing strategies enables destinations to meet the tourists' needs better than its
competition" (p. 892).

In this context, events are arising as a competitive key factor, contributing to attracting new tourists, increasing repeated visits to the destination,
and at the same time, satisfying recreational and leisure needs of the host
community. Getz (2007) discusses that events are an important motivator
of tourism and strong demand generators. Faced now with a new increasingly independent and active consumer, who is constantly looking for
authentic and original experiences, events are now more than ever the main
factor that distinguishes destinations.

Strategic destinations management, along with event tourism and the
new consumers' profile, constitutes the main topics of the literature review
of this research.

With the aim of distinguishing the Algarve and making the region more
attractive and competitive, *Allgarve* events program was launched in 2007.
During its five editions, *Allgarve* held events in the following areas: Music,
street artist events, gastronomy, sports, and art. The name "*Allgarve*" was
chosen to embrace the Algarve, not with the purpose of destroying or
replacing the brand or the Algarve designation. The idea was that tourists
could easily understand that besides offering sun and beach, the Algarve

had a coherent and interesting cultural program on offer throughout the year, and it also helped to reduce seasonality. Supported by the slogan "Lifetime Experiences," *Allgarve* events program tried to reposition the Algarve as a sophisticated and glamorous tourist destination.

The Algarve region and the "*Allgarve*" program were selected at an empirical level to analyze the importance of events as a differentiation factor of tourist destinations. Within this context the main research question is: "Will the non-residents in the Algarve, who attended 'street artist events' and pop music concerts in 'Allgarve '11', develop a positive perception of the *Allgarve* brand?" The findings of this study may be useful for improving differentiation strategies in the Algarve and in other similar destinations.

THEORETICAL CONSIDERATIONS

The events industry is still very fresh and has become stronger, especially in the nineties. However, an increasing amount of attention has been focused on the role of events in our societies and especially on destinations. Currently events are central to our culture, probably as never before. "*The event industry is a global industry with significant economic, political, and social impacts*" (Crouch & Ritchie cited by Rompf, Breiter, & Severt, 2009). Events are now supported by governments and are seen as an efficient marketing strategy to differentiate destinations.

Now tourists are interested in the experiences and attractions provided during their stay. As outlined by the European Commission (2000), modern tourists expect to find a range of activities and a variety of experiences in destinations. Besides looking for destinations which satisfy their basic needs they also want to fulfill their personal satisfaction. There is a higher need to escape from the stressful routine and to participate in different activities. The idea is to offer a diversified range of elements contributing to distinguishing destinations from their competitors. Events are so important to destinations because their essence is to offer experiences, not products. As Richards (1992) argued, the variety of experiences offered tends to make the destination more desirable to the visitor.

As argued by Getz (2007) and Richards and Palmer (2010), destinations are developing and promoting events of all kinds to achieve certain objectives: to attract tourists (especially during low season), spread a positive image of the destination, to amuse specific areas or attractions, and to diversify the cultural offer. In that sense, presenting a rich portfolio of events is one of the mechanisms that certainty contributes to reinforcing destination branding.

Also, depending on their strength, events can contribute to tourist loyalty to the destination. Many researchers in the tourism literature underlined the importance of developing a coherent and long-term marketing strategy. According to Jago, Chalip, Brown, Mules, and Ali (2003), an event could make a particularly useful contribution to branding a destination if it were tied to the same destination for 5−10 years.

In particular, coastal destinations are trying to regain their competitiveness through alternative mechanisms (Chootima & Douglas, 2013). Investing in culture and hosting events is a safe investment in order to satisfy the needs of seaside tourists, who are waiting to live unforgettable experiences at the destination.

Satisfaction and Loyalty in Tourist Destinations

If it is so important to manage tourist destinations in a strategic way, it is equally important to make tourists satisfied with their holidays. Why it is so important to ensure tourist satisfaction? Because when a tourist is satisfied, there is a greater chance of being loyal to the destination or of bringing benefits.

In fact, many studies confirmed the relationship between satisfaction obtained during the tourist experience and the intention to recommend trips to others, which subsequently will lead to tourist loyalty to the destination (Alegre & Garau, 2010; Buhalis, 2001; Kozak & Rimmington, 2000; Yoon & Uysal, 2005). The relationship between quality, satisfaction, and loyalty is presented in Fig. 1.

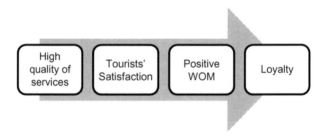

Fig. 1.   Relationship between Quality, Satisfaction, and Loyalty.

Tourists are an excellent vehicle for promoting destinations. When deciding where to travel, recommendations from other people (word of mouth) are one of the most sought after types of information (Ye, Law, Gu, & Chen, 2011).

As Yoon and Uysal (2005) underlined, tourists' positive experiences could produce repeat visits as well as positive word-of-mouth effects for potential tourists such as friends and/or relatives.

It is also important to note that in tourism literature, intention to loyalty can be measured by two variables: "repeated sales or recommendation to other consumers" (Pine, Peppers, & Rogers, 1995).

Consumer satisfaction may be a determinant to make them loyal to the destination and to ensure a competitive place in the market of travel, entertainment, and leisure.

The Algarve as a Tourist Destination

The Algarve is mostly known for its sun and sea product, due to its natural conditions. According to World Travel & Tourism Council (2003), the region benefits from a mild climate with an average of 3,000 hours of sunshine a year. It is one of the favorite holiday destinations in Europe and has national and international prestige. Its economic activity depends strongly on tourism. Also, tourism revenues coming from the region contribute greatly to the local and national economy.

In spite of its popularity, the Algarve is no longer the same competitive region like it was before, facing problems of strong seasonality, the emergence of new competing destinations, and changes in tourists' motivations (Guerreiro, Oom do Valle, & Mendes, 2011). Cruz (2010) also underlined that government authorities have been pointing out the importance of diversifying the tourist offer, with special attention to the cultural offer. The Algarve needs to create added value to distinguish itself from other competitors that are offering much more appealing conditions.

Allgarve Program

With the aim of distinguishing the Algarve and making the region more attractive and competitive, the "*Allgarve* events program" was launched in 2007 by the Ministry of Economy and the Algarve Tourism Board, in collaboration with regional agents. The main purpose of this program was to provide the Algarve with a set of alternative products such as culture, sports, and entertainment, positioning the region as a top tourist destination, associated with glamour and sophistication. In other words, *Allgarve* wanted to strengthen the Algarve's competitiveness showing that the region had much more to offer than sun and beach. Mendes, Oom do Valle, and Guerreiro (2011) argued that the name *Allgarve* was chosen to express the multifaceted character of the Algarve as a tourist destination, aimed at both national and international tourists.

The idea was to embrace the Algarve, not destroy or replace the brand or the Algarve designation. However, the acceptance of the brand was not consensual among some residents of the region, and some controversy was raised around it.

It was mainly directed at international tourists throughout the year, but also the preferences of national tourists were taken into account. However, the residents in the Algarve were the main audience.

Since today's tourists are looking for unforgettable experiences and want to be closer to the culture and values of the local population, *Allgarve* linked its events to historical locations and golf courses, also promoting the region's identity values.

Initially designed for only three years, *Allgarve* lasted five editions, ending in December 2011, and had five thematic areas: music (pop, jazz, and classical), street artist events, gastronomy, sports, and art. Policy and budget issues were the main reasons given to explain the end of the events program.

Supported by the slogan "Lifetime Experiences," *Allgarve* was intended to provide its audience with an unforgettable experience that will make them return and recommend the Algarve to others. It was also the first events program with a regional character (at a European level).

Due to its features, the *Allgarve* program was selected to analyze the importance of creating a diversified and consistent cultural offer in coastal destinations. In spite of ending in 2011, having been on the market for five editions, it allowed us to reach important conclusions, mostly because of its unique regional character.

METHOD

Data for this study were provided by the Algarve Tourism Board and carried out by CEAP (Center for Applied Statistics and Forecast of the Faculty of Economics from Algarve University). The sample comprises 224 non-residents interviewees in the Algarve, who attended "street artist events" and pop music concerts in the 2011 edition of the *Allgarve* program. From these 224 respondents, 113 attended pop music concerts and 111 attended "street artist events." Only these two areas were chosen because they were the most sought out by the audience.

Data Analysis Methods

The application of the software "Statistical Package for the Social Sciences" (SPSS 17.0) in the analysis of the collected data allowed the development of several statistical analyses. Firstly, attending the nature of the survey, organized by nominal or ordinal answers, Nonlinear Canonical Correlation Analysis (*OVERALS*), a multivariate data analysis technique, was one of the methods applied.

Originally described by Gifi (1990), Van der Burg (1988), and Van der Burg, De Leeuw, and Verdegaal (1988), this method is adequate for any type of qualitative variables, allowing the creation of standards, typologies, or topologies. As Yazici, Ögus, Ankarali, and Gurbuz (2010) argued, "*the purpose of OVERALS is to determine how similar sets of categorical variables are to each other.*" This method uses the algorithm *alternating least squares* (ALS) to transform, through optimal scales, categorical variables into metric variables.

There are several ways to measure the association between sets in a nonlinear canonical correlation analysis: the *fit* value (which tells us how well the nonlinear canonical correlation analysis solution fits the optimally quantified data with respect to the association between the sets), the *loss* value (which represents the proportion of variation in the object scores that cannot be accounted. Notice that the average loss is labeled mean) and the *eigenvalue* (which indicates the level of relationship shown by each dimension). Lastly, *weights* and *component loadings* are important too, since they allow for analysis of the relevance of the variables.

We used six variables from the survey and classified them in two sets: *intention to return and to recommend Allgarve events to others and satisfaction about Allgarve events organization* (see Table 1).

On the one hand in the *first set*, the intention variable was chosen not only because it was a loyalty indicator but also because it showed the program's quality. On the other hand, in the *second set* the satisfaction variable was selected with the purpose of verifying the type of relationship between satisfaction and intention to recommend *Allgarve* events to others.

Table 1.   Sets Analyzed.

Set 1 – Intention	Set 2 – Satisfaction about *Allgarve* Events Organization
Do you intend to attend other *Allgarve*'11 events?	Event promotion
Do you recommend *Allgarve* events?	Accessibility Information signage Parking

Also, satisfaction was studied through four variables (event promotion, accessibility, information signage, and parking) which are very important in the creation of the consumer's perception of events. Finally, it is also important to note that the variables from *set 1* are nominal dichotomous in contrast to the variables from *set 2*, graded on a five-point Likert-type scale (1 = completely disagree; 5 = completely agree).

After the *sets* definition, the OVERALS method allowed the obtainment of detailed information about data structure, finding similarities and relationships between these two variable groups, and from there realizing which are the most relevant variables for the analyzed audience.

Secondly, attending the type of the variables analyzed and the size of the sample, we also applied another method named *k-means* (nonhierarchical cluster analysis) in order to find clusters with similar behavior to the selected variables via OVERALS. As Davidson (2002) argued, the k-means algorithm is a popular approach to finding clusters due to its simplicity of implementation and fast execution. In this particular study, the main goal of using this technique was to understand if there is a relationship between satisfaction with events' promotion and the intention to recommend them to family and friends. Three clusters were created to identify which was the most relevant.

At the least, it was also possible to make a description of this audience, as well as their recommendations, suggestions, and preferences in order to determine their perception regarding the *Allgarve* brand. For that purpose, respondents were asked to associate one or two words to the *Allgarve* brand.

FINDINGS

For OVERALS analysis, the databases were worked on together. However, 13 respondents were removed from the sample because they did not answer all questions. So, this specific method was carried out on a sample of 211 respondents.

With the application of the OVERALS method, the intention was to meet two main objectives: (i) to determine the degree of dependence between the sets created and (ii) to identify the most relevant variables within each group. To achieve the first goal, it is necessary to analyze the *fit* and *loss* functions and compare them with the number of dimensions in order to evaluate the explanatory capacity of the model.

Loss values, eigenvalues, and *fit* values are presented in Table 2. OVERALS analysis produced two canonical relationships represented by dimensions 1 and 2. Eigenvalues obtained from the study were quite high (0.765 and 0.746). An actual fit value of 1.511, which is the sum of eigenvalues, was calculated for variation. For both sets we can verify a mean loss of 0.489 (2 − 1.511). Summation of average loss and fit is equal to the number of dimensions (0.489 + 1.511 = 2).

We also concluded that in the first dimension, there is a significant dependence (53%) between the two sets and a lesser dependence (49.2%) in the second dimension.

To meet the second goal we analyzed the values of *weights, component loadings,* and *multiple fit.* We found that the most relevant variables (which fulfilled all OVERALS criteria) were *"recommend Allgarve events"* and *"satisfaction about Allgarve organization − events' promotion."* Among the six variables, these two were the only ones that showed higher values in the same dimension. In this context, 59.2% from the sample were satisfied/very satisfied with the promotion of the events. In other words, that means that the individuals who were satisfied intended to recommend *Allgarve* events to others. OVERALS analysis proved to be a quite useful method in data structure interpretation, revealing similarities and relational structures among multi-dimensional categorical variable sets.

Table 2. Summary of Overals Analysis in SPSS.

		Dimension		Sum
		1	2	
Loss	Set 1	0.184	0.320	0.504
	Set 2	0.286	0.188	0.474
	Mean	0.235	0.254	*0.489*
Eigenvalue		*0.765*	*0.746*	
Fit				*1.511*

Given the importance of the relationship between satisfaction and intention to recommend to others, in the success of the destinations/events, we
chose to apply the *k-means* method. Our aim is finding groups (clusters) of
respondents with a similar opinion in relation to the most relevant variables
found from the OVERALS method.

Three clusters were created to identify which was the most relevant.
From these, we concluded that all of the 191 satisfied interviewees revealed
the intention to recommend *Allgarve* events to family and friends, as well as
the fact that 111 of them had the intention to return and participate again.

From all the methods applied (including descriptive analysis) we concluded that the greater part of the interviewees who were satisfied with
events' organization had the intention to return and to recommend
Allgarve's events to family and friends. This fact highlights the existence of
a direct relationship between satisfaction and word of mouth.

Finally, about the recommendations, suggestions, and preferences we
also concluded that the interviewees understood the message spread by
the *Allgarve* brand and associated positive words meeting the values and
the goals initially defined. They also believe that Allgarve contributes to the
growth and diversity of the Algarve's cultural offer and that it can differentiate the region. However, they suggested improvements at the promotional level.

CONCLUSION AND IMPLICATIONS

From the descriptive analyses of the collected data, it was concluded that
despite a low rate of participation in previous editions of *Allgarve*, satisfaction levels were higher in relation to the lived experience. This low loyalty
can be explained by two main reasons: only the non-resident interviewees
were analyzed, excluding the residents in the Algarve (who were the main
audience of the program), and also the absence of a coherent long-term
management strategy. Effectively, managing a destination brand in a competitive and demanding market takes time and persistence (Jago et al.,
2003; Richards, 2010; Tasci & Denizci, 2009).

The application of OVERALS and of the k-means method supported
the relationship between satisfaction and intention to recommend the
experience to others, which emphasized the importance of these variables
for successful brand management. In general, the audience built a positive

perception about the program, recognizing its prestige, attractiveness, and capacity, contributing to the growth and diversity of the Algarve's cultural offer.

Despite its flaws — mostly at the promotion level — positive conclusions were reached, and after its five editions, the program was finally able to be linked to the region's image, distinguishing it in a wide range of cultural events and entertainment.

This research has some limitations that should be mentioned. Firstly, the study focuses only on "street artist events" and pop music concerts, excluding other areas of the *Allgarve* program. Secondly, the opinions of the residents in the Algarve were not taken into account. Thirdly, there was an absence of an offer analysis. It would have been interesting to evaluate the opinions of hotels, restaurants, and local trade, regarding the *Allgarve* program.

Despite of its limitations, this paper may contribute to future research lines, especially at marketing and communication levels. Planning strategies at a regional level to improve event promotion along with the creation of new alternative attributes to refresh mature tourist destinations should be taken into account by tourism managers.

We can also conclude that events are an important mechanism for the differentiation of tourist destinations and should be integrated into strategic management. "Events are of increasing importance for destination competitiveness" (Getz, 2007).

Without the "*Allgarve* events program," the Algarve is still trying to regain its competitiveness in the tourism market. Now each local authority is making its own events program according to their possibilities and cultural designs, not always valuing the Algarve's identity because there is no coherent strategy.

If it is true that tourists didn't come to the Algarve because they were attracted by the *Allgarve* brand, it is also true that this study reveals that a consistent and appealing events program, planned and managed at the regional level, can be a determinant for the differentiation of a tourist destination.

REFERENCES

Alegre, J., & Garau, J. (2010). Tourist satisfaction and dissatisfaction. *Annals of Tourism Research, 37*(1), 52–73.

Buhalis, D. (2001). Introduction: Tourism demand and competitiveness in the globalization era. In S. Wahab & C. Cooper (Eds.), *Tourism in the age of globalization* (Vol. 10, pp. 69−96). London: Routledge.

Chootima, L., & Douglas, G. (2013). Managing a mature coastal destination: Pattaya, Thailand. *Journal of Destination Marketing & Management, 2*(3), 165−175.

Crouch, G., & Ritchie, J. (1999). Tourism, competitiveness, and societal prosperity. *Journal of Business Research, 44*(3), 137−152.

Cruz, R. (2010). *Tourism and creativity in the Algarve: An analysis of regional tourist offer as an attractor to the creative class.* MSc thesis, University of the Algarve, Portugal.

Davidson, I. (2002). *Understanding k-means non-hierarchical clustering.* Technical Report. SUNY, Albany, NY.

Djurica, M., & Djurica, N. (2010). *Tourism destinations marketing management.* Tourism & Hospitality Management, Conference Proceedings (pp. 890−901).

Echtner, C., & Ritchie, J. (2003). The meaning and measurement of destination image. *The Journal of Tourism Studies, 14*(1), 37−48.

European Commission. (2000). *Towards quality coastal tourism.* Brussels: Author.

Getz, D. (2007). Event tourism: Definition, evolution, and research. *Tourism Management, 29*(3), 403−428.

Gifi, A. (1990). *Nonlinear multivariate analysis.* Chichester: Wiley.

Guerreiro, M., Oom do Valle, P., & Mendes, J. (2011). Allgarve events: Implications for the Algarve image. *Original Scientific Paper, 59*(2), 183−202.

Jago, L., Chalip, L., Brown, G., Mules, T., & Ali, S. (2003). Building events into destinations branding: Insights from experts. *Event Management, 8*(1), 3−14.

Kozak, M., & Rimmington, M. (2000). Tourist satisfaction with Mallorca, Spain, as an off-season holiday destination. *Journal of Travel Research, 38*(3), 260−269.

Mendes, J., Oom do Valle, P., & Guerreiro, M. (2011). Destination image and events: A structural model for the Algarve case. *Journal of Hospitality Marketing & Management, 20* (3−4), 366−384.

Pine, B., Peppers, D., & Rogers, M. (1995). Do you want to keep your customers forever? *Harvard Business Review, 73*(2), 103−114.

Radisic, B., & Mihelic, B. (2006). The tourist destination brand. *Tourism and Hospitality Management, 12*(2), 183−189.

Richards, B. (1992). *How to market tourist attractions, festivals and special events: A practical guide to maximising visitor attendance and income.* Harlow: Longman.

Richards, G. (2010). Increasing the attractiveness of places through cultural resources. *Tourism, Culture & Communication, 10*(1), 47−58.

Richards, G., & Palmer, R. (2010). *Eventful cities: Cultural management and urban revitalization.* Oxford, UK: Elsevier.

Rompf, P., Breiter, D., & Severt, K. (2009). Destination selection criteria: Key success factors evolve and dominate. *Event Management, 12*(1), 27−38.

Tasci, A., & Denizci, B. (2009). Destination branding input−output analysis: A method for evaluating productivity, *Tourism Analysis, 14*, 65−83.

Van der Burg, E. (1988). *Nonlinear canonical correlation and some related techniques.* Leiden: DSWO Press.

Van der Burg, E., De Leeuw, J., & Verdegaal, R. (1988). Homogeneity analysis with k sets of variables: An alternating least squares method with optimal scaling features. *Psychometrika, 53*, 177−197.

World Travel & Tourism Council. (2003). *The Algarve — The impact of travel and tourism on jobs and the economy.* Oxford, UK: Author.

Yazici, A., Ögus, E., Ankarali, H., & Gurbuz, F. (2010). An application of nonlinear canonical correlation analysis on medical data. *Tubitak, 40*(3), 503—510.

Ye, Q., Law, R., Gu, B., & Chen, W. (2011). The influence of user-generated content on traveler behavior: An empirical investigation on the effects of e-word-of-mouth to hotel online bookings. *Computers in Human Behavior, 27*(2), 634—639.

Yoon, Y., & Uysal, M. (2005). An examination of the effects of motivation and satisfaction on destination loyalty: A structural model. *Tourism Management, 26*(1), 45—56.

FROM TOURISM SPACE TO A UNIQUE TOURISM PLACE THROUGH A CONCEPTUAL APPROACH TO BUILDING A COMPETITIVE ADVANTAGE

Kamila Borseková, Anna Vaňová and
Katarína Petríková

ABSTRACT

The main aim of the chapter is to propose a conceptual approach for the creation, exploitation and building of a competitive advantage through which it would be possible to create a unique place from tourism space. In the chapter we present theoretical basement for the issue of competitive advantage at the level of places, its types, factors and approaches for its creating, building and exploiting. In the chapter we specify one main hypothesis and one research question. They are verified through several scientific, statistical and mathematical methods. These methods are used for the evaluation of primary and secondary research results. In the final part of the chapter, a conceptual approach for identification and

Marketing Places and Spaces
Advances in Culture, Tourism and Hospitality Research, Volume 10, 155–172
Copyright © 2015 by Emerald Group Publishing Limited
All rights of reproduction in any form reserved
ISSN: 1871-3173/doi:10.1108/S1871-317320150000010012

exploitation of competitive advantage aimed at building unique and competitive places was proposed.

Keywords: Competitive advantage; conceptual approach; unique tourism place

INTRODUCTION

Several researches (Borseková, 2012; Ministry of Transport, Development and Regional Development of Slovak Republic, 2013; Pompurová, 2011) have showed that Slovakia and its regions have a huge potential for the development of tourism and a potential to become a strong tourism destination. This potential is still not being fully used and needs to be unlocked. The attractiveness of tourism destinations is possible to really increase only through the improvement of the tourism offer and its presentation in the targeted market. Lehu (2004, p. 68) explains the term attractiveness as the ability to attract larger or smaller number of customers. The attractiveness of a tourist destination means a competitive advantage of the territory which has a potential for tourism and is able to provide conditions for tourism development. The attractiveness should be expressed in relation to visitors' decision relating to the goal and purpose of their travel and stay. According to Buhalis (2000), the attractiveness is the key to influencing the competitive advantage of a tourism destination and also influences the economic effects arising from consumption of goods and services on its territory.

According to World Tourism Organisation UNWTO, world tourism currently contributes to 30% of the world services export, creates 9% of GDP and creates over 8% of the jobs. In the most well-developed countries, tourism development brings significant economic benefits. The tourism sector has an ability to create conditions for the development of other related sectors of the national economy. There exists a positive relationship between the tourism sector and labour market because the tourism is a sector with a significant absorption capacity of the unneeded excess labour from primary and secondary sectors. In Slovakia, there are a lot of possibilities for the development of tourism which are not fully exploited. However, the positive influence of tourism on the development of national and regional economies is clear and indisputable.

The most important questions which led to writing this chapter are the following: Are the representatives of regional self-governments able to identify correctly the competitive advantages in tourism within their regions —

to identify and exploit a potential of space? Are the regions able to use their advantages and transform them into real competitive advantages – create a unique tourism place? What are the most important factors that influence use or non-use of tourism competitive advantages on the regional level?

Following the general process of globalization in the world, strengthening of international cooperation in tourism has occurred at the end of the 20th century. This process was accompanied by liberalization of labour movement and growth of competitive environment. The development of tourism requires new approaches and appropriate measures at all levels. The globalization trends need to be respected also by countries of middle Europe which have to be part of globalization. The main role of tourism is and will be a preservation of national identity in Slovakia as one of the essential elements of a competitive advantage (The New Strategy of Development Slovak Republic Tourism for 2020). We absolutely agree with this statement and to our opinion tourism in Slovak regions has to be built on unique regional competitive advantages based on internal resources, such as natural potential, history, culture and traditions supported by the high quality of human resources.

According to UNWTO in 2020 the fastest growing region in tourism will be in Central and South-Eastern Europe. This is also a chance for the Slovak Republic to stand out of the shadow and become a real unique tourist destination. The Ministry of Transport, Construction and Regional Development of the Slovak Republic sets the strategic aim for tourism development in Slovak Republic for this decade as 'a need of increasing competitiveness of tourism by better exploitation of its potential with intent to balance regional disparities and create new jobs'. The Slovak Republic is typical of post-transitional economies of Central and Eastern Europe; with the collapse of the command economy system, many communities are facing a decline in industrial activity while a single destination enjoys rapid growth. This is especially the case for Slovakia as an agglomeration is being formed around the capital of Bratislava. The unique topographical layout of the country is also enhancing this agglomeration as it is extending up the Vah river valley to form what can be called the Bratislava-Zilina corridor (Cole, 2009).

The main scientific aim of the chapter is closely connected with the strategic aim of the Slovak Republic for tourism development. In the chapter we offer the conceptual approach to development of tourism in Slovak regions through proper identification and exploitation of a regional competitive advantage based on internal resources, especially natural potential, history, culture and traditions.

Our basic assumption that Slovakia has a huge potential for tourism development was confirmed by one of the world tourist guide leaders Lonely Planet that ranked Slovakia in the top 10 countries for travelling in the year 2013. The other very important advantage is that the second biggest city in Slovakia – Košice is the European capital of culture for 2013 together with French city Marseille. These two aspects help Slovakia to promote itself and to attract more domestic and especially foreign tourists to Slovakia.

Even if there is a really huge tourism potential in Slovak regions we would like to underline that unique tourism potential is not being used efficiently and there are gaps which need to be filled. In the chapter we offer the proposal of a conceptual approach to building a unique tourist destination based on regional competitive advantage stemming from unique internal resources. This approach also corresponds with the strategic priorities in Europe 2020 and supports smart, sustainable and inclusive growth. We choose this topic because the tourism competitive advantage on the regional level is the subject of our several research projects, for example, VEGA 1/0680/14 Creative industries delivering the crucial intangibles to public sector in context of innovation and smart growth and to our mind there is not enough attention being paid to this topic, especially in post-transitive countries.

LITERATURE REVIEW

According to Martin (2002), there is no single, all containing economic or economic-geographic, theory providing a generally acceptable definition and explanation of regional competitiveness and regional competitive advantage. The issue of a competitive advantage is a well-researched topic on the level of enterprises and partially on the level of nations or state, but only a few authors deal with this topic on the regional level. In the theory, three basic approaches to a competitive advantage have been identified. There are a market-orientated approach to competitive advantage (Kotler, 1992; Porter, 1994; Vaňová, 2006), an approach of competitive advantage based on resources (Barney, 1991, 1997; Hall, 1993; Pfeffer, 1994; Powel, 1992; Ulrich & Lake, 1991) and a marketing-orientated approach to competitive advantage (Barney, 1997; Kotler & Armstrong, 1992; Porter, 1999; Solomon, Marshall, & Stuart, 2006).

Between the market-oriented approach of a competitive advantage and approach of competitive advantage based on resources, there is a potential conflict because a market-oriented approach is based on its impacts, opportunities and resources that result from the external environment and their applications to the market. The approach of the competitive advantage based on resources is based on the internal environment of the region and internal resources are considered as essential. The basic differences among these two approaches are shown in Table 1.

A compromise between these two approaches is an approach based on the value networks, which should be considered as the third approach to a competitive advantage (McPhee & Wheeler, 2006). According to this approach, building of a sustainable competitive advantage is based on the positioning of subject in value networks. By this approach building of the sustainable competitive advantage is based on the positioning of subject in value networks. The required market position can be achieved through the competitive advantage of the place. The basic term of this approach is the value expected by the customer, which gives the ratio to what the customer gets, with what they have to do to obtain the desire product or service. In addition, what the customer receives is understood as the expected benefits which the product, service or its associated service brings. Furthermore, what the customer needs to spend to obtain the product or service can be understood as being direct and indirect costs that customer sacrificed in favour of a desired product (Hollensen, 2010, pp. 28–35).

This approach to a competitive advantage corresponds to most marketing concepts, in particular marketing places. Kotler defines marketing places as 'a set of activities aimed on creation, maintain or change of attitudes and behaviour to certain places. The aim of marketing places is to attract to some place, region or state new inhabitants, tourists or investors'

Table 1. Comparison of Approaches to the Competitive Advantage.

	Market-Orientated Approach	Resources-Based Approach
Basic principles	Resources adapts to the demands of the competitive environment, according to key success factors	Pro-active searching of such kind of environment which allows the best utilization of resources
Strategic analysis	Focus on sectorial structure and market attributes	Emphasis on internal analysis and conditions
Formulation process	From external environment→ inside	From internal environment→ outside
Sources of competitive advantage	Market position in relation to local competitive environment	Specific unique set of resources, potential and competences

Source: Hollensen (2010, p. 34).

(1992, p. 482). Vaňová defines marketing places as 'a continuous social management process which provides the ability to influence more effective sustainable development of the place through building sustainable competitive advantage by creating synergies among demand and supply by using specific marketing methods and tools' (2006, p. 36).

Marketing places is based on the innovative approach to the development of places – strategic marketing planning. It is needed to note that 'management of strategic marketing planning in conditions of places is much more difficult than in conditions of private companies' (Kotler, 1992, p. 106). The competitive advantage of the place is an important basis for taking the position in the market, as it makes the place more attractive. It is often a basis for setting marketing goals. Entry superiority over the competition became the core of marketing strategies that are not oriented only for customer satisfaction (Borseková & Vaňová, 2011, p. 3). Based on Porter (1999) creating the competitive advantage of a place can be considered as the core of places development. A successful place development strategy can be created by finding unique opportunities and possibilities that should bring to the place a strong competitive advantage.

The competitive advantage of the place grows in principle from the value that the place is able to create for its customers and at the same time this value exceeds costs needed for its creation. Value is what brings customers to the place greater benefit than the value offered by competing places. This offering can be of a lower price than a competing place of the same value, or in providing something special, unique or specific or certain benefits which compensate for the higher price (Porter, 1994).

The marketing concept argues that for achieving success in the market, subjects have to provide higher value and customer satisfaction than the offerings of the competition (Saloner, Shepard, & Podolny, 2001). The role of marketing specialist is therefore to do something more than just to adapt to the needs of target customers. The link between strategic marketing planning and competitive advantage is so strong that the development of a marketing strategy is often defined as searching for the competitive advantage. According to Vaňová, 'the role of strategic marketing planning is to ensure the satisfaction of commercial and non-commercial needs, requirements and expectations of existing and potential customers of the place through evaluation and optimal exploitation of place potential' (Vaňová, 2006, pp. 55–56).

We considered this approach to competitive advantage as a suitable compromise of the first two approaches, which is also well applicable to the conditions of places and development of tourism. Through strategic marketing planning and several marketing analyses which are a part of this process there are possibilities to exploit the existing tourism potential more efficiently and to build from the region a unique marketing tourism place. This approach remains consistent with the contemporary approach to territorial development, putting emphasis on specific resources, which are rooted into regional context and 'territorially tied' (Sokołowicz, 2012, p. 19). In the regions or places that are tourist destinations, often, instead of using the term competitive advantage, the term 'unique selling proposition' or 'unique selling point' is used by King (2010), Lupberger (2009), O´Leary (2000). These two terms will be considered as synonyms in our chapter. The origin of this term dates back to the forties of the 20th century when the theory of unique selling proposition was created as a new concept to promote unique products or services that bring some kind of advantage to its producers.

Originally this theory was created for corporate environment but it can also be relatively easily applied to the conditions of places like cities or regions. For the purpose of our chapter we understand that the unique selling point of the overall product place or partial products of the place which differ from other competing places and bring unique position for this place in the market. The unique selling feature can thus be understood as, in the true sense, the competitive advantage, that is to say, it is something special and unique, which differentiates the place from its competitors. In case of places as tourist destinations we understand that it is some type of unique natural environment, culture, architecture, regional gastronomy, lifestyle, traditions etc.

METHODOLOGY

In the chapter, we specify one main hypothesis, which is based on the literature review and will be verified in the conditions of the Slovak Republic. Destination management and marketing should act as tools and facilitators to achieve a complex range of strategic objectives, which will ultimately need to satisfy the needs and wants of stakeholders. Tourism marketing should operate as a mechanism to facilitate regional development objectives and to rationalize the provision of tourism in order to ensure that the strategic objective of the destinations are achieved (Buhalis, 2000). The aim of regional development and destination marketing is to build the partnerships at a local level targeting the attainment of the competitive advantage in a global market (Soteriades, 2012; Stimson, Stough, & Nijkamp, 2011).

One of the most important challenges for destination marketing management is to bring all individual partners together to cooperate and to pool the resources towards developing an integrated marketing mix and delivery system (Buhalis & Cooper, 1998; Fayos-Sola, 1996; Garmise, 2006). In other words, it is necessary to develop a comprehensive destination plan that should respect and evolve all factors of internal and external environment, especially the human resources, which help identifying the uniqueness of a destination — the competitive advantage.

Hypothesis 0. The conceptual approach to building the unique tourist destination based on internal regional competitive advantage involving all local and regional stakeholders is missing in most Slovak regions.

The importance of human resources, especially in the form of networks, clusters and partnership of various stakeholders in the tourism destination, declares the studies of many authors (Hall, 2005; Michael, 2003; Pike, 2004; Ryan, 2002; Tinsley, 2007). Destination marketing partnerships are important because most destinations have to compete in a global world (Soteriades, 2012). The partnerships and its quality influenced by human resources bring various positive benefits in tourism destinations including an increase in competitiveness of the regional tourism industry and sustainable competitive advantage (Michael, 2003; Poon, 2002; Saxena, 2005). Referring to the theory, the following research question has been settled: RQ: What is the decisive factor for the exploitation of the competitive advantage in the tourism destinations?

The research question and hypothesis are verified through a number of scientific methods as analogy, analysis and synthesis of knowledge gained by extensive secondary and empirical research. For verifying the hypothesis we also used the comparison, deduction and methods of descriptive statistics as non-parametric equivalent of two-factor analysis of variance for ordinal data-Friedman's test, depending test using chi-square test statistic etc.

Empirical research was realized in three phases as shown in Fig. 1.

In the first phase, we realized a pre-research in all NUTS three regions in Slovakia through a questionnaire. In the second phase we realized a questionnaire survey by the Delphi method with an expert group consisting of domestic and foreign experts. The third phase of empirical research was realized through structured interviews with managers and employers of all Slovak regional self-governments. The respondents were from the departments of regional development, tourism and culture and create expert group of respondents in each Slovak region. First and third phases are

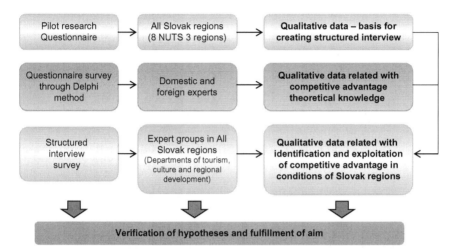

Fig. 1. Empirical Research of the Chapter. *Source*: Own workmanship.

interconnected and this research was realized on the sample of core set – all NUTS three regions in the Slovak Republic. The second phase of the research was aimed on acquiring of theoretical knowledge related to the issue of competitive advantage on the territorial level. Results from the second phase helped us by creating structured interviews realized in the third phase.

FINDINGS

The first part of the empirical research was aimed at identifying the competitive advantage. All asked respondents were able to identify competitive advantage and each person from expert groups specifies what is considered a competitive advantage or advantages. Among the competitive advantages of the Slovak regions most frequently appeared were the competitive advantage based on resources, competitive advantages of low cost and competitive advantage of differentiation. Identification of five competitive advantages was repeated in most of the Slovak regions. These competitive advantages are rich water resources, culture and historical heritage, qualitative human resources, location and natural potential.

The only one competitive advantage which occurs in the answers of respondents in all Slovak regions is a culture and historical heritage. The second most mentioned competitive advantages are rich water resources and location, then natural potential. The results of our empirical research showed that a competitive advantage is considered as important for the development of places by 100% of asked experts. Overall, 71% of all respondents in Slovak regions reported that their regions and places do not use its competitive advantage or advantages sufficiently. They also said there is a space for better and more efficient exploitation of the competitive advantages. This number is extremely high and we unfortunately believe that it reflects real situation in the Slovakia.

One part of empirical research was aimed at evaluation of factors influencing creation, building and exploitation of the competitive advantage. The importance of regional competitive advantage factors has not been investigated in the Slovak Republic yet. Factors of competitive advantage were chosen from the literature (Porter, 1999, 1994; Švantnerová, 2005; Vaňová, 2006, 2010). The importance of the factors was verified through Friedman test. Friedman test is a non-parametric test similar to two-factor analysis of variance with one observation in the subclass. The input data are arranged in a matrix of k rows and n columns.

Friedman test statistic has the following form:

$$F = \frac{12}{nk(k+1)} \; R - 3n(k+1) \quad R = \sum_{j=1}^{k} \left(\sum_{i=1}^{n} Rx_{ij} \right)^2$$

where n means the sample size, which is the same for all selections; k is the number of selections; R is the final order totals in columns brought to a square. The average order of importance of factors of the region's competitive advantage as a result of Friedman's test is shown in Table 2.

A comparison of the factor's importance of the region's competitive advantage based on the results of questionnaires and structured interviews using the Friedman statistic test showed that groups of experts from both parts of the survey considered the most important factor of competitive advantage, that is, the qualitative human resources. Results of this partial research give answer for our research question and showed that the most important factor for identification, exploitation and building of competitive advantage are qualitative human resources. The average order of importance shows that the second ranked factor for an expert in a questionnaire survey is knowledge infrastructure; further factors are innovation and

Table 2. Factors of Competitive Advantage of the Regions.

Factors of Competitive Advantage of the Region	The Average Order of Importance of Competitive Advantage Factors According to the Results of Structured Interviews	The Average Order of Importance of Competitive Advantage Factors According to the Results of Questionnaires
Quality of human resources	12.83	20.68
Knowledge infrastructure	12.67	19.56
Location	12.65	14.62
Creative potential	12.46	18.38
Information about the region	12.04	15
Quality of management in the region	12.04	13.92
Natural and geographical potential	11.63	14.62
Financial resources of the region	11.42	13.56
Innovation and innovation potential	11.27	18.47
Regional culture	10.96	11.94
Socio-demographic potential	10.29	15.23
The economic potential of the region	10.23	15.62
Socio-cultural potential	10.19	13.45
Development strategy for the region	10.02	11.91
Basic infrastructure	9.58	18.26
Foreign investment	9.58	10.27
Technological infrastructure	9.42	16.38
Market demand	8.71	9.23
Competition	8.56	12.83
Influence of central government	7.73	9.38
Chance (random effects)	5.31	8.32

Source: Own workmanship according to results of empirical research

innovation potential, creative potential and basic infrastructure. The average order of importance shows that the second ranked factor for an expert in a structured interviews survey in all Slovak regions is knowledge infrastructure, then location and further creative potential. Experts groups in both cases consider the least important factor of competitive advantage random effects or chance.

Empirical research was also aimed at processing of exploitation competitive advantage in planning and strategic documents. Overall, 58% of respondents within the expert groups indicated that their competitive advantages are processed in some kind of strategic or planning documents, 42% of respondents said they do not work with competitive advantage within these kinds of documents. According to 69% of answers, the most common document with the processing of identification and exploitation of the competitive advantage was the Program of economic and social development (PESD). We studied PESD of all Slovak regions and also all other documents which were mentioned (especially strategies for development of tourism and strategies for the development of culture on the local or regional level). Most of these documents, plans or concepts have processed analysis SWOT with strengths for selected areas, but most of these documents have analytical character. They are mainly focused on identification of problem areas in the territories, but a comprehensive approach for solutions to these problems through exploitation of competitive advantage is not included in any of them.

Within structured interviews we also asked expert groups about what they see problems of insufficient exploitation of the competitive advantage. Experts from regional self-governments (96 %) experts from the regional self-governments said they would welcome a methodological approach of identification and exploitation of a competitive advantage at the regional level which would help them in their work. All these research results confirmed our hypotheses that conceptual approach for identification and exploitation of a competitive advantage is missing. The research results also show that a proposal is needed and would be helpful in conditions of regional self-governments.

Primary and secondary research showed that in Slovak regions there are huge gaps in exploitation of regional competitive advantage in tourism caused especially by the lack of methodology and knowledge about the competitive advantage and its importance. According to several analyses, one of the biggest problems in Slovak tourism is that in Slovakia there is a lack of competent management on the local and regional level. It is quite fragmented without specifically designated authorities and responsibilities with a low level of cooperation. One of the tools that can be used for the sustainable development of tourism based on a competitive advantage is the development in education of labour employed in tourism. In this process, universities play an important role.

In the case of Slovak regions we emphasize the importance of public authorities in tourism development and the importance of a conceptual and concentred regional planning and management. The conceptual and integrated approach linking all stakeholders and all levels (national, regional and local) is more than needed. In the chapter we offer the marketing-based approach for identification and exploitation of potential regional competitive advantages in tourism and transformation of them into the real competitive advantages. In the same way, this approach leads to the creation of unique marketing places and development of tourism.

CONCLUSIONS AND IMPLICATIONS

An innovative and marketing-orientated approach to the development of tourism based on exploitation of a unique regional competitive advantage offers new possibilities for increasing employment, creating new jobs, attracting tourists and inhabitants, development of tourism-orientated entrepreneurs and overall social-economic development.

The first very important step in this approach is to identify the competitive advantage or potential competitive advantage of the region in tourism correctly. In the process of its identification, stakeholders should assume that a competitive advantage is a special, unique and exceptional quality, ability or characteristic, which represents a value for the customers of the place, in our case especially tourists (domestic or foreign). This specific, unique and exceptional quality, ability or characteristic can be identified in a place through bringing significant benefits to the place and making its position better in the market compared to competing places or competing tourist destinations. The competitive advantage should be identified through four partial analyses. To identify a competitive advantage is possible through analysis of the internal and external environment, market analysis and analysis of the competition. A SWOT analysis can be used to assist in identifying the competitive advantages, particularly the strengths. Identified strengths of the territory can serve as a basis for building unique places.

According to our research regions of the Slovak Republic prepared SWOT analysis in strategic and planning documents, which is positive. As a problem we perceive the fact that the SWOT analysis in most cases does not fulfil their functions in Slovak regions. Most SWOT analyses in Slovak regions have the general character. Strengths are not presented in order of importance, they are only listed. We recommend connecting the items according to their importance. Then it is possible to identify which strengths are strongest and thus represent a potential competitive advantage, or benefit, with the potential to become a real competitive advantage. Attributes of the competitive advantage also need to be considered for identification such as uniqueness, sustainability and profitability. The competitive advantage should be in compliance with market needs and in consistent with the external environment. The competitive advantage would arise in conditions of an imperfect competition.

The next step is an identification of the specific type and kind of competitive advantage and subsequently to select the suitable strategy for exploitation of the competitive advantage. The chosen strategy should be consistent with the vision, strategic aims and intent of the places. Considering all these aspects, places represented by its management together with all relevant stakeholders can choose from these types of strategies aimed at the creation, exploitation and building a competitive advantage which helps to create unique places from the spaces. Market-orientated competitive advantage is focused on cost or differentiation. In identifying market-based competitive advantage it should be taken into account that this kind of competitive advantage is greatly influenced by the external environment (opportunities and threats). By this approach, for sustainability of the competitive advantage it is necessary to innovate constantly, improve and move the target of the place.

The first kind of competitive advantage is a low-cost competitive advantage. The place reaches this competitive advantage if it is able to provide its customers with greater or equal value of the total product, or partial products at a lower price than the competing places. The conditions for the implementation this strategy are sensitivity of target market segments to change of prices and the inability to imitate low prices by competition. The competitive advantage of differentiation means that the place will provide an overall product or partial product/products, which is unique for customers and these represent the target segment. Due to the uniqueness of this type of product, the customer accepts a higher price, which is given by the unique supply. Under the competitive advantage of differentiation in terms of place, we therefore understand the specific or unique feature, which has the place at the level of product or sub-products and the unique feature (the ability, character) gives consumers a better value compared to competing places. In the case where the place has identified its competitive advantage, an advantage of differentiation should then be chosen for its continued use as one of differentiation strategies.

The choice of this strategy and its successful implementation have to meet the following conditions: the place offers a unique product at the overall product or partial product(s); the place meets the different needs of customers; the place must be able to adapt to market needs; competition of the places focuses on all segments of the market. By choosing the strategy of differentiation one may choose whether to focus on all target segments (undifferentiated strategy of differentiation), or choose just one or only a few target segments (differentiation strategy). Usually the costs are higher in undifferentiated strategy, but the efficiency of the response segments is also higher (Vaňová, 2006). The advantage of strategy of differentiation applied to places conditions is that the name of the place is also the brand. In case that the place has a good image, the place's customers are less sensitive to price changes. A positive fact can be taken that in the case of customer's satisfaction; they like to come back to the area which creates customer loyalty to the place, which significantly limits the entry of new competitors in the area. In case of low-cost competitive advantages, there is a risk that competing place will be able to imitate this competitive advantage (Vaňová, 2006).

The second type of competitive advantage is a competitive advantage based on resources, especially internal. The place can choose this strategy if in its area, there is some specific characteristic, unique preferential or extraordinary ability in either quality or quantity or way of use of place potential and its resources. It allows offering greater value than the competitors at the same market. The place has a higher value based on the efficient use of resources and ensures a certain advantage over competitors by owning unique resources which cannot be imitated, or that resources in the place are used in a unique way. Strategy can be chosen according to target markets or unique characteristics that need to be developed with the aim to build a strong competitive advantage. Both types of competitive advantage strategies based on marketing places can be chosen. It is understood that the competitive advantages of the region based on a marketing approach, especially marketing places, provide a significant advantage of a specific preference, exceptional ability in quality or quantity, of use of potential of the place, which has the place. This gives an advantage over its competitors which enables the place to realize greater value than what the competition could achieve in the same market. Several marketing strategies defined in marketing places can be chosen according to type of competitive advantage, target markets, aims or vision.

The next step is to realize the chosen strategy and activities and then control and evaluate them. For the whole process it is necessary to involve all relevant stakeholders and to synchronize planning and management on the local, regional and national levels. The best practice of the regions which is based on their uniqueness of a regional competitive advantages and its connection with tourism activities needs to be highlighted especially the benefits of exploitation for this approach. The conceptual methodological approach aimed at creating unique marketing places can be seen in Fig. 2.

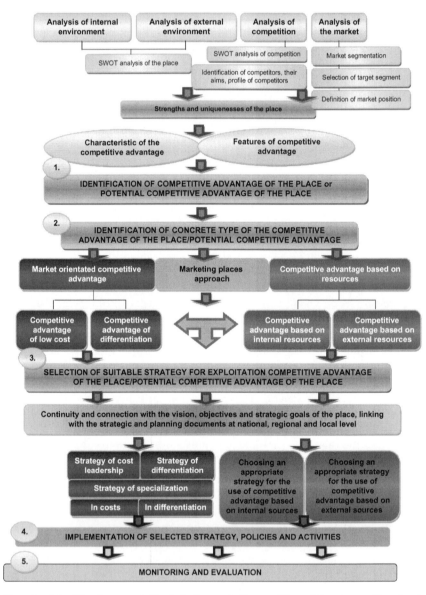

Fig. 2. Identification and Exploitation of Competitive Advantage Aimed at Building Unique Places. *Source*: Own workmanship.

The proposed conceptual approach of identification and exploitation of a competitive advantage aimed at building unique places was consulted with expert groups in all Slovak regions. As we were trying to process all their needs, requirements and remarks, we consider this approach as widely useful in practice. It should be useful to the departments of tourism in local and regional self-governments. This approach should also be used in preparing strategic and planning documents at the local and regional level but also as a tool which should help in local and regional development.

REFERENCES

Barney, J. B. (1991). Firm resources and sustained competitive advantage. *Journal of Management, 17*, 99–120.

Barney, J. B. (1997). *Gaining and sustaining competitive advantage.* Ontario: Addison-Wesley Publishing Company.

Borseková, K. (2012). *Identification and utilization of competitive on the regional level.* Banská Bystrica: Faculty of Economics.

Borseková, K., & Vaňová, A. (2011). Competitive advantage of Slovak Republic. *International Journal of Multidisciplinary Thought, 1*(4), 237–257.

Buhalis, D. (2000). Marketing the competitive destination of the future. *Tourism Management, 21*, 97–116.

Buhalis, D., & Cooper, C. (1998). Competition or co-operation: The needs of small and medium sized tourism enterprises at a destination level. In E. Laws, B. Faulkner, & G. Moscardo (Eds.), *Embracing and managing change in tourism.* London: Roudledge.

Cole, D. A. (2009). Applying utility functions to equalize regional preferences in Slovakia. *New trends in education of management: Conference proceedings* (pp. 1–13). Banská Bystrica: Občianskezdruženie Strategy.

Fayos-Sola. (1996). Tourism policy: A midsummer night's dream? *Tourism Management, 17*(6), 405–412.

Garmise, S. (2006). *People and the competitive advantage of place.* New York, NY: M.E. Sharpe.

Hall, C. M. (2005). Rural wine and food tourism cluster network development In D. Hall, I. Kirkpatrick, & M. Mitchell, (Eds.), *Rural tourism and sustainable business* (pp. 149–164). Clevedon: Channel View Publications.

Hall, R. (1993). A framework linking intangible resources and capabilities to sustainable competitive advantage. *Strategic Management Journal, 14*(8), 607–618.

Hollensen, S. (2010). *Marketing management: A relationship approach.* Edinburgh: PEL.

King, A. (2010). Point of difference. *Business Review Weekly, 36*(32), 28–29.

Kotler, P. (1992). *Marketing management.* Praha: Victoria Publishing.

Kotler, P., & Armstrong, G. (1992). *Marketing.* Bratislava: SPN.

Lehu, J.-M. (2004). *L'encyclopédie du marketing.* Paris: Édition d'Organisation.

Lupberger, D. (2009). Unique selling proposition. Qualified Remodeler.

Martin, R. (2002). *A study on the factors of regional competitiveness.* The European Commision.

Mcphee, W., & Wheeler, D. (2006). Making the case for the added-value chain. *Strategy and leadership, 34*(4), 41.

Michael, E. J. (2003). Tourism micro-clusters. *Tourism Economics, 9*(2), 133−145.

O'Leary, N. (2000). Unique selling proposition. Adweek Western Edition.

Pfeffer, J. (1994). *Competitive advantage through people: Unleasing the power of the workforce.* Boston, MA: Harvard Business School Press.

Pike, S. (2004). *Destination management organisation.* Oxford: Elsevier.

Pompurová, K. (2011). Attractiveness of Slovakia for chosen segment. *E + M Ekonomie a Management, 14*(2), 137−150.

Poon, A. (2002). *Tourism, technology and competitive strategies.* Oxford: CAB International.

Porter, M. E. (1994). *Competitive strategy.* Prague: Victoria Publishing.

Porter, M. E. (1999). *Competitive advantage of nations.* New York, NY: Free Press.

Powel, T. C. (1992). Organizational alignment as competitive advantage. *Strategic Management Journal, 13*(2), 119−134.

Ryan, C. (2002). Equity, management, power sharing and sustainability − Issues of the new tourism. *Tourism Management, 23*(1), 17−26.

Saloner, G., Shepard, A., & Podolny, J. (2001). *Strategic management.* New York, NY: Wiley.

Saxena, R. (2005). Relationships, networks and the learning regions: Case evidence from the Peak District National Park. *Tourism Management, 26*(2), 277−289.

Sokołowicz, M. (2012). Territorial context in the research on the EU cohesion. One-speed or multi-speed Europe? *Studia Regionalia, 33,* 9−28.

Solomon, R. M., Marshall, G. W., & Stuart, E. W. (2006). *Marketing: Real people, real choices.* Brno: Computer Press.

Soteriades, M. (2012). Tourism destination marketing: Approaches improving effectiveness and efficiency. *Journal of Hospitality and Tourism Technology, 3*(2), 1−23.

Stimson, R., Stough, R. R., & Nijkamp, P. (2011). *Endogenous regional development.* Cheltenham: Edward Elgar Publishing Limited.

Švantnerová, L'. (2005). *Spatial economics.* Banská Bystrica: OZEkonómia.

The Ministry of Transport, Construction and Regional Development of the Slovak Republic. (2013). *Strategy of tourism development in the Slovak republic for 2020.* Bratislava.

Tinsley, L. (2007). Small business networking and tourism destination development: A comparative perspective. *The International Journal of Enterpreneurship and Innovation, 8*(1), 15−27.

Ulrich, D., & Lake, D. (1991). Organizational capability: Creating competitive advantage. *Academy of Management, 5*(1), 77−92.

Vaňová, A. (2006). *Strategic marketing planning of territorial development.* Banská Bystrica: Faculty of Economics UMB.

Vaňová, A. (2010). Creative economy and development of places (from marketing places point of view). In J. Kloudová et al. (Ed.), *Creative economy* (pp. 59−84). Bratislava: EUROKÓDEX.

PART III
MARKETING PLACES – TOWARDS
A COOPERATIVE STRATEGY

ACHIEVING CONSISTENCY IN DESTINATION PERSONALITIES: A TRIPARTITE PERSONALITY CONGRUITY THEORY FOCUSED ON INDUSTRY PROFESSIONALS

Veronica I. K. Lam and Leonardo (Don) A. N. Dioko

ABSTRACT

Destination brand personality has been considered as an emotional relationship between a branded destination and its visitors (Ekinci, 2003). Previous studies exclusively focused on the match between visitor's personality and destination personality (Sirgy & Su, 2000; Usakli & Baloglu, 2011). However, there is a lack of investigation centered on tourism industry professionals (TIPs). This chapter is to assess the congruity between TIPs' self-assessed personality, their perceived brand personality of Macau as a destination as well as the brand personality of their tourism/hospitality-related organizations. Findings of this study reveal that TIPs' perceived Big Five dimensions of self, Macau, and organization tend to match with each other in certain dimensions.

Marketing Places and Spaces
Advances in Culture, Tourism and Hospitality Research, Volume 10, 175–191
ISSN: 1871-3173/doi:10.1108/S1871-317320150000010013

Neither their own nor their organizations' Big Five dimensions "Openness" and "Conscientiousness" matches their perceived brand personality of Macau. This chapter provides empirical evidence which may suggest to Macau policy makers to further develop branding strategies through strengthening its brand personalities.

Keywords: Destination branding; brand personality; person-organization fit; tourism industry professionals

INTRODUCTION

A destination's brand is multidimensional and influenced by many stakeholders. It is challenging to brand a destination because it comprises different sectors such as accommodation, attractions, and arts over which destination marketers have little control (Ritchie & Crouch, 2000). The existence of multiple stakeholders makes destination branding process more complex and difficult (Balmer & Greyser, 2002; Roberts & Dowling, 2002). As a result, the entire tourism experience in branded destinations will depend principally on the level of consistency between different stakeholders' values and characteristics.

In order to build a fully integrated destination brand that delivers quality visitor experience, it is necessary to form a destination vision which is consistent with stakeholders' values (Morgan, Pritchard, & Piggott, 2003). Consequently, without the consensus of destination perceptions between industry players and destination vision, destination image will be communicated obscurely because stakeholders within a destination could potentially aim in a different direction (Morgan et al., 2003).

Employees often act as an interface between internal and external brand environment (Harris & De Chernatony, 2001; Macrae, 1999; Yaniv & Farkas, 2005). Their personalities, attitude, and their views on the brand can influence customer perceptions. The role of tourism employees contributes to the overall image of a destination (Baum, Hearns, Devine, & Moscardo, 2007). Their behavior and attitude can directly influence visitors' travel experience, satisfaction, and future behavior (Freire, 2009). On the other hand, employees are recognized as people who are essential elements for the success of tourism enterprises (Baum, 2008). Therefore, it is important to achieve a fit between the employees' values and brand values of the organization and the destination which they represent.

Brand personalities have been considered as human-like characteristics of a brand (Aaker, 1997). They are important for destinations as brand personalities distinguish a destination from other competitors and emphasize the uniqueness of a destination (Ekinci & Hosany, 2006). The distinctive personalities enable visitors develop an emotional and symbolic connection with a destination (Ekinci, 2003). Most of the previous studies assessed destination brands were from the visitors' perspective, such as the congruence between visitor's own personality and destination personality (Sirgy & Su, 2000; Usakli & Baloglu, 2011). There is a lack of investigation centered on industry employees' perception of brands. The objective of this chapter is to assess the congruity between Tourism Industry Professionals' (TIPs) self-assessed personality, their perceived brand personality of Macau as a destination as well as their assessment of the brand personality of their tourism/hospitality-related organizations.

Macau has become a popular destination among visitors in Asia. The number of tourists visiting has reached 29 million in 2013 (MGTO Statistics, 2013), increased by three times when comparing with the tourist arrival in 2000. Majority of the visitors are from Mainland China, Hong Kong, Taiwan, and other Asian countries. There is also an obvious growth among emerging markets such as from India and Korea. The growing tourist figures is a result of liberalization of the gaming sectors started in 2002, when the government allowed foreign casino operators break the traditional monopoly of gaming industry lasted for more than four decades. These new developers provided a wide range of tourism products such as entertainments, exhibitions, luxury shopping arcades, high-end food and beverage services. Moreover, the Individual Visit Scheme was introduced in 2003. As a result, travelers from Mainland China are allowed to visit Macau on an individual basis, instead of being restricted to travel on group tours and business visa.

The rapid growth of tourism and gaming industries has contributed to the major part of the economy of Macau. More than 80% of the government total income was generated from the direct gaming tax in 2012 (DSF Statistics, 2012). About 105,000 people have been employed by the tourism and casino-related business in 2012, which accounts for 30% of the total workforce and 18% of the total population (DSF Statistics, 2013).

THEORETICAL CONSIDERATIONS

The study of destination branding has become a popular topic in tourism studies (Blain, Levy, & Ritchie, 2005; Cai, 2002). In order for a destination to differentiate itself against others, they need to highlight their unique identities and characteristics (Morgan, Pritchard, & Pride, 2002). Destination branding represents an image that enables a destination brand to express its beliefs, emotions, behaviors, and personalities. Blain et al. (2005) pointed out it is crucial to measure the effectiveness of a destination brand by evaluating whether the transmitted image is matched by visitors' actual experience, which leads to visitor satisfaction. This congruence between projected and perceived brand image will be based on whether stakeholders such as primary service providers, who are the ones from the reality, deliver communications and services that are consistent with the branding strategies (Hankinson, 2004).

Destination personality has been proposed as an effective component of a destination image (Ekinci & Hosany, 2006; Hosany, Ekinci, & Uysal, 2006). Through brand personalities, the human side of a branded destination can likely develop an emotional relationship with visitors (Ekinci, 2003). A destination brand which shows personalities often gives and reinforces memorable traveling experience (Ritchie & Ritchie, 1998). Furthermore, brand personality can enhance brand attitudes, purchase intentions, and higher levels of consumer trust and loyalty (Freling, Crosno, & Henard, 2011). Research in the tourism field showed that destination personalities influenced strongly visitors' preferences and satisfaction (Sirgy & Su, 2000; Usakli & Baloglu, 2011).

The role of brand personalities in consumer–brand relationship building is based on self-congruity theory (Sirgy, 1982). Customers prefer brands that are consistent with their self-concept. Hence, they can satisfy their self-consistency and self-esteem after the usage and ownership of a particular brand which share similar personalities with them. This self-congruity, the link between an individual's self-concepts with the symbolic value of brand purchased, influences tourists' behavior (Chon, 1990). Sirgy and Su (2000) stated that self-congruity involves a process that matches a tourist's self-concept to a destination visitor image. The greater this match, the more likely that a visitor has a favorable attitude toward a destination and more likely makes a visit.

There are a growing number of studies on destination personality in the tourism context. Majority of studies identified personality traits of various destinations and their relationship with destination image and future behavior (Ekinci & Hosany, 2006); visitor motivation (Murphy, Moscardo, & Benckendorff, 2007); destination personality comparison and visitor self-congruity (Murphy et al., 2007); the relationship of projected and perceived destination personality (Kim & Lehto, 2013). Most of these studies adopted Aaker's Brand Personality Scale (BPS) which originally measures 42 traits in five underlying dimensions of product brand personality: competence, sincerity, excitement, sophistication, ruggedness across products and service. Although Aaker's BPS can be applied to tourist destination, some destination dimensions on the original BPS may not be relevant due to the unique, emotional nature of tourism destination (Ekinci & Hosany, 2006).

Kaplan, Yurt, Guneri, and Kurtulus (2010) also agreed that brand personality of products are applicable to place personality, the researchers developed another personality scale for assessing personality of places based on Aaker's BPS. Their scale offered two new dimensions "Conservatism" which is a cultural-specific dimension and "Malignancy" which reflects the "Neuroticism" dimension of the Big Five model.

Though there are a considerable number of studies dealing with visitor–destination personality fit or congruence (Ekinci, Sirakaya-Turk, & Baloglu, 2007; Hosany et al., 2006), little attention has been given regarding how this theoretical relationship pertains to tourism industry professionals, who, in collectively performing their roles as service providers, act as a critical conduit for shaping and materializing destination personality. Understanding whether TIPs passively reflect or actively shape the destination's overall personality or that of their organization thus merits necessary exploration and suggests a tripartite theory of relational interaction between industry professionals, the service organization into which they are embedded and the emergent destination image.

A few established frameworks rooted in management studies provide a conceptual precedence for such a proposed tripartite relational theory. People are recognized as essential elements for the operational success in the tourism industry (Baum, 2008). Jovičić, Milanović, Todorović, and Vujičić (2011) pointed out employees in hotels and restaurants are the most important factor in the service quality as they provide identity and recognition to a facility. Previous research emphasized the person–organization (P–O) fit, which organizations should regard as a means to improve organizational performance (Yaniv & Farkas, 2005). P–O fit is one of the dimensions of person–environment (P–E) fit which can be conceptualized in different ways such as matching people with their jobs, organizations, or vocations (Kristof, 1996).

Organizations, besides hiring people based on their appropriate knowledge and skills, need to select individuals whose personalities fit with the unique corporate culture. As personality predicts job attitudes and behaviors, organizational success should be based on having employees not only technically competent; their personalities, values, interests, and individual behavior patterns need to match the characteristics of their organizations

(Bowen, Ledford, & Nathan, 1991). These authors emphasized that it should be the "whole person" who is hired to fit well into the organization's culture, instead of only their knowledge, skills, and abilities (KSAs) are hired for the requirement of specific jobs. In the study of Iplik, Kilic, and Yalcin (2011), P–O fit perceived by hotel managers was found crucial for job satisfaction, job motivation, and organizational stress. Result in another study concluded that aligning Big Five personalities of hotel employees with organization activities increases positive brand image and guest satisfaction (Jovičić et al., 2011).

METHOD

In order to obtain a deeper understanding of TIPs perceptions, a study that combines qualitative and quantitative methodologies was undertaken, which consisted of both a survey among TIPs and in-depth interviews with senior TIPs. The purpose of using a mixed-method design for this study is to seek enhancement and clarification of the results from one method with the results from the other method in order to extend the breadth and range of inquiry (Greene, Caracelli, & Graham, 1989). Meanwhile, it provides a triangulation that corroborates results from both a qualitative and quantitative study. As a result, this research method can increase the integrity of suggestions based on the findings provided by contextual understandings and quantitative result (Bryman, 2006). Above all, applying a mixed-method design in this study can help overcoming the limitation of using a brief Ten Item Personality Inventory (TIPI) scale.

The quantitative approach of this study measures TIPs' self-assessed Big Five personalities of their own, their perceived brand personality of Macau as a destination, as well as their assessment of the brand personality of their own tourism/hospitality-related organization. The Big Five model, which is also known as the Five-Factor model, is the most widely used in previous researched study in personality (Goldberg, 1990; John & Srivastava, 1999; McCrae & Costa, 1987, 1989). The model, suggested that most of individuals can be grouped into five broad personality dimensions comprising Extraversion (characterized by one's enthusiasm, talkativeness, assertiveness, and energy), Agreeableness (reflects individual has general concern for social harmony, being friendly and helpful), Conscientiousness (tendency to show self-discipline, and dependability), Neuroticism (tendency to experience negative emotions, low tolerance of stress, its polar opposite is emotional stability), and Openness (reflects one's originality, curiosity, willing to try new things).

To capture this self-, destination- and organizational-brand personality assessments, we utilized the Ten Item Personality Inventory (TIPI) scale (Gosling, Rentfrow, & Swann, 2003). Each of the 10 items in the TIPI scale was rated on a 7-point scale from 1 (disagree strongly) to 7 (agree strongly). The TIPI scale which was developed by Gosling et al. (2003) is a brief instrument and a reasonable proxy for longer instruments that measure the Big Five dimensions, such as the 240-item NEO Personality Inventory (Costa & McCrae, 1992), the 60-item NEO Five-Factor inventory (Costa & McCrae, 1992) and 40-item instrument (Saucier, 1994). Gosling argued that although the TIPI somewhat inferior to the standard multi-item Big five instruments, it reached adequate levels in four criteria: convergent and discriminant validity, test-retest reliability, pattern of external correlates, and convergence between self-and observer-ratings. Moreover, using the TIPI scale is methodologically advantageous by reducing respondent fatigue.

Though the Big Five model is widely adapted by personality psychologists to measure human personality traits, recent studies showed that this model can be extended from social psychology to brand personality. Therefore, the TIPI scale was not only used to measure TIPs' self-personality assessments in this study but also adapted to measure TIPs' perceived personality of Macau as a destination and the organizations for which they work. The quantitative data were collected through convenience sampling method: (1) a web-based survey among industry professionals assisted by researcher' personal contact who are either working in or related to the tourism/hospitality industry; (2) self-administered survey among tourism/hospitality industry employees who are studying evening tourism-related courses in a tourism educational institution. Convenience sampling was utilized at this preliminary stage of this research until funding for a more comprehensive and full-fledged data collection can be secured. Results reported in this study are therefore limited in its generality.

Qualitative data were collected in this study to facilitate interpretation of the survey results and provide contextual grounding of tourism industry professionals' emergent perceptions about Macau's destination brand, the role of their work and organizations in relation to the destination brand building of Macau. A total of eight in-depth interviews with senior TIPs were conducted in Macau. A purposive sampling technique (Patton, 2005) was adopted to principally target experienced tourism industry

professionals. The sample consisted of 4 male and 4 female senior professionals with a position ranging from managers to directors, who work in
hotels (4), travel agencies (2), events planning operations (1), and retail
management in resorts (1). Their work experience is ranged from 10 years
to 38 years. These participants were selected through the assistance of the
researchers' personal network.

Participants were asked standard and open-ended questions in the
semi-structured interviews. They were asked to express their viewpoints
and opinions on the characteristics of the Macau destination brand, their
responsibilities toward delivering the Macau destination brand as well as
the relationship between the current tourism environment and their working situation. All interviews ranged from 45 minutes to 1.5 hours and were
conducted in Chinese. They were taped, transcribed, and translated to
English by the bilingual researchers.

FINDINGS

A total of 144 usable questionnaires were collected in the survey part of the
study. Frequency analysis and paired sample *t*-test were conducted using
SPSS 19 (Statistical Package for Social Sciences) to analyze the data. The
sample of this study contained more female (76%) than male (24%).
Majority of them are working in hotel (rooms and other services) (48%)
and other sectors in the tourism industry (52%). Most of the respondents
are from the junior level (60%), followed by the level of middle management (19%), supervisory (13%), and top management (8%). Almost one
third of them (32%) have just entered the industry (less than 1 year of
industry experience); 15% of them have industry experience ranging from 4
to 6 years; 16% of them have worked more than 10 years in the same
industry.

Findings of the study reveal that respondents rated their self-personality,
perceived Macau personality, and organization personality higher than
average. Their ratings of all TIPI dimensions on their self-personality are
relatively higher than their perceived Macau personality and organization
personality, except for one dimension "Emotional Stability." Meanwhile,
their ratings of "Extraversion," "Conscientiousness," and "Openness" of
their organization are relatively higher than the ones of Macau, except for
"Agreeableness" and "Emotional Stability." Interestingly, their perceived
"Emotional Stability" of Macau is higher than the ones of their

organization and themselves. The top two Big Five dimension scores rated by TIPs on self-personality and organization personality are the same and they are "Openness" (5.17 and 4.75 respectively) and "Conscientiousness" (4.82 and 4.78 respectively). For Macau personality, TIPs' highest ratings of dimension scores are "Agreeableness" (4.48) and "Emotional Stability" (4.44), the lowest is "Conscientiousness" (3.98).

The findings reveal that TIPs' perceived Big Five dimensions of self, Macau, and organization tend to match with each other in "Extraversion," "Agreeableness," and "Emotional Stability." However, neither their own nor their organizations' Big Five dimensions "Openness" and "Conscientiousness" match their perceived brand personality of Macau (Fig. 1).

As shown in Table 1, results from the paired samples *t*-test indicate that all TIPs' self-personality scores were found significantly higher than their perceived brand personality of Macau, except for "Emotional Stability." Findings from the in-depth interviews are congruent with quantitative results. TIPs' "Extroversion" can be explained when respondents revealed that they were enthusiastic with their jobs and that led to benefiting the

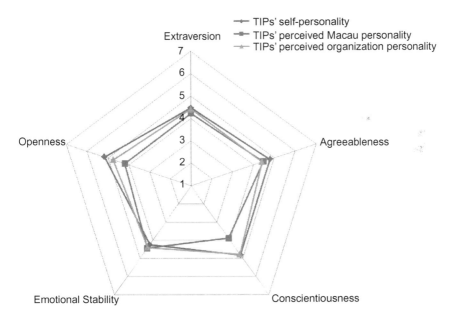

Fig. 1. The Big Five Scores of Self, Macau, and Organization Personality.

Table 1.   Result of Paired Samples t-Test Comparing TIPs' Self-Personality and Their Perceived Macau Personality ($n = 144$).

TIPI Dimensions	TIPs' Self-Personality Assessment		TIPs' Perceived Brand Personality of Macau		Dif	t	df	Sig. (Two-Tailed)
	Mean	SD	Mean	SD				
1. Extraversion	4.47	1.07	4.23	1.01	0.24	2.07	143	0.040*
2. Agreeableness	4.80	0.82	4.48	0.81	0.32	3.46	143	0.001**
3. Conscientiousness	4.82	1.21	3.90	1.03	0.92	7.17	143	0.000***
4. Emotional stability	4.25	1.28	4.44	0.81	−0.18	−1.61	143	0.109
5. Openness	5.17	1.00	4.20	1.35	0.96	6.99	143	0.000***

$*p < 0.05$, $**p < 0.01$, $***p < 0.001$.

image of Macau. For example, one of the TIPs stressed that she and her colleagues were active and enthusiastic at work to promote their products and service by inviting overseas media to write about it. The same TIP mentioned that their activities at work had contributed beyond what destination marketing organizations can perform for branding Macau. On the contrary, another TIP reflected during the in-depth interview that Macau was not active and ambitious enough as a tourism destination:

> I don't know if the government and trade originations in Macau will tell others to come to Macau. For example, to approach those event destination decision makers such as chairman of organizations, university professors and marketing directors .... If someone can answer their questions, they may consider organizing their events in Macau. They know Macau but they don't know there are things good for an event. (Events and destination management sector, male, about 30 years of industry experience)

Majority of TIPs in the in-depth interviewed considered themselves as "broad-minded." This aspect reflects their "Openness" as some of them pointed out that they were willing to take advantage to learn along with the growth of the industry. One of them revealed that the growth of the industry had given them a wider horizon for self-career development, particularly learning from senior colleagues who are overseas expatriates. This "Openness" of TIPs has a contrast with their perception of Macau. Majority of them mentioned that the city was uncreative and unimaginative because it had been a routine that new developments in Macau contain similar elements such as casinos, shopping malls, and some performance and that lacks family friendly facilities. One of them added that Macau lacks creative local business. Such phenomenon exists as TIPs explained that majority of visitors in Macau were formed by a large and single market segment from the mainland China. They revealed that those visitors were well satisfied with the offers from the casinos and retail sectors, without much of interests in other attractions such as museum, heritage, and shows.

One TIP pointed that the city lacks creativity and attributed this to the conventional education system and limited government policy related to training and education for tourism industry employees:

> I think the whole system should be changed. I think our government should learn examples of human resources management and educational system from other tourism destinations. They need to understand how education can support tourism development. It is related to our educational style. Ours is more non-creative. Children only follow what parents tell them to do .... Resources are very important especially human resources. Without creative education system, we don't have creative people to create a creative place. We need to solve the problem from its root. (Hotel operations, male, more than 15 years of industry experience)

Quantitative findings indicate that TIPs' self-personality score "Conscientiousness" is significantly higher than Macau (Table 1). As dependability and self-discipline are two distinctive characteristics of "Conscientiousness," TIPs' views related to these characteristics between themselves and Macau were found different from in-depth interviews. Almost all of the TIPs in the interviews said that they had a sense of mission to pass on to their subordinates the passion they have for working in the tourism and hotel industry. They highly realized that their industry depended on them as local people who work in the middle and top management level. However, they found that Macau lacked a long-term plan and efficiency:

> In general, I found that Macau is lacking long term plan. For example, we are surprised to see a new building which was built right next to a heritage site. (Tour operations, female, more than 20 years of industry experience)

> The problem now for Macau is that it wants to establish as a commercial city. There are only convention venues but the ferry terminal, border gates, airport are still very limited. The situation for Macau now is that it wants to offer everything but we are lacking facilities in many areas. (Event and destination management sector, male, more than 30 years of industry experience)

Macau becomes undependable in the eyes of interview respondents due to its non-internationalized and unfriendly infrastructure. According to another respondent, the city is believed not ready to sustain the tourism growth due to other limited resources such as land and man power:

> Though Macau's future looks very bright, but it makes me worry as well actually. How are we going to sustain this expansion? Basically we have very limited land and labor. I don't know how Macau is going to tackle these two problems. If we want to build more roads for coaches, we need to find land. (Tour operations, male, more than 30 year of industry experience)

Findings from the paired samples t-test showed that TIPs rated personality dimension scores "Conscientiousness" and "Openness" significantly higher in the brand personality of their organizations compared to the brand personality of Macau (Table 2). These results are consistent with the qualitative findings. During the in-depth interviews, majority of TIPs acknowledged the effort and contribution of their organizations in supporting the diversification strategy of the tourism industry set by the government, for example, the organizations where majority of them work offer new experience to visitors such as special entertainment and events. TIPs agreed that the image of Macau has moved away from a gaming-only destination to one that offers more special amenities and leisure activities than before for families and other non-gaming markets.

When comparing their own and their organizations, it is shown in Table 3 that TIPs' self-personality scores "Agreeableness" and "Openness" was found significantly higher compared to their perceived personality of their organizations. Some TIPs expressed in the in-depth interviews their loyalty and cooperativeness toward the industry. As majority of these TIPs have been working in the industry for many years, they revealed that they were being brought up in Macau, educated, and become successful in their career. Their current senior positions and achievements are fruits of progressive years of personal effort, solid hard work, and unmemorable experience. Reaching the current stage, they are more open to emotion, intellectual curiosity, cooperativeness in the areas of destination branding and ownership:

> As a citizen, the basic we can do is to be hospitable. Macau people in general are quite helpful but we see the issue of taxi drivers who reject to take visitors and to do whatever they want. This causes a bad image about Macau ... We have been thinking ... I don't see taxis came back with lost and found items like a bag or a phone. In the past we called the taxi station but nine out of ten times with no reply. For me as a staff in this industry, what I can help contribute into a tourist image of Macau is to give suggestions to my workplace in order to recognize those good taxi drivers. (Hotel operations, male, more than 15 years of industry experience)

Table 2. Result of Paired Samples *t*-Test Comparing TIPs' Perceived Organization Personality and Their Perceived Brand Personality of Macau ($n = 144$).

TIPI Dimensions	TIPs' Perceived Organization Personality		TIPs' Perceived Macau Personality		Dif	t	df	Sig. (Two-Tailed)
	Mean	SD	Mean	SD				
1. Extraversion	4.42	1.15	4.23	1.01	0.19	1.59	144	0.113
2. Agreeableness	4.42	0.92	4.48	0.81	−0.06	−0.70	144	0.486
3. Conscientiousness	4.78	1.02	3.90	1.03	0.88	7.34	144	0.000***
4. Emotional stability	4.41	1.05	4.44	0.81	−0.03	−0.29	144	0.773
5. Openness	4.75	1.40	4.20	1.35	0.54	3.58	144	0.000***

***$p < 0.001$.

Table 3. Result of Paired Samples *t*-Test Comparing TIPs' Self-Personality and Their Perceived Organization Personality ($n = 144$).

TIPI Dimensions	TIPs' Self-Personality Assessment		TIPs' Perceived Organization Personality		Dif	t	df	Sig. (Two-Tailed)
	Mean	SD	Mean	SD				
1. Extraversion	4.47	1.07	4.42	1.15	0.49	0.43	143	0.665
2. Agreeableness	4.80	0.82	4.42	0.92	0.39	4.23	143	0.000***
3. Conscientiousness	4.82	1.21	4.78	1.02	0.45	0.43	143	0.666
4. Emotional stability	4.25	1.28	4.41	1.05	−0.16	−1.38	143	0.171
5. Openness	5.17	1.00	4.75	1.40	0.42	3.60	143	0.000***

***$p < 0.001$.

Another one said:

> I 'm not boasting about my position, (in this stage) I am really working for the image of Macau ... I am so happy to help my organization to train up good employees. Although many of them leave (my organization) and go to another place, however they are still using those skills in the same industry. (Hotel operations, female, more than 20 years of industry experience)

CONCLUSION AND IMPLICATIONS

As stakeholders' values and characteristics are critical for communicating the vision of a destination brand (Morgan et al., 2003), it is necessary to explore the extent stakeholders − namely TIPs and their organizations − are identifying themselves with the destination in terms of personalities. The reason for exploring destination brand personality is largely due to previous studies which revealed that destination personality can influence visitors' preferences and satisfaction (Sirgy & Su, 2000; Usakli & Baloglu, 2011), while studying personality from the perspective of TIPs is because of they play their important roles of delivering the brand value.

Results of this study suggest tourism policy makers to reinforce the destination brand personalities of Macau in order to increase its uniqueness and differentiate it from other destinations. The incongruity of personalities between Macau and its stakeholders implies that there is a need for tourism policy makers to form a consistent destination brand by considering the values and characteristics of the people who work for the brand. On the other hand, past research suggested that organizations hiring people should consider beyond their technical competence, as their personalities and values reflect the brand values of their organizations and that are related to brand performance and guest satisfaction. Finally, the findings of this study indicates a need for destination branding efforts to achieve internal consistencies as a prior necessity before external marketing consistencies regarding destination brand is achieved.

Although the small survey population of respondents cannot generalize the results accurately or reliably to the total population, the qualitative analysis from the in-depth interviews helped explain, elaborate on the quantitative data and that provided a more refine understanding of the research problem (Ivankova, Creswell, & Stick, 2006). The current results call for a larger scale study on this topic with a more representative and generalizable sample size. In addition, this chapter only focused on TIPs' perspectives. Future research can study visitors' and local residents' perceived personality of Macau in order to draw substantial implications for destination branding strategies. Furthermore, future study can explore the relationship of person–environment fit with other constructs and the behavioral intention of employees and visitors.

REFERENCES

Aaker, J. L. (1997). Dimensions of brand personality. *Journal of Marketing Research, 34*(3), 347–356.
Balmer, J. M., & Greyser, S. A. (2002). Managing the multiple identities of the corporation. *California Management Review, 44*(3), 72–86.
Baum, T. (2008). Implications of hospitality and tourism labour markets for talent management strategies. *International Journal of Contemporary Hospitality Management, 20*(7), 720–729.
Baum, T., Hearns, N., Devine, F., & Moscardo, G. (2007). Place, people and interpretation: Issues of migrant labour and tourism imagery in Ireland. *Tourism Recreation Research, 32*(3), 39–48.
Blain, C., Levy, S. E., & Ritchie, J. B. (2005). Destination branding: Insights and practices from destination management organizations. *Journal of Travel Research, 43*(4), 328–338.
Bowen, D. E., Ledford, G. E., & Nathan, B. R. (1991). Hiring for the organization, not the job. *The Executive, 5*(4), 35–51.
Bryman, A. (2006). Paradigm peace and the implications for quality. *International Journal of Social Research Methodology, 9*(2), 111–126.
Cai, L. A. (2002). Cooperative branding for rural destinations. *Annals of Tourism Research, 29*(3), 720–742.
Chon, K. (1990). The role of destination image in tourism: A review and discussion. *Tourism Review, 45*(2), 2–9.
Costa, P. T., Jr., & McCrae, R. R. (1992). Four ways five factors are basic. *Personality and Individual Differences, 13*(6), 653–665.
DSF Statistics. (2012). Finance Services Bureau. Retrieved from http://www.dsf.gov.mo/finance/public_finance_info.aspx?FormType=3&#generalLedger2. Accessed on January 20, 2014.
DSF Statistics. (2013). Finance Services Bureau. Retrieved from http://www.dsf.gov.mo/finance/public_finance_info.aspx?FormType=3&#generalLedger2. Accessed on January 28, 2014.
Ekinci, Y. (2003). From destination image to destination branding: An emerging area of research. *E-Review of Tourism Research, 1*(2), 21–24.
Ekinci, Y., & Hosany, S. (2006). Destination personality: An application of brand personality to tourism destinations. *Journal of Travel Research, 45*(2), 127–139.
Ekinci, Y., Sirakaya-Turk, E., & Baloglu, S. (2007). Host image and destination personality. *Tourism Analysis, 12, 5*(6), 433–446.
Freire, J. R. (2009). 'Local people' a critical dimension for place brands. *Journal of Brand Management, 16*(7), 420–438.

Freling, T. H., Crosno, J. L., & Henard, D. H. (2011). Brand personality appeal: Conceptualization and empirical validation. *Journal of the Academy of Marketing Science, 39*(3), 392−406.

Goldberg, L. R. (1990). An alternative "description of personality": The big-five factor structure. *Journal of Personality and Social Psychology, 59*(6), 1216.

Gosling, S. D., Rentfrow, P. J., & Swann, W. B., Jr. (2003). A very brief measure of the big-five personality domains. *Journal of Research in Personality, 37*(6), 504−528.

Greene, J. C., Caracelli, V. J., & Graham, W. F. (1989). Toward a conceptual framework for mixed-method evaluation designs. *Educational Evaluation and Policy Analysis, 11*(3), 255−274.

Hankinson, G. (2004). The brand images of tourism destinations: A study of the saliency of organic images. *Journal of Product & Brand Management, 13*(1), 6−14.

Harris, F., & De Chernatony, L. (2001). Corporate branding and corporate brand performance. *European Journal of Marketing, 35*(3−4), 441−456.

Hosany, S., Ekinci, Y., & Uysal, M. (2006). Destination image and destination personality: An application of branding theories to tourism places. *Journal of Business Research, 59*(5), 638−642.

Iplik, F. N., Kilic, K. C., & Yalcin, A. (2011). The simultaneous effects of person-organization and person-job fit on Turkish hotel managers. *International Journal of Contemporary Hospitality Management, 23*(5), 644−661.

Ivankova, N. V., Creswell, J. W., & Stick, S. L. (2006). Using mixed-methods sequential explanatory design: From theory to practice. *Field Methods, 18*(1), 3−20.

John, O. P., & Srivastava, S. (1999). The big five trait taxonomy: History, measurement, and theoretical perspectives. *Handbook of Personality: Theory and Research, 2*, 102−138.

Jovičić, A., Milanović, T., Todorović, M., & Vujičić, D. (2011). The importance of fitting personality dimensions and job characteristics in employees in the hotel management. *Turizam, 15*(3), 119−131.

Kaplan, M. D., Yurt, O., Guneri, B., & Kurtulus, K. (2010). Branding places: Applying brand personality concept to cities. *European Journal of Marketing, 44*(9−10), 1286−1304.

Kim, S., & Lehto, X. Y. (2013). Projected and perceived destination brand personalities the case of South Korea. *Journal of Travel Research, 52*(1), 117−130.

Kristof, A. L. (1996). Person-organization fit: An integrative review of its conceptualizations, measurement, and implications. *Personnel Psychology, 49*(1), 1−49.

Macrae, C. (1999). Brand reality editorial. *Journal of Marketing Management, 15*, 1−24.

McCrae, R. R., & Costa, P. T. (1987). Validation of the five-factor model of personality across instruments and observers. *Journal of Personality and Social Psychology, 52*(1), 81.

McCrae, R. R., & Costa, P. T. (1989). The structure of interpersonal traits: Wiggins's circumplex and the five-factor model. *Journal of Personality and Social Psychology, 56*(4), 586.

MGTO Statistics. (2013). *Macau government tourist office.* Retrieved from http://industry. macautourism.gov.mo/en/Statistics_and_Studies/list_statistics.php?id=39,29&page_id= 10. Accessed on June 11, 2014.

Morgan, N., Pritchard, A., & Piggott, R. (2003). Destination branding and the role of the stakeholders: The case of New Zealand. *Journal of Vacation Marketing, 9*(3), 285−299.

Morgan, N., Pritchard, A., & Pride, R. (2002). *Destination branding: Creating the unique destination proposition.* Oxford: Butterworth-Heinemann.

Murphy, L., Moscardo, G., & Benckendorff, P. (2007). Using brand personality to differentiate regional tourism destinations. *Journal of Travel Research, 46*(1), 5−14.

Patton, M. Q. (2005). *Qualitative research, encyclopedia of statistics in behavioral science.* New Jersey: John Wiley & Sons.

Ritchie, J., & Crouch, G. I. (2000). The competitive destination: A sustainability perspective. *Tourism Management, 21*(2), 1–7.

Ritchie, J., & Ritchie, J. (1998). The branding of tourism destinations. Annual Congress of International Association of Scientific Experts in Tourism.

Roberts, P. W., & Dowling, G. R. (2002). Corporate reputation and sustained superior financial performance. *Strategic Management Journal, 23*(12), 1077–1093.

Saucier, G. (1994). Mini-markers: A brief version of Goldberg's unipolar big-five markers. *Journal of Personality Assessment, 63*(3), 506–516.

Sirgy, M. J. (1982). Self-concept in consumer behavior: A critical review. *Journal of Consumer Research, 9*(3), 287–300.

Sirgy, M. J., & Su, C. (2000). Destination image, self-congruity, and travel behavior: Toward an integrative model. *Journal of Travel Research, 38*(4), 340–352.

Usakli, A., & Baloglu, S. (2011). Brand personality of tourist destinations: An application of self-congruity theory. *Tourism Management, 32*(1), 114–127.

Yaniv, E., & Farkas, F. (2005). The impact of person-organization fit on the corporate brand perception of employees and of customers. *Journal of Change Management, 5*(4), 447–461.

MARKETING TO CHILDREN IN TOURISM INDUSTRY: DESCRIPTIVE ANALYSIS OF KID-FRIENDLY HOTELS' PRACTICES IN TURKEY

Çağıl Hale Özel

ABSTRACT

This chapter aims to determine the marketing practices of kid-friendly hotels in Turkey by utilizing descriptive analysis. A total of 77 kid-friendly hotels operating in Turkey were surveyed through the examination of their websites. This chapter adopts a descriptive approach in defining marketing practices of kid-friendly hotels. The findings showed that various facilities and services are offered in kid-friendly hotels under the categories of "room options for children," "food and beverage options for children," "activities for children," "price options," and "children's health and safety." Although the results cannot be generalized beyond the scope of the study, this chapter revealed the current status of marketing to children in kid-friendly hotels operating in Turkey.

Marketing Places and Spaces
Advances in Culture, Tourism and Hospitality Research, Volume 10, 193–208
Copyright © 2015 by Emerald Group Publishing Limited
ISSN: 1871-3173/doi:10.1108/S1871-317320150000010014

Marketing implications are provided for practitioners and recommendations for future research are also discussed.

Keywords: Marketing to children; kid-friendly hotels; Turkey

INTRODUCTION

Children have a substantial influence in household spending (Rose, 2007, p. 23). In fact, children have a wide area of influence varying from household items to media consumption preferences (Aktaş, Özüpek, & Altuntaş, 2011, p. 116). Influence of children in household spending extends far beyond the products that they consume or use. This relates to such choices as buying a house, organizing holidays, choosing holiday destinations, buying a car, or even clothes for mother or father (Mathiot, 2010; McNeal, 1999).

Three main factors can be mentioned in the emergence of marketing efforts toward kids in the recent years. First, today's children have considerable amounts of money to spend on needs and wants of their own, followed by the freedom to spend it. This makes them an important primary market (Valkenburg & Cantor, 2001, p. 61). Second, children are also a future market (McNeal, 1992). In fact, children develop brand loyalty at an early age, and favorable attitudes toward brands last well into adulthood (McNeal, 1992). For this reason, marketers intensify their efforts to develop brand relationships with young consumers, beginning when they are toddlers (Story & French, 2004, p. 3). Third, children have a dominant role in determining how to spend family's disposable income (Özata, 2007). In other words, children constitute an important market of influencers.

Children are an important part of population in Turkey. According to the address-based population registration system 2011 data, 25.2 percent of Turkey's population, which is approximately 78 million, is children between the years of 0 and 14 years (Turkish Statistical Institute website, 2011). In terms of the whole world, population under the age of 15 accounts for 26.3 percent of total population. In the United States, children between the ages of 5 and 14 control about $10 billion in food and drink sales (International Dairy-Deli-Bakery Association, 2005, p. 27). Therefore, it seems that children appear to represent a huge market potential. Children should be informed, their needs and wants should be listened to and moreover they should be persuaded by marketers. Due to these developments, marketing to children has found an important place in the literature among other types of marketing (McNeal, 1999).

Nevertheless, tourism marketing literature lacks comprehensive and up-to-date studies which focus on practices of marketing to children in hotel establishments. Additionally, there is a lack of academic research findings related to the locations and classes of kid-friendly hotels in Turkey. This chapter is believed to contribute to fill this gap. Briefly, the current chapter aims to determine the marketing practices of kid-friendly hotels operating in Turkey by utilizing descriptive analysis. This chapter is arranged in the form of a descriptive research in which literature is reviewed and marketing practices of kid-friendly hotels are introduced under predefined categories.

THEORETICAL CONSIDERATIONS

Marketing to children is a specific type of marketing which aims to create brand awareness and brand loyalty in children, increase brand recognition in children, and change children's brand preferences in favor of a specific brand. It appeals to children by taking their lifestyles, dreams, needs, and wants into account (Barlovic, 2006, p. 34). According to McNeal (1999), marketing to children begins in childhood although children are not the primary customers of products.

Children's role in influencing the level of satisfaction for the service delivered and family preferences toward kid-friendly hotels fostered many businesses in the tourism industry to adopt marketing practices for children. Accommodation businesses adopt various marketing practices for children. For instance, a hotel chain in Caribbean has teamed up with "Sesame Street" to make its resorts more appealing for children (Economist, 2006). Thus, children can enjoy their holiday with the characters from Sesame Street in this resort. Another hotel in Algarve offers a wide spectrum of activities such as soccer, t-shirt painting, magic shows, slumber parties, fashion shows, hiking, dolphin, and seal shows. In a hotel in the South of Cyprus, towels and slippers are designed for both children and parents. Additionally, children can call reception and order milk and cookies before sleep (Gönül, 2007). German Ministry of Economics and Labor determined the qualifications of a good family hotel under the sub headings of business philosophy, location of the company, garden, equipments in the room, baby extras, child extras, security, playgrounds, and cleaning units (Yılmaz, 2007, pp. 54−56).

An important concept that should be addressed in the context of marketing to children is Kid-Friendly Hotel Project in Turkey. In Turkey, the scope and conditions of kid-friendly hotels have not been determined by the Ministry of Culture and Tourism or any other government agency. For this reason, assessments of independent auditing companies, tour operators, and customers have become influential in the determination of kid-friendly hotels in Turkey by now. In order to rectify this deficiency in the field of kid-friendly hotels in Turkey, Kid-Friendly Hotel Project was launched at the beginning of 2012.

The ongoing Kid-Friendly Hotel Project is conducted by Pediatric Emergency Medicine Association and Turkish Health Tourism Organization. According to this project, hotels which provide such facilities as room options, dining options, and hotel amenities to their guests who are on holiday with their children are called kid-friendly hotels. With this project, it is aimed to take measures for the safety of children in hotels and train all the staff, particularly the personnel working in children-related sections of the hotel. In addition, the factors which constitute a risk to the safety of children in hotels will be communicated and recommendations will be made on the measures to be taken. Hotels participating in the project will be provided the title of "Kid-Friendly Hotel" (Ntvmsnbc, 2012). In today's highly competitive environment, having the nature of kid-friendly will no doubt provide a significant competitive advantage for businesses. The main reason for this situation is that travel agencies and tour operators suggest kid-friendly hotels for families for a safe and enjoyable holiday. Thus, being kid-friendly helps hotels to differentiate their products from competitors' products and pass ahead of the competition.

METHOD

The main purpose of this research is to determine the facilities and services offered by kid-friendly hotels in Turkey under the title of marketing to children. In other words, this chapter aims to identify and describe the current status of kid-friendly hotels in Turkey as it exists. Thus, this chapter has descriptive characteristics. Facilities and services offered by kid-friendly hotels are surveyed by examining the websites of these hotels. More specifically, what are the classes of kid-friendly hotels in Turkey? Where do kid-friendly hotels in Turkey locate? What are the facilities and services offered by kid-friendly hotels? This chapter aims to answer the above questions and to further extend the understanding of marketing practices toward children in kid-friendly hotels in Turkey.

The whole population of this chapter comprises of all kid-friendly hotels in Turkey. However, as mentioned earlier, a complete list of kid-friendly hotels is not available since requirements of being kid-friendly have not been constituted and declared by any government agency in Turkey. Instead, an internet search was made and kid-friendly hotels, whose kid-friendliness was determined by customer surveys and independent auditing companies' ratings, were listed. The total list of kid-friendly hotels reached summed up to 77. Thus, 77 hotels were selected as the sample of this study and descriptive analysis was conducted.

The data collection form consisted of two parts. The first part evaluated the classes and locations of kid-friendly hotels in the sample. In the second part, facilities and services of kid-friendly hotels were assessed through the examination of websites. This assessment was made in accordance with sub-categories of kid-friendly hotels' requirements explained in the presentation of the ongoing project. However, full requirements of kid-friendly hotels have not been determined by project coordinators at the time of data collection. Instead, they were summarized in a brief sentence in the presentation of project as follows:

> The term "kid-friendly hotel" usually comprises of such issues as room options for children, food and beverage alternatives, hotel amenities and price. On the other hand, the most important point in evaluating the appropriateness of a hotel or resort for children is safety. (Kid-Friendly Hotel Project, 2012)

Given the explanation above, it can be inferred that requirements of kid-friendly hotels can be grouped under five main categories. These categories are: "room options for children," "food and beverage options for children," "activities for children," "price options," and "children's health and safety." On the other hand, explanations found in the presentation of the project do not contain the full details of which facilities and services should be found under each of these categories. For this reason, identification of all possible facilities and services which can be related to each of these categories was made through a detailed investigation of websites of 77 hotels in the sample between 10 June and 17 July 2012. As a result of this investigation, a total of 100 different facilities and services were identified, each of which can be placed under one of the five categories. Thus, a structured data collection form, consisting of five main categories and a total of 100 checkpoints (facilities and services), was developed by the researcher.

Data were collected between July 18, 2012 and August 17, 2012. Websites of kid-friendly hotels were visited for the second time for data collection. Each facility and service was coded as "Yes" if it was available in the hotel. Otherwise, it was coded as "No." In order to avoid incomplete data collection forms, information given on hotels' websites was investigated in details and photographs and factsheets were also taken into consideration. Data of 77 kid-friendly hotels were collected by this means.

Descriptive statistics were used in the analysis of collected data. Frequency distributions were utilized for determining the characteristics of kid-friendly hotels and facilities and services offered in these hotels. Data about the facilities and services offered in kid-friendly hotels were interpreted considering five main categories foreseen in Kid-Friendly Hotel Project. Frequency distributions were conducted by using PASW statistics 18.

Data of this study were collected in consistence with the main categories of kid-friendly hotels' requirements. In other words, findings and results of this study are consistent with the conceptual framework of Kid-Friendly Hotel Project. Besides, detailed information was provided on each stage of the research. This can contribute to the construct validity of the research (Yıldırım & Şimşek, 2011, p. 259; Yin, 2003, p. 35). In order to provide internal reliability, data was first provided directly and without any comment to the reader and interpretations were left for later. Thus, the reader was given the opportunity to evaluate and interpret the results of this study in accordance with the collected data. This is expected to increase the internal reliability of the study (LeCompte & Goetz, 1982). Furthermore, findings and results of this study cannot be generalized to all kid-friendly hotels in Turkey since the aim of this chapter is not to achieve generalizations but rather to investigate and deeply understand the facilities and services offered in kid-friendly hotels with an exploratory approach.

FINDINGS

Characteristics of hotels showed that majority ($n = 69$) of the kid-friendly hotels are five-star hotels. There is only one four-star hotel and there are seven five-star resort hotels. Kid-friendly hotels are mostly located in Belek ($n = 22$), Kemer ($n = 18$), Side ($n = 9$), Lara ($n = 7$), Manavgat ($n = 5$), and Bodrum ($n = 5$) regions. Other locations where kid-friendly hotels are found are: Fethiye ($n = 3$), Izmir ($n = 2$), Alanya ($n = 2$), Marmaris ($n = 2$),

Konyaaltı ($n = 1$), and Kuşadası ($n = 1$). In other words, kid-friendly hotels in Turkey are mostly located in Antalya ($n = 67$), Muğla ($n = 8$), and Izmir ($n = 2$), respectively. Facilities and services offered to children in kid-friendly hotels are described below (see also Table 1).

Table 1. Facilities and Services Offered to Children in Kid-Friendly Hotels.

Facilities and Services	Available (n)	Not Available (n)
Room options for children		
1. Family room	69	8
2. Family suite	55	22
3. Baby cot on demand	19	58
4. Family apart	1	76
5. Kid-suite	2	75
6. Child reception	4	73
7. Complimentary milk	2	75
8. Comfort package for family room	4	73
9. DVD player	1	76
10. Beverages for children at the arrival	2	75
Food and beverage options for children		
11. Teenage club bar	2	75
12. Mini restaurant	22	55
13. Highchair for children in the main restaurant	17	60
14. Child buffet in the main restaurant	44	33
15. Waiter responsible from the child buffet	1	76
16. Baby corner in the main restaurant	2	75
17. Children's menu in ala carte restaurant	7	70
18. Special section devoted to children in the main restaurant	11	66
19. Priority service for children in the main restaurant	2	75
20. Barbecue party for teenagers	2	75
21. Alcohol-free mini-club bar	3	74
22. Ice-cream buffet	5	70
23. Drink bar on children's beach	1	76
Activities for children		
24. Swimming pool for children	70	7
25. Children's beach	1	76
26. Dance classes	8	69
27. Sand sculpture arts lessons	2	75
28. Indoor swimming pool for children	16	61
29. Mini football	23	54
30. Indoor swimming pool for babies	3	74

Table 1. (*Continued*)

Facilities and Services	Available (n)	Not Available (n)
31. Mini volleyball	6	71
32. Land and pool Olympics	11	66
33. Mini bowling	6	71
34. Mini club for children between the ages of 4 and 12	73	4
35. Baby club	5	72
36. Age segmentation in mini club	18	59
37. Caricature lessons	2	75
38. Mind games	1	76
39. Music lessons	2	75
40. Percussion lessons	1	76
41. Yoga lessons	1	76
42. Aquapark with slides	3	74
43. Child theater	8	69
44. Mini amusement park	15	62
45. Kids' cinema	32	45
46. Mini disco	51	26
47. Horseback riding	5	72
48. Internet café	38	39
49. Playstation room	21	56
50. Reading	4	75
51. Playground	57	20
52. Mini golf	20	57
53. Electronic game consoles	14	63
54. Trampoline	8	69
55. Ping-pong	3	74
56. Teenage club	17	60
57. Handicrafts (ornaments, plasterwork, play dough, etc.)	27	50
58. Acrobatics lessons	1	76
59. Swimming lessons	2	75
60. T-shirt painting	17	60
61. Face painting	28	49
62. Tennis lessons	5	72
63. Jacuzzi for children	1	76
64. Jetton-operated electronic mini cars	2	75
65. Driving route	1	76
66. Children's store	4	73
67. Mini basketball	10	65
68. Cooking and cocktail atelier	15	62
69. Animation shows for children	34	43
70. TV room for children	10	65
71. Mini zoo	3	74
72. Kids' shows	12	65
73. Aquatic sports	10	65

Table 1. (*Continued*)

Facilities and Services	Available (*n*)	Not Available (*n*)
74. Ball pool	2	75
75. Air hockey	2	75
76. Ballet classes	1	76
77. Thematic days	11	66
78. Birthday parties	2	75
79. DJ courses	4	73
80. Planting	2	75
81. Clowns and magic shows	4	73
82. Defense sports lessons	1	76
83. Circus	3	74
84. Playback	1	76
85. Kite fair	1	76
86. Night walks	1	76
87. Sand pool	2	75
Price options		
88. Free accommodation for children	72	5
89. Free of charge service for children between the ages of 0 and 6 in a la carte restaurant, a discount of 50 percent for the second child	2	75
Children's health and safety		
90. Antibacterial floor in mini club	1	76
91. Babysitting service	45	32
92. Doctor service	51	26
93. Nursing services	33	44
94. Baby stroller	15	62
95. Car seat	1	76
96. Camera system in mini club	5	72
97. Baby walker	1	76
98. Baby carrier seat	1	76
99. Sleeping room	11	66
100. Baby walky-talkies	5	72

Room Options for Children

Room features and amenities which facilitate accommodation with children are identified under this category. Sixty-nine of the kid-friendly hotels have family rooms. Family room can typically be described as a bigger type of room with two separate bedrooms with bathroom. These two rooms are separated from each other with an interior door. Family rooms also have a sitting area. Fifty-five of the kid-friendly hotels in the sample contain family suites, which are more comfortable and luxurious and have a wider space when compared to standard family rooms. Family suites have such as differentiating features as terrace, balcony, and wireless internet connection. Two of the hotels have kid-suites which are decorated specially for children and contain special kids' amenities. Two kid-friendly hotels have bungalow family aparts as accommodation units. In 19 of kid-friendly hotels, a cot can be placed in the room, on demand. Four hotels place comfort packages for children in family rooms, which contain bathrobe, towel, and slippers for children, milk in the minibar, baby bath and mini stools, baby shampoo, and baby powder.

Food and Beverage Options for Children

More than half of the kid-friendly hotels ($n = 44$) in the sample have a child buffet in the main restaurant. The number of kid-friendly hotels which have an independent mini restaurant is 22. In 13 of the hotels, a special section in the main restaurant is devoted to children and this section is equipped with tables and chairs suitable for children and is decorated in a way that may be of interest to children. Children can have their meals themselves or together with their parents in this section. In order to facilitate babies' feeding, highchairs are offered in 17 hotels' main restaurants. In 17 kid-friendly hotels, children's menu is offered in a la carte restaurants. On the contrary, it is remarkable that in some of the hotels in the sample children are not allowed to a la carte restaurants.

Although many restaurants have a child buffet, only one hotel employs a waiter responsible from the child buffet. Two of the hotels offer priority service for kids in the main restaurants, by using existing service staff. Again, a baby food preparation corner is found in two of the hotels, which contains a feeding bottle warmer, a sterilizer, a microwave oven, and a mixer.

Activities for Children

This category has a wide array of options. In 73 of the hotels, there is a mini club, which appeals to children between the ages of 4 and 12.

Moreover, a baby club is present for babies between the ages of 0 and 3 in five of the kid-friendly hotels. Baby clubs offer a kitchen, which is open 24 hours a day, for parents to prepare their baby's meal easily. Also, parents can take the advantage of babysitting service for a fee if they make reservation in advance. Findings also revealed that in 20 of the kid-friendly hotels, mini club is segmented based on age criteria. In other words, age segments are formed such as 4–6, 7–9, and 10–12 segments or 4–7 and 8–12 segments. As understood from these findings, kid-friendly hotels try to differentiate their facilities and services according to different age segments. Seventeen of the kid-friendly hotels have a teenage club, which targets young guests between the ages of 13 and 16.

Fifty-seven of the kid-friendly hotels have a playground, where children can have fun accompanied by mini club's staff. In some of these hotels, an indoor playground is also present, which can be utilized in cold weather. Findings also showed that mini clubs offer a large number of entertainment alternatives for children. Among the most popular alternatives are: mini disco (51 hotels), animation shows for children (34 hotels), and kids' cinema (32 hotels). In 12 hotels, kids' shows are prepared by children during the day and these shows are exhibited in front of the audience within animation shows. Thematic days are organized in 11 kid-friendly hotels such as "Pirate Day" or "Indian Day."

Sport has an important role within hotel activities. Some of the most popular sport activities offered in kid-friendly hotels are: mini football (23 hotels), mini golf (19 hotels), land and pool Olympics (11 hotels), aquatic sports (like banana boat) (10 hotels), and mini basketball (10 hotels), respectively. Findings also showed that kid-friendly hotels offer trampoline (8 hotels), mini bowling (6 hotels), and mini volleyball (6 hotels) as sport activities. Findings also indicated that many types of classes and workshops are organized under different themes in kid-friendly hotels in the sample. Among them, dance classes (8 hotels), tennis lessons (5 hotels), and DJ courses (4 hotels) are the most common ones. Another group of activities offered to children in kid-friendly hotels relates to swimming and sunbathing. Almost all hotels ($n = 70$) have a swimming pool for children while 16 hotels have an extra indoor swimming pool. Sixty-three hotels have an aquapark with slides. Likewise, three of the hotels have an indoor baby pool.

Findings of the study showed that kid-friendly hotels also offer some activities which develop children's handicraft skills. Among these activities are: face painting (28 hotels), handicrafts such as making ornaments, plasterwork, play dough, and jigsaw puzzles (27 hotels), and t-shirt painting

(17 hotels). Apart from these activities, cooking and cocktail atelier (15 hotels) and planting (21 hotels) are some other activities that children can attend. The last group of activities offered in kid-friendly hotels can be summarized under the title of computer games and electronic toys. Half of the hotels ($n = 38$) have an internet cafe. In 21 hotels, a playstation room is present while 14 kid-friendly hotels have a room for electronic game consoles.

Price Options

Kid-friendly hotels also offer price advantages for families with children. The most important advantage is free accommodation for children who accommodate with their parents. It is not surprising that almost all kid-friendly hotels ($n = 73$) in the sample adopted this application since price promotions are not solely related with the practices of marketing to children. Findings indicated that children between the ages of 0 and 14 are free of charge in 2 of the hotels while 33 hotels offer free accommodation for children between the ages of 0 and 12. Not all the hotels have such a large range of ages for free accommodation offer. Age range of free accommodation is between 0 and 11 in four of the hotels and 0 and 9 in one of the hotels.

Kid-friendly hotels also offer price promotions for their food and beverage services. However, price promotions offered for food and beverage services are limited when compared to promotions offered for accommodation. More specifically, only two kid-friendly hotels offer free of charge services for children between the ages of 0 and 6 in their a la carte restaurants. A second child can also benefit from a discount of 50 percent in a la carte restaurants in these two hotels.

Children's Health and Safety

Findings of the study revealed that kid-friendly hotels pay special attention to children's health and safety. In 51 of the hotels in the sample, there is a paid doctor service while 33 hotels offer nursing services. These services are provided only in a specific period of the day. More than half of the kid-friendly hotels ($n = 45$) offers paid babysitting service throughout the day at various times. Moreover, there is a sleeping room in 11 hotels, where children can sleep throughout the day accompanied with professional babysitters. Besides, findings revealed that kid-friendly hotels offer various baby and child equipments, which allow parents and children enjoy a safe holiday. Some of these equipments are: baby stroller (15 hotels), baby walky-talkies (5 hotels), baby walker (1 hotel), baby carrier seat (1 hotel), and car seat (1 hotel). Five kid-friendly hotels in the sample take safety a step further and establish a camera system all over the mini club building. By this means, parents can view their children live simultaneously from the TVs in their rooms or from PDA devices that could be obtained at the reception. In one of the kid-friendly hotels, floor of mini club is covered with antibacterial material in order to provide hygiene.

CONCLUSION AND IMPLICATIONS

This study aims to determine marketing practices of kid-friendly hotels in Turkey. The results of this study indicate that most of the kid-friendly hotels are five-star hotels. The reason for this can be the sufficient physical capacity and financial resources of five-star hotels. Likewise, five-star hotels are rich in human resources and they employ permanent staff, which can also be regarded as a facilitating factor.

Kid-friendly hotels are located in Antalya ($n = 67$), Muğla ($n = 8$), and Izmir ($n = 2$). One reason for this can be the accumulation of chain and independent hotels on Mediterranean and Aegean coasts. In addition, Antalya is also suitable for kid-friendly hotels due to the availability of convenient climatic conditions. Families with children usually prefer warmer seas for their children to swim; therefore they choose to stay in Antalya. Besides, tourism season is relatively longer and this constitutes a competitive advantage for kid-friendly hotels in Antalya. Here, the tourism season is about seven months from the end of April until the end of November. On the contrary, in such destinations as Muğla and Izmir, season may be reduced to five months. In general, families with children have time to go on a vacation when they are on annual leave and their children's schools are closed. On the other hand, their vacations sometimes coincide with low season in order to take the advantage of low prices or just because Eid holidays are in the low season. For that reason, the southern regions, where tourism season is relatively longer, are preferred more than other regions by families with children.

The findings of the present study showed that most of the kid-friendly hotels furnish their rooms for families with children so as to minimize the problems experienced during their stay. Furthermore, a small number of hotels focus on personal experiences such as "special welcome for children" and "decoration materials appealing to children," which make children feel themselves special, to differentiate themselves from their competitors.

Descriptive analysis of food and beverage options showed that very few kid-friendly hotels have an independent mini restaurant or a waiter responsible from the child buffet in the main restaurant. Thus, it can be inferred that adequate number of staff is not employed in the context of providing an excellent service to customers. The relatively high proportion of employee costs in total costs and tendency to cut down on employee costs in hotel establishments may have led this situation. Besides, the number of mini restaurants may be low due to additional costs such as equipments and employees. Apart from that, alcohol-free mini-club bars, barbecue parties, ice-cream buffets, and drink bars give the impression to children that they are treated like an adult. Such practices are also significant in the context of creating self-confidence in children.

Almost all of the kid-friendly hotels in the sample have a mini club. It is also remarkable that mini clubs are named with mnemonic names that recall the name of hotel. Such an effort can be interpreted as an attempt to create brand image in the minds of young consumers from an early age. Because children who are satisfied with the services of mini clubs will probably prefer to stay in the same hotel as a customer. This finding is consistent with the determination in Story and French (2004) where they indicated that brands try to reach youth, beginning when they are toddlers, to foster brand-building and influence purchase behavior. Obviously, as found in present study, various activities are available for children in kid-friendly hotels. Particularly, many activities are offered to children under the sub-categories of entertainment, sports, classes and workshops, swimming and sunbathing, handicraft skills, computer games, and electronic toys.

As understood from the findings of the present study, kid-friendly hotels in the sample pay special attention to accommodation, food and beverage, and entertainment issues related to children. Such a finding is consistent with the finding in Thornton, Shaw, and Williams (1997) where they indicated that ability of children to influence the holiday decision making and behavior of parents can be seen in two forms, which are child care requirements (sleep and meals) and a totally satisfying experience, respectively.

This chapter has determined the marketing practices of kid-friendly hotels in Turkey. At the time of this study there was no legal regulation basis for kid-friendly hotels in Turkey but findings of this study showed that there are significant developments in this area of knowledge. In other words, hotel establishments in Turkey may have taken big steps in the area of marketing to children due to the intense competition in tourism sector. However, kid-friendly hotels should recognize children and parents well and estimate their needs and wants in advance in order to be successful. Likewise, they should follow the developments and trends in children's market and include motivators for children while presenting their products. Moreover, age-based market segmentation strategy should also be utilized and age segments should be targeted with different marketing strategies.

Although this study is one of the primary studies in Turkey in the area of marketing to children, it has certain limitations. First, the scope of the study is limited to the marketing practices of kid-friendly hotels operating in Turkey. On the other hand, the number of these hotels may vary from one season to another since a legal regulation basis for kid-friendly hotels does not exist in Turkey. For this reason, some of the kid-friendly hotels may have been excluded from the study incidentally. Second, websites were examined in a specific period of time. Thus, findings of this study reflect the status of kid-friendly hotels at a specific time. Lastly, descriptive analyses were conducted under the assumption that all marketing practices will be announced on hotels' websites. Therefore, some practices which are not announced on websites may have been excluded from the study.

Some ideas for future studies can be suggested by the limitations of the current research. More specifically, data used in this study can be confirmed by interviewing with officials from kid-friendly hotels. Thus, accuracy of the findings can be tested while additional data can be obtained. Also, children's level of satisfaction with the facilities and services offered by kid-friendly hotels can be measured.

REFERENCES

Aktaş, H., Özüpek, M. N., & Altuntaş, H. (2011). Çocukların marka tercihleri ve medya tüketim alışkanlıkları. *Selçuk İletişim, 6*(4), 115–125.

Barlovic, I. (2006). Obesity, advertising to kids, and social marketing. *Young Consumers: Insight and Ideas for Responsible Marketers, 3*, 26–34.

Economist. (2006). *Business: Trillion-dollar kids; marketing to children.* Retrieved from http://www.economist.com/node/8355035. Accessed on November 13, 2013.

Gönül, F. (2007). *Lykia World, Times'ın aile dostu oteller listesinde.* Retrieved from http://www.turizmdebusabah.com/haberler/bebek-havuzu-cocuk-plaji-guvenlik-ve-kresle-puan-aldi-32956.html. Accessed on November 13, 2013.

International Dairy-Deli-Bakery Association. (2005). Free kids marketing tips. *Frozen Food Age, 53*(10), 27.

Kid-Friendly Hotel Project. (2012). *Presentation of Kid-Friendly Hotel Project.* Retrieved from http://www.cocukdostu.org/index.php/%C3%A7ocuk-dostu-otel-projesi/tan%C4%B1t %C4%B1m. Accessed on July 25, 2012.

LeCompte, M. D., & Goetz, J. P. (1982). Problems of reliability and validity in ethnographic research. *Review of Educational Research, 52,* 31−60.

Mathiot, L. (2010). Child consumption of fun food: Between deviating practice and re-appropriating food-use. *Young Consumers: Insight and Ideas for Responsible Marketers, 11*(2), 108−116.

McNeal, J. U. (1992). *Kids as customers: A handbook of marketing to children.* New York, NY: Lexington Books.

McNeal, J. U. (1999). *The kids market: Myths and realities.* Ithaca, NY: Paramount Market.

Ntvmsnbc. (2012). *Oteller "çocuk dostu" olacak.* Retrieved from http://www.ntvmsnbc.com/id/ 25330393/#storyContinued. Accessed on July 23, 2012.

Özata, Z. (2007). *Çocuklar öncelikle çocuktur, onları "tüketici" olarak tanımlayınca başlıyor sorun!* Retrieved from http://zeynepozata.blogspot.com/2007/12/ocuklar-ncelikle-ocuk-tur-onlar-tketici.html. Accessed on October 13, 2013.

Rose, K. (2007). *Kids' snack attack, new product trends.* Retrieved from http://www.prepared-foods.com/ext/resources/Special_Reports/Kids−Snack-Attack.pdf. Accessed on September 15, 2013.

Story, M., & French, S. (2004). Food advertising and marketing directed at children and adolescents in the US. *International Journal of Behavioral Nutrition and Physical Activity, 1*(3), 1−17.

Thornton, P. R., Shaw, G., & Williams, A. M. (1997). Tourist group holiday decision making and behaviour: The influence of children. *Tourism Management, 18*(5), 287−297.

Turkish Statistical Institute Website. (2011). Retrieved from www.tuik.gov.tr. Accessed on January 10, 2013.

Valkenburg, P. M., & Cantor, J. (2001). The development of a child into a consumer. *Applied Developmental Psychology, 22,* 61−72.

Yıldırım, A., & Şimşek, H. (2011). *Sosyal bilimlerde nitel araştırma yöntemleri* (8th ed.). Ankara: Seçkin.

Yılmaz, A. (2007). *Aile turizmine yönelik hizmet veren otel işletmelerinde hizmet kalitesi: Antalya Bölgesinde Türk ve Alman turistlere yönelik bir araştırma.* Unpublished Master Thesis, Eskişehir Anadolu University Institute of Social Sciences.

Yin, R. K. (2003). *Case study research, design and method* (3rd ed., Vol. 5). Applied Social Research Methods Series. California, CA: Sage.

THE INFLUENCE OF SLOW CITY IN THE CONTEXT OF SUSTAINABLE DESTINATION MARKETING

Yeşim Coşar, Alp Timur and Metin Kozak

ABSTRACT

There appears to be a close relationship between the concept of slow city and the tourism industry, in respect of sustainable life and sustainable destination marketing. Due to the lack of empirical studies focusing upon this relationship, the present chapter aims to analyze the probable effects of the trend toward slow city on tourist destinations, in terms of sustainable marketing. To accomplish these objectives, the study uses qualitative research methods, conducting interviews with domestic tourists and local residents, as well as owners and managers of tourism establishments. The results are represented as a sample across three different categories. In light of the data assessment, the chapter revisits the list of the above-mentioned objectives and provides empirical evidence emphasizing the value of slow city in maintaining sustainability in terms of destination marketing, although some objections suggest that sustainability remains at risk.

Keywords: Slow city (Cittaslow); sustainable tourism; destination marketing; tourist behavior

Marketing Places and Spaces
Advances in Culture, Tourism and Hospitality Research, Volume 10, 209–220
Copyright © 2015 by Emerald Group Publishing Limited
All rights of reproduction in any form reserved
ISSN: 1871-3173/doi:10.1108/S1871-317320150000010015

INTRODUCTION

The literature on tourism in recent years has included some research into the close nexus between the management of slow city and the application of sustainable forms of tourism (e.g., Knox, 2005; Mayer & Knox, 2006). Some of these striking applications, in various countries across the world, are discussed in a book entitled *Slow Tourism: Experiences and Mobilities* (Fullagar, Markwell, & Wilson, 2012). This book is commendable for being the first to be published in this domain. It is possible to handle the interdependence between these two terms as follows.

"Slow city" was introduced as an alternative to the concept of "the current modern life," in order to make it possible for inhabitants of particular cities to lead a comparatively comfortable life, away from noise and environmental pollution, in a naturally and culturally unspoiled atmosphere. In current modern cities, called metropolises, working conditions place great restrictions on people's time, due to the length of time spent traveling from one place to another; in addition, abiding by one's promises puts pressure on people, and transportation from one place to another causes environmental and noise pollution. As a result, metropolitan people are rarely able to come into contact with one another on common ground (Davidson & Maitland, 1997; Ratcliffe & Flanagan, 2004).

In contrast, let us imagine a settlement where the traces of industrialization are barely observable, where technology is used solely for fundamental necessities, and where natural and cultural identities are preserved. In cities of this kind, people do not lead their lives in a rush; rather, they shop in small shops or small-scale supermarkets rather than mega shopping malls, they buy natural products easily in neighborhood bazaars, and can consume these products either in local restaurants or at home. In such cities, one is much less likely to encounter unfavorable effects such as noise pollution, the stress of traffic congestion, or construction projects in town centers or suburbs that impair the view. Each of these issues is a constituent of the slow city model that has been put forward as an alternative to the mentality of the metropolitan city, which paves the wave to consuming resources rapidly instead of producing new ones, and encourages people to consume rather than conserve.

Highlighting this basic discrepancy between metropolitan life and the slow city concept can render a service to tourism, in respect of sustainability. Sustainability is a perspective aimed at conserving life standards, making it possible for contemporary people and tourists to benefit from natural, cultural, and economic assets obtained for the fulfillment of their fundamental needs (Aransson, 1994; Liu, 2003). Conversely, sustainability is also a perspective that will guarantee the fulfillments of future generations, who can be imagined engaging in similar lifestyles in years to come. This perspective has been approached quite differently in recent years and across a range of countries, both due to the way that the tourism industry operates and because natural cultural resources directly supporting tourism are restricted. These resources are not only for the use of the current generation, but will be used by prospective tourists in different periods of time as basic necessities as long as mankind exists (Garrod & Fyall, 1998).

Countries strive to apply competitive strategies in order to control regional markets in the face of increasing competition in tourism (Kozak and Baloglu, 2010). They also monitor strategies based on collaboration with other countries in certain domains. Besides this, a substantial change in the attitudes and expectations of tourists has been observed, and although the slow city concept was initially applied in relation to the life standards of local inhabitants, it was subsequently applied as a source of possible attraction with respect to tourism marketing.

It may be the case that a tourist on holiday is disturbed by environmental pollution or noise pollution, or that they must consume artificial products instead of natural ones, or that they are obliged to mediate the termination of all elements that natural and cultural life offers as basic products. It may also be the case that although a tourist on holiday is trying to escape from technology, they then return to home and to work having had a holiday filled with stress and turmoil instead of the peace and quiet they were seeking. As a result, the formation of slow city, as a new concept, has potential as an important means of guaranteeing the sustainability and continuity of tourism dynamism and supply and demand, in terms of the impact of a holiday experience upon living quality.

In recent years, destinations have faced some crucial questions with respect to sustainability. Destinations must be cleaner, greener, and safer in order to attract foreign investment, to promote the development of tourism, and to stay tuned to rival destinations, with a view to obtaining commercial benefits. The most important issue to be taken into consideration is environmentally sustainable tourism applications and asset management (Ratcliffe & Flanagan, 2004). The rapid increase in the number of tourists, the number of buses allocated for tourists, and the crowds and the chaos created by tourism-related traffic, all exert pressure on the resources of tourism (Davidson & Maitland, 1997).

As discussed above, a fairly close interrelationship between the concept of slow city and tourism is at issue. This interrelationship is closely connected with the issues of sustainable life and sustainable tourism. Regarded from a worldwide perspective, it can be observed that in recent years the phenomenon of slow tourism, as a new sort of product, has started to become more popular. Nonetheless, there has been not much research into the interrelationship between these two concepts. Thus, the aim of the present chapter is to analyze the probable effects of the trend of slow city on tourist destinations with respect to sustainable marketing.

METHOD

The questionnaire was prepared and implemented by converting the purpose of the study into research questions and soliciting expert views. Interviews were conducted with 26 domestic tourists visiting Seferihisar, a town of İzmir, Turkey (between 17 and 20 August 2012), 22 local residents in Seferihisar (between 17 August and 6 September), and 24 businessmen or administrators trading in Seferihisar (between 17 and 30 August 2012). Each interview lasted between 15 and 60 minutes. All the domestic tourists included in the interview group stayed in a resort for at least one night, and interviewees in the local residents and businessmen groups were chosen from across Seferihisar. Special attention was paid to choosing interviewees who were voluntary and who had little or no knowledge of the slow city concept.

FINDINGS

This section presents a brief discussion of the results of the study, using three sets of data. The first set includes an analysis of interviews with domestic tourists, the second addresses the results of interviews with inhabitants of the study area, and the third evaluates the interviews with managers or owners of businesses operating within the study area.

Analysis of Interviews Conducted with Domestic Tourists

The analysis of interviews with domestic tourists (the first group) yielded the following findings: the interviewees had many different occupations;

their ages ranged between 34 and 68; with regard to the frequency of visits to Seferihisar, the respondents ranges between those visiting Seferihisar for the first time and those who had visited Seferihisar 20 times. Their reasons for visiting Seferihisar ranged from the fact that it is close to Izmir to the fact that Seferihisar is a quiet city. As Table 1 shows, the 24 tourists participating in the research were a fairly heterogeneous group with regard to parameters such as occupation, age, and the frequency and purpose of their visits.

Amount of knowledge acquired about the meaning and content of slow city: Several characterizations of the slow city concept were proposed, including the following: cherishing civic culture; conserving natural assets; an understating that conserves a peaceful and quiet environment, instead of the rapid way of life brought about by globalization; evasion from urban life; evasion from hustle and bustle, as well as noise; living, eating, and working slowly. In most of these statements, slow city is associated with tranquility and silence.

Changes observed in Seferihisar after the accreditation of slow city: After the accreditation of slow city, tourists coming to Seferihisar observed some changes. The number of constructions, enterprises, and tourists coming to the city increase in relation to the previous years, seemed to trigger problems relating to crowds and parking. As for favorable observations, some of the consequences mentioned were the rehabilitation of green areas, and the possibility of a greater attachment to planning a quiet atmosphere.

Effects of slow city on tourism development in Seferihisar: Aside from the unfavorable effects of becoming a slow city (such as excessive constructional development), favorable consequences abound, such as the conservation of cultural and natural assets, as well as people's desire to visit places where slow city is available. Taking the unfavorable effects into consideration, it was stated that, parallel to the revival in the tourist demand for environs, there has also been a revival in the constructional development of environs in recent years. Considering the issue from a positive perspective, it was emphasized that local inhabitants and enterprises need to transfer the natural and cultural assets of environs by making a claim to those assets.

> There is no good or bad advert. People hear about slow city and become curious to see why people from Italy have started to come here since this city (Seferihisar) became a slow city. The title of slow city has become a way of introducing the people to the city. With its history and nature, Turkey is a very significant asset, and no matter what is to be done, it must be done by conserving these assets. (Participant 4 – Sailor)

Table 1. Profiles of Respondents (Domestic Tourists).

No.	Profession	Age	Number of Visits	Purpose of Visit	Date to Interview	Hour to Interview
1	Public relations	39	1	Word of mouth recommendation, quit atmosphere	17.08.2012	21.00
2	Lecturer	41	2	Visiting friends	17.08.2012	21.45
3	Manufacturer	56	17 years	Seaside, nature	18.08.2012	19.30
4	Sailor	46	37 years	Seaside, nature	18.08.2012	21.55
5	Dietician	64	12 years	Quit atmosphere, water temperature	19.08.2012	17.20
6	Retired	63	2	Seaside, water temperature, tourist profile	19.08.2012	17.50
7	Accountant	37	15	Seaside, nature	19.08.2012	19.00
8	Worker	38	4	Quit atmosphere, seaside, value for money	19.08.2012	19.25
9	Accountant	47	20 years	Quit atmosphere, nature, behavior of local people	19.08.2012	19.50
10	Retired	56	12 years	Nature, seaside, water temperature, wind	19.08.2012	20.15
11	Accountant	66	2	Seaside, nature	19.08.2012	20.50
12	Mechanical engineer	42	10	Value for money	19.08.2012	21.15
13	Retired	59	10	Quit atmosphere, business	19.08.2012	21.40
14	Travel agent	54	2	Seaside, quit atmosphere, accessibility	19.08.2012	22.00
15	Bank officer	42	2	Quit atmosphere, water temperature, tourist profile	20.08.2012	10.10
16	Public officer	60	1	Quit atmosphere, seaside, value for Money	20.08.2012	10.25
17	Retired	68	1	Seaside, slow city	20.08.2012	10.40
18	Custom officer	34	1	Closer to Izmir	20.08.2012	11.25
19	Advertisement agent	42	20 years	Seaside, quit atmosphere, closer to Izmir	20.08.2012	11.30
20	Bank officer	38	2	Seaside, quit atmosphere, slow city	20.08.2012	11.45
21	Artist	38	2	Word of mouth recommendation	20.08.2012	12.00
22	Trade	42	4	Quit atmosphere, slow city	20.08.2012	12.30
23	Not available (N/A)	44	4	Closer to Izmir, quit atmosphere, value for money	20.08.2012	13.00
24	Retired	57	1	Seaside	20.08.2012	14.35

Analysis of Interviews with Local Inhabitants

As regards the profile of respondents within this category (Table 2), many different occupations were represented, such as bank officers, teachers, engineers, and retirees. The age distribution was quite broad, ranging from 27 to 68. With regard to the length of residence in Seferihisar, the profile of the respondents was very mixed, ranging from light involvement (e.g., residence periods of 3−5 years) to heavy involvement (e.g., residence periods of 56−61 years).

Amount of knowledge acquired about meaning and content of slow city: From the perspective of local inhabitants, we can probably define slow city as follows: it is a project that is based on improving life standards, by means of conserving both the natural properties and the cultural values of a destination. These natural properties involve the conservation of ecological life, organized housing, silence, and so on. The cultural values are

Table 2. Profile of Respondents (Local Inhabitants).

No.	Profession	Age	Length of Residence in Seferihisar (in year)	Date to Interview	Hour to Interview
1	Fisherman	41	20	17.08.2012	22.20
2	Bank manager	46	4	19.08.2012	18.15
3	Teacher	43	43	28.08.2012	11.30
4	Public officer	31	31	28.08.2012	16.00
5	Agricultural engineer	53	12	28.08.2012	16.30
6	Farmer	44	44	29.08.2012	17.00
7	Mechanical engineer	57	14	29.08.2012	17.30
8	Teacher (retired)	61	61	29.08.2012	18.00
9	Worker (retired)	56	56	29.08.2012	18.40
10	Teacher	41	35	30.08.2012	14.35
11	Tradesman	34	34	30.08.2012	17.45
12	Teacher	38	3	30.08.2012	18.30
13	Agricultural engineer	45	25	01.09.2012	17.00
14	Doctor	45	1	01.09.2012	18.40
15	Housewife (peddler)	56	50	02.09.2012	11.00
16	Retired (peddler)	48	7	02.09.2012	11.20
17	Tailor	55	5	02.09.2012	12.00
18	Bank officer	38	38	02.09.2012	12.30
19	Bank officer (retired − peddler)	68	17	02.09.2012	13.10
20	Teacher (retired − peddler)	62	16	02.09.2012	13.40
21	Tradesman (peddler)	50	15	02.09.2012	14.10
22	Sales agent	27	27	06.09.2012	15.40

made up of customs, traditions, lifestyle, table manners, and the way people communicate with each other. It is notable that this definition coincides with the real definition of slow city.

Changes observed in Seferihisar after the accreditation of slow city: It is possible to analyze how local people perceive the change brought by slow city in three ways: Primarily, it is in a positive sense, in terms of economic, cultural, and *promotional* aspects. Value in labor has increased, housewives have started working, new employment areas have been created, organic agriculture and marketing have been encouraged, tourist arrivals have increased, the incomes of local people have been boosted, building exteriors have been rearranged, local people have become aware of environmental issues, and the number of social and cultural activities has soared.

> Tourist arrivals have increased, particularly from Istanbul. A producer's market and local market in the castle have been established, and attract great attention. On those days when markets take place, there are a lot of visitors. The value of agricultural products has increased, and the marketing of these products has been guaranteed. (Participant 5 – Agricultural Engineer)

On the other hand, a considerable numbers of participants (11 people) mentioned deeper negative effects. Some of these include population increase (immigration and visitor flow), the noise and traffic resulting from the crowds, a construction boom due to interest in the area, a resultant increase in property prices, the increase in daily visitors over the summer seasons, a spoilt environment, the use of foreign words or names as trademarks of businesses, and the rising number of investors from different places.

Effects of slow city on tourism development in Seferihisar: There are two opposing views on the development of tourism in Seferihisar with the concept of slow city. The first emphasizes that the tourism industry will develop in a positive direction, through the image of being the first slow city and through an increase in awareness, through prioritizing local products, and through operating guest houses. Members of this group express such views as the following:

> Tourism [in Seferihisar] continues to develop. Tourists come to Seferihisar to see local aspects and food. As long as these assets are protected it will attract tourists. (Participant 6 – Farmer)

> If Seferihisar develops in accordance with the criteria of slow city it will attract fewer but higher profiled tourists. In this case, Seferihisar will benefit more both culturally and economically. (Participant 3 – Teacher)

Members of the second group do not identify a positive relationship between slow city and the future of tourism in Seferihisar. They do not regard the development of tourism through the increasing number of visitors with optimism. They believe that as tourism develops, in its context of slow city the area might lose its charm and as a result they expect a degradation both in service and life quality, like that experienced in other popular destinations in Turkey, such as the resorts of Özdere, Çeşme, and Kuşadası.

Assessment of Interviews with Business Operators or Managers

The third group interviewed was composed of owners or managers of businesses operating in various fields relating to production and services, including hotels, souvenir shops, food shops, and handcraft shops. The age of respondents in this group ranged from 19 to 57, though the respondents were mainly middle age. The duration of their service ranged from 1 to 25 years, but was mainly limited to 1−2 years (Table 3).

Amount of knowledge acquired about the meaning and content of slow city: Owners and managers know as much about the slow city concept as the previous two groups. Like these other groups, they regard slow city as the symbol of a calm life. A calm life consists of a slow food culture, which puts forward the local cuisine based on organic products, the protection of natural life and structure, less building and traffic, the elimination of noise and visual pollution, and the sustaining customs and traditions. Their underlying aim is to ensure the happiness (in other words, the quality of life) of both people living in the area and of those coming to visit the area.

Effects of slow city on tourism development in Seferihisar: The managers or owners of properties in Seferihisar underline that the slow city concept has had a positive effect on the development of local tourism. According to this group, slow city has been a source of promotion of Seferihisar and, as a result, the number of people visiting the area has substantially increased due to greater curiosity. Along with the construction of new hotels, arrivals of foreign tourists are observed. Some in this group believed that the slow city concept was good for Seferihisar, and that as long as the necessary procedures were implemented, more tourists would arrive and that local businesses would benefit accordingly.

> Slow cities are loyal to each other and there is a mass of tourists as a result of this. This will attract more tourists. I think the town will be more publicized. (Participant 2 − Hotel Manager)

Table 3.   Profile of Respondents (Business Operators or Managers).

No.	Profession	Age	Length of Residence in Seferihisar (in year)	Date to Interview	Hour to Interview
1	Hotelier	46	18	17.08.2012	18.50
2	Hotelier	39	12	17.08.2012	20.00
3	Hotelier	23	18	17.08.2012	20.30
4	Business operator (cafe−bar)	49	2	18.08.2012	20.50
5	Hotelier	29	7	18.08.2012	21.40
6	Business operator	40	1	19.08.2012	16.50
7	Hotelier	39	20	19.08.2012	20.30
8	Business operator (spice−herb)	19	1	30.08.2012	12.30
9	Business operator (jewelry)	32	1,5	30.08.2012	12.45
10	Business operator (boutique)	53	1,5	30.08.2012	13.00
11	Business operator (jewelry)	47	2	30.08.2012	13.15
12	Business operator (cafe−bar)	48	2	30.08.2012	13.30
13	Business operator (cafe−bar)	37	2	30.08.2012	13.45
14	Business operator	30	3	30.08.2012	14.00
15	Business operator (jewelry)	47	2	30.08.2012	14.20
16	Business operator (cafe−bar)	24	1	30.08.2012	14.50
17	Business operator (handcrafts)	39	3	30.08.2012	15.10
18	Business operator (handcrafts)	43	2	30.08.2012	16.00
19	Business operator (handcrafts)	53	4	30.08.2012	16.15
20	Business operator (constructor)	53	4	30.08.2012	16.40
21	Trainer (diving club)	49	4	30.08.2012	17.00
22	Business operator (restaurant)	57	2	30.08.2012	17.20
23	Business operator (handcrafts)	58	3	30.08.2012	18.00
24	Business operator (patisserie)	48	25	30.08.2012	18.15
25	Hotelier	48	1	30.08.2012	18.45
26	Business operator (handcrafts)	45	2	30.08.2012	19.30

On the other hand, some claimed that slow city had not had a positive impact on local tourism, that Seferihisar had failed to meet the criteria for being a slow city efficiently, and that there was a conflict between keeping the slow city on the agenda on the one hand, and the increase in building, noise pollution, and the number of hotel construction on the other hand. These respondents do not anticipate any positive developments related to the tourism industry in the near future, because they believe that the local authorities' approach to saturation limit in terms of tourism mobility poses a risk.

> Becoming a slow city has affected the development of tourism positively. It has turned into a town with a value from scratch. If tourism grows and it gets crowded, it might be disqualified as a slow city. (Participant 6 – Tourism Manager)

Contribution of slow city to Seferihisar: The contribution of slow city to Seferihisar can be summarized as follows, in terms of positive impact: publicity of the area, all year around tourism mobility (rather than just at certain periods of the year), more social activities (concerts, festivals, etc.), landscaping (maintenance of roads, pavements and houses, electric cables being installed underground), greater employment through the development of the marina and new businesses, encouraging people to produce, and an increased quality of life as a result of increased income. All these factors meet the criteria of being a slow city. However, in terms of negative impact, rising property prices and inadequate social activities can be observed, as well as overpopulation because of publicity and a failure to observe architectural criteria.

CONCLUSION AND IMPLICATIONS

Primarily, when knowledge of the meaning of slow city is controlled, it is recognized that domestic tourists, local people, business owners and managers are familiar with the subject. Although various terms are used when defining slow city, it is commonly referred to as a "calm, quiet and serene city." A group of tourists with no previous knowledge said that that they learned about slow city while they were in Seferihisar.

The owners or managers of businesses operating in Seferihisar (along with the local people) emphasize the fact that slow city has affected the local economy positively. According to them, slow city has been an important source of publicity for Seferihisar, and has led to a significant increase in the number of people visiting the town. It is reported that because of the new hotels and guest houses constructed, there are more foreign tourists visiting the area. It is claimed that Seferihisar can take advantage of slow city, and that as long as the appropriate procedures are implemented, more tourists will arrive and local businesses will benefit accordingly.

Last but not least, Seferihisar is unlikely to meet the criteria for being a slow city adequately, and there are some related environmental issues. Keeping the slow city on the agenda on one hand, and the increase in building and noise pollution and the number of hotel construction on the other, the expectations were seen by some respondents as being in conflict.

Some did not expect any positive developments related to tourism activities in the near future because of the risk posed by local authorities' approach to the limit of saturation in terms of tourism mobility. As a result, these respondents expect service and life quality to deteriorate, as experienced in other resorts such as Özdere, Çeşme, and Kuşadası in Turkey. Such an experience may result in the overdevelopment of the town, and have a negative impact on its overall image that would also create a barrier to marketing.

REFERENCES

Aransson, L. (1994). Sustainable tourism systems: The example of sustainable rural tourism in Sweden. *Journal of Sustainable Tourism*, 2(1−2), 77−92.

Davidson, R., & Maitland, R. (1997). *Tourism destinations*. London: Hodder & Stoughton Educational.

Fullagar, S., Markwell, K., & Wilson, E. (2012). *Slow tourism: Experiences and mobilities*. Bristol: Channel View Publications.

Garrod, B., & Fyall, A. (1998). Beyond the rhetoric of sustainable tourism. *Tourism Management*, 19(3), 201.

Knox, P. L. (2005). Creating ordinary places: Slow cities is a fast world. *Journal of Urban Design*, 10(1), 1−11.

Kozak, M., & Baloglu, S. (2010). *Managing and marketing tourist destinations: Strategies to gain competitive edge*. New York, NY: Taylor & Francis.

Liu, Z. (2003). Sustainable tourism development: A critique. *Journal of Sustainable Tourism*, 11(6), 459−473.

Mayer, H., & Knox, P. L. (2006). Slow cities: Sustainable places in a fast world. *Journal of Urban Affairs*, 28(4), 321−334.

Ratcliffe, J., & Flanagan, S. (2004). Enhancing the vitality and viability of town and city centres: The concept of the business improvement district in the context of tourism enterprise. *Property Management*, 22(5), 377−395.

CUSTOMER COMMUNICATION FACILITIES WITH TOURISM: A COMPARISON BETWEEN GERMAN AND JAPANESE AUTOMOBILE COMPANIES

Yosuke Endo and Yohei Kurata

ABSTRACT

This chapter investigates a corporate branding method that is based on direct customer communication. Consumer goods companies often arrange communication platforms that are designed to attract visitors and advertise their products and corporate philosophy. Such platforms include corporate showrooms, corporate museums, and factory tours. This chapter focuses on automobile companies and their customer communication corporate activities. The chapter compares the current customer communication strategies of leading German and Japanese car manufacturers. Certain car manufacturers maintain customer communication facility arrangements. The chapter finds certain differences concerning facility utilization and the corporate policies of each company.

Marketing Places and Spaces
Advances in Culture, Tourism and Hospitality Research, Volume 10, 221–233
Copyright © 2015 by Emerald Group Publishing Limited
ISSN: 1871-3173/doi:10.1108/S1871-317320150000010016

We discuss the results of our study and consider a company's suitability and potential with respect to branding methods that incorporate tourism.

Keywords: Industrial tourism; brand strategy; marketing strategy; brand recognition; tourism marketing; tourism communication

INTRODUCTION

This chapter focuses on the incorporation of tourism in the corporate branding strategies of consumer goods companies. The production facilities of the companies are the main objects of this chapter. These facilities represent a platform from which companies can directly communicate with tourists as part of their corporate branding efforts. Many consumer goods companies operate factory tours and host exhibitions in their production facilities, and we consider that these activities are conducive to building relationships with customers.

Maintaining effective customer relationships leads to product and corporate brand loyalty depending on the customer relationship marketing strategy (Stone, Woodcock, & Machtynger, 1995). Production facility visits can provide customers with an opportunity to become familiar with the origins of a corporate brand, which might be an effective way for a company to reinforce their brand and develop a differentiation strategy. MacCannell (1999) insists that tourists are often eager to see the "back side" of locations that they visit, which he calls a "quest for authenticity." Beverland (2009) proposes that product authenticity contributes to corporate branding. We assume, given these theories, that an informational marketing event at a production facility could meet consumer demand for authenticity and satisfy the quest for the origin of a consumer product brand.

We present certain automobile companies in Germany and Japan as examples of companies that operate customer communication facilities and provide consumer services, such as factory tours and corporate museums, at their production districts. Coles and Hall (2008) introduces corporate policies for customer communications and branding using German automobile company factory tours.

This chapter examines the activities of Volkswagen Group and the exhibition facility, Autostadt, in Wolfsburg. We obtained visitor data from Autostadt and investigated Volkswagen Group's corporate policy for the facility operations from literature research. We also investigated three

Japanese companies, Honda, Mazda, and Toyota. These three companies operate factory tours similar to the Volkswagen Group's tour at Autostadt. However, we found certain differences in visitor data and the corporate purpose of the three Japanese automobile companies and Volkswagen Group. We consider that the results are attributable to differences in corporate strategy.

This chapter suggests that there is potential for expansion of this branding method with the aid of tourism, and seeks to enlighten those responsible for corporate strategy and tourism resource development. Consumer goods companies seem to be the most conducive to this branding strategy. This chapter tries to determine the cause of the company differences in approach, which are presented in the conclusion.

LITERATURE REVIEW

This chapter considers direct communication with customers to be a fundamental corporate activity that is consistent with the marketing theory of *relationship marketing* and *customer relationship management* (Brink and Berndt, 2009). Although this theory focuses on relationship building with various stakeholders from employees to business partners, the current chapter evaluates the potential of customer relationships. We consider that direct communication with customers in exhibition facilities is an effective marketing method and represents customer relationship building as part of corporate strategy. Additionally, direct communications provide consumer goods companies with an opportunity to interact with customers and can be applied to *one-to-one marketing* (Peppers, Rogers, & Dorf, 1999). Companies should pay attention to the individual characteristics of each customer, which represents a new paradigm in marketing theory.

Kent and Brown (2009) proposes that a flagship facility can play a representative role in corporate strategy, and provides examples of consumer goods companies such as fashion retailers and luxury brands. According to Kent (2009), such symbolism can be applied to brand advertising, relationship building, and corporate branding. The flagship marketing theory is applicable to the object of this chapter, automobile companies. We consider that customer communication facilities operated by automobile companies could function as vital flagship assets to boost the companies and their brands.

The targets for communication facilities are often tourists because they represent the recipients of such resources. According to Otgaar (2010), this type of tourism activity is defined as *industrial tourism*; the activity is composed of a visit to the site that facilitates visitor education with respect to the past, current, and future economic activities of the company. Gnoth (2002) evaluates a tourism-oriented branding method that considers the relevance between export and tourism destination brands. This current chapter incorporates research theories into the study, presents the marketing method associated with customer communications in tourism destinations, and applies the method to corporate strategy.

METHOD

The study objects of this chapter are exhibition facilities in production districts operated by automobile companies in Germany and Japan. The products of automobile companies have global reach and we assume that the marketing methods of these companies would be superior to consumer goods companies with limited reach. This chapter examines the marketing strategies of the companies that incorporate tourism destination factors by arranging factory tours and corporate museums in production districts. The production districts are proximate to company headquarters. If brand authenticity is associated with the location of company founding, the company headquarters represent an appropriate location to communicate advertising and the origins of the corporate brand. This chapter addresses the communication platforms of the chosen German and Japanese companies because they have arranged customer communication facilities near the company headquarters.

We adopted four survey methods in the investigation of automobile companies in Germany and Japan: literature research, Internet document searches, enterprise investigation utilizing a survey questionnaire, and fieldwork conducted in each facility. First, we investigated the current situation at Autostadt and the factory tours in Wolfsburg from literature and the Website, with a focus on the visitor data and Volkswagen Group's purpose of attracting visitors. We also examined Japanese automobile companies using a survey questionnaire and by conducting fieldwork from 2011 to 2012. These investigations focused on the utilization of exhibition facilities in production districts.

The study objects are three car manufacturers: Honda, Mazda, and Toyota. Although we initially approached five Japanese companies to participate in the survey, we obtained permission from only three companies (the response rate was 60%). The questionnaire is designed to collect data concerning the following: visitor data from the exhibition facility, the factory tours that were offered in 2010, and the corporate policies with respect to tour operation and attracting visitors. The following are examples of the survey questions. *Question 1*: How many people visited your facility in 2010? *Question 2*: What demographic constituted the majority of visitors? Please choose among the following: tourist groups, student groups, or business groups. *Question 3*: What is the purpose of facility operations? We collected the visitor data from Questions 1 and 2, and evaluated the corporate policies concerning operations from the responses to Question 3. The research results provided data for a comparison between German and Japanese automobile companies that could explain the differences in corporate policies concerning tourism-oriented branding.

FINDINGS

Volkswagen Group

Volkswagen Group is a leading German automobile company with global reach. The company headquarters are located in Wolfsburg, Germany. Volkswagen Group operates its communication platform adjacent to the company headquarters at Autostadt, which attracts substantial tourist visitors (Fig. 1).

The facility has many exhibitions designed to entertain visitors and to interact with customers (Autostadt, 2013a). A collection of pavilions acts as a corporate museum and illustrates the various automobile brands and products of the Volkswagen Group. Autostadt arranges guided factory tours during which visitors can directly communicate with employees. If customers purchase products, they can collect them at the customer center. Moreover, accommodations and restaurants are located in the grounds. The exhibition at Autostadt constitutes an attractive tourism destination that provides a variety of visitor experiences.

We examine these corporate activities and sizeable investments from the perspective of marketing theory. The theory of *experiential marketing*

Fig. 1.   Autostadt in Wolfsburg. *Source:* The authors.

assumes that a successful consumer goods experience will lead to customer satisfaction and customer loyalty (Schmitt, 2000). The visitors to Autostadt become Volkswagen Group's new customers, or remain existing customers, and they are likely to have been subject to a successful consumer experience. Therefore, Volkswagen Group would regard customer experiences as a significant element of their corporate brand and customer loyalty strategy.

Walvis (2003) insists that companies often arrange their symbolic locations for purposes of customer communication, and such communication platforms play an important role with respect to corporate branding. Walvis (2003) calls such facilities *brand locations*, and Volkswagen Group's Autostadt provides a perfect example. Volkswagen Group operates this exhibition facility for customer communication purposes, as its Website attests (Autostadt, 2013a). The Managing Director and CEO of Autostadt, Otto Ferdinand Wachs, stated "If the Autostadt is where Volkswagen Group's heart beats, and we are able to reach our customers meaningfully, then we have significantly contributed to the success of the Volkswagen Group" (Autostadt, 2013b). Volkswagen Group considers

Autostadt to be a customer communication facility based on corporate philosophy.

According to the Autostadt annual report (Autostadt, 2013c), this facility attracts approximately 2 million visitors per year, and Coles and Hall (2008) explain that 9% of visitors originate from other countries. Additionally, press releases by Volkswagen Group state that the total number of visitors to Autostadt reached 25 million in 2012 since its opening in 2000 (Autostadt, 2012). With respect to factory tours, 185,237 annual visitors participated in factory tours in 2007, among which 158,269 visitors (85%) were comprised of tourist groups, and 26,968 visitors (15%) were comprised of student or business groups (Otgaar, van den Berg, Berger, & Feng, 2010). The factory tour visitor data show that Volkswagen Group operates factory tours as a way to communicate with their main target, tourist groups.

The Japanese Companies

Japanese automobile companies also boast global reach. The companies featured in this study are Honda, Mazda, and Toyota. These companies also operate factory tours and corporate museums near their headquarters in Japan. Although Volkswagen Group tries to attract tourists to the place of production in Wolfsburg, we discovered that the three Japanese automobile companies differ from the German company with respect to the current production district communication facility.

Honda is located in Tokyo, and the company operates factory tours in Saitama Prefecture, which is adjacent to Tokyo and close to company headquarters. The respondent to our questionnaire was the Honda employee responsible for the factory tours. The total number of visitors who participated in the factory tour during 2010 was 22,070, and the majority belonged to student and business groups. The student groups are mainly composed of regional school field trips, and the business groups represent inspectors from Honda's headquarters and other company visitors for transactional purposes. The respondent stated that the main purpose of operating factory tours is social contribution, or community contributions that might improve company reputation and brand image regionally.

Mazda is headquartered in Hiroshima Prefecture (Fig. 2). The company possesses manufacturing plants that operate factory tours, and the Mazda museum is located adjacent to the factory.

Fig. 2. Mazda Headquarters in Hiroshima Prefecture. *Source*: The authors.

Factory tour visitors can also visit the corporate museum. The question-naire responses from the Mazda representative, who belonged to the General Affairs department of Mazda, revealed that the main targets are not general tourists. The majority of visitors belong to student groups. The visitor data revealed that a total of 61,613 visitors have participated in factory tours. The respondent stated that Mazda attracts visitors for social contribution purposes and to build and maintain public relations with the local community.

Toyota's headquarters are located in Aichi Prefecture. The company also arranges factory tours and operates a corporate museum in the production district (Toyota Exhibition Hall, which is adjacent to the headquarters). The total number of visitors to the museum and factory tours in 2010 was 320,000. The majority belonged to student groups, who are Toyota's main target. The Toyota Corporate Citizenship Division responded and explained that the main purpose for operating factory tours and the corporate museum is social contribution to the local community and society. Additionally, they responded, "If people have a favorable impression and trust for Toyota, it would bring about a sustainable development for the society and us." Toyota values relationships with the regional community and this encompasses the main purpose of operating the communication facilities. The three Japanese companies share this common purpose.

Comparison of German and Japanese Firms

A comparison of the four companies reveals obvious differences in exhibition facility operation purposes and the main target audiences (Table 1). For example, Volkswagen Group operates Autostadt to attract tourists and to emphasize the symbolism and origin of the company through direct customer communication. However, Honda, Mazda, and Toyota, the three Japanese companies, attract primarily student groups, and the common purpose for the Japanese companies is social contribution to the local community.

The differing visitor types are a decisive point in the comparison between the German and Japanese car manufacturer case studies. Student groups are likely to represent future new customers; however, we emphasize the significance of retaining existing customers consistent with the relationship marketing theory (Berry, 2002). If existing customers participate in factory tours, they are part of a tourist group; therefore, from a comparison between the Volkswagen Group and the Japanese companies, we

Table 1. Company Data and Purpose of Attracting Visitors to Production Facilities.

	Annual Visitors	Visitor Type	Purpose
Volkswagen's Autostadt and factory tours in Wolfsburg	2,000,000	Tourist groups	Company symbolism and communication platform for customers.
Honda's factory tours in Saitama	22,070	Student groups	Social contribution.
Mazda's factory tours and Mazda museum in Hiroshima	61,613	Student groups	Social contribution and public relations.
Toyota's factory tour and Toyota Exhibition Hall in Aichi	320,000	Student groups	Social contribution for sustainable development of the company and society.

conclude that the Volkswagen Group attempts to communicate with existing customers at its Autostadt facility and to attract global visitors.

Although we have assumed that customer communication in production districts is an effective method for relationship marketing and corporate branding, Japanese car manufacturers do not operate their communication facilities as a marketing strategy. Japanese companies operate the facilities to benefit the local community and as a social contribution. Therefore, these companies do not intend to attract visitors from abroad. This chapter analyzes the possible reasons for the different perspectives among the companies in their customer communication facility purposes.

One reason for the difference is corporate strategy. Aaker (2004) notes that a corporate brand is a significant company asset; however, a corporate brand is difficult to maintain and control. Therefore, we examine whether corporate branding can be achieved intentionally with the aid of tourism. If a consumer goods company chooses the branding method introduced in this study, then the company must also consider the cost implications and the benefits, or cost effectiveness. Whether a company chooses this method could depend on corporate strategy.

Fig. 3.   Toyota Mega Web in Tokyo. *Source*: The authors.

Another reason for the differences between the companies is the selection of the communication facility location. Certain companies choose urban locations for their showrooms to maximize the number of visitors. Toyota, for example, has its communication platform at Toyota Mega Web in Tokyo (Fig. 3).

Tokyo is the most famous city in Japan and attracts a substantial number of tourists, and the Japan Tourism Agency (2011) reports that the number of tourists visiting Tokyo exceeds that of every other Japanese city. Our survey on Toyota Mega Web reported over four million visitors to the facility in 2012, and the majority was tourist groups. When it comes to attracting a substantial number of visitors, urban districts are superior to the place of production. We suppose, therefore, that Japanese automobile companies choose urban districts for their communication facility locations.

Moreover, we consider that company recognition of the value of corporate brands is a significant factor in the differences between German and Japanese companies. The significance attached to brand recognition by a company is also reflected in the corporate decisions of each company. Many products and brands exist in the markets, and corporate brand positions vary according to the market (Aaker, 1996). Therefore, we examine whether a corporate brand is connected to a certain production area. Volkswagen Group may consider that their brand is associated with its production district origins, the German district of Wolfsburg. However, certain companies do not consider the production areas as an important factor with respect to brand recognition, such as the Japanese automobile companies examined in this study.

Therefore, we suggest that the differences between German and Japanese automobile companies can be attributed to differences in corporate strategy. The differences reflect whether companies use their production districts as communication platforms.

CONCLUSION AND IMPLICATIONS

Our study clarifies the present situation of customer communication facilities operated by automobile companies in production districts. Although we expected that customer communications can be an effective method for corporate branding, this marketing theory cannot be applied to all cases in the light of company suitability.

The respective corporate strategies of companies affect the corporate activities and determine whether a company operates communication facilities for branding purposes. The difference in the purpose is the most significant factor that influences facility operations. The operational purposes that were found in the case studies for this research were social contribution to the local community, or advertising and corporate branding. Moreover, this difference affects the targets in each facility, such as the local residents or tourist groups. Therefore, corporate strategy must first be examined to evaluate this branding method, which utilizes direct communication with customers.

We note the importance of positioning in the market, which is a basis of competitive strategy. Porter (1991) finds that attaining a competitive and attractive position increases the superior performance of companies. We suggest that the difference in market positioning between Volkswagen Group and the Japanese companies is related to the outcome of this investigation. If corporate market positioning is related to corporate branding strategy, we should clarify the brand positions that would be appropriate for the application of the branding method with the incorporation of tourism. This would justify the three Japanese companies' strategies, which are not intended to attract tourist groups to the production facilities.

Using the examples of the exhibition facilities of automobile companies in production districts, this chapter demonstrated that the companies possess different corporate strategies and different perspectives concerning corporate brand recognition. We consider that the example of car manufacturers can be applied to a broader context of other types of product manufacturers such as clothing, food, and drink. This hypothesis could be proven in a future study. The application of tourism-aided branding method to other types of products would facilitate the recommendation and development of this branding method to the consumer goods industry.

REFERENCES

Aaker, D. A. (1996). Measuring brand equity across products and markets. *California Management Review, 33*(5), 102–120.

Aaker, D. A. (2004). Leveraging the corporate brand. *California Management Review, 46*(3), 6–18.

Autostadt. (2012). *Press release: 25 million visitors to the Autostadt in Wolfsburg.* Retrieved from http://presse.autostadt.de/en/?p_p_id=presseartikelportlet_WAR_presseartikelportlet&p_p_state=exclusive&viewMode=pdf&articleId=39134. Accessed on January 29, 2014.

Autostadt. (2013a). *The Autostadt: People, cars and what moves them.* Retrieved from http://www.autostadt.de/en/ort/our-philosophy/introduction/. Accessed on June 18, 2013.

Autostadt. (2013b). *Managing director: Otto ferdinand wachs.* Retrieved from http://www.autostadt.de/en/ort/our-philosophy/otto-ferdinand-wachs/. Accessed on June 18, 2013.

Autostadt. (2013c). *Autostadt annual report 2013.* Retrieved from http://presse.autostadt.de/en/?p_p_id=presseartikelportlet_WAR_presseartikelportlet&p_p_state=exclusive&viewMode=pdf&articleId=68655. Accessed on January 29, 2014.

Berry, L. L. (2002). Relationship marketing of services: Perspectives from 1983 and 2000. *Journal of Relationship Marketing, 1*(1), 59−78.

Beverland, M. B. (2009). *Building brand authenticity: 7 habits of iconic brands.* United Kingdom: Palgrave Macmillan.

Brink, A., & Berndt, A. (2009). *Relationship marketing and customer relationship management.* South Africa: Juta and Company Ltd.

Coles, T., & Hall, C. M. (2008). *International business and tourism: Global issues, contemporary interactions.* London: Routledge.

Gnoth, J. (2002). Leveraging export brands through a tourism destination brand. *Journal of Brand Management, 9*(4−5), 262−280.

Japan Tourism Agency. (2011). *White paper on tourism in Japan.* Retrieved from http://www.mlit.go.jp/common/000221176.pdf. Accessed on January 18, 2014.

Kent, T., & Brown, R. (2009). *Flagship marketing: Concepts and places.* New York, NY: Routledge.

MacCannell, D. (1999). *The tourist: A new theory of the leisure class.* Oakland, CA: University of California Press.

Otgaar, A. H. J. (2010). *Industrial tourism: Where the public meets the private.* The Netherlands: Haveka.

Otgaar, A. H. J., van den Berg, L., Berger, C., & Feng, R. X. (2010). *Industrial tourism: Opportunities for city and enterprise.* London: Ashgate Publishing.

Peppers, D., Rogers, M., & Dorf, B. (1999). Is your company ready for one-to-one marketing? *Harvard Business Review, 77*(1), 151−160.

Porter, M. E. (1991). Towards a dynamic theory of strategy. *Strategic Management Journal, 12*, 95−117.

Schmitt, B. H. (2000). *Experiential marketing: How to get customers to sense, feel, think, act, relate.* New York, NY: Simon and Schuster.

Stone, M., Woodcock, N., & Machtynger, L. (1995). *Customer relationship marketing: Get to know your customers and win their loyalty.* London: Kogan Page.

Walvis, T. (2003). Building brand locations. *Corporate Reputation Review, 5*(4), 358−366.

TOURIST SPACES AND TOURISM POLICY IN SPAIN AND PORTUGAL

Fernando Almeida, Rafael Cortés and
Antonia Balbuena

ABSTRACT

This study analyzes the relationship between the development of tourism policy of Spain and Portugal and their effects on regional imbalances. Despite the proximity of the two countries and their specialization in tourism, there are few comparative studies on tourism of the two Iberian countries. The study focuses on the two major phases of tourism policy: the period of mass tourism and post-Fordist stage. In the conclusions we refer the debate on the existence of a model of development based on tourism to the Latin countries of Southern Europe and we note the export process of Spanish low cost tourism model to other countries.

Keywords: Spain; Portugal; tourism; policy; spaces

Marketing Places and Spaces
Advances in Culture, Tourism and Hospitality Research, Volume 10, 235–249
Copyright © 2015 by Emerald Group Publishing Limited
ISSN: 1871-3173/doi:10.1108/S1871-317320150000010017

INTRODUCTION

Tourism has contributed enormously to the economic growth of Spain and Portugal. Usually, economic benefits generated by tourism have been highlighted more than negative impacts caused on society, environment, and territory. The benefits that economists usually emphasize are the income, the improvement in the trade balance, the use of tourism as a driver of infrastructure development, and job creation (Antón & González, 2007). Among the problems that tourism can produce one of the least studied is the regional imbalance (Vera, 2011, p. 235) and this is one of the central themes of this study.

Regional imbalances are closely related to the territorial nature of tourism. We cannot forget that tourism is a spatial phenomenon that generates different economic activities in the territory (Vera 1997, p. 60). The territorial aspect of tourism has been relegated to a lower priority because of the preeminence of the economic analysis of tourism. In any way, we should not forget the importance of economic factors in the development of tourism and the generation of regional imbalances. The location of tourism is directly related to inequality, as each area has different tourist resources and the basis for development of mass tourism is the concentration of supply and demand. Tourism resources are not distributed equitably, so tourism tends to create territorial imbalances (Almeida, 2013).

An examination of Spain and Portugal's shared history reveals parallel development as far as tourism policies and models are concerned, although the tourism processes in the two countries also display certain differences due to their differing socioeconomic development. The evolution of tourism policy since the mid-twentieth century can be divided into the two main stages:

(1) *The Fordian phase.* This period was characterized by the emergence of mass tourism due to improved transport and paid holidays for the working class. Mass tourism was the end of elite tourism and strengthening of tourism as a global phenomenon. The Fordian tourism needs to standardize supply and demand to reduce production costs. These facts had a singular importance in shaping supply in destination countries such as Spain and Portugal. In this way the high concentration of the supply of accommodation is explained.

The first phase, between 1950 and 1975, brought a series of important developments. The Iberian nations now understood that tourism held the key to economic growth. Indeed, several authors maintain that this period saw the introduction of a uniquely Latin model of development which was heavily reliant on tourism (Bote, 1998).

This phase also marked the first major divergence between the two countries in terms of tourism policy: whereas the Spanish government committed itself fully to mass tourism as a means of maximizing revenue and investment (Cals, 1974), the Portuguese opted instead to maintain a more gradual rate of tourist growth (Cunha, 2009). In fact, mass tourism was the dominant theme during this period, and tourism-based development is the facet of tourism most frequently studied by both Spanish and Portuguese authors (Cals, 1974; Cunha, 2009; Esteve & Fuentes, 2000; Martins, 1997). In this period, the concentration of the hotels in certain areas of the Spanish Mediterranean coast and the Lisbon region is favored. The high concentration is related to the maximization of investment in tourism and a clear policy *laiser faire*.

(2) *The post-Fordian phase.* This period was characterized by the emergence of processes of production and marketing of tourism. Governments get involved less in the tourism sector; we observe a lower interest in the development of tourism policies (e.g., social tourism practically disappears) and regulation and use of tourism is left to the market. New forms of production are based on flexibility, deregulation, and public–private collaboration. Likewise, a strong diffusion of the tourism phenomenon is observed globally.

During the second phase, Spanish and Portuguese society began to act in unison. The dictatorships in both countries ended in successive years (1974/1975), they joined the European Union (1986), adopted the Euro (2001), and experienced similar economic ups and downs. However, their respective administrative structures and tourism planning procedures took vastly different paths. While Spain's heavily centralized policy was replaced by a decentralized system overseen by its Autonomous Communities and the tourist towns themselves, in Portugal, the exact opposite now occurred. Regional policy, the restructuring of the tourism sector, and the social and environmental impact of tourism are the aspects most commonly identified by authors as the main consequences of the protracted growth of tourism in Spain and Portugal.

This chapter provides a comparative analysis of tourism policy and its spatial effects in Spain and Portugal. This study aims to compare the evolution of tourism policies of the two countries since 1960. Also, it analyzes the territorial imbalances caused by tourism in Spain and Portugal.

LITERATURE REVIEW

Tourism is a complex product in which economic and political factors combine with those of a geographical and recreational nature (Hall, 1998). As such, tourism policy may be defined as a multidisciplinary field related with the mixed science that is tourism itself (Edgell, 1990). In this context, definitions of tourism policy vary, though it is worth noting the view of Hall and Jenkins (1995), who feel that tourism policy is whatever governments choose to do or not to do with regard to tourism – an interpretation that provides tourism researchers with a wide investigative scope (p. 8). In any event, research into tourism policy must focus first and foremost on those government measures taken with the aim of influencing tourism.

No clear consensus exists regarding the way in which the study of tourism policy should be approached, or the fields of interest that it ought to include. There is an economic angle which considers tourism policy as a branch of the economy characterized by a series of idiosyncrasies (Sessa, 1976). The growing importance of tourism, and particularly its impact on both national and regional economies, has led in turn to an increase in the number of studies into tourism policy (Hall & Jenkins, 1995). These studies have tended to adopt a neutral standpoint, focusing on the achievements of tourism rather than on the social and territorial imbalances that it brings (Lea, 1988). The difficulties encountered in generating development contrast sharply with the praise heaped by governments on tourism's contribution to economic development at both national and regional levels (Williams & Shaw, 1988). In the case of Spain and Portugal, there have been numerous studies into tourism strategy as an area of economic policy (Cals, 1974; Martins, 1997; Monfort, 2000).

Political science, too, has taken an interest in tourism policy, in spite of its initial indifference to tourism itself (Richter, 1983), which it considered a frivolous and superficial field, and of the difficulties faced by tourism specialists in attempting to define the exact nature of tourism policy. The role played by tourism policy within the larger field of political science has evolved to such an extent that some authors now claim that the former must be viewed separately from the latter (Velasco, 2005).

Research into tourism policy has generally focused on specific countries, analyzing the subject as a branch of national policy and approaching the task in large, regional blocks (Hall, 1991; Lickorish, 1991). To date, there has been relatively little analysis contrasting the tourism policies of different countries, though several interesting studies have been carried out in Europe (Swarbrooke, 1993). Spain and Portugal, however, have rarely been compared, despite their geographical proximity and the existence of socioeconomic processes that are common to both (Fig. 2). Most of the references to these countries currently available are to be found either in studies dealing with tourism in Europe in general, Southern Europe or the Mediterranean area (Akehurst, Bland, & Kevin, 1993; Apostolopoulos, Loukissas, & Leontidou, 2001), or in series of publications compiled by international organizations such as the OECD and the WTO. Worthy of special mention are the analyses of tourism policy in Spain and Portugal undertaken by Williams and Shaw (1988) and Williams (1993), which assess the role played by tourism in both national economic development and regional imbalance; however, none of these studies deal specifically with the two countries alone. Our study of Spain and Portugal adopts a similar approach to the one taken by Williams, albeit with the inclusion of other facets such as the process via which national tourism policy is constructed.

METHOD

To carry out this study, we have made a comprehensive literature review of major studies on tourism policy of Spain and Portugal. We have collected the main sources of tourism statistics. The statistical data are required to understand the evolution of tourism and to compare tourism issue of both countries. The main variable used by this study is the supply of hotel accommodation, secondly foreign tourists and foreign visitors. The main tourist factors are indicated by figures and tables. This variable was chosen because it has a close relationship with the territorial changes and it also represents tourism offer. Furthermore, the hotel supply with tourism demand is the most suitable variable to show the evolution of tourism pol-icy. The analysis period is between 1960 and 2010. At the end, we carry out an analysis that shows maps representing changes in tourism policy of Spain and Portugal. A database of the hotels has been made with a spatial reference in each of the countries (Districts and NUT III in Portugal and Province in Spain). This database was exported and referenced to the GIS base map (GvSIG).

FINDINGS

The growth of tourist activity in Europe as a whole during the decade of 1950s led to a keener interest in tourism on the part of the Portuguese

government, which took steps toward its development: (i) Financial measures such as the Tourism Fund (1956) were introduced along with others
of a fiscal nature, including the 1954 Public Utility Law, which offered tax
exemption for investors in hotel infrastructure; (ii) in 1956, the Tourism
Law was passed.

The Tourism Regions exercised greater influence over tourism management and enjoyed financial independence, thanks to the introduction of a
local tourism tax. Though eminently regional, this policy failed to bring
territorial diversity, and tourism was largely confined to the Lisbon area
until the mid-1970s, when the Algarve emerged as a popular destination for
foreign tourists. In 1963, for example, 30% of Portugal's hotels were
located in the Portuguese capital and 41% in the surrounding region
(Table 1). Beyond this established enclave, a lack of hotel facilities and the
poor state of the country's roads made it impossible for tourism to take
root (Cunha, 2009). Nevertheless, Portugal played host to 232,261 visitors
in 1956.

The 1960s and 1970s saw moderate growth in tourism demand and supply in comparison with Spain (Table 1). The main consequences of tourism
in Portugal were (i) the creation of an unbalanced territorial model (Fig. 2)
which had a significant impact on the environment; (ii) the reduction of

Table 1.   Hotel Places by Region and Major Tourist Destination.

% of Total Hotel Places	1963	1973	1983	1993	2007	2012
Lisbon Region	41.9	39.4	32.3	24.5	18.7	18.9
Algarve	5.0	19.1	33.8	39.9	36.3	35.9
Madeira Islands	3.3	14.2	10.3	8.5	10.3	9.7
Rest of Portugal	49.8	27.3	23.6	27.1	34.7	35.5
Alicante	3.8	5.9	5.9	4.9	4.9	4.7
Balearic Islands	17.8	30.9	27.2	25.6	14.3	13.1
Barcelona	13.4	8.6	7.5	7.5	6.7	8.2
Canary Islands	5.4	6.8	8.4	8.4	14.9	15.7
Gerona	17.4	10.2	8.8	7.5	4.1	3.8
Madrid	12.6	6.3	5.8	5.1	6.8	7.3
Malaga	4.9	4.8	5.7	5.3	6.0	5.5
Valencia	2.4	1.4	1.6	1.5	2.6	2.5
Rest of Spain	22.3	25.1	29.1	34.2	39.7	39.2
Spanish Mediterranean[a]	59.7	61.8	56.7	52.3	38.6	37.8

Source: INE (National Institute of Statistics, Spain and Portugal), Ministry of Information
and Tourism, 1951–1977.
[a]Provinces of Alicante, Barcelona, Gerona, Malaga, Valencia, and the Balearic Islands.

the country's balance of trade deficit (Cunha, 2003; Martins, 2007), with revenue from tourism accounting for as much as 93.5% of the coverage rate during this period (Cunha, 2003, p. 20).

The repercussions of tourism in Spain were similar, though more marked than in Portugal. Portugal's tourism strategy differed greatly from Spain's during this period in which Spanish tourism definitively took off. Portuguese tourism growth was slower than for Spain, since initially the government continued giving support to elite tourism and tourism was not considered as strategic sector for the Portuguese economy.

Spain, meanwhile, would have to wait until the mid-1950s for an upturn in foreign tourism after the decline brought about by the Spanish Civil War (1936–1939) and the post-war period that followed (Fig. 1). The 1950s saw several measures taken to encourage tourism: (i) in 1951, the Ministry of Tourism and Information was created, lasting until 1977, and in 1952, the National Tourism Plan was introduced; (ii) the same decade marked the beginning of a process of economic liberalization and adjustment that culminated in the Economic Stability Plan (1959).

Spain remained fully committed to the development of tourism during the 1960s. Certain internal and external factors ensured that the country could hardly do otherwise (Esteve & Fuentes, 2000), though it did exercise choice over the degree to which the process should be pursued, opting for maximum intensity. As in Portugal and other Southern European

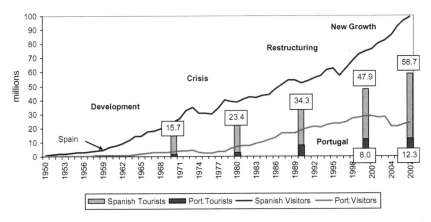

Fig. 1. Visitors and Tourists in Spain and Portugal. *Source*: INE (National Institute of Statistics) Spain and Portugal. *Note*: Methodological change in 2004 (Portugal).

countries, the model adopted was based on indicative planning designed to generate development and manage foreign investment. Objectives were centralized via the Development Plans, which focused progressively more closely on tourism, though viewing it more as a means of balancing payments than as a strategic economic sector in its own right. Between 1961 and 1969, the revenue generated by tourism covered 72% of Spain's balance of trade deficit (Vallejo, 2002).

Certain authors contend that the key role played by tourism in the growth of Italy, Spain, and Portugal points to a peculiarly Latin model of development based on mass tourism (Bote, 1998; Martins, 2007; Vallejo, 2002). The considerable revenue generated by tourism (and also by emigration) underpinned both the industrialization processes and the development plans pursued by said nations. These countries also provide the earliest instance of mass tourism playing a key role in socioeconomic development, the relationship between the two being particularly marked in Spain. Development based on tourism would subsequently be attempted by other Mediterranean and Caribbean countries, with mixed results in accordance with their differing socioeconomic climates (Blázquez & Cañada, 2011; Williams & Shaw, 1988). Several authors highlight the importance of the context (economic, social, political, geographical, and technological) in which development takes place in determining its ultimate success or failure in a particular country (Pearce, 1991). The fact that Europe provided the backdrop for the Latin model was probably a key factor in the positive socioeconomic development achieved by the aforementioned countries.

The years between 1950 and 1975 were a period of significant growth for tourism in both countries, though the firm commitment to tourism made by the Spanish government, which offered every possible incentive to private enterprise, ensured that its development in Spain was truly spectacular. However, this in turn had a profound effect upon the environment in the latter country, with coastal areas of immense natural value becoming built up, and part of the nation's historical heritage being replaced in certain cases by characterless constructions. All of this was done in the name of removing any conceivable barriers to private sector investment and increasing the number of tourists.

In 1966, the country's most heavily developed coastlines were in the Balearics (5,000 hectares), Gerona (3,000 hectares) and Malaga (2,500 hectares), followed by Barcelona, Tarragona, and Alicante with approximately 1,500 hectares. Between 1950 and 1975, an estimated 90,000 hectares of Spain's total surface area were built on in order to cater for tourism (Casanova, 1970, p. 70). These figures, the source of much concern at the time, were subsequently dwarfed by the immense development project undertaken in Spain over the following decades, a process which also took place in Portugal, though on a smaller scale. A further territorial conse- quence was the enormous imbalance in the distribution of tourism facilities, which were concentrated on Spain's Mediterranean coast (61.7%) and in Portugal's Algarve (19.1%) (Table 1 and Fig. 2).

During the post-Fordist phase, between 1980 and 1990, tourism demand rose by 46.6% and hotel accommodation by 14.1% against a backdrop of economic development accelerated by Spain's admission to the EEC. In order to limit the severe impact that tourism had been having upon the environment for several decades, a series of new laws were now introduced. Of particular note were the Coastal Law (1988), which enabled certain public domain areas along Spain's coastline to be recovered, and the Conservation of Natural Spaces Law (1989). Although these legal changes initially relieved the pressure on coastal areas, the economic crisis of 1992 dealt a crucial blow. The protective measures taken were powerless to prevent the real estate bubble between 1997 and 2007. Between 1987 and 2006, 74,417 hectares of the Spanish coast were built on at a rate of

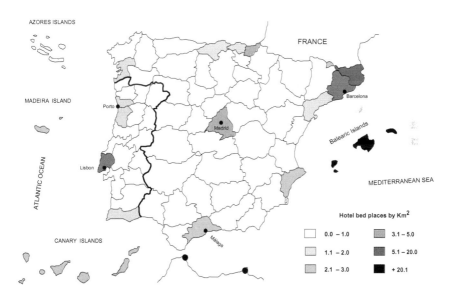

Fig. 2. Density of Hotel Places. Provinces (Spain) and Districts (Portugal) 1968.
Source: INE (Portugal), Ministerio de Información y Turismo (Spain).

244   FERNANDO ALMEIDA ET AL.

2,884 ha/year from 1987 to 2000 and 6,154 ha/year from 2000 to 2006 (Observatorio de Sostenibilidad de España [OSE], 2010, pp. 417–420).

At the beginning of the decade of the 1990s Spain was confronted with economic crisis. This time, tourism suffered the consequences directly. The Fordist traditional tourism model had finally been exhausted (Vera, 1994). The sector had enjoyed decades of growth, but was now unable to compete with the new destinations springing up throughout the world. The year 1992 saw a sharp decline in both the number of foreign tourists coming to Spain and average receipts per visitor. Between 1995 and 2000, the growth of hotel facilities was tempered, and the sector underwent a major overhaul involving the closure of less profitable hotels and a change in their categorization. The combination of the slump in tourism, the environmental problems that it has created and the new administrative order in 1980s–1990s, in which the lion's share of power now lay in the hands of the autonomous communities, forced the national Government to develop a specific program of restructuring and boosting of tourism sector: Excellence and Stimulation Plans (*Planes de Excelencia y Dinamización Turística*), besides tourism quality plans, tax incentives, etc.

These plans helped the implementation of the new post-Fordist production processes, and from the territorial point of view those plans caused a significant spread of tourism to new areas (Brunet, Almeida, Coll, & Monteserín, 2005). The latter was due to depletion of coastal land and the strong momentum of the interior areas that are supported by endogenous development policies (Fig. 3).

The political transition in Portugal was accompanied by severe social, economic, and political instability, which had far-reaching implications for the tourism sector. The remarkable recovery that took place from 1975 onward owed more to the progressive normalization of the political situation than to an increase in activity. In 1986, the introduction of dedicated planning in the shape of the National Tourism Plan signaled a change in tourism policy. The aim of this global plan was to ensure that tourism played a key role in the country's economic development (Martins, 2007). Its objectives included the reduction of territorial imbalance, the promotion of training, the protection of the country's natural and cultural heritage, and the development of cultural tourism. By the beginning of the 1990s, tourism supply and demand in Portugal had grown significantly, thanks to the country's consolidation as a medium-sized power in the sector (an increase of 60.7% in the number of tourists between 1985 and 1990, and a rise of 31.0% in accommodation facilities between 1990 and 1995).

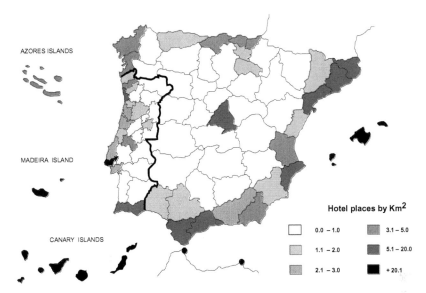

Fig. 3. Density of Hotel Places. Provinces (Spain) and NUTS III (Portugal) 2010.
Source: INE (Portugal), Ministerio de Industria, Comercio y Turismo, Turespaña
(Spain).

REGIONAL IMPLICATIONS

The tourism trend to cause regional imbalance was not prevented by pre-democratic governments of Spain and Portugal. In the 1960s, the supply of hotel accommodation was highly concentrated in the regions of Lisbon (Portugal) and Spanish Mediterranean provinces (Gerona, Barcelona, Baleares, and Malaga) (Fig. 2). This scenario was changed in the following decades. In the 1980s and 1990s, it had been a spread of tourism accommodation supply to former no tourist areas. This process was due to the need to diversify tourism sector, the lack of competitiveness in some saturated coastal areas and the interest of local and regional governments to development the inland regions and, real estate sector needs that demanded new areas for the building of second homes.

We can confirm there has been a very strong concentration of the hotels on the Spanish Mediterranean coastline, Balearic Islands, Canary Islands and Madeira in 2010. Almost the whole coastline of the Iberian Peninsula has become a tourist belt, this excludes small coastal stretches (coastal

246   FERNANDO ALMEIDA ET AL.

Alentejo in Portugal and the Spanish province of Lugo in northern Spain). The islands have a strong tourist density (Fig. 3).

Before the great development of mass tourism in Portugal and Spain between 1950 and 1960, tourist accommodation supply was quite low and was relatively equally distributed across the country. The varying range of accommodation depends on the size of the demographic area. At the time of the great tourism growth in the middle 1960s (mostly in Spain), the supply of tourist accommodation is concentrated on the Mediterranean coast (Baleares, Gerona, Barcelona, Alicante, and Malaga).

The huge growth of the Algarve was later. In the 1980s, there was a strong focus on the Spanish Mediterranean coast in both Spanish and the archipelagos (Balearic and Canary Islands). In Portugal, the areas with the highest tourism concentration were Lisbon, Algarve, and Madeira.

From the 1990, a diffusion of tourism to inland areas of Spain and Portugal was produced and this process was extended to the last undisturbed coastal areas of the Atlantic and the Mediterranean. The process is related to the development of new tourism products such as rural and cultural tourism, eco-tourism, etc. These new tourism products are connected with tourist destinations improvement plans.

In 2010, we see the consolidation of large tourist axes along the entire coastal area of Spain and Portugal and the major islands of Spain and Portugal (Fig. 3).

In summary, the distribution of tourism in the two countries was unbalanced, a fact which helped clearly the more developed regions. Tourist sector was encouraged to finance the national development of the industrial sectors.

CONCLUSION AND IMPLICATIONS

Spain's seaside tourism sector has grown with great intensity in recent years and has exported its model of mass tourism to other countries, mainly to Caribbean Sea (Blázquez & Cañada, 2011). It has generated economy of scale enough to keep its production costs low. The internationalization of the country's hotel chains, notably in the Balearic Islands, represents an exportation of this continuous process of growth and the search for low costs (Ramón, 2000). In these Caribbean countries, also it has been also repeated processes of territorial imbalance, than it follows that there is a close relationship between mass tourism and regional imbalances.

However, the Spanish tourism sector has also diversified, with cultural and culinary tourism among the alternatives now joining sun and sand vacations. Portugal, meanwhile, has turned its back on luxury tourism and is now belatedly exploiting the sun and sand market instead, though strenuous efforts have also been made to develop cultural and nature tourism. The Portuguese tourism sector is yet to reach full maturity.

Certain authors highlight the existence of a Latin model of development based on tourism. While the characteristics of this pattern are not radically different from those of subsequent methodologies implemented in tourist-receiving countries, its significance lies in the fact that this model was the first of the mass tourism era, a period which would ultimately transform the nations concerned into developed countries. In the Latin model, the role of the tourism sector was to provide resources (tourist revenue) that could be invested in industry. Spain's case is unique in that the early days of tourism saw the country open up to and rely upon foreign countries in much the same way as the small tourist nations of the Caribbean, the Indian Ocean, and Oceania would do years later. In spite of this, the situation in Spain evolved toward greater independence, with Spanish hotel chains even replicating this model of economic dependence in the Caribbean.

In territorial terms, the post-Fordist stage is manifested in Spain by increasing the hotels supply in coastal areas of the Mediterranean and Atlantic sea, in addition to dissemination to inland mountainous areas (Pyrenees and Cantabrian Mountains). Post-Fordist has been a process of touristification most of the territory of Spain. In Portugal, supply has remained concentrated around Lisbon and the Algarve, and to a lesser extent in Porto and Madeira Island (Fig. 3). In the Post-Fordian phase there has been a strong transformation of most of the Spanish territory caused by tourism. The tourism industry is constantly looking for the creation and exploitation of new tourist spaces.

Finally, it should be noted that the tourism sector now combines Fordist and post-Fordist processes in the territory and in the tourism market. Tourism seeks to introduce Fordist low cost measures in new areas and applying post-Fordist in mature destinations.

ACKNOWLEDGMENT

This research project has received funding from the Spanish Government, Fundamental Research Program (CSO2012–30840), "Geographies of crisis: analysis of urban and tourist territories of the Balearic Islands, Costa del Sol and main tourist destinations of the Caribbean."

REFERENCES

Akehurst, G., Bland, N., & Kevin, M. (1993). Tourism policies in the European Community member states. *Journal of Hospitality Management, 12*(1), 33–66. doi:10.1016/0278-4319(93)90040-G

Almeida, F. (2013). Tourism policy and territorial imbalances in Spain. *Bulletin of Geography. Socio-Economic Series, 22,* 7–19. doi:10.2478/bog-2013-0027

Antón, S., & González, F. (Eds.). (2007). *A propósito del turismo. La construcción social del espacio turístico.* Barcelona: UOC.

Apostolopoulos, Y., Loukissas, P., & Leontidou, L. (Eds.). (2001). *Mediterranean tourism. Facets of socioeconomic development and cultural change.* London: Routledge.

Blázquez, M., & Cañada, E. (Eds.). (2011). *Turismo placebo. Nueva colonización turística: Del Mediterráneo a Mesoamérica y el Caribe. Lógicas espaciales del capital turístico.* Managua: Enlace.

Bote, V. (1998). El desarrollo del turismo en España: Cambio de rumbo y oportunidades científicas. *Revista Valenciana D`Estudis Autonómics, 4,* 29–43.

Brunet, P., Almeida, F., Coll, M., & Monteserín, O. (2005). Los planes de excelencia y dinamización turística (PEDT), un instrumento de cooperación a favor del desarrollo turístico. *Boletín de la Asociación de Geógrafos Españoles, 39,* 201–206.

Cals, J. (1974). *Turismo y política turística en España: Una aproximación.* Barcelona: Ariel.

Casanova, L. (1970). *Urbanismo y turismo. La experiencia española.* Madrid: Consejo Superior de los Colegios de Arquitectos.

Cunha, L. (2003). *Perspectivas e tendências do turismo.* Lisboa: Edições Universitárias Lusófonas.

Cunha, L. (2009). *Introdução ao turismo.* Lisboa: Verbo.

Edgell, D. L. (1990). *International tourism policy.* New York, NY: Van Nostrand Reinhold.

Esteve, R., & Fuentes, R. (2000). *Economía, historia e instituciones del turismo en España.* Madrid: Pirámide.

Hall, D. (1991). *Tourism & economic development in Eastern Europe & The Soviet Union.* London: Belhaven Press.

Hall, C. M. (1998). *Tourism and politics. Policy, power and place.* Chichester: Wiley.

Hall, C. M., & Jenkins, J. M. (1995). *Tourism and public policy.* London: Routledge.

Lea, J. (1988). *Tourism and development in the third World.* London: Routledge.

Lickorish, L. J. (1991). Developing a single European tourism policy. *Tourism Management,* (September), 179–184.

Martins, J. (1997). *Economia do turismo em Portugal.* Lisboa: Dom Quixote.

Martins, J. (2007). *Planeamento e ordenamento territorial do turismo.* Lisboa: Verbo.

Monfort, V. (2000). La política turística: Una aproximación. *Cuadernos de Turismo, 6,* 7–27.

Observatorio de Sostenibilidad de España (OSE). (2010). *Sostenibilidad en España 2010.* Madrid: Ministerio de Medio Ambiente, Medio Rural y Marino y Fundación General de la Universidad de Alcalá (Spain). Retrieved from http://www.sostenibilidad-es.org/. Accessed on March 19, 2011.

Pearce, D. (1991). *Tourist development*. New York, NY: Wiley.

Ramón, B. (2000). *La internacionalización de la industria hotelera española*. Alicante: Universidad de Alicante.

Richter, L. (1983). Tourism politics and political science. A case of not so benign neglect. *Annals of Tourism Research, 10*, 313–335.

Sessa, A. (1976). The tourism policy. *Annals of Tourism Research, 5*, 234–247.

Swarbrooke, J. (1993). Public sector policy in tourism: A comparative study of France and Britain. *Insights*, (March), C33–C46.

Vallejo, R. (2002). Economía e historia del turismo español del siglo XX. *Historia Contemporánea, 25*, 203–232.

Velasco, M. (2005). Existe la política turística? La acción pública en materia de turismo en España (1951–2004). *Política y Sociedad, 42*, 169–195.

Vera, J. F. (1994). El modelo turístico del Mediterráneo español: Agotamiento y estrategias de reestructuración. *Papers de Turisme, 14–15*, 131–147.

Vera, J. F. (Ed.). (1997). *Análisis territorial del turismo*. Barcelona: Ariel.

Vera, J. F. (Ed.). (2011). *Análisis territorial del turismo y planificación de destinos turísticos*. Valencia: Tirant lo Blanch.

Williams, A. M. (1993). Tourism and economic transformation in Greece and Portugal. *Inforgeo, 6*, 7–20.

Williams, A. M., & Shaw, G. (Eds.). (1988). Tourism and economic development. Western European experiences. London: Printer Publishers.

PART IV
METHODS IN MARKETING
PLACES AND SPACES

ANALYZING SEASONAL DIFFERENCES IN A DESTINATION'S TOURIST MARKET: THE CASE OF MINHO

Elisabeth Kastenholz and António Lopes de Almeida

ABSTRACT

The present study analyses patterns of seasonal tourist consumption, based on data collected in the Minho, a rural region situated in the Northeast of Portugal. The study aims at identifying and discussing main differences regarding socio-demographic profile and tourist behavior between tourists visiting the destination in the high, medium, and low season. Results permit a discussion of implications on destination management and marketing. More specifically, the understanding of these differences, considering the existing resources, constraints, and potentialities of the destination, shall help develop strategies yielding the diversification of demand, creating conditions for attracting, satisfying, and possibly ensuring loyalty of different tourist types in different seasons of the year (Jeffrey, D., & Barden, R. (2001). An analysis of the nature, causes and marketing implications of seasonality in the

Marketing Places and Spaces
Advances in Culture, Tourism and Hospitality Research, Volume 10, 253–267
ISSN: 1871-3173/doi:10.1108/S1871-317320150000010018

occupancy performance of English hotels. In T. Baum & S. Lundtorp (Eds.), Seasonality in tourism (pp. 119–140). Amsterdam: Pergamon). That is, the here discussed results should help strategically manage demand yielding sustainable destination development (Kastenholz, 2004).

Keywords: Tourist market analysis; seasonality; management of demand; rural tourism; Minho/North Portugal

INTRODUCTION

The growing importance of tourism for the global economy and particularly for the economies of some western countries, like Portugal, whose traditional economic activities are becoming less competitive in the global market, requires a more profound knowledge of the tourism phenomenon and of the constraints to its consolidation and progress. One of the major constraints, object of concern in many emergent destinations, is the temporal concentration or seasonality of tourism demand. This phenomenon characterizing tourism demand in many destinations leads to several operational problems, mainly reflected in sub-optimal use of facilities in the low season and overcrowding, with consequent negative impacts on the destination, its resources, the community, as well as the quality of the tourist experience, in the high season (Koenig-Lewis & Bischoff, 2005). Butler (2001) calls for increased research efforts to better understand the phenomenon, leading to improved capacity of its management.

In this context, this chapter presents part of the results of a comprehensive empirical study undertaken in the Minho region/North Portugal aiming at a better understanding of the causes of seasonality as related to tourist behavior. The selection of this destination is due to four factors: first the destination presents a relative high degree of seasonality of demand $(G = 0.23)$;[1] second, the destination presents a wide diversity of supply,[2] both in terms of different types of tourist destinations (mountains, historical cities/towns, rural, and seaside) and in terms of associated tourist resources and products; third the seasonality of the larger region, North Portugal, was analyzed in a previous study with data from over a decade ago (Kastenholz & Almeida, 2008), making the study's partial replication in the more touristically developed sub-region Minho, an interesting extension of the prior study, permitting a discussion of its evolution, particularly in terms of the seasonality phenomenon. Last, but not least, the effective temporal changes of this destination's resources along the year (especially of its natural resources, such as climate and landscapes) may in fact represent a particular facet of tourist attraction in distinct seasons of the year.

The study analyses, more specifically, the distinct features and motivations of destination demand in three seasons: high, medium, and low. Additionally, the propensity of traveling in each season is also part of our analysis, trying to understand not only why certain tourists travel in each season, but also if tourists actually would also like to visit the destination in a different time of the year. This should help identify possible target markets for each season of the year, particularly potential clients for the low and medium seasons.

THEORETICAL CONSIDERATIONS

Tourism seasonality may be defined as *"a temporal imbalance in the phenomenon of tourism [which] may be expressed in terms of dimensions of such elements as numbers of visitors, expenditure of visitors, traffic on highways and other forms of transportation, employment, and admissions to attractions"* (Butler, 1994, p. 332). Alternative definitions stress the tourist flows' concentration in short periods of the year triggering, on the one hand, activity peaks often representing a hard burden to physical and social destination resources and, on the other hand, demand "valleys" responsible for productive inefficiency (Allok, 1995; Hartmann, 1986; Mitchell & Murphy, 1991; Vanhove, 2004). Particularly considering these "valleys," the negative seasonality effects imply strong revenue limitations with direct impact on tourism businesses' profitability (Cooper, Fletcher, Gilbert, Shepherd, & Wanhill, 1998; Lundtorp, Rassing, & Wanhill, 1999; Manning & Powers, 1984; Sutcliffe & Sinclair, 1980).

These negative effects explain why seasonality is often understood by Destination Marketing Organizations (DMOs) as a weakness or a problem that needs to be solved (BarOn, 1975; Butler, 1994; Donatos & Zairis, 1991; Yacoumis, 1980). Efforts conducted toward the reduction of seasonality have been put into practice without a sufficient theoretical/conceptual background, which may explain their limited success. There seems to be incapacity to understand and address the core of the problem (Baum & Hagen, 1999; Butler, 2001; Lundtorp, 2001). There are also few methodological approaches aimed to address this problem. The main approaches in the attempt to reduce seasonality consist in trying to extend the main season, the attempt to develop new seasons, supply and market diversification, differential pricing, staggering holidays, and developing special attractions in the low season (Butler & Smale, 1991; Somerville, 1987; Stäblein, 1994; Witt, Brooke, & Buckley, 1991). Nevertheless, the persistence of the problem makes us believe that a substantial number of these approaches and respective measures do not reach their goal, which eventually may reinforce the argument of the poor understanding of the phenomenon and particularly of its causes. Butler (2001) argues that more profound research is needed, especially in areas such as: detailed identification of the basic causes of seasonality, namely those related to tourists' motivations and consumption patterns.

McKercher (1995) suggests that a sound understanding and management of a destination's tourist market is more important than the management of its products. Kastenholz (2004) further suggests management of demand as a tool for enhancing sustainable destination development. Several studies revealed seasonal differences within a destination's tourist market regarding the market's age structure and presence (or not) of children; constitution of the travel group (O'Discroll, 1985; Spotts & Mahoney, 1993); as well as benefits sought at the destination (Bonn, Furr, & Uysal, 1992; Calantone & Johar, 1984; Kastenholz & Almeida, 2008). A deeper understanding of distinct motivations/constraints characterizing those tourists traveling in each season might be fundamental for achieving differentiated and successful marketing strategies for each seasonally defined (target) segment (Baum & Hagen, 1999; Commons & Page, 2001; Kastenholz & Almeida, 2008; Margaryan & Zherdev, 2011).

Particularly in the medium and low season, a better adaptation to the corresponding markets' requirements and desires may help increase destination appeal and eventually reduce seasonality, not only through product development but also through the attraction of those segments that may be easiest to attract and satisfy in each season and that actually best match the seasonally shaped destination offer, that is, through active management of demand (Kastenholz, 2004; Lundtorp et al., 1999; Spencer & Holecek, 2007). Regarding particularly the destination North Portugal, a previous study revealed significant differences between the tourist market visiting the destination in the high versus low season, specifically regarding travel motivations and destination images (Kastenholz & Almeida, 2008). In the present approach, additionally the mid-season is considered, permitting a fine-tuned and actualized analysis of seasonal differences between visitors of the Minho region, as shown next.

METHOD

The data used for the analysis were collected in the scope of a tourist market study undertaken in the second half of 2010 and January 2011, with data collected in three successive tourist seasons: the high, the medium, and the low season. An attempt was made to yield an approximately representative sample ($N = 942$) of tourists staying in each season, administrating the questionnaire personally (with a small, especially trained research team) in a cluster-sampling approach, defined by time and space, addressing all tourists encountered in selected central points of tourist attraction/stay in the region, with a response rate of 94% of valid responses/inquiries. Data from the high season (defined as the months of June to the first half of September) accounted for 51% of the sample (corresponding to effectively larger tourist volumes encountered in the region), 32% in the mid-season (from 15th of September till the end of October), and 17% in the low season (from 1st of November till the 20th of December − excluding Christmas and New year celebrations − and the month of January). The effort in time allocated to administer the survey was approximately the same in each period, with a slightly more intense effort in terms of number of interviewers involved in the high season justified by the larger tourist flows.

FINDINGS

The global socio-demographic/economic profile of the sample is shown in Table 1. Results obtained reveal statistically significant differences between seasonally defined groups (distinguishing visitors in the low from those in the mid- and high season) as far as tourists' socio-demographic/economic profile, travel behavior, and motivations are concerned, as presented next.

As far as tourists' socio-demographic profile is concerned, it is interesting to note a predominance of mid-aged tourists in the high season (24−64 years, 82.8% of the respective sample), against a relatively higher number of elder tourists in the mid (>64 years; about 15.3%) and relatively more younger tourists (16−24 years, 39.2% of the respective group) in the low season (Pearson Chi-Square = 99.266; Asymp. Sig. (two-sided) = 0.0000). The domestic market prevails in the low season (67.7% of total), while in the high and medium seasons the international market dominates, with

Table 1.   Socio-Demographic/Economic Profile of Sample.

		N	Valid %
Age	16−24	161	17.1
	25−34	228	24.2
	35−44	196	20.8
	45−54	190	20.2
	55−64	94	10.0
	65−74	59	6.3
	> 74	14	1.5
Education level	Without studies	5	0.5
	Primary	66	7.0
	Secondary	348	36.9
	Superior	407	43.2
	Post-graduation	107	11.4
	Don't know/don't respond	9	1.0
Income (month)	<500	68	7.2
	501−1,000	118	12.5
	1,001−2,000	251	26.6
	2,001−3,000	149	15.8
	3,001−4,000	45	4.8
	4,001−5,000	20	2.1
	5,001−7,000	20	2.1
	7,001−10,000	10	1.1
	> 10,000	32	3.4
	Don't know/Don't respond	229	24.3
Nationality	Portuguese	272	28.9
	Foreigners	670	71.1

80.3% and 76.7%, respectively, mirroring statistically significant differences between seasons (Pearson Chi-Square = 140.657; Asymp. Sig. (two-sided) = 0.0000). Interestingly, tourists with higher income are more present in the high season, in comparison to other seasons (Pearson Chi-Square = 69.422; Asymp. Sig. (two-sided) = 0.0000).

Also statistically significant differences between tourists traveling in the three seasons in terms of educational level are observable (Pearson Chi-Square = 13.917; Asymp. Sig. (two-sided) = 0.008). Although those with highest education level prevailing in all seasons, they are relatively more present in the high and mid-season (59% and 54.4%, respectively, vs. 44.2% in the low season). As far as the professional occupation is concerned and considering only those categories (suggested by World Tourism Organisation [WTO], 1995) with more than five cases (students; employed, and retired), a statistically significant association between occupation and season was found (Pearson Chi-Square = 114.161; Asymp. Sig. (two-sided) = 0.000). Although the category "employed" stands out in all seasons, this percentage is most dominant in the high season (83%), the retired being relatively more present in the mid-season (24.8%) and students more in the low season (33.6%).

As accommodation type, the following categories stand out most: hotel units (50% of total); with friends and family (16.3%); second home (8.8%) and rural tourism units (8.7%), with these categories revealing different levels of preference in the three seasons (Pearson Chi-Square = 51.600; Asymp. Sig. (two-sided) = 0.000). More than in the other two seasons, the hotel stands out particularly in the mid-season (64.8%), while both rural tourism units and staying with friends and family are more referred to in the high and low seasons. The second home stands out as the accommodation relatively more chosen in the high season (11%). The transportation mode used for traveling to Minho also differs for the seasons analyzed (Pearson Chi-Square = 102.659; Asymp. Sig. (two-sided) = 0.000), with particularly those coming in the mid-season using relatively more air transportation (48.2%) and relatively more of those coming in the low season (72.2%) and the high season (52.8%) using the car.

Also the travel party reveals interesting seasonal differences (Pearson Chi-Square = 61.837; Asymp. Sig. (two-sided) = 0.0000); particularly regarding tourists traveling as a couple with their children who are more present in the high (42%) and least in the low season (12.7%). Interestingly, there are statistically significant differences between seasons regarding daily expenditures (Pearson Chi-Square = 30.100; Asymp. Sig. (two-sided) = 0.000). Average daily expenditures per person registered in the high, medium, and low seasons are, respectively: 121€, 163€, and 98€/day. The mid-season shows highest average daily expenditure levels, making this an economically interesting season. When additionally considering the relatively larger travel groups (more families with children) and longer periods of average stay and of those coming in the high season, also this season appears to be quite profitable.

An important finding is that a significant part of respondents (20.5% of the sample) consider that the season of stay at the destination is *not* the ideal and that part of the respondents would like to visit the destination at a different time of the year. A more detailed analysis per season (see Table 2) shows that the percentage of those not happy with the season is largest for the low season (43%), which may suggest more constraints of respondents in this season on their freedom of choice of the travel time (with a Chi square value of 60.237 revealing statically significant differences

Table 2. Preference of Season of Stay at Destination.

Questions		[Q6][a]		[Q8][b]	
Total sample	[Yes]	749	79.5%	651	69.1%
	[No]	193	20.5%	291	30.9%
		942		942	
High season	[Yes]	409	**84.7%**	313	**64.8%**
	[No]	74	15.3%	170	35.2%
	Total	483		483	
Mid-season	[Yes]	250	**83.1%**	216	**71.8%**
	[No]	51	16.9%	85	28.2%
	Total	301		301	
Low season	[Yes]	90	57%	122	**77.2%**
	[No]	68	**43%**	36	22.8%
	Total	158		158	

[a]*Question 6 (Q6)* – Do you consider this is the ideal *season (month)* for your vacation *in this region*?
[b]*Question 8 (Q8)* – Apart from this season, would you like to holiday *additionally* in (an)other season(s) of the year?

between seasons at sign <0.005). Additionally, data reveals a trend toward the propensity of additional tourist consumption in another season of the year (69.1% of sample), being particularly high, again, for tourists coming in the low season (77.2%). Also here, a Chi square value of 10.049 (with sign <0.05) reveals statically significant differences between seasons, regarding the desire for an additional holiday season. However, this propensity is also high in other seasons, so that there might be a potential of attracting tourists who come in the high season also in the low or medium season, thereby contributing to a better seasonal spread.

Associated to the effective selection of the period of stay is the respondents' perceived freedom of choice of their travel season (timing of their holidays). Pearson's Chi-square test reveals a significant association between these variables (Pearson Chi-Square = 10.049; Asymp. Sig. (two-sided) = 0.007). There are statistically significant differences particularly between the high/mid- and the low seasons. Thus, respondents traveling in the mid, but also the high season, perceive lightly more freedom of choice of the period of stay, while those coming in the low season reveal less freedom of choice. Also the perceived freedom of holiday spread along the year shows statistically significant differences between seasonal tourist groups, especially distinguishing between the high/mid- and the low season, again (Pearson Chi-Square = 8.608; Asymp. Sig. (two-sided) = 0.014). Also in this respect, individuals interviewed in the low season report a relatively higher percentage revealing constraints regarding holiday spread along the year. On the other hand, individuals traveling in the mid-season present the highest percentage of responses (73.4%) indicating high perceived freedom of distributing the holidays along the year, that is, revealing high potential for visiting the destination in different seasons.

Length of stay is another variable showing statistically relevant differences between seasons (Pearson Chi-Square = 93.601; Asymp. Sig. (two-sided) = 0.000), with the high season visitors standing out staying relatively longest (average of 12 days), while in the mid-season visitors stay an average of 8 days and in the low season only about 6 days. There is also a relatively larger proportion of short-break visits observable in the low and mid-seasons (36.1% and 33.9%, respectively), compared to the high season (with only 14.7%). Longest periods of stay (more than three weeks), although not the dominating category, are registered mainly in the high season (9.9%). The length of stay visitors reported is considered satisfactory by most respondents, in all seasons, although differences exist (Pearson Chi-Square = 6.871; Asymp. Sig. (two-sided) = 0.032). Travelers in the mid-season reveal a relatively lower percentage of respondents considering the actual length of stay of their holidays the ideal length of stay (67.4% in comparison to 76.6% of respondents in the low season and 75.2% in the high).

Also behavioral destination loyalty apparently differs from season to season (Pearson Chi-Square = 7.835; Asymp. Sig. (two-sided) = 0.02), with repeat visitors being relatively more present in the low season (44.9%) and less in the mid-season, when first time visitors dominate (68.1%), as is also true for the high season (61.9%). Probability/reported intention to come back to the destination also differ for respondents traveling in the three seasons. Apart from a globally minor indication of this return being "improbable" (3.9%), the highest percentage of responses is registered for the option "within one year" (52.3%), this response being particularly important for travelers in the high season (56.7%). On the other hand, the probability to come back for holidays "still this year" is referred to lightly more by individuals in the low season (Pearson Chi-Square = 36.100; Asymp. Sig. (two-sided) = 0.000).

The most relevant motivations mentioned for visiting the Minho region (with visitors ranking the most important 5 from 26 predefined motivations) also differed according to the season of visit (Pearson Chi-Square = 73.468; Asymp. Sig. (two-sided) = 0.000), as visible in Table 3. Thus, in the high season and particularly the mid-season, the *opportunity for getting to*

Table 3. Rankings for the Main Tourist Motivation by Season (Five Most Important Positions).

Main Motivation (Five Important) *(Items Selected Based on Pearson Chi-square Para Sig. <0.05)*	Season		
	High	Mid	Low
Opportunity to visit friends and family	2°	5°	3°
Sun and beach	4°		
Quality of gastronomy and wine			2°
Opportunity to contact with nature		3°	1°
Local history and culture	1°	1°	5°
Architecture and monuments		4°	4°
Good climate	3°		
Discover region and its landscapes/beautiful scenery	4°	2°	

know local history and culture stand out. In the low season this motivation is less relevant, while here the opportunity of nature appreciation is the most important, followed by gastronomy and wine and the opportunity to visit friends and relatives. This *social motive* (VFR) is a most important travel motivation also in the high season (ranking second), in which additionally "*good climate*" *and* "*sun and beach*" (appreciation of the vast sandy beach areas at the Minho's Atlantic Coast) are referred to as ranks 2 and 3, respectively.

In the mid-season, after local history and culture, the second motivation most referred to is discovering the region and its landscape beauty, followed by *contact with nature* and, forth, by getting to know the region's architecture and monuments. That is, the mid-season stands out by attracting tourists interested in *exploring the region*, its culture, history, landscape, and nature. Both tourists in the high and low seasons also visit friends and relatives, with those in the high season also, different from the others, enjoying good weather and sun and beach and those in the low season also, again differing from the others, enjoying the region's *food and wine.*

DISCUSSION

Based on the results of the present research project, the profile of each seasonal market traveling to the Minho region could be described, significant differences highlighted and, based on this knowledge, corresponding marketing opportunities identified, while also acknowledging season-specific constraints. Particularly the travel market coming to Minho in the *mid-season* seems to be worthwhile catering to, with both the opportunity of extending length of stay of these travelers and of having them additionally come back in another, possibly also the low season, should be considered in this respect. This basically international, slightly older, better educated, and wealthier group of travelers also reveals higher daily expenditure patterns at the destination. Traveling in a couple for relatively short periods they mainly use hotel accommodation. However, although globally satisfied with the season at the destination, they seem not to be to the same degree satisfied with the length of their stay and might stay longer. Their main motives being the discovery of the region, its landscape, history and culture, and given the variety and quality of attractions existing at the destination and in its proximity (the city of Oporto, other rural and culturally interesting North Portuguese sub-regions, the close Central region with similarly attractive features, and last but not least, Galiza, across the Spanish border, all areas accessible in daytrips), makes this relatively well accessible destination particularly interesting for this type of destination-exploring tourists. There seem to be aspects that these tourists may also be attracted to in repeated visits, but that have not drawn their main attention as much as the (typically domestic) market coming in the low season, namely gastronomy and wine, which have been identified as relevant attractions for culturally interested tourists elsewhere (Hall, Sharples, Mitchell, Macionis, & Cambourne, 2003). These assets, the region is nationally renowned for, might require a better, internationally more visible integration in the destination's tourist offer and image (Ribeiro & Vareiro, 2010). Simultaneously travelers in the mid-season show greater freedom of choice of holiday timing and also interest in eventually changing the season, with the low season being still attractive for some of these tourists' quests. In any case, the attractiveness of this market, their interest in coming back for holidays and for longer stays, their high level of daily spending, should be viewed as an opportunity of increasing this very interesting market, to which the destination should target to through well-developed opportunities for getting to know the region's most interesting and peculiar historical and cultural aspects, but also for tasting unique quality food and wines (like the unique *green wine*), for exploring landscapes, with accessibilities, maps, signposting and information, also in English language, paramount requirements for this curious and highly educated market.

The mainly domestic travelers present in the *low season*, on the other hand, reveal relatively lower levels of income, low/mid-education level and low daily expenditures, while staying typically for short breaks in search of nature, good food, and for visiting friends and relatives. These tourists show least satisfaction with the season of travel, however reporting a high probability of coming back, and simultaneously presenting less freedom of choice regarding the season. This domestic, relatively loyal tourist market should not be neglected, but opportunities for this group to also come in other seasons should be made available (eventually through promotional offers in some accommodation units rather catering to the national market) and attractive through new product development, while destination managers should also try to increase the number of international tourists, particularly those identified in the mid-season for the above-mentioned reasons, particularly with less climate-dependent activities (e.g., wine and cultural tourism opportunities).

Finally, the *high season* reveals a predominance of international tourists, similar to the mid-season, however in this season, tourists, who mostly present mid-level income and mid-high level of education, traveling in a couple, but also frequently with children, tend to stay for longer periods than in the other seasons. The main travel motives these holidaymakers mention are getting to know local history and culture, visiting friends and relatives, but also climate and the beach, with some revealing high levels of loyalty to the destination, even owning a second home. Not all summer visitors report much freedom of choice of the holiday season (with those coming with children more conditioned by the school vacation schedule), but some may and many would like to also visit the region in another season of the year. Consequently, it would be interesting to try to make those who actually are not as constraint to choose their holiday period to also come in the mid- or low season, eventually for only a short-break and possibly to get to know other facets of the destination, making travelers also explore other regions and attraction, away from the beaches and implying a type of activity which may actually be more enjoyable in not so warm periods of the year (like hiking in the National Park of Gerês and cultural tourism offers).

CONCLUSION AND IMPLICATIONS

The profile, behavior, motivations, and attitudes of tourist demand in the Minho region reveal interesting seasonal variations. As discussed before, understanding the seasonal profile and differences between tourists traveling in different seasons at a destination should be crucial for directing effective strategies to these seasonal markets and to specifically increase demand outside the high season and thereby reduce seasonality at the destination.

Comparing results with those of a study undertaken in 1998–1999 in North Portugal (Kastenholz & Almeida, 2008) similarities in seasonal differences are observed, particularly regarding the predominance of short-break domestic travelers in the low season versus more international and longer staying tourists in the high season. Still, in the past summer holiday motivations tended to be more focused on "sun and beach," while nowadays also "exploring history and culture" stand out as motivations in the high season, reflecting more heterogeneity in summer holiday motivations. The here-introduced additional distinction of a "mid-season" (which in the previous study was integrated in the "low season") increases through the identification of a quite distinct tourist market the quality of analysis and capacity of useful marketing action. Probably through the introduction of low-cost airline connections at the Oporto airport since 2005 a new type of traveler has been attracted to the region, extending the interest of the international market from the previously dominating high to a mid-season for short-break travel, thereby introducing new travel patterns, new markets and motivations, that the region may do well in adapting to, as illustrated before.

Results should contribute to both general discussion research on the phenomenon of seasonality in tourism and to improved capacity of management of seasonal demand in the North Portugal's Minho region aiming at a more balanced and sustainable growth in demand in an emergent tourist destination. Thus, seasonal differences, both regarding the traveler market and the destination, must be understood, as well as the opportunities and challenges they imply for sustainably managing the destination through enhanced capacity of management of supply (Butler, 2001; Kastenholz, 2004).

NOTES

1. Seasonality degree accessed by Gini's Coefficient on hotel night stays at Minho Region, 2009 (North Portugal $G = 0.19$).
2. The destination supply diversification is an important reason to balance seasonal touristic flows' over the year (Almeida & Kastenholz, 2008).

REFERENCES

Allok, J. (1995). Seasonality. In S. Witt & L. Moutinho (Eds.), *Tourism marketing and management handbook* (pp. 92–104). Hert FordShire: Prentice Hall International.

Almeida, A., & Kastenholz, E. (2008). Towards a theoretical construct of tourism seasonality. In IASK (Org.), *Proceedings of Advances in Tourism Research conference* (pp. 81–93). UA, Aveiro.

BarOn, R. (1975). *Seasonality in tourism: A guide to analysis of seasonality.* Economist Intelligence Unit Technical Paper No. 2.

Baum, T., & Hagen, L. (1999). Responses to seasonality: The experiences of peripheral destinations. *Journal of Tourism Research, 1*(4), 299–312.

Bonn, M., Furr, H., & Uysal, M. (1992). Seasonal variation of coastal resort visitors: Hilton Head Island. *Journal of Travel Research, 31*(1), 50–56.

Butler, R. (1994). Seasonality in tourism: Issues and problems. In A. Seaton (Ed.), *Tourism: The state of art* (pp. 332–339). Chichester: Wiley.

Butler, R. (2001). Seasonality in tourism: Issues and implications. In T. Baum & S. Lundtorp (Eds.), *Seasonality in tourism* (pp. 5–21). Amsterdam: Pergamon.

Butler, R., & Smale, B. (1991). Geographical perspectives on festivals in Ontario. *Journal of Applied Recreation Research, 16*(1), 3–23.

Calantone, R., & Johar, J. (1984). Seasonal segmentation of the tourism market using a benefit segmentation framework. *Journal of Travel Research, 23*(2), 14–24.

Commons, J., & Page, S. (2001). Managing seasonality in peripheral tourism regions: The case of northland New Zealand. In T. Baum & S. Lundtorp (Eds.), *Seasonality in tourism* (pp. 153–172). Amsterdam: Pergamon.

Cooper, C., Fletcher, J., Gilbert, D., Shepherd, R., & Wanhill, S. (1998). *Tourism: Principles and practices* (2nd ed.). London: Addison-Wesley, Longman.

Donatos, G., & Zairis, P. (1991). Seasonality of foreign tourism in the Greek island of Crete. *Annals of Tourism Research, 18*(3), 515–519.

Hall, C. M., Sharples, L., Mitchell, R., Macionis, N., & Cambourne, B. (2003). *Food tourism around the World – Development, management and markets.* Oxford: Elsevier, Butterworth-Heinemann.

Hartmann, R. (1986). Tourism, seasonality and social change. *Leisure Studies, 5*(1), 25–33.

Kastenholz, E. (2004). Management of demand as a tool in sustainable tourist destination development. *Journal of Sustainable Tourism, 12*(5), 388–408.

Kastenholz, E., & Almeida, A. (2008). Seasonality in rural tourism – The case of north Portugal. *Tourism Review, 63*(2), 5–15.

Koenig-Lewis, N., & Bischoff, E. (2005). Seasonality research: The state of the art. *International Journal of Tourism Research, 7*(4–5), 201–219.

Lundtorp, S. (2001). Measuring tourism seasonality. In T. Baum & S. Lundtorp (Eds.), *Seasonality in tourism* (pp. 23–48). Amsterdam: Pergamon.

Lundtorp, S., Rassing, C., & Wanhill, S. (1999). The off-season is "no season": The case of the Danish island of Bornholm. *Tourism Economics, 5*(1), 49–68.

Manning, R., & Powers, L. (1984). Peak and off-peak use: Redistributing the outdoor recreation/tourism load (Vermont). *Journal of Travel Research, 23*(2), 25–31.

Margaryan, L., & Zherdev, N. (2011). *Tourism development in North Iceland – The issues of seasonality and image production.* Akureyri: Icelandic Tourism Research Centre.

McKercher, B. (1995). The destination market-matrix: A tourism market portfolio analysis model. *Journal of Travel & Tourism Marketing, 4*(2), 23–40.

Mitchell, L., & Murphy, P. (1991). Geography and tourism. *Annals of Tourism Research, 18*(1), 57–60.

O'Discroll, T. (1985). Seasonality in the trans-Atlantic vacation market. *Annals of Tourism Research, 12*(1), 109–110.

Ribeiro, J., & Vareiro, L. (2010). Portugal's Minho—Lima region as a tourist destination: Tourism operators' attitudes towards its management and promotion. *Tourism Economics*, *16*(2), 385—404.

Somerville, J. (1987). Jamaican, Swiss, U.S. independents target new markets to beat seasonality. *Hotels and Restaurants International*, *21*(11), 50—53.

Spencer, D., & Holecek, D. (2007). Basic characteristics of the fall tourism market. *Tourism Management*, *28*(2), 491—504.

Spotts, D., & Mahoney, E. (1993). Understanding the fall tourism market. *Journal of Travel Research*, *32*(2), 3—15.

Stäblein, F. (1994). School holidays. Presentation of an experience: Rolling system of school holidays. *Conference on Staggering of Holidays*. *Niedersächsisches Kultusministerium*. Düsseldorf, Germany.

Sutcliffe, C., & Sinclair, M. (1980). The measurement of seasonality within the tourism industry: An application to tourism arrivals in Spain. *Applied Economics*, *12*(4), 429—441.

Vanhove, N. (2004). *The economics of tourism destinations*. London: Butterworth Heinemann.

Witt, S., Brooke, M., & Buckley, P. (1991). *The management of international tourism*. London: Unwin Hyman.

World Tourism Organisation. (1995). *Concepts, definitions and classifications for tourism statistics*. Madrid: WTO.

Yacoumis, J. (1980). Tackling seasonality: The case of Sri Lanka. *Tourism Management*, *1*(2), 84—98.

MODELLING FERRY PASSENGER NUMBERS: IMPLICATIONS FOR DESTINATION MANAGEMENT

Carl H. Marcussen

ABSTRACT

This chapter models the number of ferry round trips per day in order to make suggestions for future ferry schedules for an island — in this case Bornholm. Calendar effects, including the effect of moving religious holidays, as well as the overall annual level of economic activity, are taken into account. The model for the number of round trips per day is also applicable to the number of passengers per day. If the number of passengers (and arrivals) per day is forecast, this may be used as a basis for forecasting daily, weekly and monthly activity levels for service providers at the destination, including service providers in the accommodations sector. For islands, data for all passengers to/from the destination may be available (ferries and airlines). Based on these daily, weekly or monthly passenger numbers, both domestic and international numbers may be modelled and forecast. Other destinations may model and

Marketing Places and Spaces

Advances in Culture, Tourism and Hospitality Research, Volume 10, 269−279

Copyright © 2015 by Emerald Group Publishing Limited

ISSN: 1871-3173/doi:10.1108/S1871-317320150000010019

*forecast daily, weekly and monthly international arrivals by air in order
to support decisions at the destination site.*

Keywords: Ferry trips; destination management; transportation;
demand modelling

INTRODUCTION

Although transportation is a necessary part of any leisure or business tourism activity, the transportation aspect is rarely the focus of tourism-related
studies. The possibilities for exploiting transportation data in order to gain
further insight into tourist behaviour, preferences and choices are under-
utilised.

The first purpose of this chapter is to use historical time series of ferry
passengers and ferry round trips per day in order to make suggestions for
future ferry schedules for an island — in this case Bornholm. The second
purpose of this chapter is to discuss the potential use of a historical time
series of ferry or airline passengers per day, as well as monthly overnight
statistics, in order to estimate the unknown daily and weekly number of
overnight guests for both island destinations and for other destinations.

The perspective of the study is a destination marketing/management perspective, including (daily) demand modelling and optimisation of supply
(ferry round trips per day), based on the same model developed to explain
demand (daily passenger numbers).

LITERATURE REVIEW

In tourism, demand modelling/forecasting generally utilises months, quarters or years as the time units. Research in tourism journals rarely involves
the modelling of daily, or even weekly, demand. However, the research by
Bartolomé, McAleer, Ramos, and Rey-Maquieira (2007), as well as by
Divinoa and McAleer (2010), is the exception to the rule. Both of these studies include the daily level. But modelling the number of ferry passengers,
and the optimisation of ferry capacity, involves further layers of seasonality, in addition to monthly variations (i.e. between days of the week, and
intra-day, as well as intra-holiday variations).

Scheduling models for ferries can be quite complex, notably under alliances (Yan, Chen, Chen, & Lou, 2007). The relationship between transportation and tourism has been the focus of a number of papers involving Gui Lohmann (Lohmann, 2003; Lohmann & Duval, 2011; Lohmann & Pearce, 2010, 2012; Lohmann & Trischler, 2012). Literature on public utility demand modelling/forecasting for products and services, such as gas, electricity and water consumption, may be relevant for modelling the number of ferry passengers (Ismail, Jamaluddin, & Jamaludin, 2008).

The discipline of revenue management is applied within the passenger transport industries, including airlines, ferry lines and cruise ships (Maddah, Moussawi-Haidar, El-Taha, & Rida, 2010), as well as within the accommodation sector, including hotels and holiday rentals. Revenue management is concerned with modelling demand at the daily level, and even at the within-day level. Revenue management systems are being offered to ferry operators by several software suppliers. Dynamic pricing is being integrated into these systems.

Ferry transportation, and in some instances, air transportation (Williams & Pagliari, 2014), is a Public Service Obligation (PSO) for some destinations, notably some islands (Angelopoulos, Chlomoudis, Christofas, & Papadimitriou, 2013; Chlomoudis, Kostagiolas, Papadimitriou, & Tzannatos, 2011). Therefore, strict adherence to the commercial principles for pricing and profit optimisation may not necessarily apply. However, being able to model daily ferry passenger numbers and tourism overnights would be useful for the tourism industry, including cottage rental agencies and other holiday accommodation options, on a weekly basis.

The number of references to 'revenue management' within a 'tourism' context in the literature is high. The inclusion of the term 'daily' combined with 'revenue management' is also high. Thus sciencedirect.com returned 265 references to these search engine terms in *Tourism Management*, 147 in *International Journal of Hospitality Management*, 138 in *Annals of Tourism Research*, 72 in the *Cornell Hotel and Restaurant Administration Quarterly*, with additional references in *Journal of Air Transport Management* and *Journal of Transport Geography*.

According to the same source, there is only one reference to 'revenue management' in conjunction with the search term 'ferries' (Anguera, 2006). This reference is not concerned with the daily, weekly or even monthly number of passengers, but instead, it is concerned with the annual numbers. Searching 'revenue management' in conjunction with the search terms 'ferries' and 'daily tourism' on Google Scholar returned 102 results.

METHOD

The number of ferry passengers is modelled based on a unique and detailed 5-year series of daily departures and passenger statistics. The time series allows for an assessment of the temporal variations in the number of passengers and the capacity utilisation within each day. However, the intra-day variations are beyond the scope of this chapter, since, from the point of view of the accommodation sector, the important thing is the number of arriving and departing passengers, rather than the timing of these within each day.

Also, the statistics of traffic streams could be elaborated by also including the number of vehicles and even cargo trailers. But again, from an accommodation point of view, the important thing is the number of passengers. It would be relevant for businesses in the accommodations sector to know how passenger numbers are split into segments, such as day-visitors, those staying in commercial accommodations, other overnight visitors, and residents. However, the time series of passenger statistics at hand does not allow for such a breakdown.

The model includes at least four sets of variables: weekdays, months, years, and holiday periods. Coding the weekdays requires $7 - 1 = 6$ dummy variables. Coding the months requires $12 - 1 = 11$ dummy variables. Distinguishing between five historical years requires four dummies. Coding the seven holiday periods requires six dummies.

Normally, dummy variables are pure $0-1$ variables, hence the name 'dichotomous variables'. To improve the explanatory power of the model, instead of $0-1$ variables, $0-$'fractions of 1' is used on the specific days within the different holiday periods. Furthermore, the interaction between weekdays and summer holiday is included as a variable, specifically Saturdays in the summer holiday (the variable 'Saturdays' and the variable 'summer holiday' including all of July) are multiplied. Residuals were scrutinised during the process of finalising the model of ferry passengers per route per day, notably for the main route, and/or for all routes, in order to get input for the process of refining the model.

FINDINGS

Fig. 1 shows that the following may be taken into account as determinants of the daily number of ferry round trips: weekdays with Tuesday as basis,

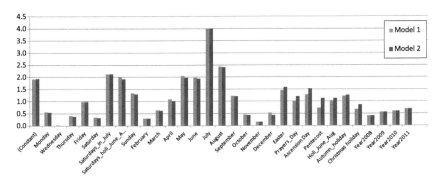

Fig. 1. Graphical Illustration of the Algorithm for Establishing the Number of Round Trips per Day on the Route Rønne−Ystad 2012, 2013, 2014.

Saturdays in July, Saturdays in June and August, months with January as basis, Easter, Great Prayers Day, Christ's Ascension Day, Pentecost, the part of June and August which is summer holiday in Denmark, autumn holiday (week 42, in Denmark), Christmas holiday and the annual level of round trips per day with 2012 as basis.

The difference between model 1 and model 2 can be explained as follows, as illustrated by the variations in the number of round trips within each holiday period, with Easter as example, cf. Fig. 2: The busiest day during the Easter period is the Wednesday before Maundy Thursday (i.e. the day before the eve of Good Friday). Good Friday is the slowest day among the Easter days in Denmark as far as the number of ferry rounds between Bornholm of Denmark and Ystad of Sweden is concerned.

In model 1, all days within a given holiday period are coded the same, as 1 as opposed to 0 for all other days. However, for example, during the 11 days before, during and by the end of the Easter holidays, each day is somewhat busier or somewhat less busy than the average. Therefore the dummy variable 0−1 differs in such a way that the '1' is smaller than the '1' for the relatively slow days and larger than the '1' for the relatively busy days. The '1' is varied until the estimated number of round trips per day fits with the actual number of round trips per day, in this example, each day during Easter.

Due to this varying of the dummy variable, $R2$, the explanatory power of model 2 is greater than the $R2$ for model 1. Specifically, $R2$ increases from 0.747 in model 1 to 0.773 in model 2, with round trips as the dependent variable, and alternatively, from 0.837 to 0.868 in models with passengers as the dependent variable based on the route

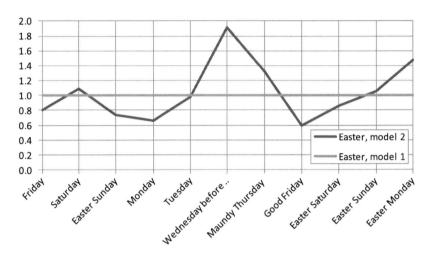

Fig. 2. Graphical Illustration of the Transition from Model 1 to Model 2 Regarding the Number of Passengers and Round Trips for the Route Rønne at Bornholm Island–Ystad – Here for Easter.

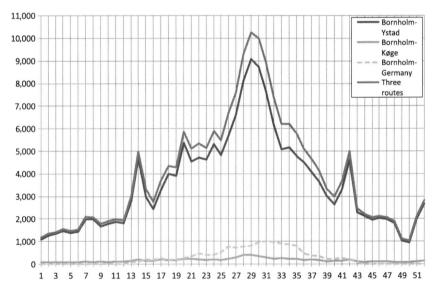

Fig. 3. Number of Passengers per Week per Route to/from Bornholm 2012. *Note*: The numbers on the horizontal line are week numbers.

Rønne/Bornholm−Ystad/Sweden. Arguably, if the purpose is to transfer the variations in passengers to variations in the total arrivals at the island of Bornholm, which subsequently may be translated into variations in the number of overnights, all three routes to/from the island should be modelled under one, rather than just the main route Rønne/Bornholm−Ystad.

It is possible to show the estimated versus the actual total number of passengers per day 2012, as well as to make forecasts per day for the years 2013−2016, based on a known calendar and an assumed level of economic activity. The daily number of passengers can be aggregated to a weekly number of passengers (Fig. 3). The known annual number of passengers can be split into individual week numbers. If the number of overnights per night or per week is not known, the number of passengers per day or per week may be used as an indicator, thus allowing for a splitting of monthly overnights into certain dates and weeks.

CONCLUSION AND IMPLICATIONS

A model of ferry passengers per day (per route) is developed. The same model (i.e. the same set of variables which can explain the number of passengers) can be used to illustrate the number of round trips per day, based on the assumption that the ferry schedules of the past were sensible in that high capacity is offered when the expected demand (number of passengers) is high.

If the number of passengers per day is known for a given destination, for example, the number of passengers per day for the past five years, this can be used as one of the inputs for estimating the historical split of monthly overnights into overnights for the night of each day, and then those estimates can be aggregated into weeks, if desired. Similarly, for the current year and for the next few years, with a known calendar (including moving religious holidays) and known expected levels of aggregate economic growth, daily passenger numbers can be forecast. This can be used as one of the inputs for estimating overnights per day, per week and per month.

One problem with sub-national overnight statistics in Denmark is that overnights for holiday cottages, one of the main categories of overnights in most of the Danish provinces outside of the capital, only are published on a monthly basis down to the NUTS2 level (i.e. for the five regions only). So, different methods can be used to estimate the holiday cottage overnights at the NUTS3 level. In this respect, the model of ferry passengers per day is one of the helpful tools.

Other indicators of the split of the holiday cottage overnights per week are the weekly price calendars for the major or local holiday cottage rental agencies (i.e. prices tend to be high when demand is expected to be high). Additional inputs for making estimates of weekly or monthly overnights, given a known annual total, include the statistics for the other types of accommodations for the same destination. If needed, the ferry passenger model may be used to split the monthly overnights into the nightly and weekly number of overnights.

One arguably inventive feature of the approach used in this chapter is the development of adjusted dummy variables for the holiday periods. The idea is that each day within each holiday period is different in terms of the expected number of passengers or tourists, and therefore the normal 0–1 variables for each holiday period are adjusted, modifying the value for each day of the holiday so that the busy days have a value of over 1 and vice versa. This is done in such a way that the average remains 1 for each holiday period, but each day within the holiday period gets a value that is proportional to the historic average number of passengers for each respective day.

The explanatory power of the ferry passenger model (which is a linear multiple regression model) increases when the holiday dummy variables differ as described. Furthermore, the t-values of almost every variable in the model increase (i.e. not only does the t-value of the holiday variables increase, but so do the rest of the variables). This indicates that the analysis is sharper, and the model can arguably better predict the optimal number of round trips that should be scheduled for any future day within the next few years. Also, the model can be used to suggest minor adjustments to published copies or drafts of ferry schedules.

In the case of island destinations, the number of arrivals and departures by sea or by air may be published. If not, then airports, seaports, airlines or ferry operators may voluntarily reveal the time series of passenger numbers. The level of detail of such information may vary. For example, the most detailed time unit may be months, weeks, days or individual departures. For non-island destinations, daily, weekly or monthly numbers for international arrivals by air may be available from airports or other data sources. International arrivals may thus be modelled and forecast in order to support managerial decision-making at the destinations.

What insights into touristic relevance, which may be gained from the time series of transportation data, depend on aspects other than the temporal level of detail? Seasonality by months, week numbers, days of the week and within-day variations may be modelled based on the historical time series. With the given calendars and assumptions about the economic development, the historical pattern of arrivals (and/or departures) may be modelled.

Apart from counting and reporting the number of passengers, in the case of ferries, the number and type of vehicles may be reported. This may enable researchers or destination management organisations to have the ability to calculate the size of each travel party, for example. A relatively high number of persons per travel party would probably indicate that children (and thereby children's families) tend to be included at a particular time.

Unless transportation is provided under the public service obligation, prices of transportation may be varied according to demand. And in any case, the list prices of accommodations may be varied according to expected demand. Some hotels, hotel chains and holiday cottage rental agencies may have advanced revenue management systems and may be able to optimise their revenue without the support of information regarding passenger flows. Other accommodations and tourism-related service providers, such as various types of restaurants and attractions, whose sales are highly correlated with passenger streams, may benefit from a projection or forecast of arrivals and/or departures for the next year or two by day, week or month.

Since calendars are known with absolute certainty, and the economic climate for the next year or two has been forecast by external parties, passenger flows can be forecast with some confidence for the most important origin markets. Such a forecast could be made publicly available for relevant decision makers at the given destinations. This may be used as background information for decisions about capacity and list prices by day, week or month. At (highly) seasonal destinations, decisions about capacity include whether the given service providers should be open at all, and if open, whether all facilities should be open to full capacity, and what level of staff capacity should be provided.

In the data matrix of a certain time series, the highest level of temporal detail may, for example, be days (as opposed to months or weeks or within days periods of time). A series of seven (or six, since the last day would be given) dummy variables can be used to indicate the day of the week, twelve (or eleven) dummy variables can indicate the month, each of a number of years can be indicated by dummy variables, shifting religious holidays or fixed holiday periods can be indicated, and even the shifting of the summer holiday periods of the most important or states nearest to Germany (Bundesländer) may be coded.

A certain economic level of activity can be associated with each past year, the current year and the next year or two. Some of these and other factors, which may be significant for demand, and in this case, the number of passengers, can be taken into account when modelling passenger numbers, if significant. Advice on how to model and forecast demand at the monthly level can be found in tourism literature, whereas demand modelling at a more detailed temporal level may take inspiration from revenue management literature, logistics and operations research.

In order to give more specific indications of the data sources of possible relevance for specific types of destinations, a few examples can be, given. For an island such as Madeira, all arrivals to the island are by either airplane or cruise ship. Cruise ship arrivals for Funchal and most other major cruise ports are known a year or more in advance, even by day. At the airport, arrivals come by either scheduled airline routes or by charter flights.

The time series covering multiple years, with days as a key temporal unit, may be available from one of the many different publicly accessible sources. In addition, it may be available on a request basis or may be reconstructed based on historical and future published time schedules. Also, the within arrival and departure pattern can be described and modelled, if desirable, which it may be for taxi operating companies or taxi centrals, as well as for hotel front desk staffing etc. Data on scheduled and charter airline arrivals and departures are known for the past, as well as for the relatively near future of maybe one year in advance.

Even without exact knowledge of the planned arrivals of airplanes and their estimated number of passengers, given the historical arrival pattern and the associated number of arriving passengers within the given calendar and the available external forecasts for economic activity, and possibly other factors, the number of arriving passengers at the airport can be forecast by day for the current year, as well as for the next year or two.

The impact of the moving religious holidays can be accessed based on the historical data, provided it is available. For any current year, a forecast number of arrivals can be compared to the actual number of arrivals. Without a model-based forecast for the number of arrivals, it would be hard to know, for example, if any deviation from the previous year is due to an early/late Easter, an early/late summer holiday in key German states, a change in GDP growth in the main market countries, or if demand has changed for other reasons requiring action from the relevant decision makers at the destination.

REFERENCES

Angelopoulos, J., Chlomoudis, C., Christofas, P., & Papadimitriou, S. (2013). Cost assessment of sea and air transport PSO services: The case of Greece. *International Journal of Maritime, Trade & Economic Issues, 1*(2), 3–39.

Anguera, R. (2006). The channel tunnel – An ex post economic evaluation. *Transportation Research Part A: Policy and Practice, 40*(4), 291–315.

Bartolomé, A., McAleer, M., Ramos, V., & Rey-Maquieira, J. (2007). Modelling air passenger arrivals to the Balearic Islands, Spain. In L. Oxley & D. Kulasiri (Eds.), *MODSIM 2007 International Congress on Modelling and Simulation.* Modelling and Simulation Society of Australia and New Zealand, December.

Chlomoudis, C., Kostagiolas, P. A., Papadimitriou, S., & Tzannatos, E. S. (2011). A European perspective on public service obligations for island transport services. *Maritime Economics & Logistics, 13,* 342–354.

Divinoa, J. A., & McAleer, M. (2010). Modelling and forecasting daily international mass tourism to Peru. *Tourism Management, 31*(6), 846–854.

Ismail, Z., Jamaluddin, F., & Jamaludin, F. (2008). Time series regression model for forecasting Malaysian electricity load demand. *Asian Journal of Mathematics and Statistics, 1*(3), 139–149.

Lohmann, G. (2003). The role of transport in tourism development: Nodal functions and management practices. *International Journal of Tourism Research, 5,* 403–407.

Lohmann, G., & Duval, D. T. (2011). Critical aspects of the tourism-transport relationship. In C. Cooper (Ed.), *Contemporary tourism reviews.* Woodeaton, Oxford, UK: Goodfellow Publishers. ISBN: 9781906884369.

Lohmann, G., & Pearce, D. G. (2010). Conceptualizing and operationalizing nodal tourism functions. *Journal of Transport Geography, 18*(2), 266–275.

Lohmann, G., & Pearce, D. G. (2012). Tourism and transport relationships: The suppliers' perspective in gateway destinations in New Zealand. *Asia Pacific Journal of Tourism Research, 17*(1), 14–29.

Lohmann, G., & Trischler, J. (2012). The failure of fast ferry catamaran operations in New Zealand and Hawaii. *Journal of Transportation Technologies, 2,* 102–112.

Maddah, B., Moussawi-Haidar, L., El-Taha, M., & Rida, H. (2010). Dynamic cruise ship revenue management. *European Journal of Operational Research, 207*(1), 445–455.

Williams, G., & Pagliari, R. (2014). A comparative analysis of the application and use of public service obligations in air transport within the EU. *Transport Policy, 11*(1), 55–66.

Yan, S., Chen, C.-H., Chen, H.-Y., & Lou, T.-C. (2007). Optimal scheduling models for ferry companies under alliances. *Journal of Marine Science and Technology, 15*(1), 53–66.

YIELDING TOURISTS' PREFERENCES

Jaime Serra, Antónia Correia and
Paulo M. M. Rodrigues

ABSTRACT

This chapter uses stated tourist preferences as a proxy of visitor yield measures, in order to analyse and understand the yield potential of different markets' preferences. A literature review revealed that there is much progress to be made in terms of discussion, consensus and stability of methodology for the measurement of visitor yield. The aim of the visitor yield analysis, in the current chapter, is also to bring another dimension into yield analysis and discussion, contributing with a new form of measuring yield potential. Since the objective is to identify yield patterns based on tourist preferences over a period of time, dynamics may be captured from the fluctuation patterns, or expressed as volatility of visitor yield and length of stay throughout the years. Destination management organisations and tourist companies may potentially adopt this visitor yield matrix in order to support future strategic decisions.

Keywords: Visitor yield; tourist preferences; competitive positioning

Marketing Places and Spaces
Advances in Culture, Tourism and Hospitality Research, Volume 10, 281–292
Copyright © 2015 by Emerald Group Publishing Limited
All rights of reproduction in any form reserved
ISSN: 1871-3173/doi:10.1108/S1871-317320150000010020

INTRODUCTION

The overall attractiveness of a destination has long been regarded as a critical criterion in tourism consumer decision making and choice (Crouch, 2011). The choice depends on preferences, and these in turn are a function of information about destination attributes.

> Preferences are not what cause the consumer to choose particular goods, rather it is the fact that certain goods were chosen (obtained) that makes those goods preferred. (Hands, 2013, p. 8)

Hence, the uniqueness of experiences relies on declared tourists' preferences (Decrop, 2000; Goodall, 1991; Hsu, Tsai, & Wu, 2009). However, another stream of research shows that tourists' preferences are of paramount importance for the positioning of destinations (Seddighi & Theocharous, 2002), and that these preferences are dynamic (Goodall, 1991).

The importance of measuring and monitoring tourist behaviour has become an issue of paramount importance concerning future management decisions at micro (companies) or macro (destination) levels. Particularly, mature destinations, more than just merely seeking to increase the numbers of tourist arrivals, should seek to diversify and retain the most profitable markets. In this way, several countries and regions emphasise the importance of marketing in capturing and retaining higher-yield tourists. An understanding of why different preferences may contribute to enhance or diminish the yield potential of tourism can underpin destination marketing by both public and private sector organisations (Dwyer & Forsyth, 2008).

Starting from this demand/supply paradigm, an analysis of the dynamics of tourism demand based on stated preferences is suggested in order to identify the preferences of the higher-yield visitors.

This chapter introduces a new way to measure visitor yield, using tourist preferences as a proxy, in order to assess the competitiveness of the destination. This assessment is performed across countries. However, one must be aware that yield from the different existing segments will show variation over time, since market elasticity will provide a response to return yields to their normal high levels.

The scarcity of discussion about the definition of visitor and tourism yield concepts or indeed the definition of a uniform methodological framework in order to measure visitors' yield patterns has provided the impetus for the present chapter. Following these aspects, the present chapter aims to materialize a visitor yield matrix based on stated preferences and contributes to the understanding of how the yield potential of

different source markets and segments can underpin destination marketing by organisations.

THEORETICAL CONSIDERATIONS

The literature provides various definitions of yield. Scott and Breakey
(2007) state that it is in common use in agriculture and finance, and that its
meaning is the amount which can be produced by one unit of capacity. The
authors examine the use of the concept of yield in tourism and discussed
how the 'yield' measure should be used at the destination level.

Academics have further extended the yield concept to refer to the generation of financial and economic gains by means of tourism. The definition
of yield differs (Pratt, 2012) and is interpreted in different ways by different
stakeholders, due to its various ways of measurement. A yield-based
approach will, nonetheless, allow stakeholders to grasp what potential
change is required and orient themselves towards it (Northcote & Macbeth,
2006).

The aviation sector was responsible for first introducing the concept of
yield into tourism, which was then followed by accommodation, car-rental
firms, cruise lines and other exponents of the travel industry in the adoption of this tool into management approaches (Mainzer, 2004; Reynolds &
Braithwaite, 1997). Thus, when applying this concept to the accommodation sector, one definition of yield that is considered is the return in euros
per room per night.

According to Dwyer and Forsyth (1997, p. 224), the definition of tourism yield is,

> the next benefit accruing to a host country from international visitors, that is, the bene-
> fits minus the complexity of identifying, at a national level, all the benefits and costs of
> tourism, each of which has differing patterns of activity and impact.

These authors have been widely followed in recent literature in their suggestion that non-economic gains in environmental, social and cultural
scope should also be included in the term. Thus, the concept of 'sustainable
yield' is now being developed by tourism researchers (Becken & Butcher,
2004; Northcote & Macbeth, 2006).

In line with this, Dwyer, Forsyth, and Spurr (2007) drew attention to
the importance of a precise definition of the concept of yield and a clear
outline of the approaches used to measure it in order for there to be consistency among stakeholders. In each destination, there will be different views

held by different stakeholders on what should be maximised. At the level of the regional tourism organisation, the goal may be the maximisation of profit generated from total visitor revenue, local councils may set their aims on improving employment figures, and the national government may focus on the profit generated by tax revenue or value added. This leads to various definitions of the term 'yield' due to the different perspective on the object to be maximised by each stakeholder (Scott & Breakey, 2007).

The inexact definition of yield in its application to destinations is also a consequence of the paucity of detailed studies relating visitor profiles and characteristics. In a study carried out by Becken and Butcher (2004), an empirical examination was made of visitor characteristics and their relation to profitability. Notwithstanding some differences in the area of expenditure and value-added patterns between different groups of tourists, the results of the study revealed that expenditure and value added produced the same final rankings, but that employment underwent a different impact. The conclusion can then be drawn that total destination expenditure and tourism jobs will be affected in different ways by a mix of different visitor profiles.

The relationship between visitor characteristics and profit has to be calculated for each specific destination (Scott & Breakey, 2007). As has already been discussed from the perspective of destinations, the revenue associated with visits is more significant than the number of visitors per se in tourism marketing. Apart from which, the greater social and environmental impacts implied by great numbers of visitors are well known.

The above definition of the concept of visitor yield is (a) more applicable to the demand than the supply side of the industry and (b) is concerned with how satisfied visitors feel with the 'value' of their experience, while at the same time consuming products and services. In the field of consumer behaviour, customer value holds great importance (Grönroos, 1997), and by focusing on this, organisations will better understand the tourist experience and so be able to provide tourists what they want, need and expect (Dwyer et al., 2006).

In a study by Northcote and Macbeth (2006), the authors propose basing the concept of visitor yield around their integrated tourism yield framework (ITY), which encompasses the number, distribution and type of arrivals. This defines a high visitor yield as one which attracts a large number of visitors. Dwyer et al. (2006) proposed another view of visitor yield, and linked it principally to the satisfaction or 'value' that the visitor experienced related not only to the consumption of products and services but also to the quality of their tourism experience. This chapter works on the basis of preferences as proxy of pull motivations, related in turn to the attributes of destinations. From the segmentation of tourists by preferences an interesting contribution may arise in terms of a proxy of the visitor yield index.

There has been some debate in the literature on the concepts of tourism and visitor yield. The first contribution from Dwyer et al. (2006) came in the form of a technical report, enabling the measurement of concepts of visitor yield based on an initial presentation and description of them. Dwyer, Forsyth, and Spurr (2007) focused on the Australian inbound market, with a yield analysis which aimed to discover which its high-yield markets were. They also presented an overview of the different concepts of yield. Primary data were used by the authors in several of these measures, and this enabled them to make a comparison of the origin markets and establish market segments which could be seen as high yield under various measures.

Becken and Butcher's (2004) contribution was to base their yield measures on expenditure per day. Dwyer et al.'s (2006) technical report contained a matrix (Fig. 1) which was supported on the length of stay and the levels of daily spending. In this way they were able to pinpoint priority market segments at any given time.

The matrix consists of four quadrants: markets that are positioned on the right-hand side of the horizontal axis are the longer stays, while

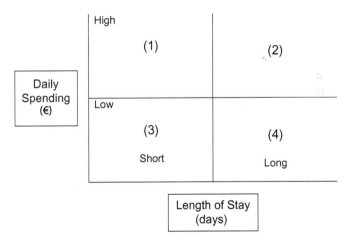

Fig. 1. Market Segments by Daily Spending and Length of Stay. *Source*: Maziteli (2003) cited by Dwyer et al. (2006).

markets positioned on the left-hand side are linked to shorter stays. Those positioned on the top of vertical axis are considered most profitable and those on the bottom are less profitable markets.

With the aim of clarifying how different markets and segments had different yield potentials, Dwyer and Forsyth (2008) set themselves the goal of showing how CGE models can be used to estimate the economic yield of a range of visitor markets for Australia. The conclusion that arose from the results of their study was that yield measures supply more valuable data in terms of destination marketing and planning development when they are based on the economic impacts of expenditure.

A discussion of tourism and of visitor yield concepts was made in two recent papers. In one, Pratt (2012) looked to identify high-spending tourist groups in Hawaii via an estimation of the economic impacts of tourism for various market segments and showed that there are different knock-on effects of each visitor's spending pattern. This chapter took up the lead of Dwyer, Forsyth, Fredline, et al. (2007), and resulted in a higher awareness of the need for further research into how to best measure visitor yield and productivity. The suggestion is that different destinations do the same for different market segments. In the other, Dywer and Thomas (2012) focused on developing new measures of tourism yield in Cambodia, South East Asia. The authors' view is that further reflection is needed on how poverty is reduced by tourism expenditure. They put forward that by measuring the economic significance of different tourist origin markets, destination marketing and management decisions can be importantly supported. Working from the perspective of the demand side, the authors established expenditure measures for the top 10 markets to Cambodia. In addition, they showed that expenditure made in the destination plays a small role in tourism's ability to improve living conditions of the poor.

As the literature review revealed, there is a lot of progress to be made in terms of discussion, consensus and stability of methodology for the measurement of tourism and visitor yield before a definition is reached. The aim of the visitor yield analysis of this chapter, therefore, is to bring another dimension into the analysis and its main purpose is to develop a methodology able to measure visitor yield based on tourists' preferences.

Tourists' preferences are the base of any choice. Revealed preference establishes the reasoning of individuals' choices within a specific context. Preferences usually arise on a scale that results from the product's attributes perceived by the consumer (Driscoll, Lawson, & Niven, 1994) and are ordered concerning tourists' declaration of intents under assumed rationality. This assumption is grounded on the Theory of Stated

Preferences (Nicolau & Más, 2006), which allows a ranking of a number of baskets or instead a number of attributes of a certain product that may lead to a final choice. In the particular case of tourism, composite product preferences are formed according to the attributes that most influence the tourist's decision. As such, yield measures should take into account the preferences that drive the whole process.

Defining yield measures through preferences means taking into consideration the importance ranking of tourists' preferences and cross tabulating these importance rankings with average stay or average spending. The main difference is that when we consider only spending or average stay we never know the reasons for the decision to stay/to spend more or less or what it is related to. By combining preferences with spending and average stay, deeper and more insightful measurements are achieved, preferably with the ability to consider preferences via panel data. In fact yield measures are also a form of measuring the volatility of demand, and panel data will allow for an understanding of how this volatility is obtained over the years.

The next section will provide methodological paths based on the tourist expenditure and average stay yield matrix (Fig. 1) in order to assess visitor yield preferences.

METHOD

Northcote and Macbeth (2006) laid out a theory whereby visitor numbers determine visitor yield, in which a market with large numbers of tourists is designated as a high 'visitor yield' market. One of the objectives of the majority of managers and operators is to increase the numbers of tourist visits, since this brings higher sales revenues. Yet, tourist expenditure per visit is the ultimate goal of tourism marketing, rather than simply the volume of tourist visits.

The visitor yield is measured for each preference based on the total overnight stays and daily tourist expenditure. This measure is based on the concept of 'visitor yield', which is relevant to the demand rather than the supply side of the industry. This concept of tourism yield relates to the declared preferences by tourists. Finally, a ranking of tourist preferences is presented by visitor yield measurements.

In order to estimate the visitor yield value, the daily expenditure on preference i, x_i, corresponding to the number of tourists considered was calculated that is,

$$x_i = \frac{\sum_{t=1}^{T} \exp_{i,t}}{\sum_{t=1}^{T} \text{over}_{i,t}} \tag{1}$$

where T is the number of time periods considered, $\exp_{i,t}$ are total tourist expenditures on preference i in period t, over_t are total tourist overnight stays in period t and $\text{over}_{i,t}$ are total tourist overnight stays indexed to preference i in period t. Hence, x_i is the average tourist expenditure per night from a tourist with preference i, and consequently, the visitor yield is given by:

$$\text{visitor yield}_i = \frac{\sum_{t=1}^{T} \text{over}_{i,t}}{\sum_{t=1}^{T} \text{over}_t} \times x_i \tag{2}$$

In order to complete the scheme of the matrix, length of stay of international tourists in the Algarve was considered as the second dimension. According to Gokovali, Bahar, and Kozak (2007), the length of stay was adopted to profile the tourists visiting one destination.

Since the objective is to identify yield patterns based on tourist preferences across a period of time, these dynamics could be captured from the fluctuation patterns, or expressed as volatility of visitor yield and length of stay throughout the years.

Further, in order to identify turn-over frontier points inside the visitor yield matrix and therefore to measure dynamic patterns, standard deviations (SDs) and coefficient of variations (CV) were computed. Thus, SD measures the dispersion of both outcomes (length of stay and visitor yield patterns over the years).

The coefficient of variation allows for the identification of volatility patterns in a measurement which standardizes various SDs over the different preferences. As a consequence, the CV of preference i in period t is given by,

$$\text{CV}_{i,t} = \frac{\sigma_{it}}{\hat{x}_{i,t}} \tag{3}$$

where, σ_{it} is the SD of each matrix axis (visitor yield and length of stay) of preference i in period t and $\hat{x}_{i,t}$ corresponds to the means of each axis matrix, represented both in the vertical axis by the visitor yield of preference i in year t; and in the horizontal axis by the average of length of stay of preference *i* in year *t*. In order to frame the visitor yield matrix the analytical steps should be as follows (Table 1).

The first step is to collect the data from a survey containing an evaluation of the degree of importance of destination attributes in order to identify tourists' preferences. Indeed, these preferences are based on destination attributes, which can be viewed as cognitive motivations (Decrop, 2000). As we are dealing with categorical variables − attributes of destinations that were assessed by tourists on a five-point Likert scale − in order to test for significant differences by year, a Scheffé test must be conducted in the second step. The third step starts with the definition of the matrix dimensions. For the horizontal axis a visitor yield measure was adopted. Therefore, as previously mentioned, overnight stays and daily expenditures by preferences are defined as variables for the visitor yield index.

For the vertical axis, the length of stay was adopted. This last dimension, as Gokovali et al. (2007) stated, is a potential indicator of what type of tourists visit a destination, and how likely they are to spend money while on holiday.

Further, a *t*-test must be conducted (step 4) in order to test the difference between the years for both matrix dimensions (visitor yield and length of stay). The definition of a volatility measure is required, in order to identify the fluctuation patterns of each matrix dimension (visitor yield and length of stay). Thus, in the fifth step, the SD and the CV must be computed.

Table 1. Analytical Steps and Methods.

Analytical Steps	Analytical Method
Step 1	Develop a preference scale: importance scale by attributes (five-point Likert scale).
Step 2	Describe and test the existence of differences by year. Apply Scheffé's multiple comparison test in order to identify preferences that present more variability over the period of analysis.
Step 3	Develop visitor yield measures criteria: Total of overnight stays by preference and daily expenditures by preference. Definition of matrix dimensions (Y = visitor yield and X = length of stay).
Step 4	Compute *t*-test in order to test the difference between the years of both visitor yield matrix items.
Step 5	Compute SD and CV for each matrix item: visitor yield and length of stay.
Step 6	Evaluate and select the higher-yield preferences.

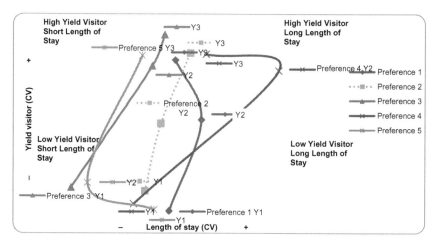

Fig. 2. Yield Visitor Preferences Matrix. *Note*: Y1 – Year 1 | Y2 – Year 2 | Y3 – Year 3.

Finally, the visitor yield matrix is constructed, where preferences that are positioned on the right-hand side of the horizontal axis are the longer stays, while those preferences positioned on the left-hand side are linked to shorter stays. Those positioned on the top of vertical axis are considered most profitable preferences and those on the bottom are less profitable. Finally, in the sixth step the matrix (Fig. 2) allows the establishment of the identification of the yield growth preferences.

CONCLUSION AND IMPLICATIONS

Tourists' preferences may reveal the yield potential of different markets. Indeed preferences are an interesting index in order to match supply to the expenditure yield and length of tourists' stay patterns and consequently support an assessment of the competitiveness of destinations. However, several advantages and limitations must be highlighted.

The following points are based on Dwyer et al. (2006). The yield approach provides a practical means to guide product development and marketing to achieve the best results from high-yield niche markets, via a more balanced treatment of stakeholders and potential investors' interests.

In addition it allows for an assessment of implemented measures and to examine how these influence yield growth that emerges from a medium- to long-term strategy for tourism. It is important that marketing strategies should identify and incorporate clear, measurable and achievable targets.

Finally, tourism operators, both at the level of the individual company and also destination managers, can implement this approach. Individual operators can use the matrix as a means of identifying which markets bring in the highest daily revenues from sales, and destination managers can make use of it to ascertain which markets are injecting the highest expenditure into the economy.

Several limitations also need to be highlighted when measuring 'visitor yield' via expenditure. Data on gross expenditure provides no breakdown of which goods and services have been purchased, and so the tourism sectors in the wider economy that receive the revenues of these sales cannot be identified. Another limitation lies in the fact that profitability for firms is not necessarily indicated simply by expenditure.

Crouch (2011) proposed a second dimension of the critical role played by destination attractions when evaluating the competitiveness of tourism destinations: namely how tourism consumers perceive the value of destination attributes. Goodall (1991) stated that tourists' preferences are dynamic, and therefore are important when analysing tourists' behavioural patterns. Determining visitor yield based on preferences could be of paramount importance when analysing future tourism destination strategies.

ACKNOWLEDGMENTS

This research is granted by national funds by FCT − National Funding Agency for Science, Research and Technology under the project UID/HIS/00057/2013.

REFERENCES

Becken, S., & Butcher, G. (2004). Economic yield associated with different types of tourists − A pilot analysis. *Proceedings of CAUTHE 2004*, February 10−13, Brisbane, Australia (pp. 73−78).

Crouch, G. (2011). Destination competitiveness: An analysis of determinants' attributes. *Journal of Travel Research, 50*(1), 27−45.

292   JAIME SERRA ET AL.

Decrop, A. (2000). Tourists' decision-making and behavior processes. In A. Pizam & Y. Mansfeld (Eds.), *Consumer behavior in travel and tourism* (pp. 103–134). New York, NY: The Haworth Hospitality Press.

Driscoll, A., Lawson, R., & Niven, B. (1994). Measuring tourists' destination perceptions. *Annals of Tourism Research, 21*(3), 499–511.

Dwyer, L., & Forsyth, P. (1997). Measuring the benefits and yield from foreign tourism. *International Journal of Social Economics, 24*(1–3), 223–236.

Dwyer, L., & Forsyth, P. (2008). Economic measures of tourism yield: What markets to target? *International Journal of Tourism Research, 10*(2), 155–168.

Dwyer, L., Forsyth, P., Fredline, L., Deery, M., Jago, L., & Lundie, S. (2007). Yield measures for special-interest Australian inbound tourism markets. *Tourism Economics, 13*(3), 421–440.

Dwyer, L., Forsyth, P., Fredline, L., Jago, L., Deery, M., & Lundie, S. (2006). *Concepts of yield and their measurement*. Technical Report. National Library of Australia Cataloguing in Publication Data, Australia.

Dwyer, L., Forsyth, P., & Spurr, R. (2007). Contrasting the uses of TSAs and CGE models: Measuring tourism yield and productivity. *Tourism Economics, 13*(4), 537–551.

Dywer, L., & Thomas, F. (2012). Tourism yield measures for Cambodia. *Current Issues in Tourism, 15*(4), 303–328.

Gokovali, U., Bahar, O., & Kozak, M. (2007). Determinants of length of stay: A practical use of survival analysis. *Tourism Management, 28*(3), 736–746.

Goodall, B. (1991). Understanding holiday choice. In C. Cooper (Ed.), *Progress in tourism, recreation and hospitality management* (pp. 103–133). London: Belhaven.

Grönroos, C. (1997). Value-driven relational marketing: From products to resources and competencies. *Journal of Marketing Management, 13*(5), 407–419.

Hands, D. W. (2013). Foundations of contemporary revealed preference theory. *Erkenntis, 78*(5), 1081–1108.

Hsu, T., Tsai, Y., & Wu, H. (2009). The preference analysis for tourist choice of destination: A case study of Taiwan. *Tourism Management, 30*(2), 288–297.

Mainzer, B. (2004). Future of revenue management: Fast forward for hospitality revenue management. *Journal of Revenue and Pricing Management, 3*(3), 285–289.

Mazitelli, D. (2003). Yield from Inbound Tourism, Industry Implementation Advisory Group (IIAG) (Unpublished).

Nicolau, J. L., & Más, F. J. (2006). Micro segmentation by individual tastes on attributes of tourist destinations. In T. V. Liu (Ed.), *Tourism management: New research* (pp. 91–122). New York, NY: Nova Science Publications.

Northcote, J., & Macbeth, J. (2006). Conceptualizing yield – Sustainable tourism management. *Annals of Tourism Research, 33*(1), 199–220.

Pratt, S. (2012). Tourism yield of different market segments: A case study of Hawaii. *Tourism Economics, 18*(2), 373–391.

Reynolds, P., & Braithwaite, R. (1997). Whose yield is it anyway? Compromise options for sustainable boat tour ventures. *International Journal of Contemporary Hospitality Management, 9*(2), 70–74.

Scott, N., & Breakey, N. (2007). Yield applied to destination management: An inefficient analogy? *Tourism Economics, 13*(3), 441–452.

Seddighi, H. R., & Theocharous, A. L. (2002). A model of tourism destination choice: A theoretical and empirical analysis. *Tourism Management, 23*(5), 475–487.

LAKE-DESTINATION IMAGE ATTRIBUTES: CONTENT ANALYSIS OF TEXT AND PICTURES

Ana Isabel Rodrigues, Antónia Correia,
Metin Kozak and Anja Tuohino

ABSTRACT

Lake tourism is a growing academic sub-field of tourism studies with an emerging body of literature. However, little research attention has been given to lake-destinations' projected or perceived tourism images. Specifically, there has been a scarcity of literature investigating the variables involved in the formation of a lake-destination image. Therefore, this study aims to explore the main attributes that might potentially influence this type of destination, and simultaneously, contribute to conceptualizing and defining lake tourism as recent research area. An explorative study was then conducted in order to generate a set of image variables through the use of textual and photographic data. The results will contribute to characterize potential lake-destinations and to develop a final list of variables specifically related to this type of destination.

Keywords: Destination image (DI); lake tourism (LT); lake-destination areas (LDA); pictorial image; content-analysis

Marketing Places and Spaces
Advances in Culture, Tourism and Hospitality Research, Volume 10, 293–314
ISSN: 1871-3173/doi:10.1108/S1871-317320150000010022

INTRODUCTION

Due to the multifaceted nature of tourism, new typologies have come into existence and many different forms of tourism have co-existed over the last decade. Particularly related to water as a tourism resource, several terms have been addressed such as marine tourism, river/canal, coastal, marina-based, and more recently lake tourism (Hall & Härkönen, 2006). This relatively unexplored research theme of tourism studies has an emerging body of literature.

Lakes are open bonds of water (natural or man-made) which can either be considered as a tourism resource, which adds value to the whole destination experience or arise as the core of the destination's attractiveness. In fact, tourism development not only on the lake itself, but in the surrounding area might constitute a valuable resource for some countries if properly developed. It is believed that due to the complexity of lacustrine tourist systems the destination image (DI), owing to its simplicity, dynamism, versatility, and capacity to integrate several factors, might represent a basis for the management of this type of destination (Rolo-Vela, 2009). Moreover, image is considered a key construct in destination positioning (Pike & Ryan, 2004), and destinations should be oriented to target positioning in their own competitiveness set (Kozak & Rimmington, 1999).

As a result, an understanding of the mental images associated with lake-environments as a tourism destination is of utmost importance. Moreover, since lake landscapes are associated with water, understanding the perceptions that tourists hold about 'waterscapes' is a starting point for marketing lake-destination areas (LDA) (Tuohino & Pitkänen, 2004). In this sense, LDA arise as an interesting topic for destination image studies after forty years of evolutionary research (Rodrigues, Correia, & Kozak, 2012) within this field.

Despite the growing number of studies related to DI as the literature review demonstrated, very little is known about destination marketing and image applied to the lake tourism context (Tuohino, 2006). A large number of studies assess DI in general, but few have attempted to measure it for any specific context. However, framed by new trends in DI research as a result of an intensive competitive environment (Stepchenkova & Mills, 2010), non-traditional entities have started to be the focus of recent studies, such as regions (Silvestre & Correia, 2005), resorts (Alcaniz, Garcia, & Blas, 2009), or types of tourism (Silva, Kastenholz, & Abrantes, 2013). Moreover, research investigating image attributes specifically related to LDA is limited. This study focuses on this particular type of destination.

The starting point to depict image scales in specific contexts grounds on construct validation theory (Gilbert & Churchill, 1979). Considering this, the main aim of this research is to generate an item pool throughout content analysis, able to depict the more accurate items to measure lake destination image. For this purpose, a review of the literature on DI and lake tourism (LT) is undertaken, in order to generate image attributes, and to investigate the nature of the LT concept. Based on the multidimensionality of the DI, functional and psychological image attributes more related to LDA are proposed. Additionally, the main characteristics and dimensions of LT concept are identified. Finally, the strategically implications of the results are discussed.

LITERATURE REVIEW

Destination Image Theory

Particularly related to the DI construct, after Echtner and Ritchie's (1991) literature review, researchers still recognized a lack of a theoretical framework (Gallarza, Saura, & Garcia, 2002; Tasci, Gartner, & Cavusgil, 2007). Therefore, a complex, multiple, relativistic and dynamic nature clearly identifies the DI construct (Gallarza et al., 2002). An examination of the main DI attributes is required in order to investigate this complex construct.

A meta-analysis paper concerning DI as a field of research since the emergence of the construct in the 1970s was examined. Having as a base line the list of the most common DI attributes proposed by Gallarza et al. (2002), an extension of the period was considered (2000–2012). As a result, 24 studies were analysed that measure image based on the following attributes: 'various activities', 'landscape surroundings', 'nature', 'culture attractions', 'nightlife and entertainment', 'shopping facilities', 'information available', 'sport facilities', 'transportation', 'accommodation', 'gastronomy', 'price, value and cost', 'climate', 'relaxation versus massification', 'accessibility', 'safety', 'social interaction', 'resident's receptiveness', 'originality' and 'service quality' (see for example, Baloglu & Mangaloglu, 2001; Correia & Pimpão, 2008; Jeong & Holland, 2012; Pike & Ryan, 2004; Shani, Chen, Wang, & Hua, 2010, among others).

The methodology of reviewing and selecting the DI attributes was the same as Gallarza et al.'s procedure (2002). The following considerations were deducted from the literature review and were very similar to Rolo-Vela (2009):

1. Destinations under study were primary large-scale entities, mainly countries. However, new entities such as cities, theme parks, types of tourism are emerging in the literature.
2. There is a lack of consensus about which attributes should be selected and included in DI scale.
3. Several authors continuously mention the lack of a standardized scale instrument for DI construct (Echtner & Ritchie, 1991, 1993; Tasci et al., 2007). Others strongly advocate a standardized scale (Deslandes, Goldsmith, Bonn, & Joseph, 2006). Nevertheless, as Rolo-Vela (2009) concluded three scales are considered to be reliable and valid: those found in Echtner and Ritchie (1993), Baloglu and McCleary (1999), and Beerli and Martin (2004).
4. It will probably be difficult to achieve a standardized scale that can adequately measure DI as a concept. As argue by Rodrigues et al. (2012), since DI is an 'umbrella construct' consensus on how to operationalize this type of constructs is rarely achieved. In this sense, shouldn't future DI scales considers the attribute differences not only based on geographical scope, but also on the type of entity/object (destination, type of tourism, event or theme park)? This chapter advocates that DI scales should progressively include attributes that really match the object under study.

In this context, the scales analysed (including the reliable and valid scales mentioned above) do not correspond well to the object under study, specifically LDA, as the literature review demonstrated. Thus, LDA have been totally absent from DI research.

A milestone in DI construct was Echtner and Ritchie's work (1991, 1993) at the beginning of 1990s, proposing a new scale to measure the multidimensional nature of this construct, shifting from a unidimensional to a multidimensional perspective. These authors postulated the existence of a continuum from the functional to the psychological, on which the different attributes were located. Analysis of DI then moves from a traditional attribute-based measurement to a broader approach, capable of capturing the *gestalt* nature.

Consequently, alternative methods of DI measurement based on qualitative techniques were recognized as useful because it captures the holistic impressions associated with a destination. By the mid-1990s, researchers started to be sceptical about the validity of attribute lists, demonstrating the benefits of using a qualitative approach (Reilly, 1990). The combination of multiple methodological practices and empirical materials in a single DI study, foreshadowed by Echtner and Ritchie (1991), was definitely legitimized. Consequently, an emerging research trend shows the use of mixed-methods, both qualitative and quantitative (e.g. Baloglu & McCleary, 1999; MacKay & Fesenmaier, 1997; Pike & Ryan, 2004). As a result, various qualitative techniques have been used for DI measurement, mostly covering techniques such as free elicitation, focus group, open-ended questions, in-depth interviews, and content-analysis (Gallarza et al., 2002).

In line with this new approach, pictorial materials were used progressively in qualitative studies. The 'pictorial turn' was underpinned by MacInnis and Price's (1987) work and the relationship between imagery processing and consumer behaviour was examined. Their primary purpose was to demonstrate that both imagery and discursive information were used in evaluating a product. Based on this assumption, visual stimuli such as travel photography have been used as a methodological approach (e.g. Greaves & Skinner, 2010; Mackay & Fesenmaier, 1997). In fact, the employment of photographs has been widely recognized as a valuable analysis method, particularly in DI studies (Jacobsen, 2007).

This study focuses on an initial perception of the cognitive image (Martin & Rodriguez del Bosque, 2008; Pike & Ryan, 2004), particularly the functional and psychological attributes of LDA (Alcaniz et al., 2009; Echtner & Ritchie, 1991, 1993). Echtner and Ritchie (1991, 1993) argued that the attribute-based and holistic components of a destination possess directly observable or measured perceptions (functional attributes) and abstract or intangible characteristics (psychological attributes).

In addition to the aforementioned efforts to understand the nature of destination image, this study adopts Beerli & Martin's rationale (2004) for whom 'the selection of the attributes used in designing a scale will depend largely on the attractions of each destination, on its positioning, and on the objectives of the assessment of perceived image, which will also determine whether specific or more general attributes are chosen' (p. 659). In the 2000s, DI studies started to be applied to particular types of destinations, (Greaves & Skinner, 2010; Rolo-Vela, 2009; Silva et al., 2013). This is in line with this new trend in DI research found in Stepchenkova & Mills' work (2010).

Lake Tourism Theory

Water is one of the most powerful symbolic resources mobilized by the human imagination and plays a central symbolic role in many forms of spiritual and social practices. Early explorers already found European lake destinations and in the period of Romanticism, the touristic value of lakes was publicized by visual artists and poets who were inspired by lake environments (Aitchison, MacLeod, & Shaw, 2000). As a consequence, there arose a demand for tourist services in lake destinations, which together with rapidly developing travel in the modern period led to the large-scale commercial exploitation of lake environments (see e.g. Ryhänen, 2001a). Against this historical background, it may be quite difficult to understand, that research literature on lake destinations as a touristic phenomenon is still relatively tricky to find (Tuohino & Dávid, 2012).

LT as a concept is multifactorial. LT is not only tourism on the lake itself, but also in the surrounding areas of the lakes (Tuohino, 2008). Lake tourism may be valued and understood in the same way as alpine tourism or forest tourism have been recognized as a subfield of tourism (Hall & Härkönen, 2006). Tuohino (2008) in turn has also positioned lake tourism as a subcategory of nature tourism due to the fact that nature as a tourist landscape and environment is an entity with different meanings (see also Koivula et al., 2005; Saarinen, 2004). Gartner (2006) correspondingly states that lake tourism is rural tourism, as the use of lakes is associated with the rural tourism experience. It can also be argued that in many cases lake tourism and water-based tourism with recreational and leisure elements are used as synonyms.

Regarding marketing perspective, textual and pictorial analysis in the context of lake tourism is used, for example by Pitkänen and Vepsäläinen (2006), who analysed the representations of Lake Saimaa and Savonlinna which were communicated and promoted in travel films and brochures, and by Carr (2006) while studying the cultural interpretations of New Zealand lakes in promotional materials and on web pages. Tuohino and Pitkänen (2004) used photos as a data while studying the mental images of Italian and Germans through promotional photos of the Finnish Tourism Board. Despite these studies more research is needed since 'successful lake-destination area marketing is tied to a strong destination image' (Erkkilä, 2006, p. 207).

METHODOLOGY

The general objective of this study is to explore the cognitive image of LDA, analysing both its functional and psychological attributes, and also investigate the nature of the lake tourism concept. This general objective is reflected in the following research questions:

1. What attributes might be involved in the image formation of LDA, as a possible basis for developing a future image measurement scale applied to this particular type of destinations?
2. What are the main characteristics and dimensions of LDA that might contribute to conceptualizing LT as a new form of tourism research?

Based on one of the goals of qualitative research (Gibbs, 2007), this study aims to develop and refine the concept of LT and LDA through the process of identifying pertinent cognitive attributes (both functional and psychological) related to this particular type of tourism. Therefore, this qualitative study was carried out in three main phases:

(1) A first step aiming to identify the most common DI attributes found in the literature for other types of destinations as previously explained. The goal here is to develop an initial set of potential image attributes which could be compared with the item sample for LDA generated later.
(2) Extract attributes applied to LDA which might potentially influence the image of this particular type of tourism through content analysis of text and photos.
(3) Examine and refine the concept of LT and LDA, identifying their main dimensions/characteristics.

Regarding the first phase a final list of attributes was obtained from the literature review. Concerning the second and third phase a content analysis of text and pictures was undertaken. Consequently, an exploratory study was conducted in an online environment by analysing contents of a lake-related website as a source of information (cf. http://www.lakelubbers.com), an online directory for lake enthusiasts containing a worldwide database of about 1,695 lakes and reservoirs spread throughout the world. Each lake contains a description by people who love lakes, true connoisseurs of inland bodies of water, named as 'lakelubbers', according to the website. It seems appropriate to deem that this is a suitable data base since the aim is to generate a sample of image attributes specifically related to the lake tourism context.

To sample the data a search was conducted to locate the descriptions of potential lake-destinations by screening the lake information within the 'lakelubbers' database. The criteria decision was based on a two-step process: first, geographical scope had to be limited to European countries ($n = 22$), due to the wide variety of lake locations; second, the two largest lakes (by surface area) in each country were considered. A total of 40 lake descriptions (units of analysis) constitute the sample of this study, which were manually browsed and scanned for their textual content. Also in line with the so called 'pictorial turn' (Feighey, 2003) this study simultaneously adopted visual information, particularly lake-related photos. A total of 124 photos from the sampled website were collected and grouped by country. In addition, the pictorial images were content-analysed in order to validate the results obtained in the textual data stage.

Content Analysis of Text

The textual data were first content-analysed using WebQDA (Web Qualitative Data Analysis), software which carries out qualitative data analysis individually or collaboratively, synchronously or asynchronously (Souza, Costa, & Moreira, 2011). In terms of coding procedure, several coding methods were used (Saldana, 2009). In fact, a direct approach was undertaken where 'the researcher uses existing theory or prior research to develop the initial coding scheme prior to beginning to analyse the data' (Hsieh & Shannon, 2005, p. 1286). In this case, the choice of the variables was determined beforehand as part of the study which means that the codebook relied on codes from the past DI literature as mentioned before. A more 'deductive procedure' was undertaken since a prior formulated theoretical schema was used (Mayring, 2000). In fact, the goal here was to conceptually validate or extend a theoretical framework of DI dimensions (e.g. 'natural resources', 'touristic infrastructures', 'tourist leisure and recreation') by using Beerli and Martin's (2004) scale, but applied to the lake-destination context.

As analysis proceeded, additional codes were developed more related to lake-destinations, and the initial coding scheme was revised and refined. The qualitative step of this analysis consists of a methodological controlled assignment of the category to a passage of text (Saldana, 2009). Since coding is a way of organizing and managing data, sub-categories were also defined.

The method of coding was now mixed with an 'inductive procedure'. Grounded on Gibbs' (2007) assumption that coding might add interpretation and theory to the data, particularly if the researcher is interested in generating new explanations and theory, a step-by-step formulation of inductive sub-categories out of the material was also developed. This procedure allowed the generation of new sub-categories specifically related to lake tourism context (e.g. 'natural features of the lake'; 'water activities, sports and recreation' or 'land-based activities, sports and recreation'). Categories and sub-categories were developed accordingly for all the items contained on lake descriptions. This procedure resulted on a refinement of the concept of LT and LDA, thus their main dimensions/characteristics was identified due to this inductive analytic process.

As a final remark, during this deductive and inductive process two coding procedures were used (Saldana, 2009). The holistic method as an initial and exploratory form of coding, and also a descriptive method in order to identify the main data's basic topics, in this case image attributes of LDA.

Content Analysis of Pictures

The most common approach to evaluating images has been content-analysis traditionally grounded on *motifs* and *themes* (Albers & James, 1988; Govers & Go, 2005). Two formal methodologies are commonly employed in the study of visual images: content and semiotic analysis. Content analysis has been widely used in media studies for decades, particularly in photographic media (Bell, 2001). In the contexts of tourism photography, content analysis provides an empirical foundation for contrasting and comparing appearances within large data-sets (Marsh, 1984 cited on Albers & James, 1988). The data-set must be composed of the overall content and composition of pictorial elements (Albers & James, 1988; Govers & Go, 2005; Markwell, 1997; Sternberg, 1997).

In this study, the photos were content-analysed using some principles of iconography. The methodology used here was based, at a first level, on Panofsky's (2006) simple distinction between primary and secondary subject matter, which is an attempt to understand the study of images in tourism. According to Panofsky, the primary level is apprehended by simply identifying certain visible forms with certain objects (*motifs*); the second level is consciously imparted by the practical action which conducted it (*themes*). The *motif* has to be tied to a *theme*, and consequently has to be thematized. Therefore, in Panofsky's sense these two levels of meaning are interrelated, since the understanding of the *motif* depends on the *theme*, and the comprehension of a specific thematization is achieved by combining all the motifs of a visual image. In other words, they are intertwined, and it is by separating the *motif* from the *theme* that one can understand the picture in question (Sternberg, 1997).

In this sense, 124 photos were content-analysed first in terms of *motifs* and then in terms of *themes*. In the first instance all the *motifs* (objects or appearances) shown in every image were identified using WebQDA software. The meaning was only perceived in an elementary view, the factual meaning, which is simply identifying certain forms (Panofsky, 2006). The *motifs* were then isolated, registered, and freely described without any constraints through the use of colourful boxes which encircle them, each one with a spontaneous comment.

Subsequently, all the *motifs* were first listed, and only after this were they submitted to a process of filtering, clustering or cut-off. Finally, an organized list of motifs was obtained (42 in total) in order to measure the frequency of each motif/object present (or not) in all photos. With each photo being a case, for each object a count was done to indicate if the specific object appeared in the picture or not. This whole procedure of freely registering and describing the *motifs* was meaningful for two reasons: firstly, it was exploratory, allowing 'chunking' of the photos into broad topics and, secondly, it captured all the relevant information.

Lastly, based on Panofsky's (2006) theory and following the procedure of other photo-based studies (Choi, Lehto, & Morrison, 2007), meaning was added to the photos connecting them to themes. Finally, a photo classification into five categories/themes was done through a combining motifs aiming to extract the main *themes* associated with lakes.

FINDINGS

The content analysis of text and pictures was conducted separately. However the results were eminently similar. The textual analysis is crucial to respond to both research questions, and the results from visuals are considered to be supportive. First reported are the results of text analysis, followed by pictures, after which the discussion brings observations together.

Results of Textual Information

Research Question 1. What attributes might be involved in the image formation of LDA, as a possible basis for developing a future image measurement scale applied to this particular type of destinations?

The initial set of image attributes extracted from the literature review reveals that they are too generic (e.g. landscape, sport facilities, culture attractions, accommodation). The list was considered inadequate and did not incorporate all salient attributes for lake-destination areas. Through a deductive approach nine image categories were determined based on Beerli and Martin's (2004) classification, namely 'natural resources', 'general infrastructure', 'touristic infrastructures', 'tourist leisure and recreation', 'culture, history and art', 'political and economic factors', 'natural environment', 'social environment' and 'atmosphere'.

Simultaneously, through a more inductive approach, 21 subcategories in total were identified for these nine categories. As an example, for the category 'natural resources' three sub-categories emerged: 'natural features of the lake', 'richness of nature' and 'weather'; for the category 'touristic infrastructures' four subcategories were defined: 'accommodation and catering facilities', 'available packages', 'signed trails and paths' and 'tourist services and information'; for the category 'culture, history and art' also four subcategories were extracted: 'history of the lake and surrounding region', 'museums and historic buildings', 'cultural attractions and events' and 'gastronomy' and so forth. Additionally, each subcategory includes several image attributes more related to LDA with the correspondent excerpts from lake description. A set of over 100 potential variables were extracted.

Conclusively, the combination of findings from an analysis of image attributes found in the literature review for other types of destinations with content-analysis of a specific lake-related website provides a more complete picture of lake image variables. Some of these attributes are illustrated in Fig. 1 based on the functional-psychological continuum Echtner and Ritchie's model (1991, 1993).

This continuum may be perceived from functional to psychological attributes about individual characteristics or more holistic impressions of a LDA. As illustrated, the upper left quadrant contains individual attributes which are directly observable (e.g. physical features of the lake, water and land activities, nautical infrastructures); the lower left quadrant includes individual attributes more difficult to observe (e.g. the beauty of the scenery around the lake, the villages on the lakeshore); the upper right quadrant contains tangible attributes, however, contributing to a more holistic impression (e.g. events on and around the lake, history of the lake and region); the lower right quadrant comprises intangible attributes essentially described as the atmosphere or mood of a lake-destination area.

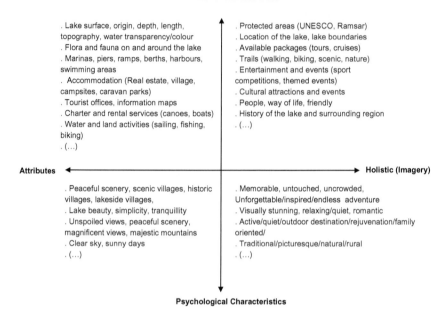

Functional Characteristics

. Lake surface, origin, depth, length,   . Protected areas (UNESCO, Ramsar)
topography, water transparency/colour   . Location of the lake, lake boundaries
. Flora and fauna on and around the lake   . Available packages (tours, cruises)
. Marinas, piers, ramps, berths, harbours,   . Trails (walking, biking, scenic, nature)
swimming areas   . Entertainment and events (sport
. Accommodation (Real estate, village,   competitions, themed events)
campsites, caravan parks)   . Cultural attractions and events
. Tourist offices, information maps   . People, way of life, friendly
. Charter and rental services (canoes, boats)   . History of the lake and surrounding region
. Water and land activities (sailing, fishing,   . (…)
biking)
. (…)

Attributes   Holistic (Imagery)

. Peaceful scenery, scenic villages, historic   . Memorable, untouched, uncrowded,
villages, lakeside villages,   Unforgettable/inspired/endless adventure
. Lake beauty, simplicity, tranquillity   . Visually stunning, relaxing/quiet, romantic
. Unspoiled views, peaceful scenery,   . Active/quiet/outdoor destination/rejuvenation/family
magnificent views, majestic mountains   oriented/
. Clear sky, sunny days   . Traditional/picturesque/natural/rural
. (…)   . (…)

Psychological Characteristics

Fig. 1. Functional-Psychological and Attribute-Holistic Components with Potential Influence on the Formation of Lake-Destination Areas. *Source*: Authors, adapted from Echtner and Ritchie (1991, 1993).

Research Question 2. What are the main characteristics and dimensions of LDA that might contribute to conceptualizing LT as a new form of tourism research?

The initial coding, using the holistic method, promptly identified two main themes in each lake's description: (i) the lake itself and lakeshore and (ii) the destination/surrounding region. The former consists of all the elements that take place on the lake and lakeshore which are directly related to it (natural characteristics, activities, infrastructures); the latter incorporated the same elements but now located in the surrounding region. The following quotation about Lake Garda in Italy (IT19) clearly illustrates this idea: '*After you have finished exploring the region, it's time to explore Lake Garda's 90,000 acres of water*'. With this in mind, three spatial levels in terms of tourism development came out: (i) development on the lake itself as the main resource of this type of tourism; (ii) development on the lakeshore, intertwined with the (iii) development of the surrounding region.

Therefore, it was possible to identify five main dimensions of LT as field of tourism studies, which corroborate the findings from the literature review stage.

Each of these five dimensions (Ryhänen, 2001b), described in more detail hereafter, are intersected by the previously defined spatial levels: (1) *Resource Dimension*, including all the natural, cultural and social resources (e.g. '*A nature reserve of over 9000 acres completely surrounds the two lakes* (...)', Lake Laguna/Spain); (2) *Supply Dimension*, referring to all the services, facilities and infrastructures which not only allow access but also add value to resource dimension (e.g. '*Access to the lake can be found at most campgrounds, and many cities and villages on the lake have public boat launches*', Lake Ijssel/Holand); (3) *Logistical Dimension*, referring to the existence of means of connections between lakes, lakes and lakeside villages, and lakes and main cities (e.g. '*Lake Maggiore visitors can take a boat from the town of Stresa to the eastern shores of the lake ...*', Lake Maggiori/Italy); (4) *Organizational Dimension*, referring to lakes as a geographic and administrative entity that crosses different territories (e.g. '*With the commitment of the three nations to the two lakes, the future is sure to include more people coming to enjoy and explore the international treasure of the Prespa Lakes*'); (5) *Representational/Meaning Dimension*, conceiving lakes as a meaningful place to which the tourist links mental images and feelings formed through experience (e.g. '*the view captures traditional Austrian architecture, historic buildings and a lush alpine setting that creates a perfect image of the Austrian countryside*', Lake Hallstatter/ Austria). In sum, the existence of lake tourism conceptualization was established which undoubtedly requires more investigation on a theoretical and practical level.

Results of Pictorial Information

The results were similar to those of the text content analysis. As explained in the previous section, the applied visual method obtained 42 motifs listed in Table 1. The motifs range from water, sky, landscape, vegetation on the lakeshore, flora and fauna to nautical infrastructures, villages, culture, monuments, activities (swimming, fishing), among others, very similar to the textual analysis results.

The most frequently appearing motifs are related to natural elements such us sky, water and landscape. Consistent with text data analysis, pictures with motifs/objects such as 'blue sky' (31.5%), 'Vegetation on the

Table 1.   Content Analysis Results of Pictures ($N = 124$).

Motifs/Objects (Total 42)	Frequency (No. of Images in which Motif Appears)	Frequency (% of Images in which Motif Appears)
Blue sky	39	31.5
Vegetation on the shoreline	38	30.6
Landscape/mountains	36	29.0
Water's blue colour	33	26.6
Water acts as a mirror	29	23.4
Open and immense sky	26	21.0
Anchored boats	18	14.5
Cultural heritage/monuments	17	13.7
Uneven waters	17	13.7
Villages on the shoreline	17	13.7
Water transparency	13	10.5
Lake sunset	12	9.7
Sailing on the lake	8	6.5
Boat slip/access to water	7	5.6
Islands	6	4.8
Air view of the lake	5	4.0
Marina	5	4.0
Ports and harbours	5	4.0
Karst topography	4	3.2
Private houses on the lakeshore	4	3.2
Road along the lake	4	3.2
Snow	4	3.2
Tourist walking on the lakeshore	4	3.2
Walking trail on the lakeshore	4	3.2
Bays, nooks and crannies	3	2.4
City near the lake/urban landscape	3	2.4
Lake's shoreline	3	2.4
Landscape/meadows	3	2.4
Lighthouse on the lake	3	2.4
Local architecture	3	2.4
Richness of fauna (birds, swans)	3	2.4
Tourists visiting the monument	3	2.4
Bathing and swimming	2	1.6
Boating	2	1.6
Richness of flora	2	1.6
Tourists admiring the view	2	1.6
Dam over the lake	1	0.8
Fishing	1	0.8
Ice on the lake	1	0.8
Idyllic countryside, picturesque	1	0.8
Man working on the lake	1	0.8
Natural beaches	1	0.8

lakeshore' (30.6%), 'landscape/mountains' (29%) and 'water's blue colour' (26.6%) are more prevalent. It is interesting to note that several motifs were highlighted in the photos related to the state of the water: 'water act as a mirror' (23.4%), 'water transparency' (10.4%) and 'uneven water' (13.7%). That suggests that what is proposed about lakes is very much water-based, as expected. Less frequently appearing, but still significant are the motifs 'villages on the shoreline' (13.7%) and 'cultural heritage/monuments' (13.7%), which are in line with the results of textual information.

Motifs related to nautical infrastructures such as 'anchored boats' appears in 14.5% of the total pictures, 'boat slip/access to water' (5.6%), 'marinas' (4%) and 'ports and harbours' (4%). This illustrates the importance of infrastructures and nautical facilities that allow access to the water and also navigating on it, leading to comfort, convenience and enjoyment. Surprisingly, water-based activities such as 'sailing on the lake' (6.7%), 'bathing or swimming' (1.6%) or 'fishing' (0.8%) are not significant at all. One more observation on the few experience-based pictures that show people making use leisure/recreational activities based on lakes: the motifs found are mainly related with sightseeing activities such as 'tourists walking on the lakeshore' (3.2%), 'tourists admiring the view' (1.6%) and 'tourists visiting a monument' (2.4%). It is supposed that this implies an inherent limitation of this study; the fact that these pictures do not fully represent the overall aspects of lakes.

Lastly, as explained in the methods section, after listing and analysed all the motifs of the photos, it was necessary to add meaning to the photos by a classification into five categories as depicted in Fig. 2.

Table 2 shows the final result of the categorization procedure of photos. Among the total of 124 photos, 47 were classified as category 1 'Natural Elements', only based on the presence of natural pictorial such as sky, flora, fauna, lake water, landscape, islands, etc. This is undoubtedly the most important category associated with lakes. Secondly, in order to confirm the relevance of nature, but also the surrounding environment of lakes, category 5 'Natural Environment' appears next, containing 23 photos. The photos classified in this category associated motifs based on the natural elements previously described with the presence of villages on the lakeshore, houses, etc. This is also an important category, as textual analysis revealed.

Thirdly, and following immediately, was category 2 'Infrastructures' containing 20 photos with this classification, mainly based on motifs related to nautical infrastructures (marinas, slips, harbours, etc.). Fourthly, 20 photos were classified in category 3 'Activities and Recreation' containing the presence of motifs such as sailing, boating, fishing, etc. This is the

Category 1 'Natural Elements': physical characteristics directly related to the lake.

Category 2 'Infrastructures': Facilities and infrastructures which allow access to and navigating on the lake.

Category 3 'Activities and Recreation': different types of sporting and recreational activities that take place on the lake and surrounding region. where the lake is located

Category 4 'Culture and Heritage': Cultural and historical attractions that provide insights into the history of the territory.

Category 5 'Natural Environment': Includes communities with visible natural elements creating an atmosphere on and around the lake.

Fig. 2. Photographs Used in Content Analysis Representing the Five Categories/ Themes. *Source*: Lakelubbers website available at http://www.lakelubbers.com. Retrieved in December 2013.

Table 2. Visual Information on the Five Sub-Categories/Themes.

Category	No. of Images	% of Images
1. Natural elements	47	38
2. Infrastructures	22	18
3. Activities and recreation	20	16
4. Culture and heritage	12	10
5. Natural environment	23	19

category that surely contributes to transforming lakes into a meaningful experience, an important dimension in the lake tourism concept as textual analysis revealed.

Finally, the least representative, category 4 'Culture and Heritage' with only 12 photos, which apparently indicates that this is not the central resource of lakes. However, this might be viewed from a different angle, demonstrating that in the future culture, heritage, and history can add value to lakes as the nuclear resource.

CONCLUSION AND IMPLICATIONS

The study examined those image attributes more related to lake-destination areas for a more accurate picture of this recent form of tourism in order to propose a future image measurement scale applied to this particular type of destinations. Hence, destination marketing organizations (DMOs) have a more precise view of the characteristics of lake areas allowing them to adequately develop an image to achieve an effective positioning in a more competitive world (Pike & Ryan, 2004). Thus, this study is underpinned by the premise that the development of an image scale, particular for newer forms of tourism such as lake tourism where information about its characteristics is lacking, requires an investigation of the nature of the concept under study.

With this in mind, this first step of a more ample work attempted to contribute to the body of knowledge in two ways: (1) by exploring image attributes more related to lake-destination areas (functional-psychological continuum) that potentially influence the image formation of this type of destination and (2) by investigating the nature of lake tourism and lake-destination areas.

With regard to the nature of lake-destination image, the results indicate that attributes related to lakes can be classified and incorporated into nine dimensions/categories and subcategories as in Beerli and Martin's (2004) conclusion. These might be used in designing a future image scale for lake-destination areas. However, in accordance with these authors, the selection of the attributes will largely depend on the type of attractions of each desti-nation, consistently with the type of tourism under investigation. Simultaneously it was evident that in this case lake-destinations are mainly formed on the basis of cognitive image (Martin & Rodriguez del Bosque, 2008), with functional (more tangible) and psychological (more abstract) image attributes, which might be more attribute-based or a more holistic impression. In fact, the existence of a functional-psychological continuum (Echtner & Ritchie, 1991, 1993) was determined for this type of destinations.

Regarding the nature of LT, this research empirically identifies the exis-tence of a LT definition and specific characteristics of this form of tourism. It is clear that the lake itself is the core resource for the development of lake-destinations enhanced by other resources and infrastructures located in the surrounding region. In fact, natural features of lakes such as its sur-face, length, origin, etc. are important elements that should be considered when promoting the lake. It was also interesting to observe that commu-nities located on the lakeshore or near the lake add an important value to lake-destinations, since in many cases they are considered a base-camp, a starting point for visiting the lake, 'gateways' as Gartner (2006) described. Simultaneously, the existence of some services and infrastructures such as accommodation on the lakeshore, available packages, marinas, ramps or slips, rental services (e.g. fishing or boating), or signed trails around the lake surely contribute to transform a neutral landscape like a lake into a meaningful experience (Tuohino, 2006).

In fact, the results of this study have provided useful insights into how lake tourism has its own particularities that can build upon an effective image and strategically use it in promotional campaigns. Given that, the findings support tourism literature when they established that lake tourism as a concept is grounded on five dimensions as previously described (Resource, Supply, Logistical, Organizational and Meaning), and should continue to be researched on a theoretical and management level.

There were some inherent limitations to this study. Content analysis is exploratory and is based on subjective judgments to some extent. Furthermore, an exhaustive examination of 42 units of analysis about lake description was made to collect image attributes related to this object. However, the findings may still not fully represent the image of LDA. At some point the units of analysis were too repetitive, containing a very similar text structure. Additionally, lake lovers' viewpoints may not be fully representative of the travelling public. Nevertheless, by analysing the contents of information provided by a lake lovers' online directory ('lakelubbers'), this preliminary qualitative study confirms that several dimensions and attributes exist specifically related to LDA. One should recall that the goal here was mainly to extract image attributes and not to analyse how lake-destinations are represented on the web, since this is a very recent form of tourism and has not yet been explored in online environments.

Lastly, this study intentionally examined lake descriptions limited to European countries considering the wide scope of geographical areas where lakes are located. For the interpretation of the content analysis results, based on a deductive category application, other steps of analysis might be used for the refinement of these DI attributes. Further research will focus on this issue and also aiming to validate the results here obtained.

REFERENCES

Aitchison, C., MacLeod, N. E., & Shaw, S. J. (2000). *Leisure and tourism landscapes. Social and cultural geographies*. London: Routledge.

Albers, P. C., & James, W. R. (1988). Travel photography: A methodological approach. *Annals of Tourism Research, 15*, 134–158.

Alcaniz, E. B., Garcia, I. S., & Blas, S. S. (2009). The functional-psychological continuum in the cognitive image of a destination: A confirmatory analysis. *Tourism Management, 30*, 715–723.

Baloglu, S., & Mangaloglu, M. (2001). Tourism destination images of Turkey, Egypt, Greece, and Italy as perceived by US-based tour operators and travel agents. *Tourism Management, 22*, 1–9.

Baloglu, S., & McCleary, K. W. (1999). A model of destination image formation. *Annals of Tourism Research, 26*, 268–897.

Beerli, A., & Martin, J. D. (2004). Factors influencing destination image. *Annals of Tourism Research, 31*(3), 657–681.

Bell, F. (2001). Content analysis of visual images. In T. Van Leeuwen & C. Jewitt (Eds.), *Handbook of visual images* (pp. 10–34). London: Sage.

Carr, A. (2006). Lakes, myths and legends: The relationship between tourism and cultural values for water in Aotearoa/New Zealand. In M. Hall & T. Härkönen (Eds.), *Lake tourism. An integrated approach to lacustrine tourism systems* (pp. 83–97). Clevedon: Channel View Publications.

Choi, S., Lehto, X. Y., & Morrison, A. M. (2007). Destination image representation on the web: Content analysis of Macau travel related websites. *Tourism Management, 28*, 118–129.

Correia, A., & Pimpão, A. (2008). Decision-making processes of Portuguese tourist travelling to South America and Africa. *International Journal of Culture, Tourism and Hospitality Research, 2*(4), 330–373.

Deslandes, D. D., Goldsmith, R. E., Bonn, M., & Joseph, S. (2006). Measuring destination image: Do the existing scales work? *Tourism Review International, 10*(3), 141–153.

Echtner, C., & Ritchie, B. (1991). The meaning and measurement of destination image. *Journal of Tourism Studies, 2*(2), 2–12.

Echtner, C., & Ritchie, B. (1993). The measurement of destination image: An empirical assessment. *Journal of Travel Research, 31*(3), 3–13.

Erkkilä, D. L. (2006). Local considerations in marketing and developing lake-destination areas. In M. Hall & T. Härkönen (Eds.), *Lake tourism. An integrated approach to lacustrine tourism systems* (pp. 207–221). Clevedon: Channel View Publications.

Feighey, W. (2003). Negative image? Developing the visual in tourism research. *Current Issues in Tourism, 6*(1), 76–85.

Gallarza, G., Saura, G., & Garcia, H. (2002). Destination image: Towards a conceptual framework. *Annals of Tourism Research, 29*(1), 56–78.

Gartner, W. (2006). Planning and management of lake destination development: Lake gateways in Minnesota. In M. Hall & T. Härkönen (Eds.), *Lake tourism. An integrated approach to lacustrine tourism systems* (pp. 177–181). Clevedon: Channel View Publications.

Gibbs, G. R. (2007). *Analysing qualitative data.* London: Sage.

Gilbert, A., & Churchill, JR. (1979). A paradigm for developing better measures of marketing construct. *Journal of Marketing Research, 16*, 64–73.

Govers, R., & Go, F. M. (2005). Projected destination image online: Website content analysis of pictures and text. *Information Technology & Tourism, 7*, 73–89.

Greaves, N., & Skinner, H. (2010). The importance of destination image analysis to UK rural tourism. *Marketing Intelligence & Planning, 28*(4), 486–507.

Hall, C. M., & Härkönen, T. (2006). Lake tourism: An introduction to lacustrine tourism systems. In M. Hall & T. Härkönen (Eds.), *Lake tourism. An integrated approach to lacustrine tourism systems* (pp. 27–42). Clevedon: Channel View Publications.

Hsieh, H., & Shannon, S. E. (2005). Three approaches to qualitative content analysis. *Qualitative Health Research, 15*, 1277–1288.

Jacobsen, J. K. S. (2007). Use of landscape perception methods in tourism studies: A review of photo-based research approaches. *Tourism Geographies: An International Journal of Tourism Space, Place and Environment, 9*(3), 234–253.

Jeong, C., & Holland, S. (2012). Destination image saturation. *Journal of Travel & Tourism Marketing, 29*(6), 501–519.

Koivula, E., Saastamoinen, O., Hentinen, L., Loikkanen, T., Määttä, M., Peltonen, A., ... Tyrväinen, L. (2005). Metsät ja luontomatkailu: Nykytila ja kehittämistarpeita. [Forests and nature tourism; the current state and development needs]. In E. Koivula & O. Saastamoinen (Ed.) *Näkökulmia luontomatkailuun ja sen tulevaisuuteen. [Perspectives on nature tourism and its future.]* (pp. 7–62). Joensuu: University of Joensuu, Faculty of Forestry.

Kozak, M., & Rimmington, M. (1999). Measuring tourist destination competitiveness: Conceptual considerations and empirical findings. *Hospitality Management, 18*, 273–283.

MacInnis, D. J., & Price, L. L. (1987). The role of imagery in information processing: Review and extensions. *Journal of Consumer Research, 13*(March), 473–491.

Mackay, K. J., & Fesenmaier, D. R. (1997). Pictorial element in destination image formation. *Annals of Tourism Research, 24*(3), 537–565.

Markwell, K. W. (1997). Dimensions of photography in a nature-based tour. *Annals of Tourism Research*, *24*(1), 131–155.

Martin, H. S., & Rodriguez del Bosque, I. A. (2008). Exploring the cognitive–affective nature of destination image and the role of psychological factors in its formation. *Tourism Management*, *29*, 263–277.

Mayring, P. (2000). Qualitative content-analysis. *Forum Qualitative Social Research*, *1*(2). Retrieved from http://www.qualitative-research.net/index.php/fqs/article/view/1089/2385. Accessed on October 10, 2013

Panofsky, E. (2006). Studies in iconology. In S. Manghani, A. Piper, & J. Simons (Eds.), *Images: A reader* (pp.86–90). London: Sage.

Pike, S., & Ryan, C. (2004). Destination positioning analysis through a comparison of cognitive, affective, and conative perceptions. *Journal of Travel Research*, *42*(May), 333–342.

Pitkänen, K., & Vepsäläinen, M. (2006). The changing historical dimensions of lake tourism at Savonlinna: Savonlinna – The pearl of the Saimaa. Lake representations in the tourist marketing of Savonlinna. In M. Hall & T. Härkönen (Eds.), *Lake tourism. An integrated approach to lacustrine tourism systems* (pp. 67–82). Clevedon: Channel View Publications.

Reilly, M. D. (1990). Free elicitation of descriptive adjectives for tourism image assessment. *Journal of Travel Research*, *28*(4), 21–26.

Rodrigues, A., Correia, A., & Kozak, M. (2012). Exploring the life-cycle model applied to 'Umbrella Constructs': Destination image as an example. *Tourism of Recreation Research*, *37*(2), 133–143.

Rolo-Vela, M. (2009). Rural-cultural conceptualization: A local tourism marketing management model based on tourism destination image measurement. *Tourism Management*, *30*, 419–428.

Ryhänen, H. (2001a). Järvi-käsitteen pohdiskelua: Mitä järvi on matkailun erityisresurssina ja järvimatkailuna? [Reflection of lake definition: What does lake means as a special resource of tourism, and as lake tourism?] *Muuttuva Matkailu*, *2*, 12–20.

Ryhänen, H. (2001b). The touristic profile and potential of European Lake destinations. Paper presented at ATLAS 10th Anniversary International Conference, 4–6 October, Dublin.

Saarinen, J. (2004). Destinations in change. The transformation process of tourist destinations. *Tourist Studies*, *4* (2), 161–179.

Saldana, J. (2009). *The coding manual for qualitative researchers*. London: Sage.

Shani, A., Chen, P. Wang, Y., & Hua, N. (2010). Testing the impact of a promotional video on destination image change: Application of China as a tourism destination. *International Journal of Tourism Research*, *12*, 116–133.

Silva, C., Kastenholz, E., & Abrantes, J. L. (2013). Place-attachment, destination image and impacts of tourism in mountain destinations. *Anatolia: An International Journal of Tourism and Hospitality Research*, *24*(1), 17–29.

Silvestre, A., & Correia, A. (2005). A second-order factor analysis model for measuring tourists' overall image of Algarve/Portugal. *Tourism Economics*, *11*, 539–554.

Souza, N. F., Costa, A. P., & Moreira, A. (2011). *Web qualitative data analyses – WebQDA (Version 2.0) [Software]*. Aveiro: Centro de Investigação Didática e Tecnologia na Formação de Formadores da Universidade de Aveiro e Esfera Crítica. Retrieved from www.webqda.com

Stepchenkova, S., & Mills, J. E. (2010). Destination image: A meta-analysis of 2000–2007 research. *Journal of Hospitality Marketing & Management*, *19*, 575–609.

Sternberg, E. (1997). The iconography of the tourism experience. *Annals of Tourism Research*, *24*(4), 951–969.

Tasci, A. D. A., Gartner, W. C., & Cavusgil, T. S. (2007). Conceptualization and operationalization of destination image. *Journal of Hospitality and Tourism Research*, *31*(2), 194–223.

Tuohino, A. (2006). Lakes as an opportunity for tourism marketing: In search of the spirit of the lake. In M. Hall & T. Härkönen (Eds.), *Lake tourism. An integrated approach to lacustrine tourism systems* (pp. 101–118). Clevedon: Channel View Publications.

Tuohino, A. (2008). *Järvi matkailumaisemana: Neutraali maisema vai elämyksellinen paikka?* [Lake as a tourism landscape: A neutral landscape or a meaningful place?]. Unpublished Licentiate Thesis. University of Oulu, Department of Geography, Oulu.

Tuohino, A., & Dávid, L. (2012). Global problems, local solutions. *Tourism Today*, *12*(Autumn), 134–150.

Tuohino, A., & Pitkänen, K. (2004). Selling waterscapes? In J. Saarinen & M. Hall (Eds.), *Nature-based tourism research in Finland: Local contexts global issues.* (pp. 129–150). Finland: Finnish Forest Research Institute. Research Papers 916.

HOW DO TOURISTS TURN SPACE INTO PLACE? – A CONCEPTUALISATION FOR SUSTAINABLE PLACE MARKETING [☆]

Juergen Gnoth

ABSTRACT

Gnoth and Mateucci (2014) develop a phenomenological point of view and explain how tourists' consciousness of their own activity determines how they experience a destination. This model is applied here to see how golf tourists might experience their destination and turn it into a meaningful place. This chapter exemplifies how destinations may develop their own uniqueness as a competitive advantage by understanding how tourists create meanings of a destination (here a golf resort). They argue that it is the tourist's individual propensity to react to a destination that

[☆]This chapter was delivered as a speech to the assembled Advances in Tourism Marketing Conference 2013, at Vilamoura, Portugal, 3 October.

Marketing Places and Spaces
Advances in Culture, Tourism and Hospitality Research, Volume 10, 315–326
Copyright © 2015 by Emerald Group Publishing Limited
All rights of reproduction in any form reserved
ISSN: 1871-3173/doi:10.1108/S1871-317320150000010023

shapes not only motivations, but also perception and evaluation of the experience.

Keywords: Experiencing; golf; phenomenology; place; space

INTRODUCTION

In this chapter, we turn to the question, 'How do tourists turn space into place and what does this mean to them'? In the face of homogenising tourism resorts across the world, offering everything from MacDonald's to Heineken, to Hiltons, to Bungee jumping, to theme-parks and beach-bars, whether with or without brand names, what is actually special about any maturing destination? In other words, 'How can we conceive of tourism marketing as an activity that enhances the destination's place values (Anderson, 2012; Young, 1999) without losing its competitive advantage, losing its uniqueness? How can a place be managed sustainably? And why is it happening so rarely'?

As marketers and researchers, we may be accused of having slowed down studying tourists seriously and failed in keeping up with how the tourist himself or herself manages the change that is created by the ongoing growth of the tourism sector. For example, we are still debating the phenomenon of authenticity and seek to understand that theme with a concept called gaze; all the while the tourist has moved to just do it! Tourists have quietly gone and created lived experiences for themselves whether marketers apply the right paradigm for understanding tourists or not. This essay applies Gnoth and Mateucci's phenomenological approach to Gnoth's Tourism Experience Model (n.d) in order to analyse different types of place involvement and engagement.

Agreeing with Uriely (2005), I maintain that tourists have quietly gone and use whatever the marketplace offers to their own ends, unbeknown to many researchers — particularly those looking through the wrong sort of glasses for this phenomenologically — rather than sociologically framed question. Tourists have begun to see destinations as malleable, transforming, something that the tourist can work with, so that they may generate their own individual satisfaction and thereby find their own happiness. I say 'their own' because marketers have not yet tried hard enough to understand how tourists actually experience and how they themselves can actually become, and be recognised as, co-creators of that happiness.[1]

Using Apter's concepts (1982), marketers rarely recognise or acknowledge tourists' meta-motivational goals, or how tourists turn destinations into tools which they use for their own ends. If marketers only knew how tourists experience places, they would most likely start developing their destination's uniqueness rather than creating the sameness of resorts that we see the world over.

In Martin Heidegger's words (1927/1962), marketers would be concerned with tourists' subjective experiencing, with their being-in-the-world, rather than just their being as customers. Responsible destination managers would become more active in helping tourists transform rather than letting them just be and consume. If we were to better understand how tourists turn space into place, marketing and service design could become more sustainable and profitable, not only financially but also experientially; firms, too, need to grow but sustainable growth builds on more than just financial growth. If a physical, natural, or cultural attraction exploits its values for mere financial profits, it will be short-lived.

I want to detail three concepts today without boring you with too much background literature. They are Place, Being and Becoming, and Experiencing; these combine as a function of consciousness and (the tourist's) activity. Although none of these concepts are entirely new, I want to suggest that if we were to have a model by which we could summarise the major ways these concepts interact, we might have a chance of improving our understanding of how we may help tourists gain more substantial satisfaction and help them achieve deeper feelings of happiness.

So how do people turn space into place? Obviously, they have to be somewhere or at least imagine being somewhere. Only when we gain a concept of something that relates to a space can we generate meaning. Meaning is then the essence of place. Place is not scalar and in its essence is not physical but meaningful and relational.[2]

I wonder: Who has wandered the grounds of that fantastic golf resort yet (at Vilamoura, Portugal) where we are holding this conference? Who has been walking the green to see the lie of the land and the positions of the holes? Who amongst you plays golf? And who would like to learn it? Who amongst you cannot be bothered with all that and just wants to relax and be, yet still 'be' within this environment, nonetheless?

The physical inspection of the space, our thoughts and feelings, as we walk the grounds create sensations. As we interact with this place all the thoughts, learnings, impressions that we acquired around the concept of 'golf-resort' now begin to be applied and in this interaction the place emerges. If I were to pretend for a moment that I knew how to play golf I might say the following:

> You know, when I played the back nine yesterday morning practicing my back-swing with a cavity back, I found that my chips were consistently failing. So I gave up and went straight to the 19th hole to tell my story to the bar tender.

What did I just do? In a somewhat clumsy way, I have created an example of how a golfer might turn space into place. The terms all refer to playing golf and containing very specific meanings. I could have just named the whole thing 'clubbing a ball across some grass out there, trying some fancy hits and swings'. Yet, what I actually tried in reality, is that I have used examples of the habitual language golfers have developed to experience their place of, and when playing golf. The sensations have created emotions that have been given specific words. Whatever way I phrase this whole experience represents another way of framing the experience. In my case it would most likely be less vivid, that is, for those whose experiences have achieved more depth and familiarity already — real golfers. Nevertheless, that expression would represent my particular way of being living the experience of golfing.

What I wanted to show you with this example is that Place emerges in people's interaction with space. We create words around it that describe how we interact with it and they reveal what we mean by the place as we see it. Place as an experience is determined by/determines emotions and creates moods. Place becomes memorable if tourists become consciously aware. A further very important fact is that the words we use are not pictures of letters that are spoken or written down on a piece of paper. Neither are they really a set of contiguous sounds that make up the spoken words. Words actually tell of processes; they indicate activities that are employed in the interaction with space as it turns into place (Wittgenstein, 1986).

If I use the word golf resort here, you probably would think and feel far different meanings than people down-town; for example, at the over-land bus stop at Vilamoura, Portugal, where the peasants and young families travel back into the hinterland to their villages and stony farmland. Their different form and lived experience of being-in-the-world, that entirely individual sensation-cum-meaning-creation would make them feel the same space as a different place.[3]

Place emerges as we interact with it. We give it names that indicate the types of interactions we have with it; we use these words in our interactions and communication more or less successfully. To phrase it more contemporary, we all know what somebody means by when they say this currently fashionable phrase: 'this place is awesome'! In our minds, we put together with these words all we know about the person who is saying it, all we see in his gestures and the intonation as we perceive it. Indeed, this currently fashionable wording expresses its meaning more in its performance than surface meaning. In this way, words reflect processes, activities of meaning creation and recreation.

When tourists experience places, they immediately construct concepts (or feelings) around them, but they themselves are often forms of lived experiences in an aggregate state that our minds reconstruct to gain a sense of them. And the more we discern and distinguish, the more will space become place. The environment, as it is perceived gains meaning. Turning space into place means, 'going there', 'doing things', 'feeling things', in your body/mind. Tourism is all about turning spaces into places.

Please note that turning spaces into places is an activity – even if just in your mind; it describes an activity. Although nobody has moved from his chair or broken into sweat when perceiving my words about golf resorts; while we were all thinking about golf, we actively recreated experiences of golf. That is because we can actually see such activity in our mind's eye as these activities may happen, more or less. It is when we are thinking memories and become aware of feelings that our minds engage in activity.

SYSTEMS AND MINDS

To detail this argument further, first let me say something about systems.

Systems consist of three basic characteristics, elements, structures and boundaries. The boundaries become the more distinct, the more the elements form unique structures. Systems exist in an environment in which the system needs (or is conditioned) to choose other, critical systems from which it distinguishes itself or which it needs to observe or interact with in order to survive. Otherwise, the environment is the source of 'chaos', from which 'danger' or uncertainty to the system may emerge. Alas, as any system must make choices as to which other system it observes, the environment can never be totally controlled or otherwise anticipated, hence it often becomes the source of unforeseen outcomes (Luhmann, 1995). Destinations such as golf resorts are systems that tourists choose to experience. They form their own systems to which tourists (as systems) need to adjust. Mal-adjustment means not functioning within that system according to norms and expectations, yet that might be of no consequence to the tourist's psychic system.

In order to function, every system has to refine its structure by constantly re-inventing itself, by repeating and honing its processes. As such,
systems are self-reflective, turning everything into means towards its own
ends. However, to survive, systems also need to learn in order to adapt.
This requires the system to explore and, as much as possible, understand
other systems it observes as systems in their own rights. That means, understanding (or learning to respond to) how other systems function and how
they consider and select other systems they observe. For example, the more
we as tourists who are new to the game of golf and seeking to understand it
in its own rights, that is, as its own phenomenon, the more likely are we to
gain essential insights of its forms and functions.

So, to apply these very theoretical yet universally applicable principles
of any living system, how do tourists maintain themselves as living systems,
biologically and socially?

Concisely, by doing things in ways that they either know and therefore
apply and repeat, or they do things in ways that let them explore and
expand.

Now, let us think of an example relating to golf and compare a pleasure-
seeking, casual, or diversionary golfer with one who is serious about her leisure. There is thus, firstly, the playful hobby golfer whom we see putting
the ball around a little, lively, it seems, but also with some evidence of focus
and interest. Although we never really know what the person actually feels
we can somehow see (empathise) when she is *not* really serious about getting a handicap today or tomorrow but, nevertheless, we seem to be able to
recognise that she enjoys a little putting, all the same.

The emotions that this person feels appear to us as being pleasant,
although they are known only to the person. The different ways this person
uses the activity of and around golf seem to create a known feeling and
outcome (fun, satisfaction etc. that we can observe through the ways they
talk or their body posture), such as one would expect from any playful
activity. Often, the ways in which the individual golfer becomes conscious
of his own activity is by following learned patterns of how to behave on a
golf course; they are thus socially acquired. They also create a known feeling of pleasure as she is making place. Although there is evidence of spora-
dic focus and avoidance of arousal, in the main, behaviour is casual,
relaxed, and scanning the environment for novel stimuli that make distrac-
tions feel welcome.

In contrast, we could also imagine somebody here on our golf course
who is seeking to recreate the fantastic success that she may have had last
year when she last played golf. During the course of these last holidays,

and through intense practice, every-day, she succeeded in getting a handicap that made her proud, and she would never stop talking about it when back home.

And, during the following year, like so many of us, she would experience a feeling of urge and of loss, as she would not have the chance of practicing what she really loves while back at home. So, now when back on the course at Vilamoura again she would try to regain her former achievements. She would be going through stroke after stroke, putt after putt, to consolidate each achievement and further improve with every stroke. The more often she achieves the more satisfied she gets. She does it by getting up early to be first on the driving range and she practices in ways that makes her feel her body, as each muscle aches. Then, in the evening, she knows she has got closer to her former golfing self.

What this golfer is doing − in contrast to the first who is 'just putting around' and having a nice time socially on and off the course, is that this dedicated golfer is 'achieving' through recreating a certain feeling of success and level of accomplishment. We can compare these activities of both to the different ritualistic processes and habit formations in social interactions that Bourdieu (1986) described and analysed so well. He thereby analysed the processes by which people then gain and employ social capital in groups and societies. Very similar principles and processes are working for the individual self as a psychic system. As she employs known activities she achieves known and desired outcomes. We may call the result of such knowledge 'psychological capital' by which a person recreates and rediscovers her former abilities, in the latter case, and funs and social approval by being sociable and friendly in the former. However, it must be noted and considered carefully, that whatever this capital is made up of in either case, it can never be the same, as Bourdieu's capital is the substance of communication while the other is the substance of thoughts and feelings.

These two golfers' activities are based on what they practiced and honed through repetition. Such activities recreate and consolidate desired and known outcomes. The tourist (as a system) who recreates and who seeks to consolidate and to revisit an image of a past self will repeat what he knows. He or she will use this knowledge as a recipe to get back to where he feels he once was, and to let the known, authentic self re-emerge. System theory thus allows us to look across different activities and explain and describe them with the same instruments. Using system language, different tourist activities become isomorphous so that we can fully focus on what their difference really is. This difference, I suggest, lies with the mode of experiencing, that is, *how* tourists experience, not *what* they experience.

EXPERIENCING

The psychologist Apter (1982) later describes the underlying motivations as being either of a telic or of a paratelic state. The telic state describes a serious goal orientation that avoids arousal. In contrast, the paratelic state has a feeling of playfulness about it that is spontaneous and pleasure-seeking. You may observe that golfers often swing between these two states as they travel across the green. Apter has detected that the feeling of flow in activities is often achieved while the telic and paratelic states alternate until the feeling of flow begins to linger for a period of time throughout the activity.

What is remarkable here is that all of Stebbin's (2007) Serious Leisure categories of hobbyist and amateurs can potentially be described in this way: the activities comprise overall known, repetitive behaviour that create a particular sense of known achievement and then may create the beautiful experience of flow. The activities here are marked not only by their repetitiveness (going through the motions while golfing, skiing, fishing, kayaking or even knitting) but also by whether it does or does not involve effort. If there is no challenge, the motions involved are often only a search for contrast, or difference in intensity of known feelings, not difference in kind. Yet if the leisure activist, that is, the golfer improves, a sense of achievement ensues and even the feeling of flow may be experienced. Recreation, when achieved, can create flow as skills begin to match challenges.

If we stay with the example of golfing and follow the tourist around the green, we may distinguish those who do not just putt along, but try and put effort into their learning. They explore different stances when hitting the ball, they listen to others which iron to take and they get immersed in the intricacies of the art of golf. They improve their stance, they refine their swing and they begin to achieve new and improving goals. So what is different between the lazy putter and the recreationist I described first and second, and this avid learner we are talking about now? The latter's engagement with the golf sport has become one of interest. No longer is the golfer thinking about just himself and how he can get a little pleasure out of shoving a tiny ball across the grass, careful, not to break into a sweat, or miss the conversation going on amongst his fellow golfers.

This EXPLORING golfer we imagine in our minds here, is now focusing on what improves, alters and shifts within his own body as he focuses on what the golf teacher is saying. And he begins to see the curves the ball is describing in the air as it is flying across the grass and around the hollows and undulating surfaces of the green. The improvement that goes beyond what this golfer might have known already and from previous achievements does result in two outcomes: the performance improves because the golfer explores new ideas and moves. He is, firstly, following role-prescribed patterns by which he learns and expands himself as a person and also for everybody else to see. This is what sociologists are able to observe and describe.

But as he improves 'objectively' he is also expanding his being. Not only is it that he grows as a person who can feel satisfied for everyone to see, as he learned all the right moves. But he himself as an individual can achieve a feeling of happiness as he can see how his new skills create a larger being-in-the-world. Life itself is becoming fuller and more wholesome, moment-by-moment and in the future. As his or her interaction with the physical space intensifies further, the golfing range also grows in its meaning and expands as a place. This third golfer, then, differs from the previous golfers as she is expanding her being-in-the-world by actively becoming. This 'becoming' emerges as she is not only becoming less self-reflective as she 'leaves' the state of flow and attempts new swings and moves but also focusing on 'the other', by listening and learning about the other without immediate self-reference. In other words, she is attempting to understand 'the other' system in its own rights. Such learning expands one's being as more of the environment is captured and understood. In our example, the golf course is being appreciated as to what it is, how it is designed, what its different conditions are at different times of the year, in different weather and different hours of the day. Its experience has made the golfer grow.

CONCLUSION AND IMPLICATIONS

By now we have discussed firstly, what place really is, beyond any physical and objective features. We then discussed how the inter-activity between mind, action, and space creates meaning of place. We also noted that activity can be known, whether as incrementally different (autopoietic) or as repetitive action, as it helps achieve certain outcomes, including sensual or hedonic outcomes, satisfaction (involving socially learned and appreciated cognitive evaluations), flow and happiness.

Tourists use their skills and knowledge to make themselves be-in-the-world. This is achieved either, by just feeling through their senses, in a plea-surable way, or by exerting effort in order to recreate in a knowing way, and regain a sense of who they were before. These activities are, of course, always evolving and emerging so that the 'knowing way' is framed or direc-ted by one's identity and a sense of authenticity (including knowing one's self). The first examples of both the casual, relaxed golfer as well as the golfer who tries to regain her former strengths are examples where tourists focus on their Being. The first just wants to be and to feel his senses in a casual, pleasurable way. In the second example, the golfer wants to recreate herself and return to who she knows she was. While that is not physically possible we know that she wants her authentic self to re-emerge, where her feelings converge with her achievements of how well she plays golf.

In the English and many other Western languages, we hit their limits here because we find it hard to express these dynamics that jump our linear understanding of time. Their linear and positivistic habitus often fails to let clearly distinct moments that are nevertheless in flux get suitably arrested in experience. Chinese, as far as I know, and which was mentioned in a little discussion on this issue on trinet,[4] is far more fuzzy on these issues and may capture this sense of emergence far easier. As Asian cultures seek calmness and harmony as their preferred emotions, people like to fit in, are more observant and more cautious with their statements and how they see things. Language thus becomes more like poetry, evocative, open, and creating more possibility of what might be meant rather than what 'is' meant. Authenticity here is thus connected with premonition and forward-directed knowing of what the self may be able to experience in the future as place has become to enrich not only the (social) person but also the (existential) individual.

By re-discovering herself the golfer is likely to learn new things about herself, if ever so slightly because she really only repeats and practices what she has already known before (this is the core of Heidegger's sense of autopoiesis). However, when challenging herself and growing beyond what she knew she was capable of, turning from merely being-in-the-world to an active becoming-in-the world, she would emerge as more than she was before. It is here where I believe happiness begins, in realising, feeling or envisioning a better future, moment-by-moment.

Happiness is an existentially authentic feeling. We can see people being happy but what they feel can only be felt by them. How tourists become aware of a destination and turn it into a place is therefore a matter of consciousness. Consciousness has no memory. It is only through perception that we filter and process what we have become aware of through our senses.

If we become aware of this golf resort following patterns of socially acceptable behaviour, we respect and we replicate certain ways of how one turns a space dedicated to golf into a place that is called a golf resort. We follow socialised norms and expectations of being. This social and observable form of being conforms to visible, implied and abstracted norms.

However, if we become aware of this space as a challenge to us as a human being, with a lack of skills and knowledge that require us to explore, we feel the place as a demand on our attention by which we are excited. If that occurs, we begin to feel our existentially authentic existence. That is, the tourist turns this space into *his* place by ways which not only lets his being-in-the-world re-emerge but also, by revealing which ways he seeks out challenges and explores this space for what it is and for what it can reveal to the tourist. This activity is turning this space into the place it can be. When that happens, then the tourist expands in his being in the world and grows.

Marketers must make sure that tourists can become aware of their destination. The question is how that should be stimulated and what sort of relationships are to be sought. Such strategy need not only speak to the tourist as a person, according to a normatively role-authentic manner that is prescribed through social etiquette and culture, but also should allow the tourist to become aware of the destination as a human being so that they can reveal to themselves what uniqueness the place holds. This is the tourism marketer's role: to facilitate co-creation by which the tourist shares what the host knows. The hosts place is, initially, merely a space of little experienced meaning and few (emic) values for which the marketer needs to prepare the tourist. These are neither the tourist's nor entirely the host's. A place, as constructed as it may be, holds its own ecological values, as well as those of all who are living there.

Marketers must guide tourists and allow them a learning process that begins with letting them be, relax, arrive, and to let them come to their senses in its true meaning; then they need help them find their being-at-the-destination. This allows not only by letting them re-discover themselves but also by motivating them to explore the destination and by revealing the unrevealed (around every bunker and at every plunk) turn space into place.

I believe that this view of conceptualising tourists' experience is also a way to encourage marketers to build and preserve the uniqueness of destinations rather than turning them into same-same. It would return to the maxim of 'understand your customer!' but at a much higher level than marketers are accustomed to. By only seeking to 'satisfy', thus focusing on service quality only, destination marketers miss out on the experiential potential that comes with 'understanding'. There are plenty of ways marketers can create places they control, but there are differences between theme-parks and people's socio-cultural and individual space which they perceive as their home; that is, the emic but also the existential space these people call their place.

If the place that is *made* by the tourist does not converge with the owner's authentic identity of the place, such a place is often replaceable or substitutable. And so will be the marketer. But if the marketer understands the place and seeks to leverage the authenticity of the place as its unique proposition, he or she may be far more likely truly interested in helping sustain the place (or make it more resilient, as Alan Lew mentioned at the same conference).

NOTES

1. Not to mislead the reader, I do not mean that functionalistic notion of happiness or satisfaction, with service quality.
2. Physicality is necessary, no doubt, but only to a certain degree and only for certain modes of mind. The virtual reality in which some of us exist when 'on-line', for example, challenges the idea of what is physical.
3. Of course, it becomes obvious that we merely agree about speaking or thinking about the same space. May be all that is 'the same' here is that we would point to the same piece of land, the same golf course; that, what simply 'is' and we can agree upon as a minimum.
4. Trinet is an internet forum for tourism researchers open to everyone. This discussion took place in the first half of 2013.

REFERENCES

Anderson, J. (2012). Relational places: The surfed wave as assemblage and convergence. *Environment and Planning-Part D, 30*(4), 570.
Apter, M. J. (1982). *The experience of motivation: The theory of psychological reversals.* New York, NY: Academic Press.
Bourdieu, P. (1986). The forms of social capital. In J. Richardson (Ed.), *Handbook of theory and research for the sociology of education* (pp. 241–248). New York, NY: Greenwood Press.
Gnoth, J., & Matteucci, X. (2014). A phenomenological organisation of the tourism literature. *International Journal of Culture, Tourism and Hospitality Research, 8*(1), 3–21.
Heidegger, M. (1927/1962). Sein und Zeit, (J. Macquarrie and E. Robinson, Trans.), *Being and Time.* New York, NY: Harper and Row.
Luhmann, N. (1995). *Social systems.* Stanford, CA: Stanford University Press.
Stebbins, A. R. (2007). *Serious leisure: A perspective for our time.* Brunswick, NJ: Transaction Publishers.
Uriely, N. (2005). The tourist experience: Conceptual developments. *Annals of Tourism Research, 32*(1), 199–216.
Wittgenstein, L. (1986). *Philosophical investigations* (3rd ed.). Oxford: Blackwell.
Young, M. (1999). The social construction of tourist places. *Australian Geographer, 30*(3), 373–389.